Global Universities
and
Urban Development

Cities and Contemporary Society

Series Editors: Richard D. Bingham and Larry C. Ledebur,
Cleveland State University

Sponsored by the
Maxine Goodman Levin College of Urban Affairs
Cleveland State University

This new series focuses on key topics and emerging trends in urban policy. Each volume is specially prepared for academic use, as well as for specialists in the field.

Global Universities
and
Urban Development
Case Studies and Analysis

Wim Wiewel and David C. Perry
editors

L LINCOLN INSTITUTE
OF LAND POLICY
Cambridge, Massachusetts

M.E.Sharpe
Armonk, New York
London, England

Published in cooperation with the Lincoln Institute of Land Policy

Library of Congress Cataloging-in-Publication Data

Global universities and urban development : case studies and analysis /
Wim Wiewel and David C. Perry, editors
   p. cm. — (Cities and contemporary society)
  Includes bibliographical references and index.
  ISBN 978-0-7656-2039-2 (cloth : alk. paper)—ISBN 978-0-7656-2040-8 (pbk. : alk. paper)
  1. Community and college—Case studies. 2. Community development, Urban—Case
studies. 3. Land use, Urban—Case studies. 4. Real estate development—Case studies.
I. Wiewel, Wim. II. Perry, David C.

LC237.G56 2008
378.1′030722—dc22   2007032404

Printed in the United States of America

The paper used in this publication meets the minimum requirements of
American National Standard for Information Sciences
Permanence of Paper for Printed Library Materials,
ANSI Z 39.48-1984.

♾

BM (c)   10   9   8   7   6   5   4   3   2   1
BM (p)   10   9   8   7   6   5   4   3   2   1

Contents

Part III
The University as a
Zone of Development

Part IV
The University and
the Contested City

Part V
Lessons Learned

List of Tables and Figures

Tables

Figures

Foreword

In recent years, researchers in the United States interested in urban revitalization have become used to thinking about the role of the university in the city. At the Lincoln Institute we bring our perspective of land policy to this work. Specifically, the goal of The City, Land, and The University project is to improve the collective capacity of leaders to achieve the multiple interests of cities, universities, and communities in ways that are mutually agreeable.

In the twenty-first century we have come to expect universities to accomplish a number of heroic feats. At the center of the university mission is knowledge creation. We expect universities to play this important social, cultural, and economic role. In addition, we expect them to train young people to enter a profession or allow the graduate to pursue advanced professional training. We also expect our university graduates to be prepared to be active participants in the social and political life of the nation.

Increasingly, we expect universities to play an important, even a leading, role in the regional economy. We do not simply expect that university-trained engineers will, for example, make productive contributions to local companies; rather, we expect that the university will play an important intermediary role as it transfers the results of the laboratory to the new firms in the university's industrial incubator.

Furthermore, we expect universities to step in and fill a void in the urban political economy. Changes in industrial and corporate structure have left cities with a different cast of corporate characters who have fewer and weaker ties to the region. Universities, with their very deep roots, are looked to as urban institutions that are unlikely to move due to mergers and acquisitions. Thus, we now turn to universities to fill the void in civic leadership created by the absence of local corporate leadership.

If the university is surrounded by a neighborhood that has received little new investment, we even expect our universities to become urban developers in a way that will achieve their core mission as well as provide positive spillovers for the neighbors. And, in many countries, universities are expected to play a central and leadership role in nation building. This is a tall order. In a world undergoing great change at great speed, universities, with their long histories, are seen as bastions of stability.

The Institute's work on this topic began in the United States, and is documented in part in the book *The University as Urban Developer: Case Studies and Analysis* (2005), which is part of this series copublished by M.E. Sharpe and the Lincoln Institute. We wanted to learn from our colleagues around the world, as well, so in 2003 we announced an international call for papers on this topic. We had no idea how or if this theme would resonate across the globe, but the cases included here attest to the interest, meaning, and potential that the city-university relationship holds for urban life in places as diverse as Helsinki, Mexico City, and Seoul.

In this volume we introduce the idea of the university as an "urban institution" and begin the process of defining that term. By urban institution we mean an organization that is not simply an enclave with literal or figurative walls, but an institution *of* the city, engaged in reciprocal cultural, social, economic, and political relationships. If university leaders are guiding their institutions to take on new roles, what does that mean for leaders in city administration and in neighborhoods and communities? We hope this book will be part of the ongoing dialogue between universities and their host communities about the roles and responsibilities of all the city's residents (i.e., individuals and institutions, public sector and private sector) in contributing to the quality of life in the city.

Rosalind Greenstein
Senior Fellow and Chair
Department of Economic and Community Development
Lincoln Institute of Land Policy

Preface

The relationship of the university and the city has become an increasingly popular topic in recent years. The growth of the knowledge economy and the renewed importance of urban areas in the global economy have prompted expansion of urban universities, increased their visibility locally and nationally, and brought attention to their physical development.

Over the past seven years we have been exploring the contributions of the university to the development of the city and, conversely, what the university gains from its developmental and broader institutional relationships with the city in which it is located. We have focused on land development as a critical nexus in which the promises as well as the conflicts of the relationships between universities and their neighborhoods and cities are played out.

Working in collaboration with the Lincoln Institute of Land Policy, we organized a series of workshops for university real estate development staff, members of community organizations, private developers, and others. That work resulted in our first book on the role of North American universities in urban real estate development, *The University as Urban Developer: Case Studies and Analysis* (M.E. Sharpe, 2005); an electronic database of more than 600 cases of university real estate development in the United States (available through the Lincoln Institute Web site, www.lincolninst.edu); and several in-depth case studies. Throughout that work, we focused on real estate development projects outside or on the edge of traditional campus boundaries, because that is where the issues deriving from the university's relationship with the surrounding neighborhood and city are most likely to occur.

Our work with scholars and administrators in North America whetted our appetite to learn more about universities elsewhere. We began with a workshop that brought together university officials and academics from countries in other regions for the express purpose of assessing the changing role of universities in cities in an era that has been described as at once global, increasingly urban, and driven by a knowledge-based economy. We had certainly found many of those characteristics in the urban universities of the United States and Canada, and we were anxious to see how they played out in higher education land policies in other cities around the world. To that end, the participants in our first global workshop constructed case studies of university real estate development in eleven countries in Europe, the Middle East, Asia, and Latin America.

As with our work in North America, we discovered that university-based land development in these countries is a significant element of urban formation—colleges and universities are becoming increasingly active in acquiring and developing property, adding not only land and buildings but also commercial ventures to their asset base. Beyond that, we discovered that such activities illuminate current transformations in the practices of the state, at both local and national levels. Universities outside the United States are most often public entities, and their development practices exemplify how the modern state operates. The role of the knowledge economy in urban and global development has, in turn, forced a new consideration of universities as elements of the state and has provided an empirical position from which to assess the changing role of the state in this dynamic new era.

Such an ambitious project could not have been accomplished without the strong support, intellectual direction, and participation of Rosalind Greenstein and the staff of the Lincoln Institute of Land Policy. As chair of the Department of Economic and Community Development at Lincoln, and our founding partner in The City, Land, and The University project, Roz has earned our immense gratitude. Her colleagues Harini Venkatesh and Anne Battis have also been integral to the project. A special word of thanks goes to Ann LeRoyer, publications director at the Lincoln Institute, and to copyeditor Jill Mason for their work on the text. The book is far better for their contributions—but all substantive misdirection is surely ours.

At the Great Cities Institute, the work and support of Marilyn Ruiz, Jonah Katz, Jessica Thompson, and Barbara Sherry have been critical to the project. For the past two years, Ratoola Kundu has played a central role in the organizational and editorial success of the book.

At the University of Baltimore we are grateful to Rita Aissi-Wespi for editorial and administrative assistance, as well as to John Kupcinski, Kara Kunst, and Ray Dubicki, whose work on the Urban Real Estate Database will provide a lasting empirical basis for this project.

At M.E. Sharpe we appreciate the constant support and guidance of executive editor Harry Briggs and Dick Bingham, editor of the series in which this book appears.

At the personal level, we are grateful to each other. Happily, we view the topics in this book from different perspectives, and, as a result, we learn as much, if not more, from each other as we do from any source we might cite. It is both fun and edifying to work on such projects together.

Finally, on the home front, we are grateful to our wives and partners: Wim to Alice Wiewel and David to Judith Kossy. Alice and Wim would not have known each other but for this project, and they are forever thankful. Judith Kossy contributes to David's understanding of the urban every day—ready to support, critique, and "purvey great ideas." David's task here is to remain receptive and make such ideas come to life. Hopefully, it will appear that he has done so with Wim and the contributors in this book.

Wim Wiewel   David C. Perry
University of Baltimore   Great Cities Institute
                                        University of Illinois at Chicago

Global Universities and Urban Development

Part I

Introduction

1

The University, the City, and Land

Context and Introduction

David C. Perry and Wim Wiewel

The Centrality of the University and the City in the Twenty-first Century

This book is about the university and the city and the ways the relations between the two "come to ground" in land development practices. In his introduction to an influential collection of essays actually titled *The University and the City,* historian Thomas Bender points out how attractive the overall topic is. It is, he observes, "as capacious as it is important" with a "compelling" rhetorical ring to it because there is no doubting the important *historic* linkage of the two—from their "mutual medieval origins" forward (Bender 1988, 3; Pirenne 1925). In an international collection of essays, Herman van der Wusten (1998) focuses on the contemporary importance of universities to cities, and vice versa, underscoring the cultural significance of urban universities as physical features of the urban morphology and as institutional partners or, in some cases, agencies of the modern state.

While scholars such as van der Wusten and Bender find historic and contemporary mutuality between universities and cities worldwide, there is certainly not perfect institutional symbiosis (Shapiro 2005). In fact, the relationship of university to city is often quite complex and conflictive—especially in the United States, where the "pastoral" features of the university campus in cities (Bender 1988; Turner 1984) are seen as evidence of the decidedly "anti-urban bias" (Jackson 1987; Bender 1988) found in U.S. culture. The relationship of universities to cities in the United States has been defined as much by what separates them as what binds them and is expressed in concepts such as the ivory tower, the political contentiousness of town-gown relations, professional legitimations based on disciplinary autonomy and academic governance, and land-use and physical design rules of campus planning and real estate development (Dober 1991; Perry and Wiewel 2005).

Moving from the United States, it is somewhat ironic to note that while universities and cities have reached new levels of political and analytic importance in the present era of what is called "globalization,"[1] the relationships *between* universities and cities have not been the subject of much serious study. The roles of cities in the globalizing environment are studied essentially independent of the institutional place of their universities. For example, an ambitious range of studies points to the increasing importance of cities in globalization (Scott 2005; Brenner 1999), stressing their place in the networks of production and distribution of the new world economy and their increasing prominence relative to the nation-state (Swyngedouw 1997). Conversely, in the literature more directly focused on higher education, it is argued that this changing global and local climate requires more of the tertiary sector throughout the world, as evidenced in studies of new management practices in universities (Gaffikin and Perry 2006; Gaffikin, McEldowney, and Perry 2006), as well as in new assessments of their economic import.[2] The cities of which these universities are a part, have, in many cases, achieved new and reconfigured global prominence (Sassen 1991, 2002), but the role of their universities in such urban ascendancy is rarely the focus of study.

Put another way, both of these literatures, on cities and on universities, speak clearly of the importance of their topic to the modern global order, but the mutuality of relationship between cities and universities referred to by Bender and van Wusten, among others, is not well articulated.[3] In the main, where the linkages between the urban and the global and the informational are made very well (Castells 1997, 2004; Sassen 1991, 2002; Scott 2001, 2005; Roy 2006), the role of the university in the city in such a dynamic and forceful context is not made well at all.[4] In the scant literature that does turn its attention to the relationship of the university to the economy of the city, the discussion is as much prescriptive (Grogan and Proscio 2000; CEOs for Cities 2002; Clusters on Innovation Group 2004) as it is descriptively analytical (Perry and Wiewel 2005). More to the point of this book, these few studies of universities and the urban environment do not focus on the significance of land development as a critical nexus between the economic promise and political conflicts that shape relationships between universities, their neighborhoods, and the other institutions of cities (Perry and Wiewel 2005). In this book we set out to address such topics, intending to contribute, on the one hand, to the burgeoning institutional study of higher education (Breton and Lambert 2004; Bender 1988; Harkavy and Puckett 1994; Rhodes 2001) and, on the other, to the role of universities in city real estate development, urban land-use planning, and politics.[5]

In this chapter, we set the stage for the remainder of the book. To do so, we will first, briefly, discuss the prominence of universities and cities in these times. Second, since this is an international collection of cases, our intention will be to place the case studies in the broader global context of change enveloping cities and higher education in both developed and developing economies. At the most general level, our argument will be that, for cities, at this global moment, universities matter. Third, we want to show how cities, in turn, are formative environments for universities, suggesting how university land development is better understood in a broader, urban, land development context. Our final goal for this chapter is to show how each of the following chapters contributes to this approach to the study of university real estate and land development. We believe that each of these studies of the university and the city offers its own particular window through which to view and better understand some of the institutional factors of city building in the present era of globalization.

To help accomplish all this, we have organized the book into several parts. Following this introductory one, Part II concerns university land development policies and the changing features of *the state;* Part III, university land development practices and *the market;* Part IV, university land development practices and *the politics* of globalizing cities. Part V comprises a single chapter, organized around key questions of development, the answers to which serve as a summary of the entire topic.

We are clearly interested in the role of urban universities as real estate developers; we are also interested in their role as agencies of the "state" and the "market" in urban restructuring. For example, while higher education in the United States is split between private and public institutions, higher education elsewhere has historically been overwhelmingly public in its funding and institutional development. Given this, it would initially appear that the substantially *public* universities outside the United States would perform in ways quite different from the privatizing (Shapiro 2005) and commodified practices (Slaughter and Rhoades 2004; Rhodes 2001) of the mixture of public and private universities in the United States. However, as several chapters in this book will suggest, that is not always the case. Universities are changing in most parts of the world in response to, among other things, the changing role and diminishing fiscal support of the state, the increasing "public-to-private" or "entrepreneurial" roles of the public university (European Commission 2006), the growing number and roles of private institutions of learning in the tertiary education sector, and the shifting politics of access to higher education brought on by major urban patterns of student "massification," especially in cities in developing economies (Altbach and Umakoshi 2004; Scott 2005). The remainder of this chapter refers to such changes and more as we set the global and institutional context for our discussion of "the university, the city, and land."

Universities: How They Matter in the World and in Cities

In 1963, in his influential *Uses of the University,* Clark Kerr (1972, 86ff.) argued that the period following the Second World War constituted a "second great transformation" in American higher education. He placed the first transformation in the last quarter of the nineteenth century, when the land grant movement in the United States and German intellectualism's emphasis on the university as a research institution combined to bring about "extraordinary change."

The stuff of Kerr's second great transformation was part governmental, part market driven, and part political. Governmentally, the American university, both public and private, was the beneficiary of what Kerr called the building of the "federal grant university"; the national government was stimulating, through grants and contracts, a "new federalism" with education at its core. In this second transformation of the university, the success of the liberal democratic state and its institutions of higher education were bound "inextricably" together.

Economically, the decades following the Second World War were a time when the universities were called upon, as never before, to "merge their activities" with industry, pushing the "extension" traditions of the land grant mission to new levels of university-industrial partnerships in professional training and in research. And politically, the university was "called upon to educate previously unimagined numbers of students," creating new goals of democratic access and constituency for higher education.

If all these societal requirements—of state, market, and liberal democracy—were met, Kerr predicted the rise of "a truly American university, an institution unique in world history, an institution not looking to other models but serving, itself, as a model for universities in other parts of the globe." For Kerr this was not a boastful statement but rather the outcome of adherence to institutional "imperatives" for the development of the modern (American) university. The university that emerged in such an institutional setting would, perforce, have formative impact on university systems around the world.

There is no disagreement: The "great transformation" that Kerr predicted has come about. In general, higher education in the United States sets the standard—both in technology, with its scientific and engineering base, and in its overall array of tertiary educational options of public and private liberal arts and professional and training institutions. A recent European study, *The Future of European Universities: Renaissance or Decay?* (Lambert and Butler 2006), points to the centrality of top U.S. research and teaching institutions in American technological and economic achievements and the correlation "between a country's higher education attainment levels and its economic prosperity."[6]

The study's authors worry about the current position of European universities relative to the technological and scientific superiority of U.S. institutions and suggest that without great effort the universities of Europe will fall further "behind in terms of innovation and technical excellence" (p. 1). For the commission and its researchers this is all the more difficult to imagine considering that universities in Europe, already in an "uncompetitive" intellectual and scientific position, employ more than one-third of the continent's researchers and produce over 80 percent of its basic research (European Commission 2003). Ironically, this dominance of universities in European research and development circles is perceived as a weakness, with the regional economy being overly dependent on universities for new knowledge. This weakness is especially clear when a comparison is made with the United States, which exhibits a much more balanced pattern of R&D, in which about half of all basic research is university based, the rest coming from commercial and other non-university settings.

If the leaders of European universities are worried by their comparative technological and scientific inferiority (European Commission 2006; Gaffikin, McEldowney, and Perry 2006), leaders in the United States are showing concern over the future place of the U.S. tertiary educational sector in this new global era, as well (Domestic Policy Council 2006). Shirley Ann Jackson, the 2004 president of the American Association for the Advancement of Science and the president of Rensselaer Polytechnic Institute, suggests that while U.S. universities still fuel "the leading engine of innovation in the world . . . with the best graduate programs, the best scientific infrastructure and the capital markets to exploit it . . . there is a quiet crisis in U.S. science and technology that we have to wake up to" (Friedman 2005, 253). Jackson's statement sets the stage for a discussion of the growing fragility of the American research university's position of prominence in a changing global network of universities and research capacities.

What both scholars and political observers are pointing to is a change in the global context of higher education. Their sense of the changing competitiveness of higher education signals the potential for another "transformation" in higher education: from the primacy of the American university model to a more worldwide accession of universities in increasingly important global cities. In this new era of "globalization," education has taken on even more importance in all regions of the world. The aforementioned studies of higher education in Europe find it to be the "prime" feature of Europe's economic future. While the United States remains the magnet for capital and students in such a competitive environment, other parts of the world are now equally involved in building universities and attracting students. In a comparative study of Asia, Altbach and Umakoshi (2004) find "enormous resources" being deployed to expand and upgrade university systems. The two million graduates coming from Chinese universities every year have surpassed the U.S. number and are fast closing on the three million graduating from all countries in Europe (Altbach and Umakoshi 2004; Lambert and Butler 2006). Breton and Lambert (2004, 27) describe such conditions as part of the "new global space" of higher education—one where the challenges and opportunities represented in higher education are "no longer the concern of only national or even regional education policy . . . but are now global in significance."

The world may or may not be "flattening" in just the ways that Thomas Friedman (2005) so dramatically claims, but globalization is, to return to our major argument, creating the conditions for major changes in higher education. UN educator Hans van Ginkel puts it this way: "Globalization . . . with the gradual decline of the relevance of borders and the emergence of the 'network society' . . . has led to a *Copernican change* in the positioning of individual universities" (van Ginkel 2003, 76; emphasis added). Van Ginkel and others referred to here suggest that new institutional changes and challenges to the state, market, and politics in an era of "globalization" are influencing a new global set of patterns in higher education—like Clark Kerr's assertion of a "great transformation" of universities built upon their response to the challenges and changes of state, market, and politics of postwar industrialization and cold war nationalism. The changing political economic relationship between city and nation-state, the cross-border movement of information and the new knowledge economy, and the new demographies of diversity in cities all set the stage for new institutional practices in the service of new models of higher education in both the developing and developed economies of the world.

Modern "geographies" of learning, the "new global spaces of higher education" (Breton and Lambert 2004), now often exceed campus and national borders, as they become the product of university-community linkage in urban and global networks of research and learning produced by faculty and students who are equally "global." When this global learning "touches down," it does so, most often, in an urban area—the city is now the location for more than half the world's population, and "global city regions" are the centers of what have come to be called the leading "networks" of capital, information, and knowledge (Clark 2002; Scott 2005; Sassen 2002). The massification of human settlement in urban areas and the concomitant advance of technology and science at the core of the knowledge economy combine to make the university a key element of both the training and preparation of new urbanites (in the developed and developing world, especially in Asia and Latin America) and the transnational science, technology, and innovation of new economies.[7]

Cities: How They Matter in an Urban World of Globalizing Cities

The heading of this section is borrowed from a book on the rising worldwide importance of cities by geographer David Clark entitled *Urban World/Global City* (2002). Clark, writing just before the millennium, was referring to an important pending transformation of the human species from rural to urban. As we said above, more of us in the new millennium live (for the first time in our existence) in urban settlements than in rural areas. Clark identified a second important feature of modern development, namely, that certain key urban places on the planet—called variously "global cities," world cities, city-states, and global city-regions (Scott 2001; Sassen 1991, 2002)—were becoming demographically, economically, and politically the most dominant and important geographies on the planet.

A host of scholars have written about this move of large cities to global prominence. By dint of their increasing size; economic transformation; power; and linkage to technology, information, and knowledge, these cities have achieved a global status that has allowed them at times to supersede, if not efface, nation-states—in the "cross border" creation of the new informational society (Scott 2005; Swyngedouw 1997; Brenner 1999; Castells 1997) and the networks that are the infrastructure of what is termed "globalization" (Breton and Lambert 2004). *Globalization* is best understood here as a term that registers the distinctiveness of the present patterns of global, urban, and national reordering of economics, politics, and governance when compared to prior core-periphery systems of world order (Wallerstein 1979; Scott 2005). Cities are the prime centers of new materiality and economic development, as well as sites of material contradiction, ethno-religious division, and deprivation for new immigrants and long-standing generations of residents alike (Sassen 1991; Castells 1997, 2004). For universities and the global geographies of learning of which they are a part, these conditions and changes in their urban context do matter. The conditions of opportunity and social and political crisis give cities a recurring level of importance in the building of modern universities (Kerr 1972; van Ginkel 2003; Lambert and Butler 2006).

Recent studies show that changes in the structural relations of global markets (Castells 1997), demographic patterns (Clark 2002; Scott 2005), and political relations (Harvey 2005; Roy 2006) have led to changes in the ways the state intervenes in cities worldwide. Some have called this a move to "neoliberalism," and others have called it a managerial and political shift from "government" to "governance" (Harvey 2005; Gaffikin and Perry 2006). Whichever way this is viewed, it has large effects on the real estate practices of state-supported universities (see chapter 13). The chapters in this volume show—that from Finland (chapter 2) to Korea (chapter 7); and from the United Kingdom (chapters 4 and 12) to South America (chapter 8)—urban universities and their land policies are being altered by declining state funds and shifting public-private relations. Thus, the analysis of urban university land development is not only a much needed new study of urban-university real estate planning, policy, and development, it is also evidence of the over-all changing institutional practices of cities in this global era (Swyngedouw 1997). It follows, therefore, that reading the chapters in this book in a context that recognizes the new place of the urban in our human world and in the competitive geographies of capital and governance should help us to better understand the changing practices of university land development in such urbanizing global geographies.

The University, the City, and Land

Harking back to the beginning of this chapter, if Bender (1988), van der Wusten (1998), and their colleagues are correct in their assessment of the mutuality found in the relations of universities to the urban, the time is way past due to advance a critical evaluation of universities as urban institutions in a worldwide, comparative context. There is a paucity of scholarship on the university as a fully vested urban institution, particularly in regard to real estate development practices, which are substantially different in different parts of the world. Like other sectors involved in the production of public good, education is caught up in differing patterns of public-private and social development around the world: employing new and varied roles and definitions of state investment and regulation of the academy, reacting to mounting challenges of "massification and access" represented by the growth of student populations and their demand for space, responding to new impulses to "privatize" the academic function (Geiger 2004; Breton and Lambert 2004; Slaughter and Rhoades 2004; Lambert and Butler 2006), and producing forceful programs of "commodification" of the "products" of the academy (Rhodes 2001; Geiger 2004). All of these patterns contribute to the institutional and entrepreneurial contexts of university real estate and the ways such development, in turn, affects institutional academic initiatives. Viewing university-city relations through the lens of land development, and doing it in a comparative, global set of case studies, will certainly offer evidence of the strength of the relation-ship of universities and cities and give us some further understanding of the ways that *institutional* changes of the state, market, and politics are played out in changes in the university —changes that, at a minimum, have global as well as urban import, whether or not they ultimately constitute a *third* "great transformation" or "Copernican shift."

The University, the City, and the State

The chapters in Part II study the role of universities and their responses to the changing political economy of the state: its political and fiscal support (Haila, chapter 2), its structural devolution (Anacker and Altrock, chapter 3; and Peel, chapter 4), and its economic restructuring (Takeuchi, chapter 5), as reflected in their development of urban land and buildings. On one level, every case study in this book concerns itself with the role the state plays in university land policy and the role university real estate development plays in the social economy of the city. But the chapters included in this section are representative of the broader range of state policies and their impact on urban university land practices. How universities develop land and buildings to meet the demands represented by changing numbers of students, new technologies and knowledge clusters of cities, and the shifting support and policy responsibilities of the state forms the basis of much of this volume in general and the chapters in this part of the volume in particular.

Perhaps there is no better starting point from which to review the shifting role and participation of the state in university real estate development than Finland, where the role of the state in education and in social democracy, more broadly, is very strong. Anne Haila, in her chapter on the conflictive conditions that make up the role of the University of Helsinki as "developer," reminds us that all universities in Finland are "state universities and their premises are owned and managed by the state real estate company, Senate Properties, that seeks to make the most efficient use of its real estate." Therefore, even though the University of Helsinki, founded in 1640, has historically adhered to an academic mission of "higher education and academic research," it has recently been tasked with new market-driven, or what Haila calls "entrepreneurial," purposes through its institutional relationship with its property manager, the Senate Properties board. Haila argues that this reconfiguration of the state purposes of "academic" land for market-oriented uses is significant not only for what it tells us about university land use, but also for what it tells us about the changing state. She finds that even in social democracies like Finland, the state seeks to make the most efficient use of its real estate, applying market-oriented strategies to the selection of public uses of university real estate. She also finds that such practices have come into conflict with "use value-driven" policies of university property development, policies that previously had reserved land use for exclusive educational and research purposes. This chapter points to conflict in the relationship between the university and the increasingly entrepreneurial state—a state that urges the university to treat its premises as a competitive urban "commodity" as well as a traditional space or enclave of educational attainment.

Chapter 3 adds to the discussion of the urban university and the changing state, focusing on what the authors, Katrin Anacker and Uwe Altrock, describe as "conversion" of the uses and institutional form of both the university and its property. They find that at the University of Lüneberg, in the Lower Saxony region of Germany, the notion of *conversion* has a double meaning: first, as a form of state policy in the newly unified Germany that allows for the conversion of an underutilized or redundant military base into a new campus for the University of Lüneberg; and, second, as an example of state higher education policy that converts the university's public institutional status to one of formal independence from the state, thereby establishing the university as a "foundation" in charge of its own fiscal and institutional identity and able to negotiate its own real estate deals. For the authors, these changes are part of a larger shift from the federal and state levels to the state and local levels, and there have been efforts to coax the private sector to the funding table. For Anacker and Altrock, the (re)development of the University of Lüneberg is an example of the evolving state, what they call an "appropriate form of governance" for a higher education process that requires new levels of collaboration between citizens, the city and private companies in costly development activities. The conversion of the public university thus paves the way, predict the authors, for the university's participation in important public-private partnerships required to play at the international level. They suggest that the university, as foundation, is no longer "entrepreneurially constrained" when it comes to land-use negotiations. The chapter questions whether this university-as-privatized-foundation approach can be considered as a role model in both the German planning context and the international fiscal context.

One example of the larger imprint of the model of the entrepreneurial university is found in recent higher education policy in the United Kingdom. Deborah Peel, in her chapter, "Varsity Real Estate in Scotland: New Visions for Town and Gown?" uses case studies of two Scottish universities—at Dundee and Aberdeen—to extend our understanding of state policies that not only restructure the development tools of the university but do so in a context that is as much global as it is urban. In contemporary Scotland, universities have been identified as playing a critical role in helping to meet the national government's wider policy objectives for modernizing the Scottish economy by ensuring that it is "knowledge driven." Using an assessment of institutional infrastructure, funding, and real estate, this chapter considers state policy that reconfigures the role of the university as what Peel calls an "economic engine": How has the role of university-as-city-developer been influenced by new public university real estate strategies and centralized measures of real estate management? Important to this is the realization in Scotland that building the "competitive knowledge infrastructure" of the twenty-first century requires a mix of what Peel calls "hard" (real estate) and "soft" (knowledge and relational) institutional dimensions.

These first three chapters in Part II concern themselves with the ways the policies of the state have influenced and, in some cases, restructured the developmental practices of the university, because the university is actually a unit of the state. Of significant note is the extent to which much of the new state higher education policy has purposely attempted to build a more engaged relationship between the university and the economy, especially with regard to land development. This analysis is continued in chapter 5, but Yuichi Takeuchi's study of Hosei University is different in at least one key way: The university is not a state entity; it is the oldest and most distinguished private university in Tokyo. In "Toward Downtown: Spatial Growth and University Location in the Tokyo Metropolitan Area," Takeuchi shows how national and urban land policies governed the location and development of all university properties in Tokyo, including private ones, for much of the last half of the twentieth century. He describes how government policy in Japan linked the location of factories and institutions of higher education to hyper-urban and -suburban concentration and therefore initiated policies prohibiting new university buildings and institutional expansions from being built in the intensely urbanized southern Kanto area around Tokyo. As a result, new university development occurred on urban land at the outskirts of and outside the southern Kanto area, stimulating growth at the urban rim.

This growth stopped when the long-term recession arrived at the start of the 1990s, and "urban regeneration" at the city center was hailed as one of the new "structural reforms." Under the new state-directed regeneration policies, collaboration between industry and the academic world was encouraged, national universities were incorporated, and, as a result, investments in central city real estate flourished. Chapter 5 describes these trends and concentrates especially on this linkage of state-sponsored regeneration policy and university development in the "glo-calization" strategies of the Tokyo city region.

The University, the City, and the Market (Zones of Development)

In introducing the previous section, we suggested that every chapter in the book could have been included in Part II, on the university, the city, and the state. The same could certainly be said for Part III, on the urban university and the "market," or the economy. Each case study in the book recognizes the role of the university as an important feature of the urban and global economy. In the United States and Europe, in Asia and Latin America, each city and its universities have their version of a political economic rhetoric that views the university, to use Deborah Peel's term, as an "economic engine." However, the chapters in Part III focus more directly on the direct and indirect economic import of university development. For example, across the world, university R&D functions are increasingly viewed as productive features of urban corporate development, leading to university property development strategies that are a mixture of proprietary and academic uses (chapter 7, Yonsei University in Seoul). At the same time, a university's land development often stimulates, in unintended ways, land speculation and real estate investment at the edge of, or in near proximity to, the campus (chapter 6, UNAM in Mexico City). Compared to the ways universities indirectly leverage or stimulate development are the ways they more directly produce and otherwise engage themselves in the construction of cities—producing whole "zones of development," as one of the authors in Part III calls them. These zones are retail, cultural, residential, and industrial, as well as academic. The universities' roles in building these "zones of urban change" are under studied, and yet today they are perceived to be increasingly important elements of the future, not only of the education sector but of the cities of which they are a part.

The first chapter in Part III, chapter 6, by Carlos Morales Schechinger and Sara García Jiménez, tells the story of one of the world's largest such zones—University City—the main campus of the National Autonomous University of Mexico (UNAM). University City is an important symbol in Mexico not only of higher education but also of the *independence* of an institution that is otherwise heavily dependent on subsidies from Mexico's federal government. The campus, covering over 733 hectares, is one of the largest single pieces of urban property, worldwide, in one of the world's largest cities, Mexico City, with almost 19 million inhabitants, owned by one of the world's largest universities, with a community of almost one-third of a million members. The development of a university of such a scale has been accompanied by equally well-established territorial feelings and control over the campus. The chapter shows how all this—both the campus and its social importance—is a product of a complex history of property struggle, design achievement, land development and speculation, taxing ambiguities, and *self-regulation* of land use. The authors provide an overview of this history, describing how politics and academic purpose combine to create a zone of university development in the city with almost full self-sufficiency of urban services, as well as economic and environmental contributions to the city. The long history of University City may be unique in its scale and politics, but in producing long-term conditions of beneficial urban development based not on land development strategies of maximization of economic surplus but on the direct and indirect economic benefits that derive from land development that supports the academic enterprise, more broadly, it is exceedingly instructive. The case demonstrates a land development strategy of stimulating proprietary and speculative real estate development all around the university but choosing to practice land development itself without speculation, in exchange for political and economic autonomy.

If the case of the UNAM is a clear example of the power of the intellectual mission as a centerpiece of land-use development, the case of the private Yonsei University in Seoul, South Korea, Senate Properties board is almost the polar opposite. In chapter 7, "Partnering with Private Corporations to Build on Campus: Yonsei University, Seoul, Korea," Gwang Ya Han and Wann Yu tell the story of a mixed-use development strategy executed through the increasingly entrepreneurial model of a major private research university.

The authors begin with a brief overview of the history of campus development at Yonsei University and the surrounding neighborhood, ShinChon, to set the context for a case study of university mixed-use development of a major research facility. Early on in the case, the authors chart the decline in national funding of R&D at Yonsei. They show how the university has "pragmatically" adjusted to this decline through the "development of partnerships with private corporations, such as Daewoo, Hyundai, LG, and Samsung, which allow for the creation of privately operated corporate R&D facilities on the university's property." The path to this institutional and programmatic change in the university is a complex one. The chapter studies the motifs, stakeholders, constraints, development approaches, and decision-making processes that led the university and the city to new financing and zoning arrangements that could accommodate a full blend of academic and corporate development interests. The chapter concludes with a critical assessment of the university's advance into entrepreneurship and mixed-use development. Perhaps the key finding is that such corporate-university partnerships assume that "the university will play two proactive roles: first, as 'project initiator,' to build an institutionalized channel for commercial undertakings; and, second, as 'land provider' in partnership development with private corporations who make contributions to project cost." The authors conclude with the suggestion that these changes of institutional roles represent, if not a great transformation, at least an alteration of the way the public views the university's function in society, as well as the way the public sector controls campus development—leading to inevitable conflicts between academic and proprietary interests.

The tension between academic and proprietary interests is modified somewhat in Abner Colmenares's case study in chapter 8, "Urban and Real Estate Development of the Central University of Venezuela's Rental Zone." Conflicts of public purpose may arise over the development of university R&D facilities for proprietary corporate uses on the core campus of Yonsei, but at the Central University of Venezuela in Caracas, in principle, at least, those conflicts are mitigated by the designation of the "Rental Zone." Colmenares points to the university's contribution to the growth of the city of Caracas through its construction, in the 1940s, of the Caracas University City campus. The campus master plan allowed for the creation of a campus of over two hundred hectares, including the development of the Plaza Venezuela Rental Zone, an extra ten-hectare area for real estate development planned to generate resources to financially support the scientific activities carried out by the university. To this end, in 1974, the Venezuelan government created a special entity for the single purpose of ensuring that the Plaza Venezuela Rental Zone would become a city-scale business, commercial, and recreational center. Chapter 8 offers a critical assessment of this development strategy, assessing the planning and design processes and the challenges the university faced in generating support for its academic purposes though such an entity. For a good portion of the chapter, Colmenares writes of an unsuccessful development zone dependent on "governmental financial backing." He suggests that the potential for the university and the zone to realize success increases only when the zone becomes a truly proprietary market zone: when it is managed, beginning in the late 1990s, as a nonprofit real estate company secure in private law and independent from university administration, planned and organized as a real estate entity with proper fiscal and regulatory authority over the zone.

In chapter 9, "Development of the Jatinangor University Area, Indonesia: Growth Problems and Local Solutions," Wilmar Salim changes the focus of this part of the book substantially. Whereas Colmenares focuses on a relatively small area, the ten-hectare rental zone, Salim recounts the development of an entire new university town, analyzing the ways government uses the siting and development of new university campuses to affect urban development in general and higher education in particular. Salim is also concerned less with the successful management of the university as an economic entity than with the unintended consequences of university development for economic development. He tries to make the case that "university land development in developing countries is not always first and foremost about higher education; and where university and government policies are undertaken in such a matter, there are often as many negative as positive consequences, especially for the existing local community" surrounding the sites of university campuses. The chapter arrives at this conclusion after assessing the new university town plan, the development of the universities and the town, and the decidedly mixed impacts of the development on the area. The author finds that the most deleterious effects of such strategic use of university land development practices are felt by those living closest to the new institutional sites.

Salim's study of "mixed impacts" leads to the final chapter in Part III. In chapter 10, Isabel Breda-Vázquez, Paulo Conceição, and Sónia Alves study the "ambiguous relationship" of the University of Oporto and the city of Oporto, Portugal, in urban economic development. While there are certainly differences between Salim's findings and those of the authors here, both chapters supply rich and critical case studies of the intended and unintended impacts university land policies can have on urban economic development. In this chapter, as much as any in this book, we find that the often conflictive and poorly coordinated relationship between university land policies and urban development plans suggests how important universities and their land policies can be to the future development (or *under*development) of the cities of which they are a part. The authors characterize the university in Oporto as an important "operator" in urban change; however, they suggest that the relationships established between the university's real estate policies, the neighborhoods where urban land development is to take place, and the city's policies are "ambiguous" and marked by conflict between the university's strategies and the specific problems of the urban area where the university is located. The authors find that a chief reason for this conflict and ambiguity of relationship is the lack of integration of university land investment policies (such as its disinvestment in the central area of the city and the resulting physical decay and social unevenness) into stabilizing urban land-use, zoning, and functional policies in the planning system developed in Oporto. The case clearly points out the benefits and liabilities that come from linked urban and university development policies and practices.

The University and the Politics of the Contested City

Universities' land development policies are more than decisions of institutional purpose between academic and market decision makers. In certain cities in the world, universities' land development decisions, their physical location, and their campus evolution can be key political elements of urban partition and conflict. As much as those of any other urban institution, the development practices of the university can be viewed as features of the communal and identity politics of cities. In certain cities, university land policies help produce "walls" of division and urban partition every bit as much as they develop campus "walls" of exclusion. Alternatively, they can become elements of community building that help transcend traditional boundaries and fault lines (Harkavy and Puckett 1994; Gaffikin and Morrissey 1999). The chapters in Part IV are studies of the politics of university land development policy. They show how university land development can be part containment policy and part campus development—dividing the academic community from the city or reinforcing the political contestedness of cities by dividing ethnicities from each other. The contributors to this section of the book also show what it takes for the tertiary educational sector to address communal conflict in the city.

In chapter 11, a study of Hebrew University in Jerusalem, Haim Yacobi traces the development of an institution that emerges as something of a colonizing "fortress"—serving as an example of how universities can perform rather dramatic and important roles in shaping not only urban space but what he calls "national urban space." He shows how the location and development of Hebrew University was a fundamental feature of the larger political strategy of what he calls the "Israelization" of Jerusalem. The chapter breaks the study of this role and the impact of university development into three parts: the national territorial role, the architectural symbolic role, and the urban functional role. At each level—of development politics, university planning and placement policies, and architecture and community relations—Yacobi shows how Hebrew University's land policies are key national as well as urban policies.

The chapter essentially begins with the reconstruction of the university after the 1967 war, which served as a formative political element or trigger for the "extensive development of Jewish neighborhoods on Palestinian expropriated land." The chapter suggests that the "mega structure scale" of the university and its location on Mount Scopus created an architecture of domination of the East Jerusalem skyline, establishing a Jewish presence that successfully competed with the "Mount of Olives skyline, where towers that mark non-Jewish monuments such as churches and hospitals existed." Through this interconnection of location, architecture, and everyday life, the politics of university development and its contribution to urban identity and politics are clearly described. The university became not only a center for and site of education but also an element of intervention and territorial control over conflicted ethno-national urban space.

What joins Frank Gaffikin's study of the proposed Springvale campus of the University of Ulster in Belfast, Northern Ireland, to the study of Hebrew University in Jerusalem is in certain ways very clear: Belfast, like Jerusalem, is a contested city, where conflicted conditions of ethno-national and religious urban space are well defined. Both are also examples of deliberate attempts to locate universities in sites of urban contestedness: Hebrew University on Mount Scopus, one of the most prominent areas of Palestinian East Jerusalem, and the University of Ulster in Springvale, a neighborhood where "deeply contested space confounds the politics of land and community." Put more precisely, the Belfast case reflects the university's decision to place a much needed expansion campus right on the "peace line" dividing two of the most contentious Catholic and Protestant communities in Northern Ireland.

But beyond these general comparisons between the two cases the similarities end. Hebrew University is one of the major research universities in the world, and Springvale never happened. Hebrew University fully privileged one side in the urban politics of identity, while the Springvale campus fell victim to unsuccessful institutional attempts to resolve the contentious identity claims of both sides. If Hebrew University is an example of the ethnic dominance of contested space, the Springvale case is more an example of the power of divisiveness. The mixed-site campus was deliberately planned to ameliorate urban ethno-nationalist conflict and to engage its adjacent neighborhoods in a new form of partnership between academy and community.

Such an ambitious project was informed by two processes: the *universal* trends affecting all UK universities and also described in chapter 4; and the *particular* circumstances of Belfast, a "contested" city scarred by over three decades of political violence. In the case of the former, Gaffikin tells us that the University of Ulster, the research university partner in the case, is challenged, like universities throughout the UK and the world to "restructure" in order to meet "rising student demand" and the challenges of "an elevated role in the new economy as prominent creators and repositories of knowledge." Both of these changes in the political economy of the university required more money and a new campus. Ironically, the University of Ulster's access to funds was greatly bolstered not by an a priori claim to educational funds but by the argument that a new university could be a site of peace in an area of violent, ethnicity-driven "Troubles" between Protestant Loyalists and Catholic Republicans. The resulting complex agenda of political responsiveness and educational transformation appeared to be the formula for major support for the University of Ulster in the globalizing era of educational competitiveness and declining state funding. But this complexity, Gaffikin shows us, was a recipe not for political success but for policy overload, leading ultimately to the failure of the Springvale project. The land and university issues and the accompanying political, economic, and institutional claims were all too much, leading to a good case study of the political limitations and changing institutional requirements placed on university land development in the contested space of modern urban settings.

Lessons Learned

With each chapter in this collection we hope to add a bit more to the understanding of the changing role of universities in cities globally and to what is known about the institutional climate affecting the practices of land development throughout the world. In the last chapter of the book, we step back and try to determine what can be learned both from the detail of each case and from what the cases have to tell us about the overall place of urban universities in the modern global context.

The contemporary conditions of globalization are nowhere more evident than in the massive demographic and economic growth of urban areas, and we find in the cases in this book recurring evidence to support the parallel "argument . . . that the growth of universities is a result of sheer population growth, as well as a manifestation of the increasing importance of the knowledge economy, including the strengthened role of urban regions (essentially agglomerations of knowledge sectors and workers) as units of global economic competition" (chapter 13). We suggest that this "core" role of universities in social change in the city is reflected in the physical appearance of universities and in the functions (academic, economic, and civic) carried out in the new physical development of urban campuses.

From these general conclusions derived from an overall assessment of the findings in the cases of the book, the final chapter proceeds to drill into the particulars of the cases to determine how they help us answer key questions, including the following:

- *Why* are universities expanding in some globalizing cities, and how are they responding to urban decay in other cities?
- *Where* is university development taking place, and is such development a product of its own priorities, of the priorities of the state, or simply of following the local real estate market?
- *How* does a university structure its land development practices?
- What is the *impact* of university growth? How successful is the development strategy in light of the university's goals?
- What can be learned about not only the *successes* but also the *failures* of university land policies?

In responding to these questions, we suggest that the cases taken as a whole provide a starting place for further study, as well as a conclusion: Universities are important institutional actors in the growing city-regions of the global era, experiencing change in both mission and scale in almost every area (from the expanding number of students to the technological transformation of education and its delivery, to rapid and sustained changes in their relationships with the state). The way urban universities develop worldwide and the scale of such development may truly be the stuff of a third great transformation[8] in higher education, in which "global" models of the urban university develop in parallel with the near hegemonic "American model." While the American model may be the prevailing one, it certainly is not fully applicable elsewhere. We suggest that comparative study between the U.S. model and universities throughout the world can be especially instructive—especially in the ways leadership and community movements appear to play a more important role in the U.S. development process than the far more "institutionalized" process of university land development elsewhere.

All of this leaves us with an observation we made in the concluding chapter of our previous book, *The University as Urban Developer:* that university real estate development is a rich area of inquiry—constituting not only a new academic way of studying the city, but also a new area of applied study of the university (Wiewel and Perry 2005), especially comparative study.

Notes

1. See Castells (1997), Sassen (1991, 2002), Scott (2001, 2005), and Roy (2006) on the rising importance of cities in new world systems of information, technology, and communication—systemic spaces of flows of capital, people, knowledge, and consumption. See also, for example, policy studies by the Clusters on Innovation Group of the Council on Competitiveness (2004), CEOs for Cities (2002), Council on Competitiveness (2006), Domestic Policy Council (2006), and National Commission on the Urban Agenda (2006), plus Breton and Lambert (2004), Bond and Lemasson (1999), Slaughter and Rhoades (2004), and Shapiro (2005), among many others on the rising importance of universities in the new global environment.

2. For example, see: Breton and Lambert (2004) or Bond and Lemasson (1999).

3. Rarely, if ever, do they set out to directly explore the contributions of the university to the development of the city and, conversely, what the university gains from its developmental and broader institutional relationships with the city. Exceptions are found in the "urban university" literature and the more historical studies, previously introduced, along with the rich array of university-community development studies and community politics case studies of U.S. universities, good examples of which include Nash (1973) and Maurrasse (2001).

4. One exception is the new collection of case studies on universities in cities in North America by Perry and Wiewel (2005).

5. Over the past five years we have sought to address these issues through a project that studies the role of the urban university as a developer. Working in collaboration with the Lincoln Institute of Land Policy, we developed a curriculum and set of cases that resulted in a book that provides a synthetic and descriptive analysis of the role of American universities in urban real estate development (Perry and Wiewel 2005).

6. A quote from a European Commission in the appendix to "Developing a Knowledge Flagship: The European Institute of Technology," a working document of the commission, March 2006, as used in Lambert and Butler (2006, 1).

7. More detailed versions for this argument of a third great transformation in higher education can be found in Gaffikin, McEldowney, and Perry (2006) and Gaffikin and Perry (2006).

8. To borrow again from Clark Kerr's notion of a previous "second great transformation" of the American university in the decades after the Second World War. See Kerr (1972), and on the topic of a "third great transformation" see Gaffikin and Perry (2006).

References

Altbach, Philip G., and Toru Umakoshi, eds. 2004. *Asian Universities: Historical Perspectives and Contemporary Challenges.* Baltimore: Johns Hopkins University Press.

Bender, Thomas, ed. 1988. *The University and the City: From Medieval Origins to the Present.* New York: Oxford University Press.

Bond, Sheryl, and Jean-Pierre Lemasson, eds. 1999. *A New World of Knowledge: Canadian Universities and Globalization.* Ottawa, Canada: IDRC.

Brenner, Neil. 1999. "Globalisation as Reterritorialisation: The Re-scaling of Urban Governance in the European Union." *Urban Studies* 36, no. 3: 431–51.

Breton, Gilles, and Michel Lambert, eds. 2004. *Universities and Globalization: Private Linkages, Public Trust.* Paris: UNESCO.

Castells, Manuel. 1997. *The Rise of the Network Society.* Malden, MA: Blackwell.

———. 2004. *The Power of Identity.* 2nd ed. Malden, MA: Blackwell.

CEOs for Cities. 2002. *Leveraging Colleges and Universities for Urban Economic Revitalization.* Boston: Author.

Clark, David. 2002. *Urban World/Global City.* 2nd ed. New York: Routledge.

Clusters on Innovation Group, Council on Competitiveness. 2004. *Regional Foundations of U.S. Competitiveness.* Washington, DC: Author.

Dober, Richard P. 1991. *Campus Design.* New York: John Wiley.

Domestic Policy Council. 2006. *American Competitiveness Initiative: "Leading the World in Innovation."* Washington, DC: U.S. Office of Science and Technology Policy.

European Commission. 2003. *The Role of Universities in the Europe of Knowledge.* The Hague: Author.

———. 2006. *Developing a Knowledge Flagship: The European Institute of Technology.* The Hague: Author.

Friedman, Thomas. 2005. *The World Is Flat: A Brief History of the Twenty-first Century.* New York: Farrar Straus Giroux.

Gaffikin, Frank, and Mike Morrissey, eds. 1999. *City Visions: Imagining Place, Enfranchising People.* London: Pluto Press.

Gaffikin, Frank, and David C. Perry. 2006. Discourses and Visions in the Contemporary U.S. Academy. Unpublished paper, Contested Cities/Urban Universities Project, Queens University, Belfast.

Gaffikin, Frank, Malachi McEldowney, and David Perry. 2006. The Planning Discourses of Higher Education: A Comparative Study. Unpublished paper, Contested Cities/Urban Universities Project, Queens University, Belfast. September.

Geiger, Roger L. 2004. *Knowledge and Money: Research Universities and the Paradox of the Marketplace.* Stanford, CA: Stanford University Press.

Grogan, Paul S., and Tony Proscio. 2000. *Comeback Cities: A Blueprint for Urban Neighborhood Revival.* Boulder, CO: Westview Press.

Harkavy, Ira, and John L. Puckett. 1994. "Lessons from Hull House for the Contemporary Urban University." *Social Service Review* 68, no. 3: 299–321.

Harvey, David. 2005. *A Brief History of Neoliberalism.* New York: Oxford University Press.

Initiatives for a Competitive Inner City. 2002. *Leveraging Colleges and Cities for Urban Economic Development: An Action Agenda.* Boston: CEOs for Cities.

Jackson, Kenneth T. 1987. *Crabgrass Frontier: The Suburbanization of the United States.* New York: Oxford University Press.

Kerr, Clark. 1972. *The Uses of the University.* With a Postscript 1972. Cambridge, MA: Harvard University Press. (Orig. pub. 1963.)

Lambert, Richard, and Nick Butler. 2006. *The Future of European Universities: Renaissance or Decay?* London: Center for European Reform.

Marcuse, Peter. 2005. "Columbia University's Heights: An Ivory Tower and Its 'Communities.'" In Perry and Wiewel 2005.

Maurrasse, David. 2001. *Beyond the Campus: How Colleges and Universities Form Partnerships with Their Communities.* New York: Routledge.

Nash, George. 1973. *The University and the City: Eight Cases of Involvement.* New York: McGraw-Hill.

National Commission on the Urban Agenda. 2006. *A New Urban Land Grant Act.* Washington, DC: NASULGC. Summer Meeting.

Perry, David C., and Wim Wiewel, eds. 2005. *The University as Urban Developer: Case Studies and Analysis.* Armonk, NY: M.E. Sharpe.

Pirenne, Henri. 1925. *Medieval Cities: Their Origins and the Revival of Trade.* Princeton, NJ: Princeton University Press.

Rhodes, Frank. 2001. *The Creation of the Future: The Role of the American University.* Ithaca, NY: Cornell University Press.

Roy, Ananya. 2006. "Praxis in a Time of Empire." *Planning Theory* 5, no. 1: 7–29.

Sassen, Saskia. 1991. *The Global City: New York, London, Tokyo.* Princeton, NJ: Princeton University Press.

———. 2002. *Global Networks, Linked Cities.* New York: Routledge.

Scott, Alan J. 2001. *Global City-Regions: Trends, Theory, Policy.* New York: Oxford University Press.

———. 2005. *City Regions: Economic Markers and Political Actors in the Global Stage.* Los Angeles: UCLA, Department of Public Policy and Department of Geography.

Shapiro, Harold T. 2005. *A Larger Sense of Purpose: Higher Education and Society.* Princeton, NJ: Princeton University Press.

Slaughter, Sheila, and Gary Rhoades. 2004. *Academic Capitalism and the New Economy: Markets, State, and Higher Education.* Baltimore: Johns Hopkins University Press.

Swyngedouw, Erik. 1997. "Neither Global nor Local: 'Globalization' and the Politics of Scale." In *Spaces of Globalization: Reasserting the Power of the Local,* ed. Kevin R. Cox, 137–66. New York: Guilford Press.

Turner, Paul Venable. 1984. *Campus: An American Planning Tradition.* New York: Architectural History Foundation.

Van der Wusten, Herman. 1998. *The Urban University and Its Identity: Roots, Locations, Roles.* Boston: Kluwer Academic.

Van Ginkel, Hans. 2003. "What Does Globalization Mean for Higher Education?" In *Universities and Globalization: Private Linkages, Public Trust,* ed. Gilles Breton and Michel Lambert. Paris: UNESCO.

Wallerstein, Immanuel. 1979. *The Capitalist World-Economy.* Cambridge: Cambridge University Press.

Wiewel, Wim, and David C. Perry. 2005. "Ivory Towers No More: Academic Bricks and Sticks." In Perry and Wiewel 2005.

Part II

The University, the Devolving
State, and Development

2

The University of Helsinki as a Developer

Anne Haila

The State, City, and University

The University of Helsinki is an old university, founded in 1640 in Turku, then the capital of Finland, as the Academy of Turku, to educate clerks. At the beginning of the nineteenth century, Sweden lost Finland to Russia; Finland became an autonomous grand duchy of the Russian Empire, and Helsinki was made its capital. The university was transferred from Turku to Helsinki and renamed Imperial Alexander University, in honor of Tsar Alexander I, who granted Finland its autonomy and decreed Helsinki as the capital. One reason for moving the university away from Sweden and closer to the Russian capital of St. Petersburg was the tsar's desire to control the radical movements that had become popular in European universities (Suolahti 1950). A fire in Turku in 1827 provided the official excuse.

In Helsinki the Imperial Alexander University was given a role in educating civil servants for the state administration. The university buildings represented this important duty, as well as the new imperial nationality. The main building of the university was built in 1832. Together with other administrative buildings in the city center, it was designed by C.L. Engel, an architect invited from Berlin. Engel's commission was to build the city center of Helsinki to imitate the city the tsar regarded as the most beautiful city in the world, St. Petersburg. Engel gave the buildings in Helsinki an imperial look, representing a role Helsinki never had. In Hollywood films, like *Reds,* Helsinki's imperial glory was used to represent Leningrad.

The main building of the University of Helsinki is still located at the heart of the city, opposite the capitol and next to the main church. These three main institutions and symbols of the Finnish society—the state, the church, and the university—surround the main square of the city, Senate Square, in the middle of which the statue of Tsar Alexander I still stands (see Figure 2.1). The university's location at the center of the city represents the duty it adopted

Figure 2.1   **The Main Building of the University of Helsinki**

from the European university tradition cherished by European princes: The aim of the university was to integrate students into the society (Vuori 1999).

Helsinki was founded in 1550 by Swedish King Gustav Vasa. Like the university it was also a pawn in power politics. Its founding was part of the king's military strategy against the eastern threat (Russia) and the Hanseatic League (Suolahti 1950, 127). Competition between cities was a known phenomenon already in the sixteenth century, and Helsinki was founded as a rival city to the flourishing Hansa city Revell (today Tallinn, just opposite Helsinki across the Baltic Sea).

From the city's point of view, placement of the national capitol, the church, and the university, not City Hall, at the most central and important location was embarrassing. In the beginning of the twentieth century the City of Helsinki established a claim on that symbolically most prestigious location and tried to establish the City Hall where the university is now and locate the university in the suburban neighborhood of Meilahti. This attempt implied a new vision of the university, not as an integral part of the city and society, mixing students and professors in the city life and socializing students to the society, but as a separate community. The Meilahti plan explicitly contrasted the old

Figure 2.2   **The Functionalist Forest House (Metsätalo)**

Heidelberg type of university with the modern American type of university that is close to nature. University professors were envisioned living in villas far from the city and forming a monastery type of scholars' community with their students. The Meilahti plan was also an attempt to relax the state's grip on the university (Knapas 1990, 615). A government committee abandoned the Meilahti plan, however, and the university remained in the city center.

In 1917 Finland became independent, and in 1919 the name of the university was changed to the University of Helsinki and the university began expanding. In 1934 it decided to concentrate the institutions of the Faculty of Agriculture and Forestry in the city center and drew up a construction plan for several colossal buildings. The plan broke with the tradition of the St. Petersburg imperial style and required a change in the town plan. Architects criticized the plan and argued that enormous buildings did not fit into the low-rise cityscape. Despite the criticism the government accepted the change of the town plan in 1936, and in 1939 Metsätalo ("Forest House") was finished (see Figure 2.2). The other buildings included in the plan were not built, however, because the money was needed to prepare for the Olympics of 1940 (which, ultimately, were not held because of the war). Metsätalo marked a change in the style of university buildings. Resembling an office building or hospital or barracks, it is a good example of functionalism (Knapas 1990, 590), which replaced the classicism and imperial look and became the main ideology and style of Finnish architecture for decades.

The University of Helsinki at the center of the city and opposite the capitol manifests two characteristics of Finnish universities. The first is the European tradition of having higher learning and education in cities, in the middle of urban life, not in campuses in suburbs. Second, universities in Finland have a close relationship to the sovereign: They are financed by the state, they educate civil servants to the state administration, and their professors are nominated in state committees. The state of Finland later continued the tradition begun by the tsar, of supporting universities and sciences (Bell and Hietala 2002). The state also intervened on behalf of the university; it appropriated land for university buildings, prevented the City of Helsinki's attempt to locate the university in the suburbs, and approved the Metsätalo plan.

Two decentralizing forces began to undermine the central position of the university, however. First, the university moved some faculties to the suburbs and introduced a campus development strategy. Second, the state established universities outside Helsinki, and the policy of the state real estate company, Senate Properties, created pressure on the university to pay attention to the market value of its premises.

Campus Strategy: University as a City Builder

In the 1960s the number of students began to grow. The university buildings could not meet the increased demand for space, and the university began renting lecture rooms from schools and other buildings near by. The situation was not only inconvenient for scholars, but also uneconomical for the university. To remedy the situation, the university drew up a development plan for the years 1992–2010 that introduced the idea of four university campuses: "One of the long-range goals of the university is to concentrate all the departments presently—and partly inadequately—housed all over Helsinki into four areas: the city centre, Kumpula, Viikki, and Meilahti" (University of Helsinki Development Plan, 1992–2010). The latter three places are neighborhoods in Helsinki, located inside a seven-kilometer radius from the city center.

Under the new strategy, titled the University of Campuses, the three suburban campuses and the city center campus would specialize in different disciplines: the city campus in administration, social sciences, law, theology, and the humanities; the Meilahti campus in medicine; the Kumpula campus in natural sciences; and the Viikki campus in forestry and agricultural sciences. Campus services like libraries, restaurants, and administrative services would be shared by various departments within each campus.

Figure 2.3   **The City Center Campus in the Middle of the Metropolis**

Developing campuses is a new concept for the University of Helsinki. The concept of the "City Centre Campus," as adopted by university officials, is a contradiction in terms, as the word *campus* in its original sense means a field outside a town (Knapas 1999, 15). The city center campus of the University of Helsinki, however, blends into the cityscape (see Figure 2.3).

Finland's constitution grants municipalities autonomy. When Helsinki was founded, the king donated lands to the city, increasing the possibilities of how the city would use its lands. According to the Planning and Construction Law, passed in 1958, municipalities have what is called a planning monopoly: Only municipalities can draw up plans. Before 1958, cities could draw up town plans only for land in their possession; after the 1958 law was passed, the planning powers of the city extended to land not in their possession. The state challenged the sovereignty of the city to decide its land use by preventing the establishment of City Hall at Senate Square and by accepting the Metsätalo plan. Now the university's campus strategy is testing the planning monopoly of the city. If the city had plans to develop Helsinki as a monocentric city, the strategy of the university, with its forty thousand students and teachers, would clearly contribute to what Nevarez (2003) has called a metropolis of campuses.

The campus strategy of the university was well suited to the city, however, and the university's real estate department worked with city planners to develop Helsinki. In the 1990s the city adopted a new strategy: to develop Helsinki as an innovative city based on science and research. The Trade and Industrial Policy program in 1998 introduced seven clusters: biotechnology, food, information, culture, tourism, health care, and the environment. Three projects were developed to implement the clusters: Viikki Science Park, Biomedicum, and Art and Design City Helsinki. The first two are on the University of Helsinki campuses. In the program Successful East Helsinki, accepted by the City Council in 2001, Viikki is identified as a region specializing in biosciences; and in the strategies of the city, the Viikki neighborhood around the university campus is called a new science neighborhood (Manninen 2002).

The University of Helsinki campuses are among the most prestigious neighborhoods in the city. They do not have a higher poverty rate than other neighborhoods, as was found out by Cortes (2004) in a study in the United States. At the time of the Meilahti plan, at the beginning of the twentieth century, Meilahti was a distant suburb. Today the neighborhoods of Meilahti and Kumpula are in the inner ring of the city. Kruununhaka, the location of the city center campus, is among the five most prestigious neighborhoods in Helsinki. Housing prices in Meilahti, Kumpula, and Viikki are above the Helsinki average.

In all four campuses the University of Helsinki has extensive development projects. Among the projects in the city center carried out between 2002 and 2005 are the following: Fabianinkatu 28 (the learning center), €8,710,000; Eläinmuseokortteli (museum in the zoology block), €23,550,000; Siltavuorenpenger 20 (behavioral science faculty), €17,700,000 (figures from the university budget 2003). Investment in these projects, totaling €49,960,000, forms a significant part of Helsinki development. A comparison with the city's own investments shows the important role of the university. The investments of the City of Helsinki in 2004 were €274.7 million (City of Helsinki budget 2004). In the budget of 2003, city investments in schools were €51,092,000, in libraries €1,352,000, in social welfare buildings €28,500,000, and in health sector buildings €25,800 000. The University of Helsinki is also a significant city builder. In 1999, it occupied space in 394 buildings in 34 municipalities. In addition to the premises in Helsinki, the university has estates, experimental stations, and buildings in other cities. Total floor space was 640,000 square meters. At the end of the 1990s, the university's expenses for development and real estate purchases increased significantly, from 18 million Finnish marks in 1997 to 79 million in 1999 (University of Helsinki, Annual Report 1999).

The decision to decentralize its faculties among the four campuses was important for the university, of course, as well as the city. One new issue for the university is how faculties and departments on different campuses can best communicate with each other and how to make sure that the institution as a whole benefits from being a multidiscipline university. To connect its various campuses and also the other universities in the Helsinki metropolitan region—most importantly, the Helsinki University of Technology and its science park, Innopoli, located in the neighboring city of Espoo—the University of Helsinki and the other universities created a public transportation plan called the Science Way. Thus, the university is not just a developer and city builder but also a traffic planner. The Science Way will connect the neighborhoods of Viikki, Arabianranta (University of Arts and Design), Meilahti, and Otaniemi (Helsinki University of Technology and Innopoli Science Park). The City of Espoo issued a statement praising the Science Way for connecting the centers of expertise in the Helsinki metropolitan region, increasing the attraction of the area for private firms, supporting the networking of universities and firms, and facilitating flexible learning as per the decisions of the City Council in 2002.

The State as Real Estate Entrepreneur

In the 1960s the state began a policy of founding new universities in less developed regions of Finland. This supplemented policies of decentralizing the state administration and founding state-owned enterprises in the northern and eastern regions of Finland aiming at promoting growth in those less developed regions. The University of Oulu, founded in 1958 at the gates of northern Finland, was the first regional university. In 1969 Lappeenranta University of Technology and the University of Joensuu were established close to the eastern border, and in 1979 the University of Lapland was founded farther to the North, on the Arctic Circle. In 1980 the School of Economics and Business Administration at Vaasa was made a university and expanded to include humanities and social sciences. The founding of these regional universities meant fewer resources for the University of Helsinki.

In 1977 all universities and institutes of higher education were made state institutions. The state owns and manages the majority of universities' real estate. The real estate of the state is owned and managed by four real estate companies: Engel, Senate Properties, Kapiteeli, and Sponda. Engel and Senate Properties originated in the Office of Intendant, established in 1811 to supervise the planning of government buildings. In 1865 the Office was renamed the Board of Public Buildings, and in 1936 the name was changed again to the National Board of Public Building. In 1995 the National Board of Public Building was closed, and the State Real Property Agency was established.

In the 1990s, the state's real estate ownership and management were reorganized. Engel was established in 1995 to take care of the development of government buildings and real estate services in those buildings. In 1999 the State Real Property Agency became a government-owned enterprise to manage the state properties the state needs for its own use; it was renamed Senate Properties in 2001, and its most important asset is the real estate of universities. Kapiteeli is the state's fully owned real estate investment company, established in 1999 to manage the state property the state does not use; it owns properties all over Finland. Sponda is a real estate investment company only partly owned by the state; it was listed on the Helsinki Stock Exchange in 1999. Kapiteeli and Sponda got their portfolios from properties the state confiscated from banks during the recession in the 1990s; Sponda's properties are mostly in the Helsinki Metropolitan Region.

One important reason behind the restructuring of the ownership and management of the state's real estate assets was the deep recession Finland faced at the beginning of the 1990s after the collapse of the Soviet Union and the loss of Finland's economically privileged position. The state confiscated a significant amount of real estate in its attempt to rescue banks, firms, and households that became bankrupt. The confiscated properties became the property of the state. The recession was also an impetus for the state to adopt a new rationality: to save and use public resources in the most efficient way. The recession also swept away several construction companies, private real estate firms, and real estate investment trusts that had been recently founded. For the emerging state real estate companies the market could not have been better: There were hardly any rivals.

All these state real estate companies—Engel, Kapiteeli, Sponda, and Senate Properties—are under the Ministry of Finance. They have adopted entrepreneurial strategies and seek to make the best and most efficient use of the state real estate, which means maximizing rental income. Kapiteeli is one of the biggest property investment companies in Finland. Its investment strategy is to "increase its asset value and to establish itself in the Finnish capital market as a profitable property investment company with a good cash position" (www.kapiteeli.fi). Because of their entrepreneurial strategies, the state real estate companies have been driven into conflicts with their tenants, employees, cities, and other public organizations. Critics have argued that the Ministry of Finance does not understand the land-use needs of the army, the universities, and the prisons; only authorities of those institutions can understand what kind of premises are needed to make good defense policy, educate students, and rehabilitate inmates.

The Use and Value of University Premises

The reorganizing of the state real estate assets and the state's new real estate policy affected the University of Helsinki immediately. At the end of 1994 the University Council decided that university departments should pay rent for their premises, and in 1999 it ordered that departments should pay the full rent for the additional space they use. They must pay this rent from their operational expenses. If they use less space, they are compensated in full. Before these regulations, payment was one-third of the cost of the space (University of Helsinki, Annual Report 1999, 17). The new regulations led to a strange situation in which departments were financially rewarded if they decreased their activities and punished if they expanded their activities. The university's real estate department argues that the point is to get rid of the thinking that space is free, to make departments understand that they have to find new funds to finance new projects.

The majority of the premises of the University of Helsinki are owned and managed by Senate Properties. One-third is owned by the University Fund. For example, the main building of the university is owned by Senate Properties, but the Administrative Building in the city center campus is owned by the University Fund. The University Fund gives the university a little flexibility in the use and development of its premises. Because of the complicated history of appropriation and donated city lands, there have been legal controversies concerning the ownership of university buildings. In one such controversy, the court ruled that the owner of the Botanic Garden is the City of Helsinki, not the university.

Senate Properties, with its rent-seeking strategy, came into conflict with universities concerning the rents they have to pay. Senate Properties demands the market rent, and the universities argue that there is no market for premises like the main building of the University of Helsinki and that the university departments have no option to rent lecture rooms from other markets. Universities are, as Maurrasse (2001, 4) has called them, "sticky capital" and cannot move and relocate as easily as enterprises. As a supplier for the university premises, Senate Properties has a monopoly position. The university cannot ask for tenders as some other public users have done. An example is policy and prosecutor offices in some municipalities that have asked for competing bids and selected a private real estate company instead of Senate Properties. They have claimed that private real estate companies build better and are cheaper than Senate Properties (*Helsingin Sanomat,* September 23, 2003).

The four campuses of the University of Helsinki have different options for meeting the demands of Senate Properties. The city center campus consists of university administration and the faculties of humanities, social sciences, law, and theology. These faculties have fewer possibilities for renting out space to private companies than the faculties of sciences and medicine, which collaborate with private companies. Also, because of the growth and globalization of Helsinki, the rise of land values places the city center campus—which occupies the most prestigious and valuable land in the city—in a more difficult position than suburban campuses.

The conflict between Senate Properties and the university is a conflict between two logics of using space. To defend the market rents–based policy of Senate Properties, Secretary of State Juhani Turunen in the Ministry of Finance, has said, "The state cannot support universities by charging less than the market rent because nowadays private companies finance an increasing amount of the research done in universities" (*Kontrahti,* Senate Properties customer newsletter, March 20, 2001). To argue against the market-based logic of Senate Properties, the university claims that its real estate policy is based on the uses of its premises, whose main functions are higher education and academic research.

The conflict culminates in the question of how to value the university premises: whether university real estate is a commodity or not. Shoukry T. Roweis and Allen Scott (1981, 142) suggested, "Urban land is clearly a noncommodity in the sense that its intrinsic use value—differential locational advantage—is produced not by individual capitalists, but through the agency of the State and the collective effects of innumerable individual social and economic activities. Specifically, urban land is produced in a complex collective dynamic where the State provides major infrastructural services as well as various public goods which cannot be adequately produced in the commodity form." It is true that urban land is a noncommodity in the sense that its value is contributed by the investments of the state; however, the University of Helsinki case suggests modifying the statement by Roweis and Scott in three senses. First, the state is not a single actor. Senate Properties, with its entrepreneurial strategies, can have contradictory interests with other agencies of the state, like state universities and the Ministry of Education. (Senate Properties has also come into conflict with the army, which argues that Senate Properties and Kruunuasunnot, the management company of the army's housing stock, do not understand the army's needs for land.) Second, the state can have a role in pushing the users to treat their properties as a commodity. By asking the market rent from the university premises, Senate Properties urges the university to develop a market-oriented real estate strategy. Third, in Finland, the state, in the guise of Senate Properties, did not adopt the role of providing infrastructure and promoting public good but intervenes in the use of space by universities.

The conflict between Senate Properties and the users of state properties like the university and the army has an interesting political dimension. When the law concerning Senate Properties was voted on in the Parliament in 2003, both the right and the left suggested that it should allow reductions in value for universities and army real estate. The Parliament rejected the proposal.

The party that voted against it was the Central Party (former Peasant Party), which has always been the major advocate of regional policy.

From Public to Private and Smart Space

The relationship of the University of Helsinki to the state has been close, whereas its relationship to the city, despite its location at the center of the city, has been far more distant. City people only caught a glimpse of what was happening inside the university walls in the ceremonious promotion processions and public lectures (Suolahti 1950). In the 1990s, however, the City of Helsinki and the University of Helsinki began working together in several partnerships. Among these are the Helsinki Science Park on the university's campus in Viikki and the establishment of urban studies professorships at the university.

The change in university buildings from the imperial-style main building to the functionalist Metsätalo represented new ideas about space. In Finland, as Sharon Zukin has argued, the middle class does not inherit houses or castles and therefore with its housing reflects each time period (Zukin 1982, 67); in Finland the public buildings have such a role. In the 1990s, the partnership between the university, the state, and the city produced a new type of suburban private and smart campus space.

Meilahti and Viikki are examples of new suburban campuses representing a new type of space. The first one specializes in medicine, and the second one hosts the Helsinki Science Park, which specializes in biomedicine. The first building of the Helsinki University Central Hospital, the Department of Obstetrics and Gynecology, was built in the 1930s in Meilahti. The Meilahti Hospital building and the Faculty of Medicine department buildings were completed in 1966. In 1998 the National Library of Health Sciences was added, and in 2000 the new medicine faculty building, Biomedicum, was finished. The University of Helsinki moved its clinics from the city center and concentrated its medical research on the Meilahti campus. To describe the importance of this medical campus in the city of Helsinki, the chancellor of the university, Kari Raivio (1999), has called the area Medilahti (*lahti* meaning "bay").

In the Helsinki Science Park in Viikki, the university and the City of Helsinki have established a limited-liability company, Helsingin Tiedepuiston Asunnot Oy, to provide rental housing for the staff working in the science park. The provision of housing has had a positive effect on the whole campus neighborhood and prevented the negative external effects universities might otherwise have in neighborhoods. Cortes (2004) determined that a university's decision to build new student housing has important external effects and partly explains why universities have positive effects in some neighborhoods and negative external effects in others. "If student enrollments increase and the university does not provide new student housing, then an overall pattern of neighborhood downgrading would possibly result near the university" (Cortes 2004, 369).

The erosion of public space has been a popular topic among urban scholars. Shopping malls, gated residential communities, closed parks, raised pedestrian bridges, and underground tunnels (Sorkin 1992), together with increased privatization of spaces that were once public domain; increased surveillance of public space and control of access; and increased use of playful design that employs theme park simulations and breaks connections with local history and geography (Cybriwsky 1999) have been taken as evidence of the end of public space. The history of the University of Helsinki also shows the changing nature of public space.

The main building of the University of Helsinki, the city center offers a public space that anyone can walk into to listen to a public doctoral defense or a concert. Biomedicum and the Viikki Science Park mark a departure from the public space anyone can enter freely. To enter requires an invitation, purpose, and contact. However, although the new spaces in Meilahti and Viikki are not public, they are not completely private, either. An appropriate name for this new category of space is "privileged space," a term used by designers of the future workplace Wheeler, Hauer, and Rose and implemented by modern companies like Nokia. Privileged space is accessible only by invitation. The university suburban campuses with their smart, clean, and secure space are harbingers of this new type of space.

Acknowledgments

I would like to thank Anna-Maija Lukkari for an excellent interview, and Robert Beauregard and David Perry for their valuable comments.

References

Bell, Marjatta, and Marjatta Hietala. 2002. *The Innovative City: Historical Perspectives.* Helsinki: Gummerus Jyvaskyla.

Cortes, Alvaro. 2004. "Estimating the Impacts of Urban Universities on Neighborhood Housing Markets: An Empirical Analysis." *Urban Affairs Review* 39: 342–75.

Cybriwsky, Roman. 1999. "Changing Patterns of Urban Public Space: Observations and Assessment from Tokyo and New York Metropolitan Areas." *Cities* 16: 223–31.

Knapas, Rainer. 1990. "Rakennettu ja rakentamaton yliopisto." In *Helsingin yliopist 1917–1990,* eds. Matti Klinge, Rainer Knapas, Anto Leikola, and John Strömberg. Helsinki: Otava.

————. 1999. "What Campus?" In *University of Helsinki: University of Campuses*, ed. Eija Vuori. Helsinki: Edita.

Manninen, Asta. 2002. "Talouskasvua tarvitaan." *Kvartti*, no. 2.

Maurrasse, D. 2001. *Beyond the Campus: How Colleges and Universities Form Partnerships with Their Communities*. New York: Routledge.

Nevarez, Leonard. 2003. *New Money, Nice Town: How Capital Works in the New Urban Economy*. New York: Routledge.

Raivio, Kari. 1999. "The Cutting Edge of Medical Research and Practice." In *University of Helsinki: University of Campuses*, ed. E. Vuori. Helsinki: Edita.

Roweis, Shoukry T., and Allen Scott. 1981. "The Urban Land Question." In *Urbanization and Urban Planning in Capitalist Society*, eds. M. Dear and A. Scott. London: Methuen.

Sorkin, Michael, ed. 1992. *Variations on a Theme Park: The New American City and the End of Public Space*. New York: Noonday Press.

Suolahti, Eino E. 1950. *Vantaan Helsinki: Helsingin kaupungin historia I osa*. Helsinki: Suomalaisen kirjallisuuden seuran kirjapaino Oy (Society of Finnish Literature).

University of Helsinki. Development Plan, 1992–2010.

————. 1999. Annual Report.

Vuori, Eija. 1999. *Helsingin yliopisto: Kampusten yliopisto*. Helsinki: Edita.

Zukin, Sharon. 1982. *Loft Living: Culture and Capital in Urban Change*. Baltimore: Johns Hopkins University Press.

3

From Conversion to Cash Cow?

The University of Lüneburg, Germany

Katrin B. Anacker and Uwe Altrock

Over the past few decades publicly funded universities have faced increasing pressure from their constituents. They have encountered funding problems at the national level and, even more so, at the state level in both the United States and Europe. In addition, as economic and social objectives have come into play, constituents now expect more than just teaching, research, and public service activities. The role of universities as a vehicle for regional development has been discussed extensively under the so-called third role rubric: Universities are now expected to cooperate with their various stakeholders and promote technology transfer and innovations in all their fields (Goddard, Teichler, et al. 2003; see also Goddard, Asheim, et al. 2003; Charles 2003; Lazzeroni and Piccaluga 2003; Etzkowitz and Leydesdorff 2002; Peck and McGuinness 2003; Smith 2003; Pimat 1999).

The role of the university as a vehicle for urban development (and redevelopment) is a new topic. In a large city, development would have an impact on a neighborhood (i.e., one or several census tracts). For example, the development of the Campus Gateway in Columbus, Ohio, is anticipated to have repercussions in the neighborhood surrounding the site. In a smaller city, development would have an impact on the entire city (see also Gumprecht 2003).

Urban development by the public sector has been practiced since the beginning of the 1950s in the United States. In the 1950s and 1960s the U.S. federal government engaged in massive urban renewal projects throughout the entire nation. States and municipalities have also engaged in urban development projects. Over time there seems to have been a shift from higher levels of funding (the federal level) to lower levels of funding (the local level). In addition, the public sector has begun trying to coax the private sector to the funding table. Public-private partnerships as a funding strategy have been discussed extensively in the planning and land development literature (see Schneider-Sliwa

1996, among others). The discussion started in the United States, then moved to the United Kingdom during the Thatcher era (Bailey 1994; Brindley, Rydin, and Stoker 1989), and finally spread to other countries, including Germany, in the 1990s (Heinz 1993; Kirsch 1997; Kletzander 1995).

Universities have engaged in urban development for several years, although discussions about it in the academic literature have just begun (Glasson 2003). One reason for university participation in urban development is the increased accountability for spending of public funds, coupled with decreased public funding. Another reason is the need for additional space for research and student residences, recreation, and entertainment. Moreover, universities are interested in improving their surrounding neighborhoods for image and safety reasons. Also, if universities own property in surrounding neighborhoods, property values may appreciate due to community development they initiate or implement.

Urban development by universities often takes place off campus, such as in nearby neighborhoods. For example, the neighborhood adjacent to the campus of Ohio State University in Columbus was an active site of university real estate development even though it is characterized by multiple challenges: an old housing stock in need of repair and maintenance, a low homeownership rate, a high rate of transition, very low median household incomes, and one of the highest crime rates in the city.

Urban development by universities can also be undertaken on campus. In the 1980s the University of Lüneburg, Germany, experienced an increased enrollment rate, which resulted in a shortage of classrooms. University buildings were scattered all over the city, requiring faculty and students to commute between different areas.

At the same time, because the Cold War was coming to an end, there was a reduced need for soldiers and barracks. Lüneburg's Scharnhorst Barracks (*Scharnhorstkaserne*) were scheduled to be vacated by soldiers, offering the university an opportunity to redevelop the facilities, thereby addressing both the rise in student enrollment and the shortage in the classroom pool. However, this plan was threatened by a federal and state funding crisis in Germany in the late 1990s, especially in the state of Lower Saxony, where Lüneburg is located. This led to extensive fiscal, administrative, and political restructuring efforts in the university, which had direct impacts on the real estate portfolio of the University of Lüneburg.

In sum, within only one decade, the University of Lüneburg experienced not only military conversion but also the transition from a publicly funded institution to a foundation. The first part of this chapter deals with the university's military conversion and its economic impact. The second part deals with the financial restructuring of the university. The conclusion discusses aspects of the University of Lüneburg that can be considered as a role model in both the German planning context and the international fiscal context.

Military Conversion in Germany and in Lüneburg

After the German reunification, military presence in both East and West Germany decreased and many military bases were closed. On the one hand, this created large, unused areas in the countryside, such as former training bases, military airports, and ammunition storage sites. On the other hand, smaller sites in urban areas, such as barracks for drafted soldiers and residential areas for permanent soldiers and staff, were now available for development.

When the armies left sites at the beginning of the 1990s, those sites became the property of the national government represented by the Federal Properties Administration (*Bundesvermögensverwaltung* [BVV]), which is subsumed under the Federal Ministry of Finance. The Federal Properties Administration is concerned with properties that are owned by the federal government but not used by it. One of the agency's main tasks is to sell sites that were formerly used by the military. It checks whether there is potential future military use of a site, and if not, it formally declares the end of military use for that site. It then determines who owned the site before the military use began. This is a particular concern for those sites where the military established its presence between 1933 and 1945, during the reign of Adolf Hitler and his National-Socialist Party, when eminent domain was typically used as a means of pursuing political goals, including discriminating against the politically unwanted such as Jewish citizens.

The Federal Properties Administration next asks the states and then the municipalities if they have any interests in each site. If a state does not declare an interest, then municipalities can declare theirs and start working on analyses, comprehensive plans, or zoning plans—even before the property is formally transferred. The Federal Properties Administration sells the property for its market value, although many buyers have taken advantage of the Discount Program (*Verbilligungsprogramm*), a temporary program that offered discounts if future use of a property would benefit the public (e.g., public housing, hospitals, facilities for senior or challenged residents, homeless shelters, shelters for women and children, educational facilities, sports facilities).

Many municipalities said that they were not informed of imminent military conversions or that they waited for BVV's decisions and instructions for a long time, sometimes in vain. Also, many have alleged that BVV was selling the sites for inflated prices, making it difficult for local stakeholders to purchase them even though the national government offered subsidies for affordable housing projects, student housing projects, and other public uses.

In some cases, political or administrative issues hindered regional and local stakeholders from becoming partners. Another problem was that regional and local planners had not been allowed to interfere during the time of the military presence, but now they were supposed to work in areas where the usual planning regulations and activities did not apply.

Many of the former military sites within urban areas were converted into new residential and mixed uses. At the beginning of the 1990s, Germany's housing shortage was one of the top items on the nation's political agenda. The German reunification led to many Eastern Germans' moving to Western Germany because of job opportunities and other reasons. This migration put additional pressure on the already tense housing market. Many conversion projects offered opportunities to develop mixed-use projects—as opposed to residential projects with one function only—favored by planners.

Other former military sites within urban areas were converted into business parks and similar entities. There are only a few examples of conversions into university facilities (Forschungs-und Informations-Gesellschaft 1997; Rother and Schwarte 1997). For example, a part of Bornstedter Feld Barracks in Potsdam (www.bornstedter-feld.de) was converted into a second campus for the local university of applied sciences, the former French military hospital André Genet in Trier was reused as an expansion of the existing university nearby (also a second campus);[1] and the former U.S. military hospital Birkenfeld was converted into an "environmental campus" of the university of applied sciences in the same city.[2]

The low proportion of former military sites converted into educational and research facilities can be explained by the fact that addressing shortages in the housing market was considered more important than addressing some needs in the education sector, which had seen expansions in the 1970s. Thus, former barracks were highly desirable to developers and planners who wanted to build new housing units.

An evaluation conducted by the state government of Rhineland-Palatine, one of the German states most affected by conversion issues, illustrates the importance of military conversion: The greatest share of the state's 85 conversion projects, about 22 percent of all projects, went to residential use; followed by mixed use, about 21 percent; commercial and retail use, about 15 percent; business parks, about 9 percent; and educational and research facilities, about 3 percent, among other uses.[3]

The location of Scharnhorstkaserne on the southern fringe of Lüneburg would have made it an attractive place for the development of suburban housing, but the relatively long distance to the freeway system, the residential character of the neighborhood, and other factors spoke against a development for commercial or manufacturing uses. Also, the existing barracks in the northern part of the site could be reused, making single-family housing implausible. Therefore, the old college that had gotten the status of university in 1987 and expanded in size found a surprisingly swift conversion environment. During the entire process, public officials turned out to be much more flexible than expected, allowing an unusually smooth and fast realization process.

The military conversion in Lüneburg can be considered a successful example of a mixed-use conversion, as well as a role model for a swift conversion. The reasons for this particular conversion are manifold, as there are both push factors and pull factors. In the 1980s the university considered expanding its campus by buying adjacent land that was used by gardeners. Germany is characterized by a low homeownership rate of about 40 percent, so many people lease small pieces of land close to their homes, where they can grow fresh produce and relax during warm summer days and evenings. Some of these garden plots that used to be at the urban fringe are now located in inner cities. Garden plots are cultural icons of Germany, so many of them are protected by a law (*Bundeskleingartengesetz*) that guarantees the gardeners low rental fees and a permanent status in the general land-use plan. Where they are not protected, political resistance by gardeners against redevelopment of their sites is usually so enormous that politicians fear to reclaim them.

Although the university had considered an expansion next to its existing site, it soon became apparent that the political opposition to that would be enormous. At the same time, the classroom shortage worsened. Alternatives had to be found quickly. Although political opposition was vast in the case of potential expansion of the university campus into the garden plots, it was surprisingly almost nonexistent to the conversion of Scharnhorst Barracks to the new university campus. The three local politicians that had seats in the federal parliament (*Bundestag*), the local politicians that had seats in the state parliament (*Landtag*), Lüneburg's lord mayor, the president of the University of Lüneburg, and other local stakeholders endorsed the project wholeheartedly. The fact that the federal government pays a subsidy of up to 75 percent of the assessed value of military conversion sites when they are reused by universities also worked in favor of the conversion.

Another point that worked in favor of the project was that at the end of the 1980s local architect Carl-Peter von Mansberg had designed a model for an expansion of the old campus. Although his model did not apply to military conversion, it did help the university to think about a comprehensive plan for its facilities instead of a piecemeal plan. This was because von Mansberg had set up a comprehensive vision and calculated the total need of classroom and administrative space for the university in the long run. This vision showed the university that there would be a severe need for additional space that was not apparent during the rapid growth of student enrollment throughout the 1980s.

Aside from the Scharnhorst Barracks there were few alternatives for relocating the university campus. One, the Lüner Barracks (*Lüner Kaserne*), would have become available only after 1996, whereas the Scharnhorst Barracks were available several years earlier. Another possible alternative was a smaller area to the north of the old university campus. However, future use by the university would have been tricky because of ownership issues and because of the high density of the area in question. Developing the Scharnhorst Barracks seemed to be the only feasible step to improve the university's situation.

Planning in general, and planning a new campus in particular, usually requires a complicated procedure in Germany. The process calls for a comprehensive coordination of stakeholders in the public sector and participation of the general public. Public entities responsible for implementation of the planning results—in most cases the State Office for Structural Engineering (*Staatshochbauamt*)—are often criticized for their inflexibility, slowness, and cost inefficiency. In this case, though, thanks to the transfer of the construction process to NILEG (today Northern German State Development Agency, *Norddeutsche Landesentwicklungsgesellschaft*), at that time a state-owned private development corporation, the process was accelerated and the costs curtailed.

One reason for the swiftness of the conversion was the effective communication and cooperation exhibited among the important stakeholders in the process, including the state parliament, State Department of Science and Culture (*Ministerium für Wissenschaft und Kultur*), State Department of Finance (*Finanzministerium*), University of Lüneburg, and residents and landlords in the university neighborhood. In addition, a high-ranking official of the State Department of Science and Culture, Baureferent Flebbe, assumed a special role in the process, pushing the development forward and speeding up the process as much as possible.

The conversion was split into three phases. Phase 1 (DM 25 million), from 1993 to 1994, comprised a quick renovation of former barracks buildings, provision of technical infrastructure, and construction of new lecture halls and the first part of the cafeteria. The completion of this first phase in only one year allowed parts of the university to move quickly to the new campus. Phase 2 (DM 37 million) started in 1995 and increased the number of students on the new campus to four thousand in one year. During phase 3 (DM 78 million), started in mid-1996 and completed in late 1997, major buildings, such as the second part of the cafeteria and the library, were erected and other existing buildings were converted (Vogel 1997).

In Germany, regulations set a certain amount of office space for employees. For example, professors are allowed larger offices (20 square meters) than their secretaries (12 square meters). Flexible application of the regulations for the larger university offices and seminar rooms (35 square meters) prevented expensive reconstruction efforts and potential conflicts with preservationists. Contrary to one of the main standards of public policy, efficiency (i.e., concern for the taxpayer), public officials involved in this project paid attention to quality, including interior design, making implementation of the project more expensive but also more aesthetically pleasing (interviews with Klaus Flebbe and Dieter Gawlik, February 20, 2004; Henning Zühlsdorf, December 19, 2003).

In summary, the significant factors in the fields of planning and real estate development that led to the successful conversion of the Scharnhorst Barracks are as follows: first, a pressing need to expand university facilities due to an increase in enrollment and insufficient and infeasible alternatives at the old site; second, a general consensus by a wide range of stakeholders who considered the conversion a feasible opportunity; third, significant federal funding opportunities; fourth, a fit between the vision suggested by a local architect and the proposed site; fifth, the pressing need to act quickly because of the concern that the window of opportunity might close; and sixth, the selection of NILEG, a development corporation, to manage the conversion process.

Economic Impact of the Scharnhorst Barracks Conversion

This study has two components, the military conversion of Scharnhorst Barracks and the restructuring of the university. While the military conversion was completed at the end of the 1990s, the financial restructuring of the university is still in progress and therefore is not discussed here. A future comprehensive discussion of the economic effects of the move to Scharnhorst Barracks should differentiate between the impact on the university and the impact on the local and regional economy. With respect to the university level, it is almost impossible to distinguish between the effects of the move itself and those of the general development of the university in the 1990s and beyond. Evaluating an economic impact usually requires the availability of and access to data, preferably before and after a significant change. Unfortunately, the data available for an evaluation of the economic impact of Lüneburg's military conversion are not sufficient.

Primary economic effects are generated through expenditures by the university on salaries and goods. The University of Lüneburg has about 400 employees (gross income: DM 29.3 million; net income: DM 17.9 million) of whom about 70 percent live in Lüneburg County and about 40 percent live in the City of Lüneburg (Pimat 1999). Other primary economic effects are generated through expenditures by students (expenditures by all students: DM 66 million during the entire year 1997 (personal communication from Henning Zuehlsdorff, December 22, 2006). In addition, there are expenditures by the Student Union (*Studentenwerk*), a national association that advises and supports students. The Student Union provides dormitories and cafeterias on or near university campuses (total expenditures: DM 540,000). Although primary economic effects are important for the university, we question whether the move changed them and, if so, to what degree.

Secondary economic effects are those that depend on the expenditures mentioned under primary effects. According to Pimat (1999), secondary effects range between DM 17.2 million and DM 60 million of generated income and between 79 and 275 generated jobs. The university has an important role with respect to improving the city's image and attractiveness. Therefore, it contributes indirectly to the economic prospect of the region.

The vitality of the campus grew as a consequence of both the move and the increased number of students at the university. The new campus provides improved facilities, such as the newly constructed auditorium in which large meetings and conventions can be held in Lüneburg. Whereas Lüneburg used to be virtually nonexistent on the German map of trade fairs and conventions, the university now seems to be an attractive place for national meetings. A cultural center established in the former gym is home to a number of exhibitions, concerts, and other events that have importance for the entire city. The university library is used by the general public, as well. Also, a retail and service building in the center of the campus is now home to businesses such as a copy shop and a bookstore that cater to students' needs. Without a doubt, the businesses in that building profit from its location in the heart of the campus and from the increased size of the university.

There are also spillover effects; local businesses might be interested in employing students and graduates, and students might start small enterprises. For example, e.novum, a center for start-ups founded in 2000, now offers graduates of the university support for establishing innovative business ideas in town (www.ihk24-Lüneburg.de).

Another economic effect is an increased number of visitors to the university, including professors and friends and families of students, who demand goods and services provided by local businesses in the fields of retail, service, and accommodation. The "feel" of the city has changed. The soldiers are gone, but the number of students has increased, so Lüneburg now has more entertainment facilities geared toward students. Students with backpacks walking or riding their bikes are a common sight in the streets (interview with Klaus Dützmann, December 18, 2003).

In summary, the move has resulted in an improved image of both the university and the city and region. The new, or at least rehabilitated, university facilities are more attractive to students, faculty, staff, and visitors, and they have increased the vitality of the campus. Also, the move put Lüneburg on the map of trade fairs and conventions, resulting in increased revenues for hotels, restaurants, and other establishments.

University Partnerships in Germany and in Lower Saxony

Whereas the first part of this study deals with the military conversion, the second part deals with the financial restructuring of the University of Lüneburg. For the past several years, Europe's higher education community has been in a state of flux. The creation of the European Higher Education Area, based on the Bologna process, has increased pressure that education and research be of high quality and foster national competitiveness in their fields. It has also increased the focus on demographic trends and developments, labor market trends, and the emergence of global educational markets. Universities are now required to take on a so-called third role, in which they are expected to cooperate with their various stakeholders and promote technology transfer and innovations in all their fields (Goddard, Teichler et al. 2003). Lüneburg, for example, has received the status of Lower Saxonian model university in the Bologna process, which requires all EU universities that award bachelor's and master's degrees to make their degrees comparable internationally.[4]

Another significant change in the field of higher education is in the area of funding. There has been a shift from the federal and state levels to the state and local levels, and there have been efforts to coax the private sector to the funding table. The increasing importance of public-private partnerships in international debates about governance reached Germany in the late 1980s and gained momentum after reunification in the early 1990s. Since then, several public services once considered the province of the state—such as public infrastructure, telecommunication, and the public railway system (*Deutsche Bahn*)—have been privatized or considered for privatization. Private companies and foundations have been established to run these former state entities (Richter 2002).

Foundations are considered the appropriate form of governance when it comes to costly activities in the joint interests of citizens, the state, and private companies (Miegel 2002; Teufel 2001; Zimmer and Nährlich 2000). The prerequisite to governance by foundation was a reform of German law to allow multiple sources of funds. Before that reform, a foundation could accept monies from one person only; now a foundation is allowed to accept monies from several people (Bundesverband Deutscher Stiftungen 2000). This holds for fields of policy making as diverse as the preservation of monuments, the development of ecologically important habitats, and the promotion of research into prevention and medical treatment of widespread diseases. In addition, foundations are attractive forms of organizing public-private partnerships in Germany due to the advantageous tax rates they receive.

Thus, although there are numerous foundations in the cultural and social fields,[5] their importance and role in Germany differ from those of United States foundations, which often step in to support universities and other institutions. In the United States it is more legitimate and acceptable than in Germany not only to donate but also to be recognized for donating—for example, many U.S. university buildings are named after their donors. Due to both a different understanding of the state and significantly higher tax burdens, however, most Germans traditionally expect the public sector to step in and conduct many activities that are often undertaken by foundations and other nonprofit organizations in the United States.

Until the early 1990s, public universities in Germany were funded almost exclusively by the states (*Länder*), which were in turn supported by the federal government. Because nationwide reforms or changes in the education system normally require comprehensive procedures that take a long time, the federal government sets up a legal framework that is filled by the *Länder*, which compete with each other for funds. The Permanent Commission of the State Ministers for Public Education and Arts (*Kultusministerkonferenz*) is a voluntary body formed by the states to coordinate their affairs, although it does not always work effectively.

The budget crisis that affected most German states and the federal government in the 1990s forced both entities to be proactive. Widespread deregulation and the privatization of particular services of the public sector were discussed. The ministers for public education suggested introducing policies such as benchmarking for effectiveness and efficiency in academics and administration, stronger competition for research monies, and bilateral agreements between state governments and universities. Although many of these measures have not been and may never be implemented, they were intended to reduce the financial and political dependence of the universities on their states' budgets. For example, in the past a contract between a university and its state government detailed a fixed amount to be awarded to the university for three to five years, allowing the university more independent planning than if it received money for a single year. However, a state government can now theoretically force its universities to reduce their budgets before the end of a three- to five-year term in times of crisis. In return, universities receive ownership of their real estate portfolios, which were formerly owned by the state.

The situation in Lower Saxony, however, was slightly different from the general situation described above. In 2001 Thomas Oppermann, the minister of education, went even further than most ministers in Germany and offered universities and colleges in his state the option of being converted into foundations (*tageszeitung*, June 13, 2001). This differs from the situation in the United States, where universities set up their own foundations, financed by private donors, but do not become foundations themselves. The general idea behind Oppermann's reform was to give Lower Saxony universities a status similar to that held by universities in the United States, where foundation culture was well established and provided universities with considerable income from private sources. In Germany, however, one could not expect such a funding philosophy to be established overnight. When some universities in Germany began discussing the possibility of legally becoming foundations, Oppermann created the legal framework in Lower Saxony in the so-called Innovation Pact II (*Innovationspakt II*) in May 2000[6] and the reformed Higher Public Education Act (*Niedersächsisches Hochschulgesetz*) in June 2002[7] followed by the Lower Saxonian University Foundations Act (*Gesetz betreffend die Errichtung und Finanzierung von Stiftungen als Träger niedersächsischer Hochschulen*) in November 2002.

Some obstacles for the success of the foundation model in Germany do exist. Unlike famous American universities with enormous endowments that make them somewhat independent from state funding, German universities will have to depend on the public sector for decades to come. In 2002 the public sector contributed 98 percent of Germany's university budgets, a share that is not expected to be reduced significantly by any foundation monies in the near future (Reinhardt 2002). Observers criticize how the universities/foundations are initiated by the state and will remain under indirect state control (Palandt 2003). Also, tax exemptions for private donations to foundations are limited to 10 percent of the donor's income (Richter 2002). This might deter private sponsors from contributing large amounts of money to university endowments.

Since the reunification, a stronger involvement of the civil society in political and social affairs has taken place in Germany, and it has resulted in a veritable boom of foundations.[8]

Several significant factors influenced the State of Lower Saxony to transform a university primarily funded by the state into a university with additional funds generated due to its foundation status. One of the factors is the American university landscape with its emphasis on third-party funding through foundations. Another is the general German budget crisis in the public sector, along with the discussion on benchmarking for effectiveness and efficiency in academics and administration. Lower Saxony was one of the few German states that took the very innovative approach of stepping forward and converting many of its publicly funded universities into foundations initially equipped with their real estate assets as endowment. This turned them into independent players on the real estate market.

Universities and Real Estate Development

The centuries-old tradition of universities in Germany has sometimes resulted in campuses that lie in the hearts of cities and towns. This means that many universities have valuable real estate portfolios and are on their way toward gaining financial independence from the public sector. With the restructuring of Lower Saxony universities to foundations, the ownership of university buildings was transferred from the state to the universities, which, as foundations, are now legally independent from the state. This makes German universities, which have been cash poor for several decades, first equity rich and later possibly cash rich.

Theoretically, universities are allowed to reorganize their real estate portfolios by selling their properties in downtown areas and moving to the peripheries, using the profits for investment and other purposes. However, this strategy is criticized for various reasons. For instance, the argument has been made that since public funding will still be required to sustain the now independent universities, profits should be partially shared with the public until the universities are self-sufficient (fundraising management through university development officers has not been common in Germany). In addition, universities located in unattractive areas will not be able to generate much profit through land sales (*Der Tagesspiegel,* June 22, 2001; *tageszeitung,* June 13, 2001). Universities might be able to obtain some additional profits by leasing their buildings to private users for congresses and other events.

Notwithstanding the difficulties, in January 2003 the following five Lower Saxonian schools became foundations: the universities of Göttingen, Hildesheim, and Lüneburg; the School of Veterinary Medicine Hannover (*Tierärztliche Hochschule*); and the University of Applied Sciences Osnabrück (*Fachhochschule*). These universities received a total initial amount of €2 million to build up their fundraising management (Palandt 2003). Their status is now as follows[9]:

- The foundations own each university's buildings and estates. These real estate assets are meant to contribute permanently and increasingly to the budgets of the universities.
- The universities have become more independent from the state—especially when it comes to budgeting and the recruitment of faculty members. They have to set up their own constitutions. They fulfill their research, teaching, and public service tasks responsibly.
- The foundations are backed by a foundation council (*Stiftungsrat*), which adds external expertise to decision making at the university level. Regulations for the administration of each foundation's assets contribute to more efficiency within the universities and mobilize additional funds.

The decisions about what in each real estate portfolio would be considered necessary for the operation of each university were controversial. Contrary to recommendations by the most important German management consultant and adviser to Minister Oppermann, Roland Berger, cafeteria buildings and sports facilities were included. The official total real estate property value of the five Lower Saxonian universities amounted to €850 million, at the time of transferring the assets to the foundations in early 2003, but the market value has been estimated to be much higher. The universities are now responsible for facility management and the rehabilitation of their building stock, both of which had formerly been part of the state's tasks. However, funding is included in the state's subsidies to cover rehabilitations, investments, pensions, and the federal support all universities receive for their construction activities (Palandt 2003).

To date, nobody knows whether the independent status of the universities will help when it comes to substituting public monies with private monies. Opponents of the foundation model fear that the state might simply reduce its financial contributions to the university budgets even further. Signs that this might happen already exist. The University of Lüneburg had to save €675,000 in 2004, and in the context of the Innovation Pact II it faces a state-initiated merger with the University of Applied Sciences North East Lower Saxony (*Fachhochschule*), which is primarily located in Lüneburg. Ironically, this merger would mean that the (scattered) buildings on the old campus that had been transferred to the University of Applied Sciences North East Lower Saxony after the move would be in the real estate portfolio of the University of Lüneburg again. In this case, the new portfolio would be that of the two merged schools. Whether the merger will allow further funding negotiations between the university and the State Department of Education is unclear. The president of the university officially supports the merger. Behind the scenes, however, even the most optimistic advocates of the foundation status heavily criticize the merger as a disheartening budgetary cut.

Conclusion

The notion of conversion has a double meaning in the case of the University of Lüneburg. The first part of this study dealt with military conversion, when the University of Lüneburg sought stabilization in a critical period of severe budget restrictions of the state governments throughout the 1990s, which later seemed to increasingly threaten smaller universities. The second part of this study dealt with the conversion of the legal status of the university to a foundation formally independent from the state. The military conversion was a role model in several ways, especially in its speed, its partnership arrangements, its integration of the university into the surrounding neighborhood, and its significant change of both the image and the economic and symbolic importance of the university campus for the entire city. The construction process was transferred to the state-owned private development corporation, which is characterized by flexibility, swiftness, and cost efficiency. Also, important stakeholders in the process communicated and cooperated efficiently and effectively through successful management by Baureferent Flebbe, the State Department of Science and Culture.

The military conversion can also be regarded as a role model in the partnerships among the main stakeholders at national, state, and local levels. Specifically, the cooperation between the public officials in the Ministry of Education, the City of Lüneburg, and the university contributed to a smooth planning procedure that optimized reuse of the existing barracks. Without affecting the adjacent residential areas, the establishment of the university in former Scharnhorstkaserne both solved its shortage of classrooms and allowed infill residential development in the southern part of the area, which created a high-density, mixed-use neighborhood and avoided further greenfield development. It seems especially noteworthy that the university was able to overcome its fragmented spatial existence and move to the new campus as a whole.

Adding new university buildings, such as the cafeteria, the library, and the auditorium, in the center of both the campus and the reused military buildings improved the spatial relationship between the different parts of the university considerably. Besides that, the conversion from military barracks to a university campus reduced the amount of funds needed, due to successful negotiations with the national government and the use of all potential ways to avoid inefficiencies in the redevelopment process. The development perspectives of the university improved even in times of budgetary cuts at the state level that might have endangered the existence of smaller universities. Functionally, symbolically, and promotionally, the university gained a new image. Its size and its economic importance now make it a competitive player in an environment in Lower Saxony that continues to be characterized by budgetary challenges. In the context of mergers of universities and colleges, the university is a stable and renowned unit that has withstood attempts to reorganize its facilities once again. Therefore, one can certainly call the move a significant contribution to a stable future for the university.

The legal framework for the conversion of an entire university into a foundation was established in the beginning of the 2000s. It is not expected that the share of public funding will decrease significantly, yet it remains to be seen whether foundations and other sponsors will increase their funding in the near future.

Thus, it is too soon to predict whether the financial conversion can be considered a success (and how success can be defined). Nevertheless, converting an entire university to a foundation is a bold step in a society that has long been characterized by conservative strategies. In a time characterized by an increased devolution of public funding and an increased accountability of publicly funded universities, universities are encouraged to initiate innovative solutions for their funding challenges. Converting to a foundation is a very innovative strategy, especially when the outcome is uncertain.

The independence from the state foreseen for the Lower Saxonian universities, the one in Lüneburg, in particular, seems to be incomplete. The university can now act more independently in staff development and the establishment of new programs, but the conversion did not contribute much to a mobilization of the real estate portfolio of the universities and colleges in town. Although so far the intended independence of the university has not led to major sales of real estate or major private donations, the university has become an important site as a conference venue and gains revenues from those events. Therefore, it has succeeded in improving both its own prestige and that of Lüneburg itself.

Notes

1. See www.uni-trier.de, www.uni-protokolle.de/nachrichten/id/16014/).
2. See www.konversion.com/main.asp?was=az, http://www.uni-protokolle.de/nachrichten/id/119872/.
3. See www.konversion.com/themen_detail.asp?id=18.
4. See www.bildungsserver.de/zeigen.html?seite=1824.
5. See for example www.stiftungsindex.de/deutschland.htm.
6. See www.hof.uni-halle.de/steuerung/zv/ni.htm.
7. See www.mwk.niedersachsen.de/master/0,,C627194_N6969_L20_D0_1731,00.html.
8. See www.stiftungen.org/index.php?strg=87_124_141&baseID=148&PHPSESSID=1eba018d65518e47d55cf53ba5c25c6e.
9. See www.mwk.niedersachsen.de/master/0,,C627194_N6969_L20_D0_I731,00.html.

References

Bailey, N. 1994. "Towards a Research Agenda for Public-Private Partnership in the 1990s." *Local Economy* 8: 292–306.

Brindley, T., Y. Rydin, and G. Stoker. 1989. *Remaking Planning: The Politics of Urban Change in the Thatcher Years.* London: Unwin Hyman.

Bundesverband Deutscher Stiftungen. 2000. *Bürgerstiftungen in Deutschland.* Berlin: Author.

Charles, D. 2003. "Universities and Territorial Development: Reshaping the Regional Role of UK Universities." *Local Economy* 18: 7–20.

Etzkowitz, H., and L. Leydesdorff, eds. 2002. *Universities and the Global Knowledge Economy.* London: Continuum International Publishing Group.

Forschungs- und Informations-Gesellschaft für Fach- und Rechtsfragen der Raum- und Umweltplanung mbH–FIRU. 1997. *Konversion–Stadtplanung auf Militärflächen.* Bonn: Bundesministerium für Raumordnung, Bauwesen und Städtebau.

Glasson, J. 2003. "The Widening Local and Regional Development Impacts of the Modern Universities: A Tale of Two Cities (and North-South Perspectives)." *Local Economy* 18: 21–37.

Goddard, J.B., and P. Chatterton. 1999. "Regional Development Agencies and the Knowledge Economy: Harnessing the Potential of Universities." *Environment and Planning C: Government and Policy* 17: 685–99.

Goddard, J., B. Asheim, T. Cronberg, and I. Virtanen. 2003. *Learning Regional Engagement: A Re-Evaluation of the Third Role of Eastern Finland Universities.* Helsinki: Edita. http://www.kka.fi/pdf/julkaisut/KKA_1103.pdf (accessed March 14, 2007).

Goddard, J., U. Teichler, I. Virtanen, P. West, and J. Puukka. 2003. *Progressing External Engagement: A Re-evaluation of the Third Role of the University of Turku.* Helsinki: Edita. http://www.kka.fi/pdf/julkaisut/KKA_1603.pdf (accessed March 14, 2007).

Gumprecht, B. 2003. "The American College Town." *Geographical Review* 93: 51–80.

Heinz, W., ed. 1993. *Public Private Partnership—Ein neuer Weg zur Stadtentwicklung.* Stuttgart: Kohlhammer.

Kirsch, D. 1997. *Public Private Partnership.* Cologne: Immobilien Informationsverlag Rudolph Müller.

Kletzander, A. 1995. "Public-Private Partnership als Gefahr für lokale Demokratie und Verteilungsgerechtigkeit?" *Archiv für Kommunalwissenschaften* 1: 119–35.

Lazzeroni, M., and A. Piccaluga. 2003. "Towards the Entrepreneurial University." *Local Economy* 18: 38–48.

Miegel, M. 2002. *Die deformierte Gesellschaft. Wie die Deutschen ihre Wirklichkeit verdrängen.* Munich: Ullstein-Heine-List

Palandt, K. 2003. "Das niedersächsische Stiftungsmodell: Idee und Bewertung aus politischer Sicht." Paper presented at the conference of the Verein zur Förderung des deutschen und internationalen Wissenschaftsrechts e.V., March 27–29, in Weimar, title: Neue Entwicklungen im Hochschulverfassungs- und Personalrecht.

Peck, F., and D. McGuinness. 2003. "Regional Development Agencies and Cluster Strategies: Engaging the Knowledge-Base in the North of England." *Local Economy* 18: 49–62.

Pimat, A. 1999. Die regionalwirtschaftliche Bedeutung der Universität Lüneburg. Ergebnisse der Diplomarbeit. Summary of master's thesis, University of Lüneburg.

Reinhardt, U. 2002. Introductory speech given at the symposium Stiftungshochschulen—Wege zur Entstaatlichung der Hochschulen, Fachhochschule Hannover, January 16.

Richter, A. 2002. Für eine neue Stiftungskultur an Hochschulen. In HRK Online-Newsletter der Hochschulrektorenkonferenz für Dozenten, no. 5, November 27.

Rother, Wolfram, and Christof Schwarte. 1997. *Konversion militärischer Liegenschaften: Planungsprozesse und Rahmenbedingungen.* Dortmund: Institut für Landes- und Stadtentwicklungsforschung.

Schneider-Sliwa, R. 1996. *Kernstadtverfall und Modelle der Erneuerung in den USA: Privatism, Public-Private Partnerships und sozialräumliche Prozesse am Beispiel von Atlanta, Boston und Washington, D.C.* Berlin: Reimer.

Smith, H.L. 2003. "Universities and Local Economic Development: An Appraisal of the Issues and Practices." *Local Economy* 18: 2–6.

Teufel, E., ed. 2001. *Von der Risikogesellschaft zur Chancengesellschaft.* Frankfurt (Main): Suhrkamp.

Vogel, Wilfried. 1997. "Hochschulstandort Lüneburg—Chancen durch Konversion." In *Mitteilungen BV der LEGen* 1: 28–30.

Zimmer, A., and S. Nährlich, eds. 2000. *Engagierte Bürgerschaft: Traditionen und Perspektiven.* Opladen: Leske und Budrich.

4

Varsity Real Estate in Scotland

New Visions for Town and Gown?

Deborah Peel

There are currently 174 higher education institutions in the UK, which provide, manage, and maintain a significant estate of buildings and land—some 25 million square meters of premises space in addition to site and land resources. In England there are 135 institutions of higher education, of which 71 are universities, 16 are individual institutions of the University of London, and 48 are colleges of higher education. Wales has 14 institutions (of which 5 make up the University of Wales), Northern Ireland has 4 (of which 2 are universities), and Scotland has 21 (of which 13 are universities) (Higher Education Funding Council for England 1998). The direct economic importance of the higher education sector on the performance and development of the national economy has been acknowledged (Kelly et al. 2002; McNicoll 1995), and continued expansion of the sector is anticipated in view of the government's targets for encouraging participation (Wolf 2002). In parallel, recent evidence suggests that considerable investment in the research, teaching, and wider physical infrastructure is required if the UK is to remain competitive (JM Consulting 2004; 2002a; 2002b; 2001; National Committee of Inquiry into Higher Education 1997). Clearly, these circumstances suggest that the university real estate resource is an important one.

In order to understand the issues around the nature of university real estate in Scotland, two caveats are important. First, the maintenance, refurbishment, and expansion of the universities' portfolio of land and property holdings have to be understood in the light of the UK-wide educational policy. From this perspective, the role of the university as city developer is influenced by the relatively recent introduction of university real estate strategies; the creation of a centralized benchmarking approach to estate management statistics; demands for increased accountability to the respective funding councils; a growing awareness of the potential role of universities in the knowledge economy;

and a commitment to encourage universities not to rely on a single (public) source of funding. Second, the processes and outcomes of devolution are important. Political devolution in the UK took effect in 1999 and in Scotland led to the establishment of the Scottish parliament and enhanced legislative and executive powers of the Scottish executive (Bond and Rosie 2002). These new cultural arrangements have accentuated potentially substantive differences in UK higher education practice in the "new" nation states, such as the decision in Scotland not to introduce student fees, unlike the position in England (Burnside 2003). Scotland provides a distinctive example of university real estate being exposed to powerful external influences and a changing domestic role in relation to emerging political and national economic agendas.

This chapter examines the real estate strategies of the universities of Aberdeen and Dundee, two autonomous higher education institutions located on the northeastern seaboard of Scotland. Case studies of these two schools are used to provide insights into the evolving nature and role of real estate management practices in particular city contexts and to illustrate the differential urban contexts in which universities operate, the determining factors that circumscribe their real estate strategies, and their relationship to their locality. Some background points on the UK educational policy context are appropriate to understanding the Scottish case.

Higher Education in the UK

Universities in the UK form a critical part of a largely public-sector university infrastructure. This provides a very specific milieu for considering the particular teaching, learning, and research environment and also for understanding the planning and development role of the university as a potential developer in any individual city. Expenditure on buildings and estates represents some 12 percent of total expenditure across the higher education sector (Higher Education Funding Council for England 2000). It is, therefore, the second-biggest single component of an institution's costs after staffing. A concern with public-sector reform has focused attention on the management of these public assets. The perceived efficiency and effectiveness of varsity real estate has become increasingly subject to government scrutiny.

The Further and Higher Education Act (1992) established four separate funding bodies responsible for Scotland, Wales, Northern Ireland, and England. The Funding Councils are principally responsible for assessing the quality of the education and research of funded institutions (Wolf 2002). Further, in 1993, universities were required to submit a real estate strategy to their appropriate Funding Council. This was effectively the first time that the varsity real estate resource had been placed under such examination and given such an important role in the overall higher education policy framework. The approach developed was driven by an assertion that accurate and comparative statistical data were crucial in order to keep records, develop strategy, make "quicker and better" decisions, monitor progress toward stated targets, and demonstrate added value to (prospective business) partners (Scottish Higher Education Funding Council 2002b). The objective was simply stated as to encourage better performance (Higher Education Funding Council for England 2002). This, it should be noted, is in line with a wider concern with improving the management of public-sector real estate more widely (Housley 1997; National Health Service 1996) and the reconfiguration of higher education in the broader welfare state (Duncan Rice 2004; Stevens 2004).

In 1999, the individual UK Funding Councils commissioned the Estates Management Statistics Service to collate comprehensive university estates information to a common framework and to a set of agreed definitions. The objective of this project was to build a centralized and authoritative picture of the scale, characteristics, and associated costs of the operation of university real estate (Higher Education Funding Council for England 2002). On an ongoing basis, annual data for two hundred different comparative measures relating to estates functions are assembled from all UK higher education institutions. The objective is to identify best practice, to determine where universities stand in relation to each other, and to inform the ways in which individual institutions may develop future strategy (Scottish Higher Education Funding Council 1999a, 1999b). This approach is intended as an important government management tool for benchmarking and vetting the entire process of real estate management, with a view to promoting consistency and strategic thinking across the university sector as a whole.

This particular reasoning reflects a business-model approach to the management of the real estate resource in the context of UK higher education. The National Committee of Inquiry into Higher Education, for example, was specifically charged with the remit to consider how the "value for money and cost-effectiveness [in higher education] should be obtained in the use of resources" (1997, para. 15.2). Its findings and recommendations, which were published in the influential Dearing Report, capture contemporary educational policy thinking:

> The demand on institutions' staff, estates, and equipment and other resources has increased markedly as the number of students has risen faster than the level of public funding. In some areas, such as libraries, this has caused severe problems for students. The efficient use of resources has been promoted by the Funding Bodies. For example, institutions share their strategic plans, including an estates strategy, with the three Higher Education Fund-

ing Councils; and the financial memoranda require institutions to secure value for money in the use of their assets and to follow a maintenance plan for their estates. Several institutions have developed ambitious projects to redevelop their estates, guided by the need to maximise efficiency in their utilisation and running costs as well as their suitability for new learning and teaching methods. (National Committee of Inquiry into Higher Education 1997, para. 15.8)

There is another contemporary dimension to the perceived significance of university real estate. Universities play an increasingly important role in the elaboration of economic development networks. Significantly, these operate at a variety of spatial scales, such as in the development of regional alliances (Charles 2003; Tomes and Phillips 2003), or at the local level in the context of university activities with small- and medium-sized enterprises (Howells et al. 1998). This perspective draws attention to the higher education sector's potentially significant contribution to local and regional economies (Glasson 2003). Indeed, the creation of Scotland's knowledge economy is presented as a nation-building exercise (Hepworth and Pickavance 2004). These factors and ambitions provide a very particular context for exploring the specific city developer role that an individual university can play in urban and city-regional economic development, and within different devolved nation regions across the UK.

Higher Education in Scotland

The distinctiveness of the Scottish education system in terms of philosophy, curriculum, participation, and structure has been acknowledged for some time and has been singled out for critical attention (Raffe 2004; Paterson 2003; Report of the Scottish Committee 1997; Irvine 1995; Jones 1992). It is argued that the concept of lifelong learning is a modern articulation of the Scottish commitment to the tradition of the democratic intellect (Denholme and Macleod 2002; Paterson 2003) and is central to the remaking of Scottish education.

Some explanation of the title of this chapter is appropriate. The term *varsity*, reflecting an archaic pronunciation of the word *university*, is often used in Scotland in preference to the more universal term. It is used here so as to acknowledge and celebrate Scotland's individuality and reflects the argument that, in rediscovering its specific traditions, Scotland can better serve its unfolding political future (Ascherson 2002). Varsities have existed in Scotland's main population centers for centuries, whereas in England, universities existed only in Oxford and Cambridge until the nineteenth century. In addition, there has been a long-standing tradition of links between varsities and their local communities and economies in Scotland. They have been seen not only as supplying an educated workforce, but also as having an important role in supplementing the provision of community facilities—by sharing theaters and libraries, for example—and providing an active local culture of applied research, design, and development services (Universities Scotland 2002). Colloquially, this relationship is referred to as "town and gown."

Scotland is a relatively small nation of approximately five million people. Some 97 percent of its territory is defined as rural, and 75 percent of the population lives in the Central Belt area between Glasgow and Edinburgh. Recent statistics suggest that the population size has stabilized. There is evidence to show that its composition continues to change, however, particularly because of the out-migration of young people, low fertility, and aging of the population (General Register Office for Scotland 2004). In 2002–2003 there were 267,000 students in the Scottish higher education sector—a marginal decrease from the previous year that, nonetheless, represented a nearly 25 percent increase over the number in 1995–96 (Scottish Executive 2004b). The scale of the varsity sector is influential in terms of institutional organization and attempts to share best practice. Cooperative working arrangements, such as through the shared resource and communications network, is a case in point. Indeed, it is argued that the relative compactness of the higher education sector in Scotland makes possible rapid and effective communication between the individual institutions, the government funding body, and the Scottish Executive (Report of the Scottish Committee 1997). This suggests a particular form of associational economic behavior (Cooke and Morgan 1998) and, again, provides a specific operational context.

In Scotland, there is an important established educational tradition of providing practical or vocational qualifications that are intended to feed directly into the development agendas set down for the Scottish economy. This relates to realizing economic competitiveness, fostering growth and development, and facilitating skill enhancement and training (Scottish Executive 2003a). Statistics indicate that a higher proportion of students attending Scottish universities are from Scotland than from elsewhere, and that the completion rate is one of the highest in the world (Universities Scotland 2002). Following Morgan (2002), for example, the implication is that the Scottish university falls within an outreach- or diffusion-oriented model of regional development. Its purpose is defined as "serving society: making a significant contribution to the health, wealth and culture of a thriving and creative Scotland," and thereby meeting the objectives of "a smart, successful Scotland" (Scottish Executive 2001a, 7). This suggests that Scottish higher education is seeking to deal with a particular and diverse set of political priorities.

The Varsity State in Scotland

Scotland's thirteen varsities may be grouped into the categories of ancient, old, and new (Table 4.1). They are the result of a relatively complex story of evolution and merger (Scottish Office 1995). The "ancient" group of universities, comprising Aberdeen, Edinburgh, Glasgow, and St. Andrews, are over four hundred years old. The oldest is St. Andrews, where teaching began in 1410. In Aberdeen, King's College was founded in 1495 and Marischal College in 1593. Their fusion in the late nineteenth century created the present-day University of Aberdeen. These varsities, as well as those of Edinburgh and Glasgow, were founded on ecclesiastical and classical traditions.

The "old" universities—Dundee, Heriot-Watt, Stirling, and Strathclyde—were the result of the UK-wide expansion of higher education in the 1960s, which reflected prevailing political priorities (Wagner 1995). Even here, however, individual institutions developed in a variety of ways. The Robbins Report in 1963 explicitly recommended an expansion of UK student numbers, a move that was welcomed with considerable excitement. Wright (1974, 233), for example, noted that "the growth of our universities in number and size since 1945 may really be called wonderful, when one considers how slowly universities changed in the past." The expansion of student numbers was secured in a number of ways, and for particular purposes, witnessing both new buildings and the granting of university status to the existing Colleges of Advanced Technology. Hence, the University of Stirling was the result of a new purpose-built campus on a greenfield site. In contrast, the University of Dundee, which was already in existence as a college of the nearby ancient University of St. Andrews, gained its independence. In the meantime, established universities, such as Aberdeen, were also able to develop new buildings as a result of the government-driven expansion.

The "new" universities—of Abertay, Glasgow Caledonian, Napier, Paisley, and Robert Gordon—form part of the expansion in the higher education sector that occurred when the so-called binary divide that had separated universities and polytechnics was removed in 1992. This expanded sector reflected a specific set of political ambitions aimed at promoting greater economic competitiveness in business, industry, and finance (Wolf 2002). This typology of origin, purpose, and focus has a range of implications for the scale, condition, age, value, and fitness-for-purpose of varsity real estate in Scotland today. The diversity of the varsity real estate is reflected in the fact that some of the buildings are medieval and others are Victorian or early twentieth century or reflect the expansion of the 1960s and 1970s.

The progressive evolution of varsity real estate has left a specific built legacy that, in many cases, is unsuitable for contemporary university teaching,

Table 4.1

Higher Education Institutions in Scotland

Ancient varsities	Old varsities	New varsities
University of Aberdeen	University of Dundee	University of Abertay (Dundee)
University of Edinburgh	Heriot-Watt University (Edinburgh)	Glasgow Caledonian University
University of Glasgow	University of Stirling	Napier University (Edinburgh)
University of St. Andrews	University of Strathclyde (Glasgow)	University of Paisley (Glasgow)
	The Open University in Scotland	The Robert Gordon University (Aberdeen)

Figure 4.1   **UK Varsity Real Estate by Period of Construction**

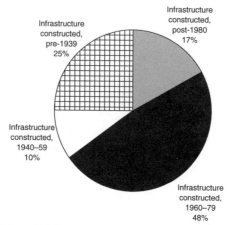

Source: Adapted from JM Consulting (2001).

research, and "third stream" activities; cannot accommodate technological developments; or is in need of substantial remedial intervention (JM Consulting 2001). Figure 4.1 graphically presents the UK real estate infrastructure by date of construction and shows that only some 17 percent was built after 1980.

The geography of the varsity state in Scotland is illustrated in Figure 4.2. This mirrors and reinforces the potential role of the principal cities in facilitating and supporting Scotland's anticipated economic growth. The inherited spatiality of the varsity state emphasizes the dominance of the Central Belt and the location of the institutions along the east coast, including Dundee and Aberdeen. The urban location of the universities means that many, such as Glasgow, are effectively landlocked and have resorted to in-fill development (JM Consulting 2001). It is necessary, then, to take account of prevailing conditions in the availability and location of land and property for the purposes of individual varsity growth and expansion. Indeed, local land and property markets may serve to inhibit any intended activity by the institutions. These considerations bring together combinations of inherited land and property assets, the outcomes of subsequent merger and takeover activity, and the specific aspirations and contextualized responses to a changing higher education policy framework and evolving financial regime.

Jewels and Duals: Aberdeen and Dundee

Scotland's long-term rate of economic growth has been documented as being lower than that of the UK, while the importance of knowledge, skills, and

Figure 4.2   **Scotland's Varsity State**

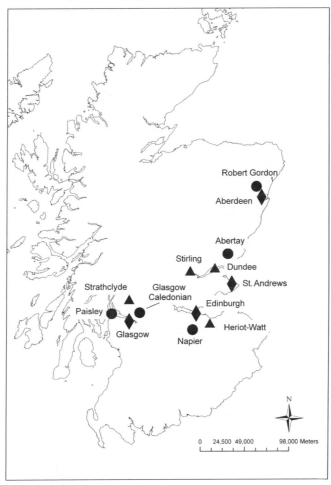

Key:

◆   Ancient: Aberdeen, Edinburgh, Glasgow, St. Andrews

▲   Old: Dundee, Heriot-Watt, Stirling, Strathclyde

●   New: Abertay, Glasgow Caledonian, Napier, Paisley, Robert Gordon

Source: This work is based on data provided through EDINA UKBORDERS with the support of the ESRC and JISC and uses boundary material which is copyright of the Crown and the Post Office. Prepared by John Marsden, University of Liverpool

Note: The Open University in Scotland is not included here; it is not funded by the Scottish Higher Education Funding Council. The UHI Millennium Institute and Queen Margaret University College (Edinburgh) anticipate university status in 2007. UHI is based on a network of existing further education facilities located across northern Scotland and serving the highlands and islands.

creativity and the transfer of knowledge from the science and engineering base into the marketplace have been emphasized (Scottish Office 1999). The prioritization of the knowledge economy is viewed by the Scottish Executive and the university sector as the basis for securing economic growth and development (Scottish Executive 2001b; Universities Scotland 2002). Current economic development policy, for example, establishes the role to be played by the principal cities in promoting economic ambitions for Scotland (Scottish Executive 2000). These considerations place universities and research institutes at the core of the government's strategy to modernize the Scottish economy (Scottish Executive 2003b). The promotion of economic competitiveness, growth, and development, together with that of social inclusion, has emphasized the importance of Scotland's principal cities, including Dundee and Aberdeen. This defines a new role—or visibility—for individual varsities.

Yet, in terms of relative economic performance, a recent analysis of Scotland's cities identified marked socioeconomic disparities between the individual settlements and their regions (Scottish Executive 2002). Hence, for example, while the political and financial capital, Edinburgh, is undergoing relative economic growth, Dundee, some one hundred miles north, is experiencing population decline and continuing economic and industrial restructuring. Aberdeen, the "oil capital of Europe," is poised to rethink its conventional energy production by shifting to renewable energy, while Glasgow continues to experience protracted industrial and physical restructuring and seeks to present itself as a city at the cultural edge (Peel and Lloyd 2005). As a consequence, the Scottish Executive (2000) has acknowledged that the public policies held to be appropriate for Aberdeen, Edinburgh, and Inverness will differ from those for Dundee and Glasgow. Explicitly, then, varsities in Scotland are operating in two different contexts. The differences have prompted a distinction between the perceived city "jewels" in the Scottish economy, Aberdeen and Edinburgh, which are characterized by expansion, and the perceived "dual" cities of Dundee and Glasgow, where economic growth and decline coexist (Scottish Executive 2002). This presents challenges for the different universities seeking to manage and develop their real estate. Table 4.2 presents some relevant comparative data of Aberdeen and Dundee.

The contrasting historical context and economic performance of Aberdeen and Dundee provide some further comparative insights into the formulation and implementation of the varsities' individual real estate strategies. Aberdeen, the so-called granite city, was founded in the twelfth century by King David I at the mouth of the River Dee. Its industrial heritage includes the quarrying of granite for export in a variety of forms, although that finally ceased in 1971. Deep-sea fishing was important, together with the manufacture of

Table 4.2

Selected Comparative Data for the Cities of Aberdeen and Dundee

Criterion	Aberdeen	Dundee
Population	212,000	145,000
Population change 1981–2001	3.9%	−19.4%
Projected population change to 2016	−11%	−19%
Change in number of jobs since 1995	−1%	−6%
People in paid employment (2002)	82%	76%
Average weekly wage (2002)	£494	£409
Unemployment rate	2.1%	6.1%
Proportion of Scotland's deprived postcode sectors (1998 index)	0%	5%
Residents with a degree	22%	11%
Proportion of Scotland's derelict land	1%	3%
Households with access to a car	62%	51%
Projected traffic growth by 2001	34%	22%
Proportion of city area that is green space	26%	22%

Source: Derived from Scottish Executive (2002).

textiles, including wool, linen, and cotton. Papermaking was also a long-established industry. The significance of these manufacturing industries was that they were based on the natural resources in Aberdeen's broad economic and physical hinterland.

In more recent times, Aberdeen has become established as the principal servicing-base for the offshore oil and natural gas exploration and production activities in the North Sea (Newlands 2000). This has had a powerful economic impact on the growth and development of the city, and on establishing a particular identity, but it has also included a number of displacement effects on the more traditional industrial activities, including fishing and boat building (Harris et al. 1988; Lloyd and Newlands 1993). In overall terms, the effects of oil have been beneficial. Although only 4 percent of the Scottish population lives there, Aberdeen has 8 percent of the country's spending power (Robert Gordon University 2003). Notwithstanding the changes in the energy sector, the economy of the city is still relatively prosperous, and Aberdeen retains the "hallmarks of a near full employment economy" (Scottish Executive 2002, 41). In April 2001, for example, the average wage was 18 percent higher than the Scottish average (Scottish Executive 2002).

In contrast, the average earnings of those who work in the city of Dundee are 3 percent lower than the Scottish average, with unemployment rates rising above 14 percent (Scottish Executive 2002). The city of Dundee continues to experience population decline, high unemployment, social deprivation, and significant areas of vacant and derelict land. Dundee has enjoyed a long-established heritage as a whaling and maritime trading center. Its coastal and estuarine location was critical to its ship building, engineering, and ancillary port activities (Whatley 1991). Changing market conditions, together with relatively higher-cost modes of production and distribution, however, contributed to a process of decline, and the severity of the economic restructuring of the city was reflected in its social and demographic conditions, particularly with respect to mortality, housing, and health (Rodger 1996). This persisted into the 1990s (Doherty 1991). Between 1995 and 2001, employment declined in most sectors, and overall employment fell by 6 percent. In 2000, 55 percent of households in Dundee contained no one who was working (Scottish Executive 2002). It is generally acknowledged that Dundee has experienced the most difficult economic trajectory of all the Scottish cities through the restructuring of its traditional manufacturing activity, principally around jute.

Since 1945, a number of parallel interventions have been put into place to address the issues associated with the processes of industrial restructuring and economic contraction. These included early attempts at managing Dundee through city regional planning, and urban regeneration initiatives that were driven by legislative arrangements. This prompted a focus on rebuilding through the preparation of a master plan for Dundee, a series of physical renewal and environmental improvements targeted at different neighborhoods, and the development of specific industrial improvement areas. A number of these activities were secured through active partnerships (McCarthy and Pollock 1997; Lloyd and McCarthy 2003).

Certainly, the municipal authority, along with the business and voluntary sectors, has explicitly engaged in a major program to give the city a new image. Active partnerships, which include the participation of the two universities and the local enterprise company, are important in promoting Dundee as a city of learning, of discovery, of culture and a city interested in the creation and maintenance of a local knowledge economy (Dundee City Council 2003). The prospect of giving Dundee a new image has focused on revitalization of the city center and investment in retail and cultural facilities. Moreover, clusters of new economy sectors, including biotechnology, medical science, and multimedia software development are emerging. For example, Leibovitz (2004) demonstrates that, in 2002, Dundee had the third-highest number of core firms, organizations, and total employed in biotechnology in Scotland.

Varsity Real Estate in Practice

Aberdeen and Dundee universities are representative of the ancient and old categories of higher education institutions in Scotland. Their institutional maturation has taken place over different time frames, as a consequence of evolving educational policy and funding opportunities. Thus, for example, the general expansion in the university infrastructure in the 1960s and 1970s witnessed Dundee receive its university charter, while Aberdeen, with its longer-established tradition as an ancient center of learning, was able to expand on an established portfolio of buildings.

Notwithstanding these different historical and contemporary economic contexts, the universities of Aberdeen and Dundee exhibit some common characteristics with respect to the formulation and implementation of their respective contemporary real estate strategies. Both have recently engaged in physical mergers with colleges of further education, and both have recently recorded unlet student bed space. Both are in receipt of investment funds from the central government and the Scottish Funding Council to improve their scientific research infrastructure. Finally, both are engaged in exploring third-stream incomes and the provision of shared educational resources. This section considers each varsity's estate strategy in more detail.

The University of Aberdeen

The University of Aberdeen is primarily located on four main sites within Aberdeen: King's College, Foresterhill, Marischal College, and Hilton. Other facilities, most notably some student residential accommodations, are located outside these principal sites. Other facilities, including the student's union and the university playing fields, are dispersed across the city. Much of the university is located in Old Aberdeen and is protected by a designated conservation area. The university holds approximately 293,000 square meters of operational buildings located on around 125 hectares of land (University of Aberdeen 2001). All the buildings within the conservation area are subject to land-use planning guidelines and restrictions, which extend not only to the historic buildings but also to the buildings constructed between 1950 and the late 1970s. Of the 175 buildings that have "listed building status" in the conservation area, 56 are owned by the University of Aberdeen. Their listed building status reinforces the land-use planning controls affecting them.

During the mid- to late 1960s, the university developed a number of new buildings as a result of the expansion promoted by the government. The stringent financial constraints of the 1980s, however, halted the physical expansion. Indeed, this changed financial context led to a review of the university's real estate holdings and resulted in the sale of buildings in and around King's College; the selective disposal of real estate continues as the university reviews property and buildings as potentially surplus. Moreover, there are a limited number of sites with potential for future university development in this area, and intensifying use of the site has to be balanced against any adverse environmental impacts within the conservation area. Also, incremental development over time means that the individual land titles for this ancient institution vary in size and detail. This complicates land dispersal and land development.

King's College occupies 34.5 hectares two miles north of the city center. All nonclinical teaching with the exception of education is carried out at this site. It also includes the main administration and other support facilities for the university. It represents 67 percent of the total varsity built estate. Marischal College is a unique building located in the city center. Its present buildings were constructed between 1836 and 1845, although extensions were subsequently added. It is held to be the largest granite building in Europe. A significant part of the building, however, is nonoperational, although civic and ceremonial events take place there. Its location in the city center and its standing as a local landmark represent a considerable challenge to the university.

Foresterhill and Hilton lie to the west of King's College. The Foresterhill site is the location of the university medical school. A substantial proportion of the site is jointly owned by the University of Aberdeen and the Grampian University Hospital Trust. The two partners work together in managing and administering the Foresterhill estate. When the University of Aberdeen merged with the Aberdeen campus of the Northern College in 2001 to include a new faculty of education, it included acquisition of the Hilton site, a significant proportion of which is leased to external organizations.

In assembling its current real estate, the University of Aberdeen has benefited from the inherited infrastructure associated with King's College and Marischal College. The additions to its real estate then materialized as part of its academic development strategic plan, such as the acquisition of land and buildings at Foresterhill. The academic merger with Northern College to enhance its education faculty also resulted in an expansion of its real estate. At times, financial constraints have led to the disposal of land and buildings, together with residential premises that the university owned. In the context of King's College, for example, the physical characteristics of the residential neighborhood resulted in the university adopting an explicit consolidation of its real estate. Here, the university would strategically acquire properties to consolidate its holdings. Rationalization of the land and property portfolio forms a critical objective of the real estate strategy. Hence, the university has largely disposed of its off-campus student accommodations to the private sector. The oil-related activities of the 1970s resulted in pressures on the local housing market and an increase in private-sector rental prices. The university responded by expanding its portfolio of student accommodations. Due to reduced demand for these accommodations in recent years, the university has determined to dispose of its surplus portfolio and underwrites student bed space through the private sector. It is further engaged in a process of consolidating its remaining student accommodations at—or in close proximity to—King's College. In parallel, the university has sought to realize development potential where appropriate. The Hilton site, for example, has been assessed with a view to sale and the relocation of students and staff to the main King's College site.

In 2000, the University of Aberdeen reviewed the condition of its estate and considered its development options to support the strategic plan and its associated financial strategy. This resulted in the *University Estate Strategy, 2002–2007* (University of Aberdeen 2001). The strategic review suggested that the university has sufficient space for its immediate requirements and sets out to consolidate, rationalize, improve, and develop the existing resource. Aberdeen explicitly recognizes the broad range of benefits to be achieved through collaboration in order to secure cost effectiveness. In particular, it is discussing opportunities for further collaboration with other higher education institutions, including Robert Gordon University, the Scottish Agricultural College, and the UHI Millennium Institute. It has also developed strong relationships with all tiers of local government in the northeast, including Aberdeen City Council, Aberdeenshire Council, and local community councils. Moreover, the university is represented at board level on a range of local interest groups. This, then, forms an explicit part of the institution's commitment to strengthening the region's identity and competitiveness as set out in the University of Aberdeen's mission statement: "The University will seek to enhance its position as the major institution of higher education in the North of Scotland and to develop its role as a local, regional and national cultural center to benefit both the academic and the local and regional communities" (University of Aberdeen undated).

Another important dimension of the estate strategy is to explore commercial property market opportunities. In the past, little emphasis was placed on the involvement of the private sector, but recently Aberdeen has explored initiatives such as a new student health center to be built by the private sector and leased by the university, which continues to retain ownership of the site.

The University of Dundee

The University of Dundee began life in 1881 in four detached town houses as Queens College, affiliated with the University of St. Andrews. As an educational model, it reflected the emergence of "university colleges" in the English industrial cities and stemmed from the perceived necessity to satisfy the city of Dundee's scientific requirements in subjects such as chemistry, mathematics, and engineering (Shafe 1982). Indeed, it was the only university college founded in Scotland in that period (Sanderson 1972). The necessary funding to establish the college was principally provided through local industrial philanthropic endowment. In 1967 the University of Dundee received its royal charter. It came, therefore, at the end of the 1960s' boom of university expansion, and thus the university's development and planning process operated in very uncertain circumstances (Shafe 1982). This had a direct effect on its real estate. From its inception, the University of Dundee undertook construction of new buildings—for example, for biological and medical sciences. This building program extended to a student's union, a library, and sports facilities. Continuing uncertainties in government funding, however, affected building plans. The university also extended its real estate resource by converting adjacent buildings to use by academic departments. By 1980, the main precinct of the campus was largely well defined and benefited from green space and landscaping (Shafe 1982). The suitability of the accommodation in size, teaching and learning space, information and communication technology, and statutory requirements relating to disabled access, for example, nevertheless prompted the university to rethink its real estate resource. As is the case with many UK universities, the University of Dundee faces a number of problems, including a substantial and escalating backlog of maintenance, insufficient teaching space, a shortage of communication and information technology facilities, some poor-quality buildings and fragmented departments, a shortage of parking, security problems, and a lack of amenity and social space (University of Dundee 2000).

The main campus of the University of Dundee forms an integral part of the city center. At present, some of the university's teaching and administrative space continues to be located in former residential accommodations, a reflection of the evolving character of this institution. The university also has real estate within the wider city-region of Dundee as a consequence of its mergers with other institutions of further education. This includes the Dundee campus of Northern College at Gardyne Road and a site at Ninewells Hospital, which houses the university's medical school on the western edge of the city. The university's School of Nursing and Midwifery is currently based in Kirkaldy, some thirty miles south of Dundee, a site that is being considered for consolidation with the main Dundee city campus.

In developing its real estate resource, the University of Dundee did not benefit substantially from any inherited infrastructure. In the mid-1960s, for example, a public planning inquiry zoned land suitable for university development adjacent to the city center. The twenty-four-hectare section comprised residential and commercial properties in a relatively poor state of condition. This essentially provided the nucleus from which the University of Dundee began its growth and development. On the main campus site, it has undertaken new construction; refurbishment of existing buildings; and extensions to accommodate its teaching, research, and administrative activities. In recent times, this has meant intensification of building use on the site and loss of parking. By engaging in mergers, notably with the Duncan of Jordanstone College of Art and the Dundee campus of Northern College, the University of Dundee has expanded its available building space. Around the main campus precinct, the university has continued to consolidate, thereby creating a distinctive academic identity to the west of the city center. This process has included disposal of less suitable buildings. The university has also explored the development potential of its real estate, as with the Gardyne Road site. The proposal to develop this for residential purposes was rejected by the local planning authority, however, and the site is now in the process of transfer to another educational institution of further education.

The local statutory land-use plan zones the main university campus area as part of Dundee's emerging "cultural quarter." The University of Dundee's real estate strategy asserts that "the success of a university city depends on the interaction of city and university" (University of Dundee 2000), and this finds its physical articulation through the explicit creation of pedestrian-friendly routes through the campus, which are open to the public. An important objective of the master plan is connectivity and establishing new routes to link varsity and city (Peel 2005). Public participation has formed an important part of this process. In addition, "the University intends to deepen its liaison with the City Council" (University of Dundee 2000). Hence, the university is keen to support the city's commitment to knowledge transfer and to the economic development policy strapline, or advertising slogan, of "Dundee: City of Discovery." These connections are firmly enshrined in the campus plan, which links the city's waterfront with the main area by way of a landmark building and a flight of steps. Nevertheless, the "Campus in the City" plan acknowledges that the university's success inevitably will stimulate adjacent development, reducing the long-term flexibility of real estate expansion (University of Dundee undated-a). The density of current development would appear to preclude further development on the city center campus site.

The University of Dundee's current real estate strategy (University of Dundee 2000) asserts the importance of a close interaction between the city and the university. This has involved a public consultation process around its new master plan, which is concerned with the "heart of the campus," reflecting its city center location, and takes account of adjacent planned developments being promoted by the city, including riverside developments, extensions to the cultural quarter, and a number of schemes on the campus perimeter.

Dundee is considered to be a leading institution in the areas of biomedical research and cancer studies. As a consequence, development of the Medipark on the campus of the Ninewells Hospital and Medical School offers companies the opportunity to create laboratory, production, and office space on a greenfield site close to Dundee Airport and the city center. Equally important is the Center for Medical Education, a worldwide distance-learning program—the largest in the UK. The links with the pharmaceutical industry have been identified as particularly significant. In this particular spinout context, the royalties from the associated sales of pharmaceutical products not only support future research opportunities and commercialization, but also can contribute to the infrastructure at the university (Scottish Executive 2001a). Collaboration with other institutions is also being explored in order to address space requirements. This includes potential cooperation with the universities of Abertay and St. Andrews and extends to links with Tayside University Hospitals. Shared ownership or lease-back arrangements are a feature of these initiatives. The University of Dundee clearly sees its role within the region as important. For example, a new sports facility to promote health and well-being and intended as a venue for training schoolteachers and for cardiac and diabetes rehabilitation programs will also be made available to the wider community.

New Visions for Town and Gown

Both the varsity real estate strategies discussed in this chapter explicitly confirm the central role quality land and property play in delivering their respective corporate objectives, despite their different economic contexts. Each university sits in a different city-wide context in terms of economic activities and land and property markets. As noted, Dundee is an archetypal postindustrial city that today is experiencing the combined processes of industrial contraction, redundancy, and new growth. Certainly, the university is playing a big part in the process of new growth. In contrast, Aberdeen has, in more recent times, enjoyed relative economic buoyancy related to its role in North Sea oil and gas exploitation and development, which saw it evolve from essentially a market town and administrative center. Both institutions affirm the benefits of managing space better, strengthening external relations, and working to a wider community agenda. The explanations for their behavior derive from a combination of generic and specific circumstances. Thus, for example, although funding and taxation arrangements affect all universities, how those effects are mediated by any individual institution depends on a number of circumstances. This final section considers these points.

First, it is evident that, over time, universities in the UK have responded to the changing political and social priorities for higher education (Sanderson 1972; Schuller 1995). Indeed, Halsey (1995, 302) goes so far as to claim that "British higher education has undergone a more profound reorientation than any other system in the industrial world." In a critical discussion of the transformation of higher education in the UK since 1944, Stevens (2004) draws attention to the ever-increasing impact of globalization on student recruitment and research funding, and to the attempts by universities to assert themselves as world-class institutions. Market values, competition, quality assurance, and accountability have become the touchstones of a more explicitly business-led approach to university management and a concern with improving efficiency and performance in all aspects of varsity life (Scottish Higher Education Funding Council 2001, 2002b; Housley 1997). Yet this has to be understood in the context of a specific public-sector attempt at a cultural change in state-related practices. This generic context clearly impacts both the varsities discussed here.

Second, and as a direct consequence of the contemporary political climate, an additional pressure on varsity real estate managers has arisen through new legislative and statutory requirements, particularly with respect to disability discrimination and health and safety (Scottish Higher Education Funding Council 2000; JM Consulting 2002a). This external legislative effort, such as the recent introduction of Houses in Multiple Occupation legislation, is dynamic and continues to constrain the ability of resource-limited varsities to innovate beyond quite specific government objectives. The changing context in which universities are seeking to discharge conventional public-sector responsibilities is taking place within a centralized interest in university real estate management and practice. Indeed, this generic approach to managing the wider university real estate resource explicitly encourages benchmarking between institutions. This context of quality assurance and control provides a prism for examining the role of the university as a potential city developer.

Third, the active management, use, and development by UK universities of their facilities, properties, and wider real estate resource are relatively recent developments (Locke 2004). Indeed, the Commission for Architecture and the Built Environment (2005) notes that universities have not traditionally explicitly focused their attention on the value of good building design in terms of enhancing the overall performance of higher education institutions. In addition, the principles of sustainable development have assumed an importance in an institution's capital projects, estate management, and procurement practices. This extends to new buildings, refurbishment, and the existing built estate and requires paying attention to sustainable construction practices, use of resources such as energy and water, waste management, transport, planning, and landscape and townscape issues (Scottish Funding Council 2006). The sustainability lens focuses attention on the duty of universities as public bodies to consider the scope for promoting green space and biodiversity within their estate management strategies, and to set key performance indicators and targets that allow progress to be measured, reported, and tracked over time. The potential of the varsity to demonstrate leadership in sustainable practice is critical. This is a particular social construction of the role of a varsity city developer. Individual institutions respond in specific ways to these demands, constrained, in part, by the nature and age of their available built and natural infrastructures.

Fourth, the UK Funding Councils now demand that universities think strategically about the performance of their real estate as part of their institutional strategic planning (Scottish Higher Education Funding Council 1999b). The various guidance documents assert that in physical terms a vibrant university campus is an integral part of any successful university marketing strategy and critical to creating a good first impression to the academy at large (Price et al. 2001; Higher Education Funding Council for England 2000). As a consequence, real estate is now an explicit and central feature of varsity corporate strategies (Jarvis 2001). Yet, again, how individual institutions respond is context specific.

Fifth, the financial context is critical. In many instances, the funding for new infrastructure is allocated on a competitive basis between institutions. In general in Scotland, there has been a gradual decline in the varsity real estate condition and a significant overall decrease in estate development expenditure (Scottish Higher Education Funding Council 2000). As a consequence, varsities typically face common problems of insufficient accommodations, unsuitable buildings and spaces or buildings in poor condition, and a lack of available space for expansion (Scottish Higher Education Funding Council 1999b). In recent times, there has been a deliberate attempt by individual varsities to address these deficiencies. Current emphasis is placed on rethinking the provision and standards of student accommodations, remodeling space for teaching and research, and generally ensuring that varsity real estate is fit for its purpose. This suggests a rather more inward-looking approach to estate management that is, in many ways, constrained to deal with internal requirements. There is a sense in which universities are playing "catch-up." Indeed, in many universities, tackling the backlog of maintenance of the research and teaching infrastructure is the most pressing requirement for those managing the real estate resource (Department for Education and Skills 2003). Here, the individual institutional response may fall short of the government's ambition for establishing the necessary teaching, learning, and research infrastructure to compete globally.

Figure 4.3 **Sources of Varsity Funding in Scotland, 2001–2002**

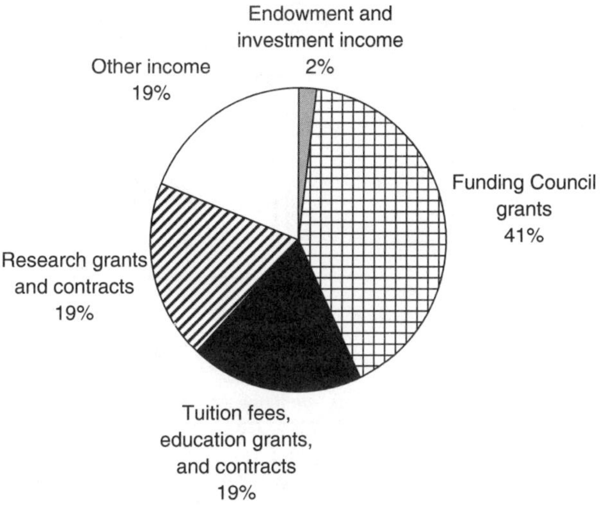

Source: Adapted from Burnside (2003).

All higher education institutions in Scotland are funded principally by the Scottish Funding Council (Figure 4.3). There is relatively little funding emanating from endowments and private funding sources. The Sutton Trust, for example, has drawn attention to the higher degree of financial autonomy enjoyed by North American universities in contrast to their British counterparts. The relative financial disadvantage faced by UK universities is held to be, in part, a consequence of endowment giving and philanthropy being less customary in the UK and university fundraising not being an established part of university leadership practice (Duncan Rice 2004). The situation is compounded by the differential unit funding per student, which is higher in the United States, for example (Sutton Trust 2003).

As a consequence of the changing external environment, varsities are increasingly required to be more financially autonomous and profit generating. In effect, a business model now prevails for varsity management in general and for its associated real estate in particular. Hence, there is an emphasis upon research and consultancy to supplement student income (JM Consulting 2004). Moreover, individual projects for varsity real estate development may be financed through private finance initiatives, contracting out, joint ventures, and sponsorships (Scottish Higher Education Funding Council 1999b). This is consistent with the concept of the "entrepreneurial university," which embodies such strategies as the commercialization of research (Lawton Smith 2003; Lazzeroni and Piccaluga 2003; McNay 1995) and the social and economic

Figure 4.4   **A Varsity Planning Triangle**

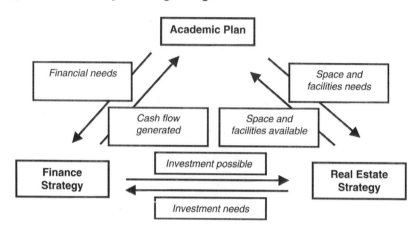

Source: Adapted from University of Aberdeen (2001).

benefits to be derived from consultancy and business-driven spinouts (Scott et al. 2001; Scottish Higher Education Funding Council 2001).

The recognition of a more internationally competitive environment has prompted the government to examine how the higher education sector can become less dependent on any single source of funding (Department for Education and Skills 2003). Endowment funds are specifically identified as an important mechanism for enabling the necessary investment in teaching, research, and, critically, the refurbishment of facilities. In the two case studies, this has resulted in building programs in the expanding life and medical sciences and tentative collaborative ventures to minimize risk.

Sixth, directors of estate of individual universities operate at the corporate decision-making level and therefore sit at the core of university business. Typically, the varsity real estate strategy is now an integral part of a management triad, along with the institutional corporate strategy and financial strategy (Figure 4.4). This reflects a wider professionalization of estate management within the sector, as evidenced by the work of the Association of University Directors of Estates. It also forms part of an assertive agenda to enhance university management practices and leadership (Scottish Higher Education Funding Council 2002a).

Conclusions

The two case studies in this chapter demonstrate the particular land developing behaviors of two varsities in Scotland in light of the new focus on estate management strategies. It is important to acknowledge, however, that varsity land development may have been more implicit or less visible prior to the changing higher educational policy and funding context. In the case of Dundee, for example, specific circumstances precipitated an opportunistic approach to the land assembly required to shape its growth and development. Change in Dundee was also informed by the city's wider industrial restructuring, the availability of brownfield sites, and transport infrastructure developments that effectively created pockets of land for development. In Aberdeen, the varsity's land purchases effectively exhausted land supply at its main campus site, King's College. It has to work within the statutory land-use planning requirements with respect to its property portfolio in two ways. First, development has to be considered in the context of a conservation area. Second, many of the university buildings form part of Scotland's historic built heritage, which also potentially limits development.

In terms of hard behaviors relating to physical land development, specific property acquisition and disposal, leasing and joint ventures are deployed according to locality and circumstance. Collaborations and mergers are also increasingly informing strategic thinking and bring with them real estate opportunities. In the cases of both Dundee and Aberdeen, respective mergers with the two campuses of Northern College created opportunities to dispose of the land and buildings to realize a potential development gain. The emphasis on consolidation, rationalization, and refurbishment on central urban sites, however, suggests a clear attempt to demonstrate the efficient management of the real estate resource to the funding authorities and to potential future investors.

The realization of a varsity real estate strategy does not take place in a vacuum, and the Scottish Executive explicitly encourages synergies and collaboration. This highlights the need to engage in relatively more "soft" relational behaviors. Institutions are required to consider their local community, industry, and commercial relationships when presenting their real estate proposals (JM Consulting 2002b). In addition, the Scottish Higher Education Funding Council (1999a) encourages varsities to prepare development frameworks in the form of master plans, or townscape or landscape plans. These can flesh out university real estate strategies and articulate the role of the university as a city developer, as in Dundee. This can provide the rationale for the development of local authority land-use plans, support funding grant applications, and provide the stimulus for private investment. The important point here is that this is a relatively new approach to managing town and gown relationships specifically encouraged through the funding councils and government controls and necessitated through interuniversity competition. It would appear that more explicit relationships between varsities, local planning authorities, and local property markets are emerging as a consequence. This could be mutually beneficial, in that both universities and municipal authorities could achieve better forward planning.

Devolution has provided an opportunity for Scotland to define more clearly its own political and policy agenda and to devise appropriate responses to its particular needs. Cooke and Clifton (2005), for example, have argued that Scotland exhibits a visionary variant of devolution in the context of proactively developing its knowledge-based economic policy. The higher education sector is identified as having an important leadership role to play in asserting Scottish distinctiveness and academic distinction, and in supporting economic development around the city-regions. The latter is advocated in Scotland's first *National Planning Framework* (Scottish Executive 2004a). This strategic policy document describes the objectives of Scotland's long-term territorial development and highlights the location preferences and clustering tendencies of government, business, and industry. On the one hand, it signals the importance of the principal urban centers as the focus of future economic growth. On the other hand, it identifies the growth of specialist, knowledge-dependent activities around research institutes and universities. Taken together, these factors accentuate the importance of the principal cities of Aberdeen, Dundee, Glasgow, Edinburgh, Inverness, and Stirling and their respective varsities. It will be interesting to follow how this is translated into practice and how individual varsities interpret their role as a city developer in specific contexts. Will it result in greater collaboration or attempts to assert distinctiveness in order to be more competitive?

The explicit and proactive stewardship of the varsity real estate resource is a new development in UK higher education. At a generic and instrumental level, it requires individual varsities to demonstrate efficiency, effectiveness, and value for money in the use of their land and buildings. The Scottish case studies would suggest that institutions are responding appropriately, in reviewing their property portfolios and devising core real estate strategies in light of specific constraints and opportunities. Inevitably, there are pressures for institutions to develop their strategies on an individual basis in order to satisfy the changing context in which they operate. There is no guarantee, however, that such institutional restructuring necessarily fits with their particular locality, or with the national objectives for Scotland as a whole. This suggests that as real estate strategy formulation and implementation mature, greater attention to developing the relational links with local and strategic governance will be needed.

References

Ascherson, N. 2002. *Stone Voices: The Search for Scotland.* London: Granta Books.

Bond, R., and M. Rosie. 2002. "National Identities in Post-Devolution Scotland." *Scottish Affairs* 40: 34–53.

Burnside, R. 2003. *Funding Higher Education in Scotland and England.* SPICe briefing 03/67. Edinburgh: Scottish Parliament.
Charles, D. 2003. "Universities and Territorial Development: Reshaping the Regional Role of UK Universities." *Local Economy* 18, no. 1: 7–20.
Commission for Architecture and the Built Environment. 2005. *Design with Distinction: The Value of Good Building Design in Higher Education.* London: Author.
Cooke, P., and N. Clifton. 2005. "Visionary, Precautionary and Constrained 'Varieties of Devolution' in the Economic Governance of the Devolved UK Territories." *Regional Studies* 39, no. 4: 437–51.
Cooke, P., and K. Morgan. 1998. *The Associational Economy.* Oxford: Oxford University Press.
Denholme, J.W., and D. Macleod. 2002. "Educating the Scots: The Renewal of the Democratic Intellect." In *Anatomy of the New Scotland: Power, Influence and Change,* ed. G. Hassan and C. Warhurst. Edinburgh: Mainstream Publishing.
Department for Education and Skills. 2003. *The Future of Higher Education.* London: Author.
Doherty, J. 1991. "Dundee: A Post-Industrial City." In Whatley, 24–39.
Duncan Rice, D. 2004. "Successful Fundraising for Universities: North America Compared with Europe." Keynote speech presented to the seventeenth International Conference on Higher Education, Luxembourg, August 27.
Dundee City Council. 2003. *Dundee: A City Vision.* Dundee: Author.
General Register Office for Scotland. 2004. *Scotland's Population 2004: The Registrar General's Annual Review of Demographic Trends.* Edinburgh: Author.
Glasson, J. 2003. "The Widening Local and Regional Development Impacts of the Modern Universities: A Tale of Two Cities (and North-South Perspectives)." *Local Economy* 18, no. 1: 21–37.
Halsey, A.H. 1995. *Decline of Donnish Dominion: The British Academic Professions in the Twentieth Century.* Oxford: Oxford University Press.
Harris, A., M.G. Lloyd, and D. Newlands. 1988. *The Impact of Oil on the Aberdeen Economy.* Aldershot, Scotland: Avebury.
Hepworth, M., and L. Pickavance. 2004. *The Geography of the Scottish Knowledge Economy: A Report Prepared for Scottish Enterprise.* London: Local Futures Group.
Higher Education Funding Council for England. 1998. *Private Investment in Higher Education.* (Circular Letter 98/18.)
———. 2000. *Estate Strategies: A Guide to Good Practice.* (Reference 00/04.)
———. 2002. *Estates Management Statistics Good Practice Annual Report 2002.*
Housley, J. 1997. "Managing the Estate in Higher Education Establishments." *Facilities* 15, no. 3/4: 72–83.
Howells, J., M. Nedeva, L. Georghiou, J. Evans, and S. Hinder. 1998. *Industry-Academic Links in the UK: A Report to the Higher Education Funding Councils of England, Scotland and Wales.* Manchester: University of Manchester, PREST.
Irvine, J.M. 1995. *The Distinctiveness of Scottish Higher Education: Future Prospects.* Report of COSHEP First Annual Forum. Edinburgh: COSHEP.
Jarvis, P. 2001. *Universities and Corporate Universities: The Higher Learning Industry in Global Society.* London: Kogan Page.
JM Consulting. 2001. *Study of Science Research Infrastructure: A Report for the Office of Science and Technology.* Bristol: Author.

———. 2002a. *Arts and Humanities Research Infrastructure.* Report to the Higher Education Funding Council for England. (Issues Paper 2002/35.) Bristol: Author.

———. 2002b. *Teaching and Learning Infrastructure in Higher Education.* Report to the Higher Education Funding Council for England. (Issues Paper 2002/31.) Bristol: Author.

———. 2004. *Study of University Infrastructure for Science and Research: A Report for the Office of Science and Technology.* (Update study.) Bristol: Author.

Jones, P. 1992. "Education." In *Anatomy of Scotland: How Scotland Works,* ed. M. Linklataer and R. Denniston. Edinburgh: Chambers.

Kelly, U., R. Marsh, and I. McNicoll. 2002. *The Impact of Higher Education Institutions on the UK Economy: A Report for Universities UK.* London: Universities UK.

Lawton Smith, H. 2003. "Universities and Local Economic Development: An Appraisal of the Issues and Practices." *Local Economy* 18, no. 1: 2–6.

Lazzeroni, M., and A. Piccaluga. 2003. "Towards the Entrepreneurial University." *Local Economy* 18, no. 1: 38–48.

Leibovitz, J. 2004. "'Embryonic' Knowledge-Based Clusters and Cities: The Case of Biotechnology in Scotland." *Urban Studies* 5/6: 1133–55.

Lloyd, M.G., and J. McCarthy. 2003. "Urban Regeneration in Dundee." In *Urban Regeneration in Europe,* ed. C. Couch, C. Fraser, and S. Percy, 56–68. Oxford: Blackwell.

Lloyd, M.G., and D. Newlands. 1993. "The Impact of Oil on the Scottish Economy with Particular Reference to the Aberdeen Economy." In *North Sea Oil and the Environment,* ed. W. Cairns, 115–38. Barking: Elsevier.

Locke, W. 2004. "Visions of 21st Century University Environments: The Significance of Estates Strategies." *Perspectives* 6, no. 1: 5–10.

McCarthy, J.P., and S.H.A. Pollock. 1997. "Urban Regeneration: A Comparative Evaluation of Practice in Glasgow and Dundee." *Land Use Policy* 14: 137–49.

McNay, I. 1995. "From the Collegial Academy to Corporate Enterprise: The Changing Cultures of Universities." In *The Changing University,* ed. T. Schuller, 105–15. Buckingham, UK: Society for Research into Higher Education and Open University Press.

McNicoll, I.H. 1995. *The Impact of the Scottish Higher Education Sector on the Economy of Scotland: Summary.* COSHEP.

Morgan, B. 2002. "Higher Education and Regional Economic Development in Wales: An Opportunity for Demonstrating the Efficacy of Devolution in Economic Development." *Regional Studies* 36, no. 1: 65–73.

National Committee of Inquiry into Higher Education. 1997. *Higher Education in the Learning Society: Summary Report.* (Dearing Report.) London: HMSO.

National Health Service. 1996. *An Exemplar Estate Strategy.* London: National Health Service Estates.

Newlands, D. 2000. "The Oil Economy." In *Aberdeen, 1800 to 2000: A New History,* ed. W.H. Fraser and C. Lee, 126–52. East Linton, Scotland: Tuckwell Press.

Paterson, L. 2003. "The Survival of the Democratic Intellect: Academic Values in Scotland and England." *Higher Education Quarterly* 57: 67–93.

Peel, D. 2005. "Putting Heart Back into the Campus in the City." *Town and Country Planning* 74, no. 5: 172–73.

Peel, D., and M.G. Lloyd. 2005. "City-Visions: Visioning and Delivering Scotland's Economic Future." *Local Economy* 20, no. 1: 40–52.

Price, I., F. Matzdorf, and L. Smith. 2001. *Where to Study: The Importance of the Physical Environment to Students in Choosing Their University.* FM Research Application Forum, April.

Raffe, D. 2004. "How Distinctive Is Scottish Education? Five Perspectives on Distinctiveness." *Scottish Affairs* 49 (August): 50–72.

Report of the Scottish Committee. 1997. *Submission to the National Committee of Inquiry into Higher Education.* Edinburgh: SHEFC.

Robert Gordon University. 2003. *Course Prospectus 2003–4.* Aberdeen: Author.

Rodger, R. 1996. "Urbanisation in Twentieth Century Scotland." In *Scotland in the Twentieth Century,* ed. T.M. Devine and R.J. Finlay, 122–52. Edinburgh: Edinburgh University Press.

Sanderson, M. 1972. *The Universities and British Industry, 1850–1970.* London: Routledge and Kegan Paul.

Schuller, T., ed. 1995. *The Changing University.* Buckingham, UK: Society for Research into Higher Education and Open University Press.

Scott, A., G. Steyn, A. Geuna, S. Brusoni, and E. Steinmueller. 2001. *The Economic Returns to Basic Research and the Benefits of University-Industry Relationships: A Literature Review and Update of Findings.* Report for the Office of Science and Technology. Brighton: University of Sussex.

Scottish Executive. 2000. *Review of Scotland's Cities: The Analysis.* Edinburgh: Author.

———. 2001a. *A Science Strategy for Scotland.* Edinburgh: Author.

———. 2001b. *A Smart, Successful Scotland: Ambitions for the Enterprise Networks.* Edinburgh: Author.

———. 2002. *Building Better Cities: Delivering Growth and Opportunities.* Edinburgh: Author.

———. 2003a. *A Framework for Higher Education in Scotland: Higher Education Review Phase 2.* Edinburgh: Author.

———. 2003b. *The Lifelong Learning Strategy for Scotland.* Edinburgh: Author.

———. 2004a. *National Planning Framework.* Edinburgh: Author.

———. 2004b. *Statistics Publication Notice: Students in Higher Education in Scotland, 2002–03.* Edinburgh: Author.

Scottish Funding Council. 2006. *Sustainable Development Guidance.* (SFC/17/2006.) Edinburgh: Author.

Scottish Higher Education Funding Council. 1999a. *Estate Strategy Guidance.* (Circular Letter HE/18/99.)

———. 1999b. *Scottish Higher Education Institutions Estate Management Action Plans: Analysis of 1999 Returns.* (Circular letter HE/59/99.)

———. 2000. *Scottish Higher Education Institutions Estate Management Action Plans: Analysis of 2000 Returns.* (HE/45/00.)

———. 2001. *Higher Education–Business Interaction Survey.* (Circular letter HE/60/01.)

———. 2002a. *The Modernising Agenda in Scottish Higher Education Institutions: Addressing Leadership and Management.* (Circular letter HE/20/02.)

———. 2002b. *Scottish Higher Education Institutions Estate Management Action Plans: Analysis of 2001 Returns.* (Circular letter HE/04/02.)

Scottish Office. 1995. *Scottish Higher Education Institutions.* Edinburgh: Scottish Office Information Directorate.

———. 1999. *Scotland: Towards the Knowledge Economy.* Edinburgh: Author.

Shafe, M. 1982. *University Education in Dundee 1881–1981: A Pictorial History.* Dundee: University of Dundee.

Stevens, R. 2004. *University to UNI: The Politics of Higher Education in England since 1944.* London: Politico's.

Sutton Trust. 2003. *University Endowments: A UK/US Comparison.* (Discussion paper.) London: Author.

Tomes, A., and M. Phillips. 2003. "Product Development through University-SME Collaboration: Lessons from Reactive and Proactive Approaches." *Local Economy* 18, no. 1: 91–95.

Universities Scotland. 2002. *The Knowledge Society: A Submission to the Scottish Higher Education Review.* Edinburgh: Author.

University of Aberdeen. 2001. *University Estate Strategy 2002–2007.* Aberdeen: Author.

———. Undated. *University of Aberdeen Strategic Plan 2004–2009.* Aberdeen: Author.

University of Dundee. 2000. *Estates Strategy: Final Draft.* Dundee: Author.

———. Undated-a. *The Campus in the City for the 21st Century.* Dundee: Author.

———. Undated-b. *The Vision Towards 2007.* Dundee: Author.

Wagner, L. 1995. "A Thirty-Year Perspective: From the Sixties to the Nineties." In Schuller 1995, 15–24.

Whatley, C.A. 1991. "The Making of 'Juteopolis'—and How It Was." In *The Remaking of Juteopolis,* ed. C.A. Whatley, 7–22. Proceedings of the Abertay Historical Society's Octocentenary Conference, Abertay Historical Society, Dundee.

Wolf, A. 2002. *Does Education Matter? Myths about Education and Economic Growth.* London: Penguin.

Wright, M. 1974. "The Design of Universities: Plans, Buildings and Relationships." *Town Planning Review* 45: 233–58.

5

Toward Downtown

Spatial Growth and University Location in the Tokyo Metropolitan Area

Yuichi Takeuchi

The Tokyo metropolitan area (TMA) is located in the Kanto plain, almost at the center of Japan. TMA consists of the capital, Tokyo, and the prefectures of Saitama, Chiba, and Kanagawa. Although the plain covers only 3.5 percent of the total area of Japan, its population is some 33 million and accounts for 26 percent of the nation's total. The metropolitan area also contains almost one-quarter of all businesses in Japan, employing over 27 percent of the nation's workers, especially in the high-skilled sectors of finance, real estate, and insurance. In short, Tokyo, and its metropolitan surroundings, is one of the economic centers of the nation. Therefore, it is not surprising that many colleges and universities are concentrated in TMA. As Table 5.1 shows, 319 colleges and universities, accounting for 26 percent of the nation's total, were located in the TMA, with 183 colleges and universities sited in Tokyo, as of 2003. The number of college and university students in the 319 institutions in the TMA is 1.2 million, or almost 40 percent of the nation's total.

After World War II, and especially in the period of high economic growth after the 1960s, intense urbanization occurred and much of the nation's population became concentrated in this area (Takeuchi 2000). In order to solve the urban problems associated with the rapid urbanization, the government, which maintained that the factories, colleges, and universities in the area were causing the concentration, prohibited new buildings and extensions from being built in the TMA.[1] Therefore, they were located on the outskirts of and outside the TMA. The rapid urban growth stopped when the long-term recession arrived at the start of the 1990s, and "urban regeneration" was introduced by the government as one of its "structural reforms."[2] Various deregulation measures were carried out, land-use controls were eased or abolished, and the location of institutes of higher education at sites near or at the core of the TMA was

Table 5.1

Statistical Comparison of Tokyo Metropolitan Area with Japan and Tokyo

Categories	Japan	%	TMA	%	Tokyo	%
Area (in square kilometers)	377,877	100.0	13,280	3.5	2,102	0.6
Population, 2000 (in thousands)	126,926	100.0	33,418	26.3	12,064	9.5
GDP (FY2000)	515,478	100.0	156,243	30.3	85,230	16.5
No. of establishments, 2001	6,350,101	100.0	1,507,778	23.7	724,769	11.4
No. of employees, 2001 (in thousands)	60,158	100.0	16,673	27.7	8,609	14.3
No. of finance, insurance, real estate, and services companies, 2001	382,966	100.0	139,426	36.4	85,056	22.2
No. of colleges and universities, 2003	1,227	100.0	319	26.0	183	14.9
No. of students, 2003	3,054,042	100.0	1,199,527	39.3	722,020	23.6

Source: Statistical Bureau, Ministry of Internal Affairs and Communications, and Ministry of Education, Culture, Sports, Science and Technology, Tokyo, Japan.

reintroduced. Moreover, the structural reforms embraced the promotion of science and technology in the reformation of colleges and universities and encouraged active collaboration between industry and the academic world. National universities were incorporated, and, as a result, investments in real estate flourished, including the establishment of new facilities and campuses and the redevelopment of old campuses, including new university facilities in existing urbanized areas, particularly urban centers.

The purpose of this chapter is to examine the processes of suburbanization and recentralization of colleges and universities in relation to higher education reform, national land policy, and urban regeneration policy with respect to the TMA; specifically, the issues to be studied are as follows:

- What recent changes in the economy and in education led to the structural reformation policy that brought about the city center recurrence?
- What kind of behavioral principles in management and administration did the universities apply with respect to such changes?
- University reformation and location were deregulated on the basis of structural reformation, but what kind of impact did they have on the relationship between the universities and the city?

The following section provides a case description of the effects of university reform and "urban regeneration" on Hosei University, a big, popular, private university in the TMA. In the background of university reform are three big challenges in Japan: advances in economic and urban globalization, the increased popularization and commercialization of universities, and demographic changes in the Japanese community. These factors are viewed as the driving forces of university reform, and we focus on the role of universities as foundational institutions of urban regeneration.

Urban Regeneration and University Reform

The system of higher education in Japan had been developed by around 1900; national and public universities; teachers colleges; and agricultural, commercial, and technical schools were placed across the nation in a balanced way under national educational policy.[3] The current Tokyo University, the Tokyo Institute of Technology, and other national universities were placed in the TMA. Private colleges and universities were established in the same period, but no distribution policy was adopted for them, and they located in large, populous cities. Current private universities established during this period in the TMA were Keio, Waseda, Meiji, Chuo, and Hosei. In the latter half of the twentieth century, higher education was expanded in Japan, as in the United

States and Europe. In Japan, however, demand for higher education was met by an increase in private colleges and universities (Ushiogi 2004). Without planned control, many of them were concentrated in the TMA (Ichikawa 1989). The suburbanization of colleges and universities was brought about during this period because of the land-use controls in the TMA. However, the trend of college and university location has recently changed. Let us examine the case of Hosei University and the process of reformation that has been developed to cope with the changes.

Reforming Hosei University: Open University–Hosei 21

Hosei University is one of six powerful universities located in the TMA.[4] Its precursor organization, the Tokyo Hogakusha, was established in the present location in Chiyoda Ward in 1880. With the postwar enactment of the Private School Law, Hosei University was established in 1951, and the Ichigaya Campus was located in a district that straddles Shinjuku and Chiyoda wards. In the subsequent period of university expansion and development of science and technology, the Koganei Campus in the City of Koganei was completed in 1964, followed by a rapid increase in student numbers and the completion of the Tama Campus in Machida City, in the western suburbs of Tokyo, in 1984, resulting in a university of 43,000 students and a teaching staff of about 1,100.

Hosei University set up an in-house council in 1994 to draw up a vision for its future development. By 1997, the council had completed a plan called "Open University–Hosei 21," whose basic concepts were as follows (Kiyonari 2003):

1. Globalization: Extend remote education across borders; compete with overseas universities.
2. Exchanges with society: Increase exchanges with citizens, nonprofit organizations, companies, and administrators.
3. Promotion of lifelong education: Promote continued education to a wide age group.

To move in the direction outlined in this plan, the following projects were set up:

- Establishment of four new departments that meet the needs of the times,
- Expansion of the postgraduate school,
- Reform of night school education,

- Reform of correspondence education, and
- Establishment of a new extension center and expansion of information systems and facilities.

To carry out these projects, the university is redeveloping the campus. It will construct a high-rise school building in the center of the Ichigaya campus, in downtown Tokyo, where low-rise buildings have so far stood. The university has also obtained the site of a neighboring high school to expand into, and new buildings have been completed in Koganei and Tama.

Open University–Hosei 21 and Relationship to Society

As globalization of the economy blurs national borders, vertical demarcations in the field of learning have also become less distinct, and in the 1990s various boundaries and walls in universities such as Hosei began to collapse. To cope with such changes, the university has had to be opened to the outside. The diversification of education and research is viewed as essential for cultivating independent thinkers and for deepening associations with society, respectively. While improving the quality of research is promoted on the one hand, diversification is required on the other hand. Open University–Hosei 21 was drawn up with an awareness of these issues (Kiyonari 2003).

Therefore, the main elements of the plan include new faculties, the reorganization and establishment of graduate schools, and the establishment of research institutes. It is said that American universities suddenly became commercialized from the 1970s into the 1980s, but more than ten years later the commercial wave swept over the academy in Japan, also (Bok 2003). Particular importance has been placed on so-called industrial relations and social services and on building close bonds between research, education, and society, and Hosei University's reformation reflects that.

Sports, research, and education are the three main fields of university commercialization, but, since university sports in Japan are not sufficiently significant to produce a cash revenue, moves toward commercialization are mainly in the fields of research and education. Research strengthens relations with industrial circles and regional communities, and new educational research institutes and activities are established for that purpose. The university's relevant proposals can be expressed by five categories: the environment, information and telecommunication technology, career formation support, globalization, and specialized graduate schools (Nikkei BP Planning 2004). The primary components of each category are listed below.

The Environment

- Enactment of the Hosei University Environment Charter
- Acquisition of ISO (International Organization for Standardization) 14001 certification and commencement of campus environmental management
- Creation of the Green Campus; making planning decisions and facilitating cooperation and interchanges by the Environment Center with other organizations such as businesses, administrative agencies, and regional organizations
- Combining of social science and natural science with environmental policy; establishment of the Faculty of Humanity and Environment
- Establishment of the Graduate School of Environmental Management to cultivate talented people for environmental business (development and training of high-grade professionals)
- Establishment of the Laboratory of Regional Design with Ecology for the social and cultural integration of science and technology with urban and regional regeneration

Information & Telecommunication Technology

- Construction of the Hosei University Academic Science network system (Net2003) for simultaneous three-campus (Ichigaya, Koganei, and Tama) teaching
- Establishment of the Faculty of Computer and Information Sciences for training IT (information technology) specialists

Career Formation Support

- Establishment of the Faculty of Lifelong Learning and Career Studies aimed at the education of business people and managers
- Establishment of the Faculty of Social Policy and Administration for the training of management specialists in welfare, communities, and clinical pathology
- Establishment of the Graduate School of Business Administration (night-time graduate courses for adults)

Globalization

- Establishment of the Hosei University Research Institute, California (Silicon Valley), and bidirectional real-time teaching between Japan and the United States
- Inclusion of overseas studying in departmental curricula

Specialized Graduate Schools

- Establishment of the Hosei Business School of Innovation Management (one-year course), combining business with IT
- Establishment of the Accounting School for the large demand to train accounting specialists
- Establishment of the Hosei University Law School (a professional graduate school) for lawyer training according to the reform of lawyers' educational systems

Changes in University Behavioral Principles

To strengthen the relationship between Hosei and the society under Open University–Hosei 21, management of the university needed to be changed. The university could easily manage with the increasing revenue from the rapidly growing number of students in the period of university expansion, but it also needed to be able to maintain stability in periods of declining demand. To promote the five strategies mentioned above, Hosei adopted the following measures to strengthen its management and administration systems: clarification of governance by the board of directors, establishment of a third-party evaluation committee, and evaluation of financial affairs by the acquisition of credit ratings.

Governance of Board of Directors

Traditionally, Japanese universities have been considered "knowledge communities." It is said that students and teachers belong to the community called a university, studying together. However, the increasing number and diversity of students, as well as major changes in the existing learning systems, caused the university to take the attitude that the higher the wall between the community and the university, the better. At present, close ties between university and community are again being sought, and the walls are being eliminated. The university has become a "knowledge management body" and continues to diversify. The bigger the university, the stronger, according to this trend; and the age of the "multiversity" has arrived. The reformation of Hosei University is also aimed at creating an "advanced multi-functional university" (Nikkei BP Planning 2004).

A university that has become a multiversity cannot function with a bottom-up system of administrative management like a traditional community type of university. A top-down system of administrative management must be developed, instead. Moreover, from the viewpoint of business, universities are becoming an unstable industry in the midst of a declining demand for higher education. Therefore, in order to fulfill its social responsibilities, Hosei University will reinforce its governance and clarify the responsibilities of the board of directors.[5]

Third-Party Evaluation Committee

The third-party evaluation committee was established in April 2003 to (1) evaluate the effectiveness of university governance, (2) evaluate the objectivity and transparency of management, and (3) develop a new management model for student retention. This is associated with aiding stakeholders, including students, patrons, teaching staff, employees, alumni, contributors, and national and regional governments, as well as ordinary citizens, in their comprehension and judgment of Hosei University and its improvements. In a sense, the evaluation committee may be likened to the outside directors of a joint-stock company.

Acquisition of Credit Ratings

In February 2003, Hosei University was the first Japanese incorporated educational institution to be granted a double-A minus, senior long-term credit rating by Rating and Investment Information, Inc., the largest domestic credit rating organization. The reasons for the rating were given as (1) reduced cost of procurement of funds for the qualitative improvement of the educational environment, (2) market assessment of public revelation of university financial affairs, and (3) improved image of Open University–Hosei 21 (Kiyonari 2003).

The medium-term target for which funds are needed is the redevelopment of the Ichigaya and Koganei campuses. At Koganei Campus, about 1.9 hectares of neighboring land were purchased in preparation for the renovation in 2003 of the Faculty of Engineering, where the Micro and Nano Technology Research Center is being built, so that Hosei University can compete in the fields of science and technology. At Ichigaya Campus, adjoining high school land and school buildings were purchased. The credit rating would have enabled university debts to be issued, but these real estate acquisitions were covered by the procurement of funds from financial institutions without any debts being issued. Because of the credit rating, the cost was half the previous cost of borrowing (Nikkei BP Planning 2004).

If one looks at what kind of universities saw the number of applicants increase over the past ten years, those that established new departments and courses that met the interests of the times are the ones that have been successful.

In addition, universities that completed their management and administration system to accept students saw a rise in the number of applicants. Following Hosei University, a growing number of universities obtained evaluations from credit rating companies to show that their management is stable.

Driving Forces Behind Reform

University reformation appeared at the same time in many Japanese universities, including Hosei University, based on three major factors: advances in economic and urban globalization, the increased popularization and commercialization of universities, and demographic changes in the Japanese community. Independently and reciprocally, these became powerful forces in stimulating the reformation of higher education. (See Table 5.2 for a summary of urban and university changes after the war in Japan.)

The Impact of Globalization

Following the rapid development of information and communication technologies, globalization became the most important factor, besides the economy, in the spread of communication networks. At the same time, after the bursting of the bubble in the early 1990s, the Japanese economy entered a long period of stagnation. To engage globalization and resist economic stagnation, alongside the revival of finance and industry, two issues in the reform of higher education were regarded as key.

One issue is urban renaissance. The urban economy, especially the economy of the metropolitan district, has been said from the outset to lead the national economy (Scott, et al. 2001). The TMA is said to be a global city-region whose economic scale might exceed that of an entire country and whose trends are closely associated with the world economy. In order to abolish the stagnation of the Japanese economy, an urban renaissance, especially the revitalization of the TMA, has become a major issue from the end of the twentieth century. For that renaissance to happen, two things must occur: (1) The entire Japanese economy must be stimulated by removing regulations and measures that prevent the movement of resources from areas of low productivity to the highly productive TMA. (2) Land in the center of the city that is being used inefficiently should be used more effectively so that the agglomeration economies of the global city-regions, such as the sharing of skilled subcontractors and specialized service firms; the formation of skilled labor pools; better access to technological and market information; and the sharing of a common infrastructure, including transport facilities, can be pursued (Fujita 1989).

Table 5.2

Summary of the History of Urban and University Changes in Japan

Stage	Establishment of new university system ~1960	Expansion of the number of universities 1960–75	Restructuring of higher education 1975–90	Diversification of university 1990–	Competition among universities Now
Percentage of students who go on to higher education	10%	10–38%	35%	35–50%	stable around 50%
No. of applicants	small	increased	stable → increased	increased → stable	decreased
University type by Trow model	elite	elite → mass	mass	mass → universal	universal?
Type of society	confused period after WWII	industrial society	industrial society	transition period	knowledge society
University location in TMA	23 wards and major suburban cities	suburbanization	suburbanization	suburbanization	23 ward areas
Land-use control	loose	strictly restricted in urbanized area	strictly restricted in urbanized area	deregulation	deregulation and special districts
National land policy	recover WWII damage	correction of regional imbalance	dispersion	dissolving Tokyo concentration	urban regeneration
Trend of economy	recovery from WWII damage	high growth	stable → bubbling	recession	highly competitive

In order for the regulatory reforms to expedite the effective use of land in the central and waterfront parts of Tokyo, Priority Urban Redevelopment Areas were specified and arrangements were made for deregulation of urban planning in those areas. As a result, urban redevelopment projects that had been stalled were expedited. Other reforms totally abolished regulations for factories and universities located in existing urban areas.

A review of national land and education policies from the prewar and postwar periods until the present (see Appendix 5.1, "Changes in University Location Policy After the War") reveals that they consistently discouraged the concentration of higher education institutions in major cities and favored dispersing them to more exurban local districts. The policies stated that the distribution of higher education institutions would not only achieve a regional balance in higher education but would also be a means of solving the economic difference between cities and farming villages and the urban problems caused by concentrations of the population in major cities. In the postwar period, the regulatory law *Shutoken no Kiseishigaichi niokeru Kougyoutou no Seigen ni Kansuru Houritsu* (the law concerning the restrictions on industries, etc., in the existing urban areas of metropolitan regions), enacted in 1959, points to the location of universities most clearly. The law placed restrictions on the twenty-three wards in Tokyo; all parts of Musashino City; and parts of the cities of Kawaguchi, Mitaka, Yokohama, and Kawasaki. Construction of classrooms larger than fifteen hundred square meters became impossible in those areas.

Postgraduate schools were taken off the list of restrictions in 1999, and the law was abolished in 2002. Reasons cited for abolishing the law were that the birthrate had declined, the percentage of students going to a higher level of education had decreased, and the number of incoming students at universities and junior colleges was expected to drop. At the same time, because the opportunity to obtain a higher education in the local areas had become pervasive, there was no longer a reason to restrict location using the law.

The urban renaissance not only brought about the redevelopment of university campuses in existing urbanized areas due to the abolition of placement regulations, but also had the effect of making colleges and universities powerful players in urban redevelopment in the TMA.

Another issue of reforming higher education is that the research and development activities of colleges and universities should be in closer cooperation with society, particularly industry, to strengthen competitive power in the fields of science and technology. Competition among nations in science and technology has intensified as a result of globalization. Consequently, a science and technology renaissance has been promoted by the government as a national policy.

If economic globalization can be divided into financial globalization and industrial globalization, up to the 1980s the main drive behind globalization in Japan was the wealth brought about by industrial production and its exportation. The TMA was successful in treading the path toward an industrial world city, but it was faced with economic stagnation due to the collapse of the financial bubble. And, in the 1990s, global competition in the areas of science and technology became intense. For Japan to be revitalized, it was important to restore its science and technology, its areas of expertise. The organizations responsible for technical competition are the universities; a national technical policy has been put in place as a national strategy.

In 1995 the Fundamental Law of Science and Technology was enacted, and two basic science and technology plans were formed based on that law. Universities have been given the central role in the plan to develop science and technology. According to the plan, their role calls for promotion of basic studies and training of human resources; cooperation among industries, government, and universities; and promotion of regional science and technology. Such a policy for science and technology has had a major impact on universities in the form of allocation of competitive study funds; cooperation among industries, government, and universities; and regional contribution. Competition is intensifying as private universities face a decline in the eighteen-year-old population. In the process, universities have had to start many new programs, such as joint study programs, programs for training human resources, extension courses, and postgraduate courses for communities. And as facilities for such programs, new campuses are being set up in buildings in urban centers of TMA, near railway stations, which facilitates transportation, and in large-scale urban redevelopment areas.

The Popularization and Commercialization of Universities

The second factor that precipitated university reform was a change in higher education itself. This involves two developments that began in the United States and Britain in the 1980s and spread to Japan in the late 1990s.

The first development is the popularization and commercialization of universities. *Popularization* refers not only to the increasing numbers of students but also to the diversification of education. In particular, it seems that the undergraduate school has become compulsory, while the graduate school has been expanded and diversified. *Commercialization* means that communities demand appropriate outcomes from colleges and universities, which reflects the cost that communities are willing to pay. Commercialization has created closer relationships between communities and colleges and universities.

The sudden expansion of the scale of higher education, and the accompanying qualitative changes and diversification of the students associated with it, resulted in changes that were unavoidable for the universities. According to Martin Trow (2000), the change from mass type to universal type brought the ratio of students who go on to higher education to more than 50 percent, and it persists near that level in Japan today.

For the transition from the mass type to the universal type in the Trow model to take place, structural changes in higher education had to occur. That is to say that it was not just an increase in the number of young people going to universities after graduating from high school. Diversity in student groups and patterns in going to a higher level of education had to take place, as well as changes in study patterns. Trow's model does not work as well for Japanese cases as for U.S. cases. In Japan, two different possibilities exist intermingled in the shift toward universal type. One has to do with higher education in Japan being virtually compulsory. Students are currently forced to enter universities and colleges immediately after graduation from high school, which means that there exists a type of universal attendance in the society. If the eighteen-year-old population declines and the ratio of students who go to universities increases further, it is predicted that only a majority of students will go on to higher education, and it will become semi-compulsory. The other possibility is that there would be a universal-access society, where opportunity for higher education would be available at some time of life, according to the wishes of every individual. Such diversification is not the mainstream yet, but it appears to be moving ahead rapidly in the 2000s. In particular, following the expansion of postgraduate schools, the number of adult students and part-time students has increased sharply at such schools. The establishment of postgraduate schools for working people and specialists could be the next logical step.

Between 1990 and 2003, the number of postgraduate schools in Japan increased by 71.7 percent, from 311 to 534, and the number of students rose by 156.6 percent. The quantitative expansion was remarkable. Focusing on postgraduate schools sharply increased the size of the student population because universities that did not have postgraduate schools added them and opened them to the public.

The second development is the commercialization of universities. With the advent of the 1980s, marketing principles became dominant in the world of higher education due to the gradual increase in the cost of higher education. The idea that in addition to its role in higher education a university is also a business enterprise that pursues benefits relative to the invested cost was taken up.

The Ministry of Education, Culture, Sports, Science, and Technology made a proposal to the Council on Economic and Fiscal Policy in June 2001. The proposal referred to the policy for the structural reform of national universities and the plan to activate the Japanese economy using universities as a base; it had three components. The first component was to carry out thoroughly the principle of competition based on evaluation, to accelerate the creation of new industries from universities, and to build world-class universities by introducing private-sector management systems into national universities. The second component was to train world-class specialists by strengthening postgraduate schools and train human resources that can cope with changes in society; the aim was to create a major nation in regard to human resources. The third component was to regenerate cities and city-regions by changing universities within them.

Demographic Changes

In a period of high economic growth, and together with the population increase over the whole of Japan, large populations shifted from the country to the city. In effect, because of the shift of resources from areas of low productivity to the highly productive cities, the incomes of the people increased, and the GDP increased. As a result, today almost all of Japan's population lives in cities, and urban economic activities control the Japanese economy. However, the population increase will approach a peak early in the twenty-first century, after which it will decline, and by 2050 the total population is expected to have fallen to the 1960 level. Since much of the population is concentrated in cities, the overall decline in the population means a decline in the urban population. Competition between the TMA and other cities will intensify. For private universities entrusted with the basic management of the rise and fall in student numbers, being established in a city with a large population will be a condition for survival. Moreover, even if there is no marked population decline over the whole of the TMA, areas of decreased population will appear within the TMA. In particular, the suburbs, which expanded at the time of the population increase, already have increasing numbers of elderly and decreasing numbers of children. Established city areas with a concentration of young people and business people become strategic bases for locating a university.

Urban redevelopment projects not only provide opportunities for new jobs in established urban areas but also pursue the benefits of an agglomeration economy by providing opportunities for new educational functions. By providing residential functions, for example, redevelopment projects will call the population back from the suburbs to established town areas. This makes the relocation of universities in established urban areas and the redevelopment of the central urban campus inevitable.

Figure 5.1   **Japan's Population at Age 18, 1960–2015**

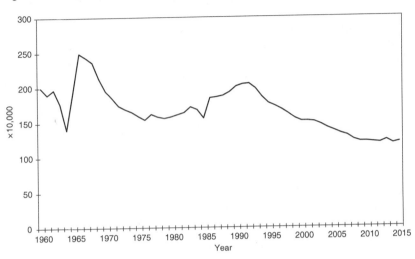

Since people in Japan have a strong inclination for formal education and university management is greatly dependent on students' fees, demographic change, primarily the movement of the young population and especially the eighteen-year-old population, has a direct impact on university management.

Competition among universities has intensified since the beginning of the 1990s, primarily because of the decline in the eighteen-year-old population (see Figure 5.1), a trend that emerged before the increase in the population of the Japanese society began to stop. When the second baby boom peaked in 1992, the eighteen-year-old population totaled 2.05 million. It has been declining rapidly since and had dropped to 1.44 million by 2003. According to a forecast by the National Institute of Population and Social Security Research, this trend will continue over a long period.

As the percentage of students in higher education has remained around 49 percent in recent years, the decline in population means fewer applicants and incoming students. Before World War II, the proportion of students in higher education was about 3 percent. It remained around 10 percent for some time after the war, when universities were established under a new system, and increased sharply in the 1960s and 1970s, when the first baby boomers came of age. After that, the proportion stayed steady at between 35 and 36 percent. In the 1990s, it increased sharply again, nearing 50 percent and remaining there. The second group of baby boomers arrived in 1992. Although the percentage of students did not decline, the number of people aged eighteen, which is the age for entry into universities, has decreased gradually since.

If these changes are overlapped with Trow's higher education development level model (see Table 5.2, p. 94), the postwar period of about ten years, when formation of universities under the new system took place, corresponds to the period of elite-type universities, as the ratio was still around 10 percent during that time. It was in 1963 that the ratio exceeded 15 percent, which is the benchmark at which universities change from the elite type to the mass type. The number of Japanese universities increased rapidly in that period. And although the ratio has not exceeded 50 percent, at which point universities change from mass to universal type, it is quite close.

Universities as Fundamental Elements of Urban Regeneration

The relationships of colleges and universities to the cities of which they are a part are strongly influenced by the aforementioned three driving forces of university reform. First, some universities located in the suburbs during the era of university expansion have recently relocated in downtown TMA, and their presence has a major impact on the demand for urban redevelopment. Second, this shift in their location requires them to develop strong and productive relationships with their surrounding communities. Such new community-oriented behaviors can be a part of community revitalization and represent important roles for the universities in their urban communities. Third, through these kind of activities, colleges and universities are expected to play large institutional roles in shaping how the TMA, as a global city-region, can be a stage for development of the knowledge-based economy that is viewed by many as the future for Japan.

University Relocation to Downtown

Many of the universities in the TMA that have a long history were established between the 1870s and the 1900s. In the early days, they were set up on the premises of the feudal lords or in the facilities of the Tokugawa regime of the Edo period. After that, the number of universities increased gradually. But the railway network that now provides service to the suburbs had not yet been developed in the urban area of Tokyo, and the universities were located on heights surrounding the city center at the time. Basically, they were inside the current Yamanote railway line.

During the latter half of the Meiji period and the Taisho period, suburban trains were developed. This is when the suburbs of Tokyo started to form, and at the same time, the number of university students increased and relocation of universities began. What accelerated this movement was the Great Kanto Earthquake of 1923, during which many of the university campuses burned down. Simultaneously, many Tokyo residents moved to the suburbs on the western side to avoid the dangerous lowland on the eastern side of the city (Takeuchi 2000). Because of this, universities also moved to the western side. Railway companies such as Tokyu Corporation and Seibu Railway Company tied this movement to the development of real estate. They invited universities to come to where their railway lines were and aimed to increase the number of passengers. They also developed land for housing by attaching a cultural image of a "town with a university" to the development of residential land. This is how the current Tokyo Institute of Technology, Keio University, Tokyo Metropolitan University, Tokyo Gakugei University, and Hitotsubashi University found their locations along suburban railway lines. Furthermore, such developments led to the garden city movement at the time.

Many of the universities that did not move to the suburbs following the Great Kanto Earthquake were burned down during World War II. Their reconstruction, the establishment of universities under the new system, and the rapid increase in the number of students after the war led to the location of many universities in the suburbs. At this stage, as already mentioned, regulations controlled the location of factories and universities in the urban areas of Tokyo. So the areas that attracted the establishment or expansion of universities were those that were not subject to the regulations and featured land of relatively low price. It was also necessary to secure sites large enough for the establishment of a university. Universities looked for locations along railway lines, which provided students with easy access to Tokyo and allowed the teaching staff to commute between the suburbs and existing urban areas. Areas that could meet these needs were within approximately 50 kilometers to the west of Tokyo or about 30 kilometers to the east.

In the period of university expansion, many local governments enthusiastically invited universities to promote the regional economy and urban development (Research Institute for Urban and Environmental Development 2002; National Land Agency 1995). By this means many universities built large campuses in the outer areas of the TMA, and many universities new and old—including Hosei University's Tama Campus in Machida City and others in the cities of Hachioji, Tama, and Inagi, where there are places that have been called University Town by the local government—were located in Tokyo's satellite cities.

In periods of university suburbanization, local governments expected that the university would act as one of the centers of regional development. Even national land policies enthusiastically supported university transfers. This was how the expansion of higher education was absorbed in this period. However, the university and the local community were not so closely related, and the local community, which expected the population to be increased by the university, was often not satisfied that the university was using its human and intellectual assets effectively. The university, on the other hand, rarely questioned the significance of its incursion into the region, simply going where it could find a suitable site.

Hosei University arrived at its present situation after rebuilding; its prewar location in Chiyoda Ward (now the Ichigaya Campus) had been burned out in World War II (see Table 5.3). In a period of increasing numbers of students and the suburbanization of universities, the Koganei Campus was established on the outskirts of Tokyo (20 kilometers from the center of Tokyo), and the Tama Campus was established on a site straddling Machida and Hachioji cities (30 kilometers from the center of Tokyo).

Koganei Campus was built in 1962 at City of Koganei because the Higashi-Koganei station was to be installed on the National Railway Chuo Line (at the time) and would resolve the problem of commuting. The Faculty of Engineering and the Graduate School were shifted onto a 4-hectare site (since expanded to 5.8 hectares). This was comparatively early in the period of university suburbanization, when educational institutions were promoting relocations along the Chuo Line. Moreover, leading industries such as electricity and machinery were promoting the establishment of factories and laboratories there, and the western Tokyo high-tech area was gradually being created. Relations between universities and local governments were not strong at this time.

Tama Campus was built on a 82.4-hectare site, and transfers of the Faculty of Social Science, Graduate School, and Laboratory were completed in 1984. It was a composite campus including teaching and research facilities, communal facilities, and physical education facilities. In the 1980s, many universities advanced into this region, and in a short time a university city was formed, as mentioned before. Because many university campuses were built on large, empty tracts of land separated from the existing urban areas in this district, relations between university and town were not always good. For the university, services such as housing, meals, and amusements for teaching staff and students were insufficient; and a train ride to the existing town area had to be taken to obtain them. For the local community, on the other hand, administrative facilities were overloaded due to the sudden population increase, and the community was dissatisfied with the campus, with which it had little contact. With the passage of time, and university reformation movements, relations between the community and the university improved. Systems were established for intermingling between the high-tech industries, which became a feature of these areas; the university; the local government; and the townspeople.[6]

In the university reform of the late 1990s, the urban concentration of uni-

Table 5.3

A Brief History of Hosei University

Year	Academic reform	Campus development
1880	Tokyo Hogakusha founded in Surugadai, Tokyo	
1889	Tokyo Hogakusha renamed Wafutsu Law School	Kudan-ue Building (1,040 m^2) constructed
1920	Hosei University founded with 2 faculties	
1921	Hosei relocated to Kojimachi, now Ichigaya Campus	
1945	Most buildings burned down in WWII	
1949	Hosei University founded under the new system of education	
1950–65	New faculties and graduate schools established (Faculties of Engineering, Social Sciences, Business Administration; Graduate Schools of Engineering, Social Sciences, Humanities)	
1964	Koganei Campus (4 ha) completed; Faculty and Graduate School of Engineering moved	
1980	100th anniversary	
1984	Tama Campus (82.4 ha) completed	
1992	Graduate School of Social Sciences began lectures day and night	Building of Graduate School of Social Sciences constructed in Ichigaya Campus
1994	South Building completed in Koganei	
1996	Open University–Hosei 21 drawn up	
1999	Faculties of Intercultural Communication, and Humanity and Environment established	"Egg Dome," multipurpose building, completed in Tama Campus
2000	120th anniversary; Faculties of Social Policy and Administration, and Computer and Information Sciences established	Building of Boissonade Tower in Ichigaya Campus, Department of Social Policy and Administration in Tama Campus, and Department of Computer and Information Sciences in Koganei Campus completed
2001–2	Graduate schools expanded	
2003	New faculties, graduate schools, and institutes established; senior long-term credit rating, AA-, assigned	Hosei bought the 0.5-ha site from Kaetsu High School adjacent to Ichigaya Campus and the 1.9-ha site near Koganei Campus for Micro and Nano Technology Center
2004	Business School and Law school established	Buildings for Law School in Ichigaya Campus and Micro and Nano Technology Center in Koganei Campus completed

Source: Adapted from information at www.hosei.ac.jp/gaiy02/history.html.

versities overlapped with the urban renaissance. Instead of professors locking themselves away in laboratories and young students living in dormitories, visiting professors and scholars with close community ties were visiting each other inside and outside the university, diligent in the pursuit of knowledge while promoting projects in common with the local community. A campus in a readily accessible place is an important condition for community members to fully participate in education and research.

To win in the competition among universities, it was important to gain the acceptance of the community. Many universities redeveloped their campuses in city centers, expanded their postgraduate schools, and opened extension colleges. Hosei University promoted the redevelopment of Ichigaya Campus in the center of Tokyo as a link in university reformation. Its symbol is the twenty-seven-story Boissonade Tower that was erected as a 120th anniversary project (see Figure 5.2). Moreover, for the completion of the graduate school, the adjoining high school ground and buildings were bought, and the Hosei University Law School building was erected.

In some cases, universities have moved into buildings that are part of large-scale city redevelopment projects. For example, Waseda University has moved into a building in the Nihonbashi 1-Chome project, which redeveloped the site of a famous department store in the city center. Tama University is using a development project on the site of a railway yard on the eastern side of the Shinagawa Station. Tokyo University, Harvard Business School, and Stockholm School of Economics moved into the Marunouchi Building, a representative office building from prewar days located in front of the Tokyo Station and redeveloped by the Mitsubishi Estate Company. Hotels, shopping centers, and art museums, in addition to offices, normally move into such development buildings, but facilities related to universities are becoming strong tenants to respond to growing demand for city-center university campuses.

Contribution to Community Revitalization

In the age of university reformation it is important that establishing relations between the university and the community be a two-way affair. It is considered to be the university's third mission after research and education. Instead of simply offering its intellectual assets to the community, the university can benefit from the skills, systems, knowledge, and talented human resources of community business enterprises, administrative authorities, and townspeople.

Cooperation between industry and the academic world becomes extremely important in discussing the role of the university as a base for intellectual production. For the university, cooperation with business can mean making

Figure 5.2   **Boissonade Tower on the Ichigaya Campus, Tokyo**

connections with many stakeholders, such as investors, entrepreneurs, employees, and customers. Business, on the other hand, had for a time a central research institute where basic and applied research could be developed; that system was gradually abandoned, however, and funds for the research seem to have been outlaid on the university's basic research (Amano 2004). Nevertheless, two-thirds of the research funds spent by Japanese businesses go to overseas research organizations. Japan's universities must become integrated with the industrial world and do more to promote cooperation between industry and the academic world to improve Japan's science and technology and productive strength. In addition, the creation of new industries and the development of technical venture companies to support them are urgent issues. Hosei University's aim is to form an intellectual cluster for inauguration and innovation in which the university and research laboratories will become the nuclei for gathering intellectually talented people to expedite intellectually creative activities and commercialize the results. Hosei University Research and Development Center is being established as the point of contact for cooperation between industry and academe, and commissioned and contributory research studies are being carried out in the Faculty of Engineering. Furthermore, the Research Institute of Innovation Management has been established in the Ichigaya Campus as an incubation facility for the initiation of ventures (Kiyonari 2003).

A growing number of universities have established satellite campuses in Marunouchi and Shinjuku, which are urban business districts.[7] Saitama University and Keio University have satellite campuses in Marunouchi. Tokyo Metropolitan University, Obirin University, and Tokyo International University have campuses in Shinjuku. Kyoto University and other non-Tokyo universities also have satellite offices in the TMA that are used not only for the education of working people but also as liaison offices for securing research funds and collecting information related to cooperation among industry, government, and university. The Ministry of Education, Culture, Sports, Science and Technology is looking for campus innovation centers that would rent space to be used as a satellite campus or liaison office.

For Hosei University, which has published the Open University–Hosei 21 vision, cooperation with the local community is indispensable. Its Center for Regional Research—whose missions are (1) to support the drawing up and evaluation of policies with respect to the local administrative authority, nonprofit organizations, the third sector, and government organizations; and (2) to support and help with starting the small to medium businesses that shoulder the core of the local economy—is cooperating with all of the university's faculties and research departments, associated research laboratories, and external organizations. As a center of community revitalization, it has become the driving force for regional promotion and is constructing a system called HURIN (Hosei University Regional Information Network) to provide regional research data and a regional communication network. A typical project is the Small to Medium Business Comprehensive Consulting Network, which cooperates with the regional research center in consulting with Taito Ward, one of twenty-three wards in Tokyo Metropolis, on a great variety of problems involving small to medium companies. The Faculty of Social Policy and Administration has also been opened in line with educational research to cooperate with the community.

One of the plans for realizing the Open University–Hosei 21 vision is to promote lifelong learning. Hosei University Extension Lifelong Learning for Professionals (HELP) was established in 1998 in response to needs related to lifelong learning, which have been increasing recently. At present, courses are being established in the fields of project initiation, administration and business, information technology, culture and education, acquisition of qualifications, and language study. In 2004, a system to actively get over the barrier between faculties was created by establishing a subsidiary, Hosei Knowledge Create Co., Ltd., aimed at education and research projects.

The "internship" to deepen one's comprehension of an occupation holds an important position in career education in universities. In the Faculty of Career Design, which was established in fiscal 2003, internship is a formal subject. Destinations are varied, from large venture companies to local government, industries, and nonprofit organizations and also include options such as information technology, hotels, advertising, and education.

In 2003, a basic agreement was made between the university and Chiyoda Ward, which is home to the Hosei University Ichigaya Campus, relating to cooperative collaboration with the university within the ward. Under the agreement, collaboration is to be promoted through a system of conferences between Chiyoda Ward and the university. Projects that have been implemented include (1) commerce and industry associations participating in internships with the university, (2) extension lectures sponsored jointly by Chiyoda Ward and the university, (3) collaboration at times of major disaster such as earthquakes, (4) events for Tokyo cultural promotion, (5) mobile consultation on the care of handicapped children, (6) town planning workshops, (7) collaboration on environmental beautification, and (8) university students teaching at primary and junior high schools within the ward.

Global City and the Role of the University

As an industrial world city, Tokyo was a pillar of the economic globalization base in the world economy in the 1980s, but with the strengthening of the monetary nature of economic globalization since the 1990s, it has lost its position (Kamo 2000; Machimura 2002). In particular, with the reduction in the costs of moving people, goods, and information, at all levels the dispersal of traditional industries is advancing, indicating deindustrialization. However, as before in the world economy, Tokyo is a place where financial activities are brought together. Moreover, in knowledge creation activities the power to accumulate is increasing (Fujita and Thisse 2001). Actually, far from dying out as simple social and geographic entities with the development of globalization, global city-regions such as Tokyo are becoming increasingly centralized bases in the world (Scott et al. 2001). Furthermore, if we look at the current trend for the global advancement of knowledge economies, Tokyo's role in accumulating human capital and information is increasing.

TMA is a global city-region not only because it hosts the head offices of great business enterprises that act globally but because the organizations that provide "nervous systems" for the specialized technical work of companies that develop projects throughout the world are accumulated there (Sassen 1991). Recently in Tokyo there has been an increase in such organizations, that is, in companies that provide specialized support in areas such as law, accounting, consulting, and information services. Instead of large-scale, fixed-production systems, such companies are extremely indefinite, rapidly changing, complexly entangled, specialized systems of horizontal networks. The result of such an accumulation economy is to improve the efficiency of the entire system and also to increase creativity, learning ability, and innovation. The consequent growth of the urban area is becoming a motivating force for the economy of Japan and the world (Fujita and Thisse 2001).

The importance of higher education and the research functions of universities in an agglomeration economy has been pointed out before (Heenan and Perlmutter 1979; Beeson 1992); but in a global city-region, technical skills, human resources, and intellectual assets demand high-grade specialization, and their development demands constant investment in human capital (Taylor, Walker, and Beaverstock 2002). The development of a knowledge economy increases the need for formal and informal education to cope effectively with new technology and environmental change (Kuratani and Endo 2003).

Since the global urban area is a stage for the development of the future knowledge economy, let us examine the role to be fulfilled by higher education.

First, saying simply that a city has a dense population says nothing about the diverse specialties of that city and its consequent ability to create knowledge and information, for which a means of effectively exchanging knowledge and information is required. By making maximum use of its human assets, the university can become an important actor in creating such means. In the short term, cooperation between industry and academe, which is currently being promoted, is a means of procuring research funds for the university, but in the longer term, it is a means of exchanging knowledge and information in science and technology.

Second, cooperation between industry and academe is a response to the rising need for formal and informal education as part of the development of a knowledge economy. The importance of opportunities such as graduate school, business school, and extension college for employees is obvious. These are easily understood from the viewpoint of university administration, but instead they should be viewed as new moves for shifting to a knowledge society. The university's human and intellectual assets should be used from such a viewpoint, and the university must take up again the matter of supplying the human resources required for a knowledge society.

Third, the needs for specialist occupations do not stop with technology and economics. The components of agglomeration economies include intellectual assets from wider areas—for instance, the accumulation of culture, politics, society, and basic research. Compared with the world's other global urban areas, Tokyo has accumulated a larger number of universities. The "special knowledge" created by this group of universities covers an extremely wide range, and universities should keep on providing such special knowledge.

Fourth, the specialized activities accumulated in this urban area must provide global services (Sassen 2001), which means they must be part of, or work in cooperation with, a global network of related activities or other associated activities. A university can contribute to the knowledge economy activities of an urban area with a network that transcends a city or national boundary.

Concluding Remarks

In the Tokyo metropolitan area, both redevelopment and new construction of a university campus in the urban center were recently accomplished. Factors behind these activities included (1) moves toward an urban renaissance through deregulation due to the impact of globalization and a policy of promoting science and technology, (2) a world trend toward the popularization and commercialization of universities, and (3) demographic changes in the population of Japan typified by a decline in the number of eighteen-year-olds. In this process, the universities, while deepening their cooperation with the public, became the main actors in an urban renaissance and activation of the community. For the Tokyo metropolitan area to become a stage for development of a knowledge society as a global urban area, the role of the universities is extremely important.

Nevertheless, at present, the universities have barely arrived at reformation. Let me select just two issues. First, since Japanese universities have ambiguous boundaries between research and education, many of them tend to be comprehensive teaching and research universities. In order to contribute to the building of a knowledge economy society, it is essential to clarify the division between education and research. Second, the results of education and research promoted by the universities have not been those demanded by the public. Although the steps toward university reformation and cooperation between industry and academe now being promoted include steps to resolve this disassociation, time is needed to achieve results.

Appendix 5.1. Changes of University Location Policy After the War

Outline of Changes

Development of postwar higher education in Japan took place gradually. An overview of the location policies for universities and colleges at each stage will show the types of macro locations (Ichikawa 1989; Kitamura 2001; Osaki 1999; Ozaki 1999; Yamamoto 2002).

Period of Formation of Universities Under the New System

During the period from the beginning of the 1900s to immediately after World War II, the principle for distribution of government schools was one for each prefecture due to the necessity for equal opportunity of higher education. When the universities started under the new system after World War II, this principle continued, leading to one national university for each prefecture. Looking at the old system shows that distribution of imperial universities was made by establishing different types of schools in central local cities: high schools in the old regime (which correspond to present junior colleges) in castle towns; business vocational schools for industries, commerce, and agriculture in industrial cities; vocational schools for art in either Tokyo or a city in eastern or western Japan; and schools for education and medical science in every prefecture. After the war, they were all turned into universities under the new system. Schools in the same prefecture were integrated under the principle of one school for one prefecture.

For such a distribution, the ideal location for higher education was determined by the level of cultural attainment in the castle towns, with excellent access to information for study and education. Other conditions for the ideal relocation were to strengthen traditional local industries; to dissolve educational differences among communities for the welfare of the residents; and to meet special, localized targets.

Private schools that had been established before the war became universities during this period under the new system. Most of them had already been located in Tokyo and other large city areas. Since it was not possible to move private universities to local areas from a policy standpoint, 52.6 percent of private universities and 34.8 percent of junior colleges were in Tokyo in the 1950s.

Period of Expansion of Universities Due to High Growth

A rise in both the ratio of students going to a higher level of education and the eighteen-year-old population increased demand for universities sharply.

Furthermore, high economic growth policies strongly sought the strengthening of higher education, mainly for science and engineering departments. The result was that it became impossible to meet the sharp increase in demand with the expansion of national universities. An increase in private universities was made to cope with this situation, but because many of the private universities were concentrated in large urban areas, there was an imbalance between the area capacity and the number of applicants. Furthermore, large urban areas were in the midst of a rapid concentration of population, and even the private universities were not able to expand capacity sharply enough.

Reflecting such factors, policies of area distribution of universities during the period were

- To reform the area unit from 46 prefectures to 8 nationwide blocks in considering the distribution of universities,
- To take in at least 60 percent of the block in considering the capacity of national and private universities in each block, and
- To establish areas in large cities, where, in principle, new expansions of universities would not be made.

Integration of various schools took place as national universities and campuses were spread out in the same prefecture. To meet the sharp increase in students, integration, restructuring, and even total removal of some campuses took place in prefectures, but capacity did not increase sharply. Private universities played a major role in easing pressure on attaining a higher level of education. The criteria for establishing private universities were eased, and many new universities were built. These were located in the outskirts of large urban areas. Existing private universities actively increased the number of their students and established new departments in the suburbs of large urban areas or moved ahead by expanding departments across the nation.

Period of Restructuring Higher Education

The period between the first baby boom and the second one saw a decline in the eighteen-year-old population and a gradual fall in the ratio of students going to a higher level of education. But based on the forecasted increase and the necessity to control new establishment and expansion in large urban areas, the central government aimed to achieve area balance and to secure quality. In addition, the new demand for higher education from working people, foreign students, and returning students had to be met. Special schools were established for higher education and a cooperative method between government and private sectors was introduced for the establishment of higher education institutes. During this period, demand for higher education was steady, and expansion of universities continued due to the increase in demand for science and engineering departments and postgraduate schools.

Period of Diversification of Universities

The period of diversification of universities was one in which the eighteen-year-old population declined sharply, the percentage of students going to a higher level of education increased steeply, and the need for lifelong study rose; competition intensified mainly among private universities. And socially, expectations for academic study rose. Diversified needs began to be sought from higher education, such as making fundamental research activities substantial, training future workers to have comprehensive judgment ability and creativity, and expanding the occupation area of intellectual contents to meet changes in industrial restructuring to knowledge-based industries. There was also a need for workers with general international traits and the ability to cope with a technology-intensive society.

Critics of the area distribution pointed out that the policy of restricting locations in large cities prevented free development of higher education, that going to a higher level of education tended to be difficult in large cities, that universities in the suburbs posed problems for students and teaching staffs, and that coping with the increase in demand for lifelong education was difficult. Consequently, the policy of restricting locations in large cities was eased.

Diversified needs for higher education and the easing of the restricting policy for large cities have led to private universities carrying out redevelopment of existing campuses in urban areas. New education formats for postgraduate schools and extension colleges and courses have been developed. Universities have also become tenants of buildings near railway stations, which are convenient from the standpoint of transportation.

Difference in Location by Parties Responsible for Establishment

The decision to relocate a campus or university activity differs widely with each type of university.

Private Universities

Private universities are, in principle, free to choose a location anywhere; nevertheless, there are conditions that affect the location. The first one is that an area should be able to supply the number of students needed to produce the necessary amount of income. Because of this, locations tend to be around large cities with large populations and where transportation is convenient. Furthermore, private universities rely heavily on part-time teachers, who are more available in large cities. Consequently, many private universities have historically converged on the Tokyo metropolitan area. Of the private universities that are concentrated in the TMA, the large-scale ones have expanded their campuses in this area, and some of them have also dispersed to major cities throughout the country.

Public Universities

The parties responsible for the establishment of public universities are basically local governments. As the purpose of their establishment is to expand studies in relation to the region, as well as opportunities for education, the location will be within the administrative districts. There has so far been a strong view that the government holds the role of providing higher education, and the number of public universities that have been established is small. They are also specialized in areas such as medical science and technology in reflection of their close relationship with their regions. Furthermore, municipal bodies that can establish universities need to be rich, and such locations are in large cities such as Tokyo and Yokohama City. Recently, a method has been developed whereby universities are established through cooperation between government and the private sector. That is to say that municipal bodies develop the facilities, such as school grounds and buildings, and the private sector manages them. As a result, the number of public universities has increased nationwide.

National Universities

As already mentioned, national universities are established according to plan with the aim of making higher education available across the entire country. Basically, there is one national university in each prefecture. In the TMA, a host of universities exists: some to advance the health and development of industries such as commerce, manufacturing, and agriculture; others to improve welfare through education and medical science, and special purposes of music and art.

In recent years, the integration of national universities has made progress because reform has been carried out. Universities are considering integration with others that have similar objectives. Many are considering abolishing the principle of one university to one prefecture. National universities have been incorporated, and this is expected to lead to further integration. Small-scale universities will be integrated with large-scale ones. Those that have complementary departments will have a better chance of integrating.

Notes

1. New buildings and extensions of university facilities were prohibited in the Kinki Region, as well.

2. The Cabinet Office's Structural Reform of the Japanese Economy in June 2001 included seven programs.

3. See Appendix 5.1.

4. There are five private universities, Keio, Waseda, Rikkyo, Meiji, and Hosei, and one public university, the University of Tokyo.

5. Many professors on the board held two posts, research and education and management, concurrently; few members were experts in university management.

6. In the western Tokyo region, where Tama Campus is located, Hosei University, as well as about one hundred associations—including universities, local governments, relevant organizations, businesses, and nonprofit organizations—are participating in Academic, Cultural, and Industrial Network Tama.

7. To carry out industry-university cooperation, there are some other instances of new campuses being set up at a slightly larger site on the outskirts of urban areas. Keio University established jointly with Kawasaki City a leading-edge research facility at a site for a railway yard development zone in the Shin-Kawasaki District.

References

Amano, I. 2004. *Daigaku Kaikaku.* Tokyo: University of Tokyo Press.

Beeson, P. 1992. "Agglomeration Economics and Productivity Growth." In *Sources of Metropolitan Growth*, ed. Edwin S. Mills and John F. McDonald. New Brunswick, NJ: Center for Urban Policy Research, Rutgers University.

Bok, D. 2003. *Universities in the Marketplace: The Commercialization of Higher Education.* Princeton, NJ: Princeton University Press.

Elliot, P.G. 1994. *The Urban Campus.* Phoenix, AZ: Oryx Press.

Fujita, M. 1989. *Urban Economic Theory: Land Use and City Size.* New York: Cambridge University Press.

Fujita, M., and J. Thisse. 2001. *Economics of Agglomeration: Cities, Industrial Location, and Regional Growth.* New York: Cambridge University Press.

Fujita, M., P. Krugman, and A. Venables. 1999. *The Spatial Economy: Cities, Regions, and International Trade.* Cambridge, MA: MIT Press.

Heenan, D., and H. Perlmutter. 1979. *Multinational Organizational Development.* Boston: Addison-Wesley.

Ichikawa, S. 1989. "Shougai Kyouiku no Kanten kara Mita Daigaku Ricchi Seisaku." *University Studies* 4. Tsukuba City: University of Tsukuba.

Kamo, T. 2000. "An Aftermath of Globalization? East Asian Economic Turmoil and Japanese Cities Adrift." *Urban Studies* 37, no. 12: 2145–66.

Kitamura, K. 2001. *Gendai Daigaku no Henkaku to Seisaku.* Tokyo: Tamagawa University Press.

Kiyonari, T. 2003. *Daitotajidai no Daigaku Jiritsu Kasseika Senryaku.* Tokyo: Toyo Keizai Shinpo-sha.

Kuratani, M., and Y. Endo. 2003. "Tokyou ha Chishiki Keizaika no Shubutai to Nariuurka." *Chiteki Shisan Souzou*, no. 4. Nomura Research Institute.

Kurobane, R. 1989. "Senzenki karano Daigaku Ricchi Seisaku no Hensen." *University Studies* 4. Tsukuba City: University of Tsukuba.

Machimura, T. 1994. *Sekai Toshi Tokyo no Kouzoutenkan.* Tokyo: University of Tokyo Press.

———. 2002. "Sekai Toshi kara Guro-baru Shithi he." In *Ethnicity and Changing Japanese Society*, ed. T. Kajita and T. Miyajima. Tokyo: University of Tokyo Press.

Ministry of Education, Culture, Sports, Science and Technology. 2004. *White Paper on Education, Culture, Sports, Science and Technology 2003.* Tokyo: Author.

Ministry of Land, Infrastructure and Transport. 2000. *Shutoken–Hakusho* (Annual Report on Development of Shutoken Area) *2000.* Tokyo: Author.

———. 2004. *Shutoken–Hakusho* (Annual Report on Development of Shutoken Area) *2004.* Tokyo: Author.

National Federation of University Co-operative Association in Japan. 2003. *Campus Life Data 2002–2003.* Tokyo: Author.

National Land Agency. 1995. *Daigakuricchi to Chiikidukuri wo Kangaeru.* Tokyo: National Printing Bureau, Ministry of Finance.

Nikkei BP Planning, Inc. 2004. *Housei Daigaku.* Tokyo: Author.

Osaki, H. 1999. *Daigaku Kaikaku 1945–1999.* Tokyo: Yu-hikaku.

Ozaki, M. 1999. *Nihon no Kyouiku Kaikaku.* Tokyo: Chuou-kouron Shinsha.

Promotion and Mutual Aid Corporation for Private Schools of Japan. 2003. *Konnichi no Shigaku Zaisei 2004.* Author. Tokyo.

Rating and Investment Information, Inc. 2003. "Hosei University: R&I assigns AA-(2003/02/26)." News release no. 2003-C-061. Tokyo: Author.

Research Institute for Urban and Environmental Development. 2002. *Daigaku Kaikaku to Toshi—Chiiki no Saikouchiku ni Kansuru Anketo.* Author: Tokyo.

Sassen, S. 1991. *The Global City: New York, London, Tokyo.* Princeton, NJ: Princeton University Press.

———. 2001. "Global City and Global City-Regions: Comparative Analysis." In *Global City-Regions*, ed. Allen J. Scott. Oxford: Oxford University Press.

Scott, A., J. Agnew, E. Soja, and M. Storper. 2001. "Global City-Regions." In *Global City-Regions*, ed. Allen J. Scott. Oxford: Oxford University Press.

Shimokobe, A. 1994. *Sengo Kokudo Keikaku no Shougen.* Tokyo: Nihonkeizaihy-ouronsha.

Takeuchi, Y. 2000. "The Tokyo Region." In *Global City-Regions: Their Emerging Forms,* ed. Roger Simmonds and Gary Hack. New York: Spon Press.

Taylor, P., P. Walker, and P. Beaverstock. 2002. "Firms and Their Global Service Networks." In *Global Networks, Linked Cities*, ed. Saskia Sassen. London: Routledge.

Trow, M. 2000. *From Mass to Universal Higher Education.* Tokyo: Tamagawa University Press.

Tsukahara, S. 2002. "Hendouki no Shinsei Daigaku." *Hiroshima Daigaku-shi Kiyou,* no. 2. Hiroshima: Hiroshima University.

Ushiogi, M. 2004. *Sekai no Daigaku Kiki.* Tokyo: Chuou Kouron Shinsha.

Yamamoto, S. 2002. *Daigaku no Kouzou Tenkan to Senryaku.* Tokyo: Jiasu Kyouiku Shinsha.

Part III

The University as a Zone of Development

6

Mexico City and University City

A Story of Struggle for Autonomy through Land

Carlos Morales Schechinger and Sara García Jiménez

The National Autonomous University of Mexico (UNAM) is one of the largest universities in the world, with a community of 329,740 people.[1] It owns University City (CU: *Ciudad Universitaria*), probably one of the most extended university campuses and one of the largest single tracts of urban property in the world, at 733 hectares.[2] It is located in the metropolitan area of Mexico City, which has a population of 18,591,527 inhabitants[3] over an area of 146,034 hectares.[4]

The university and the city have shared a long history, involving not only the CU campus but also a wide variety of buildings that the university has owned or occupied in the metropolitan area, currently 126 separate properties on 1,199 hectares (Dirección General de Patrimonio Universitario 2004). Many of them have an interesting history in their relations with their immediate surroundings, yet the most fascinating has been the acquisition, development, and transformation of CU, the main campus in the southern part of the metropolis, a long process that started at the beginning of the twentieth century.

The CU campus played an important role in the university's ideal of achieving autonomy. It had a deep impact on the urban structure at the time, triggering speculation and development of different sorts and transforming the land's potential uses by the end of the century. CU now plays a different role in the metropolis than that for which it was intended when the campus was officially endowed in March 1954. To understand this, we must study its beginnings, including the origin of the metropolis as such.

Mexico City, like most capital cities in Latin America, has played a preeminent role not only in the political life of the country but also in the economic, social, and cultural arenas—from the time of the Nahuatl civilization, during the Spanish domination, through Mexico's independence in the beginning of the nineteenth century, and again after the 1910 Revolution. During the industrialization in the second third of the twentieth century, Mexico City was the main recipient of private and public investments and of migration flows, which, together with lower mortality rates, triggered population growth

Figure 6.1   **Population of Mexico City Metropolitan Area and UNAM, 1935–2003**

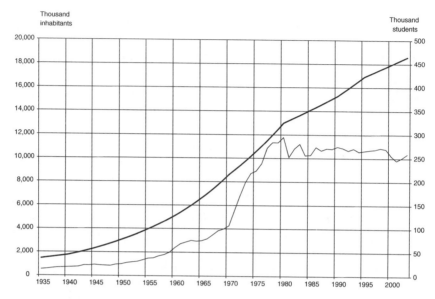

Source: Developed by the authors based on Anuarios Estadísticos (1960–1981), Presupuestos (1982–1988), y Agendas Estadísticas (1989–2003), and Negrete Salas (2000), Garza and Ruiz Chiapetto (2000).

Note: UNAM population for years 1939–1940, 1967, and 1970, are estimated as records are not available.

from 1,757,530 in 1940 to 17,956,313 in 2000 at an average rate of 3.96 percent annually (see Figure 6.1). Until the 1940s, the city remained within the boundaries of the *Distrito Federal* (DF), but sprawling growth in the 1950s impinged upon the surrounding municipalities of the State of Mexico. In the 1980s, DF population stabilized, with 8,591,309 inhabitants in 2003. Settlement is now increasing in the municipalities, though at present the DF government has tried to increase density in the city center with aggressive housing policies.

Mexico City's historic center was once the central business district. This district then spread, with high-rise corporate office buildings to the southwest, along Reforma and Insurgentes avenues, and beyond, to the Perisur in the Pedregal and Santa Fe neighborhoods. Also, toward the west and southwest, upper-income, low-rise housing extended to the hillsides of the Chiconautzin and Ajusco mountains, a protected environmental zone, all within the DF. The industrial districts spread in opposite directions—toward the northwest, northeast, and east, along the main roads and railways that lead to other

Figure 6.2   **Federal Government Subsidy to UNAM and Expenditure per Student, 1935–2003**

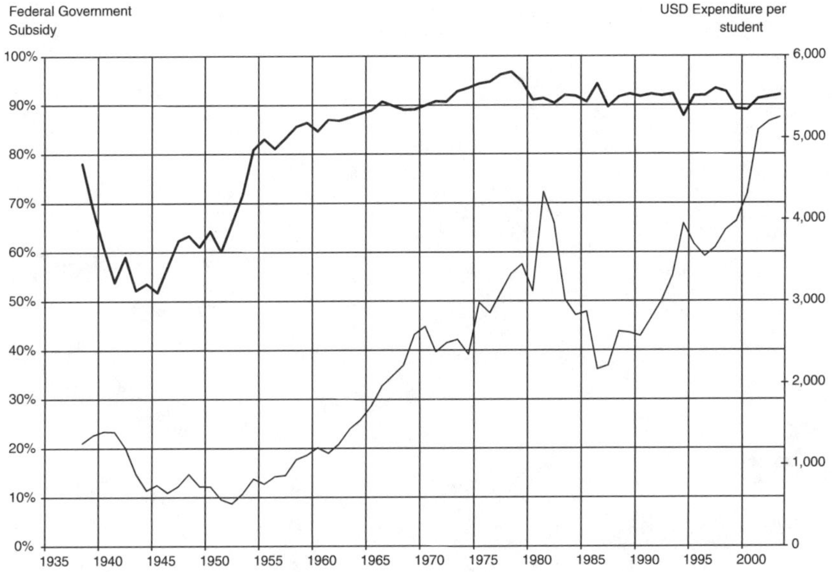

Source: Developed by the authors based on Anuarios Estadísticos (1960–1981), Presupuestos (1982–1988), and Agendas Estadísticas (1989–2003).

Note: Subsidy and expenditure per student for 1939–1940, 1967, and 1970, are estimated as records are not available.

industrial cities and eventually to the border with the United States and the Veracruz seaport.

To fill those industrial corridors, extensive informal settlements have developed that account for two-thirds of the total housing stock, as well as scattered high-density, low-income, public or subsidized housing, mostly spreading into the municipalities of the State of Mexico. Two middle-income housing sectors, one stretching toward the southeast within the DF, the other toward the northwest, act as boundaries between rich and poor. In addition, due to the rough topography of the mountainous zone, pockets of poor and middle-class areas mark the otherwise affluent southwest.

UNAM is a heavily subsidized public university that provides very low-tuition education (see Figure 6.2).[5] Today, most of its students come from middle- to low-income brackets. The CU campus is located in the affluent southwestern area, but other campuses are found in low-income areas, and UNAM still owns most of the original buildings in the historic center (see Figure 6.3). To understand better how this came about, we now review the early story.

Figure 6.3   **University City (CU) within the Mexico City Metropolitan Area (MCMA)**

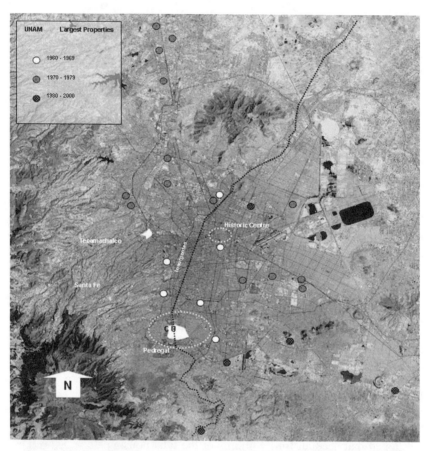

Source: Developed by the authors based on an MCMA satellite photograph, Landsat 7, March 21, 2000, Laboratorio de Información Geográfica y Percepción Remota, Instituto de Geografía, UNAM.

The university traces its ancestry back to 1551, when the Real y Pontificia Universidad was founded, and to the eighteenth century, when many other institutions of higher education were created under the Spanish Bourbonic reforms. All were incorporated in 1910 to become the National University of Mexico. For three and a half centuries, the university accumulated buildings in a valuable central location, and until 1954, scattered throughout the oldest part of the city, it had an important impact on community life, not only because of the students' intense activities and the many amenities they demanded, but

development was becoming scarce at the city's periphery. Lázaro Cárdenas had staged an important rural land reform affecting more than half the DF surface area—821 square kilometers out of 1,499 square kilometers—to turn them into *ejido* property, a type of communally owned land that at the time was forbidden for uses other than agriculture, leaving scarce room for urban expansion (Perló Cohen 1981, cited in Davis 1999).

It is difficult to know why the university made such a bad deal when it desperately needed money and the market seemed favorable. The federal government bought the land at a price established by an appointed assessor, who could have considered the traditional agricultural market value by ignoring the speculative price that the agrarian reform was creating. However, perhaps that is not the issue; the question is why did the university sell the land to the federal government in the first place? One can only suppose that the sale was part of a more complex deal with the government. The new rector, Luis Chico Gorne, who sold the property, was less radical than his predecessors were, and he was able to improve relations with the government. In fact, he was responsible for eventually renewing the subsidy flow.

The improved relationship implied that the university would give political support to Lázaro Cárdenas's subsequent structural reforms, particularly the nationalization of the petroleum industry (Ramírez López 2001). In this scenario we must point out that Cárdenas was consolidating what eventually was to become the Partido Revolucionario Institucional (PRI),[10] which governed the country for seven decades. To do that, he had to reduce drastically the influence of the military within that party; therefore, he negotiated for some material privileges, like creating the military city. The Tecamachalco property became a very convenient piece of land with which to close the deal.

The sale of the Tecamachalco property did not diminish the dream of creating a university city. Not only did the appeal for funds continue, but in 1938, the University Council also approved the creation of a university neighborhood in the Anzures area, an intermediate zone to the west, between middle- and high-income communities. The neighborhood would house nearly 10,500 residents, mostly teachers, research fellows, and their families with a select group of students. The property would have a new type of semi-social tenure—a combination of privately owned dwellings with communally owned areas, with university control over property transfers, to preserve the purely academic population, and over selling prices (Díaz de Ovando 1979). The project required financial aid from the DF government, which is strange considering that subsidies were a delicate issue at the time. The project was never implemented, yet it shows the strong desire for autonomy, in this case expressed as a territorial segregation from society. A similar concept would eventually influence how the CU campus was conceived.

The goal of autonomy, the appeal for funds, the limited subsidies, and the deteriorating condition of the historic buildings continued; yet much time elapsed before actual steps were taken to improve the situation. In 1943, Rector Rodolfo Brito Foucher personally searched the entire periphery of Mexico City for appropriate land for the new university city. Many options were discarded, including those in the working-class northern periphery (Díaz de Ovando 1979), a strange decision since students from that social stratum were expected to become part of the university community. Finally, the Pedregal zone in the southeast was chosen.

The Pedregal is a vast area characterized by centuries-old volcanic rock from the nearby Xitle volcano. It had no agricultural value, little worth as a quarry, and urban growth in fact had bypassed it. The chosen location revealed an ambivalence as the university tried to rid itself of its middle- and-upper-class image; the university was insistent about attending to the needs of the working class. UNAM needed this new focus to maintain the subsidy flow, particularly as it competed with the more working class–oriented IPN. Nevertheless, it chose to locate its future campus within the sector of a growing upper-income residential area. IPN remained in the lower-income northwest.

The Pedregal area represents a microcosm of agrarian reform in Mexico and how that reform influenced the way land has been developed for urban purposes. Rural land, organized in haciendas, was heavily concentrated in the hands of very few families before the 1910 Revolution; thereafter, it was redistributed among peasants in the communally owned properties known as ejidos.[11] Former hacienda owners became small proprietors and were allowed to choose whatever sites they desired; if they were near urban areas such as those in the DF, they chose land that was suitable for urban development. Poor land such as the rocky Pedregal became ejido land. Ejido property was at the time inalienable,[12] but it could be expropriated by the president himself or exchanged for private property, in which case the land received would be incorporated into the ejido regime and the land given would become private property.[13]

When UNAM had to select a specific site in the Pedregal area, it picked 733 hectares belonging to four ejidos: Tlalpan, Copilco, Padierna, and San Jerónimo Aculco.[14] It did not choose a large strip of land next to the urban area, some of which belonged to the former president Pascual Ortiz Rubio (Zubirán 1946a) and to the Margain family, owners of the old Copilco Hacienda. Some of this property would eventually be located between the CU campus and the existing urban area, becoming very valuable land that would be developed in the 1960s and 1970s. Private property in the area, such as the neighboring Margain property, was expensive, since it had to be bought in the open market, reflecting urban use expectations. Its expropriation at low fiscal values was ruled out.[15] By that time, President Manuel Avila Camacho had substantially diminished the agrarian reform program, and a new policy of industrialization was set up with a delicate interclass alliance between workers and owners of capital, strongly based in Mexico City.[16] The expropriation of such a large tract of land would have had an unfavorable political impact on the president's new industrialization program.

The expropriation of the 733 hectares of ejido land proceeded at a slow pace; it was not completed until three years later, in 1946. Responsible for the delays were the DF government, which argued that it wanted to ensure available water (Zubirán 1946c), and the agrarian department, apparently acting on behalf of the peasants' confederation, which wanted better compensation than the agricultural value of the land, $0.03 per square meter.[17] The new rector, Salvador Zubirán, sat down with the ejido peasants and negotiated a package. As a result, UNAM had to create a village, eventually named Copilco el Alto, with forty-three dwellings, 260 plots, and one school. It would provide free education up to the university level for the peasant children, as well as employment for construction workers during the building stage and for university employees thereafter. Moreover, the university would allow the peasants to continue to cultivate the land and use the quarry as the construction got under way.

At this point, the ejido peasants had not developed a speculative sense about land, which they acquired later in the century. Their relationship with the land was that of use value; thus, once they lost their land, their main concern was obtaining equivalent use values: a place to live and a way to sustain themselves and their families. They had been landowners for only a brief period; the property was given to them under the recent agrarian reform, and they certainly must have had a difficult time trying to cultivate anything on the rocky land in the Pedregal area.[18]

UNAM's goal of autonomy was being achieved not through financial but through territorial independence. The land expropriated was far more than it needed for its 22,337 students. The strategy was to use two hundred hectares to construct academic, administrative, and sports facilities (including an Olympic Stadium for 110,000 people);[19] some student dormitories; and academic and administrative staff housing. Half of the rest was to remain as an inalienable patrimony with the possibility of producing income, apparently in the form of a long-term lease; the other half would be developed and sold in the open market. This explains why the site was chosen: The city was growing toward the southwest area, with the most profitable land fetching at least in the range of $15 to $18 per square meter.[20] The ejido land was acquired at a low price, an average of $0.05 per square meter,[21] paid with a last-minute subsidy from the president; thus, the profit expected was very large.

Figure 6.4   **UNAM's CU Campus**

Source: Fondo Carlos Lazo/Saúl Molina, Archivo Histórico, Centro de Estudios sobre la Universidad, UNAM.

To achieve autonomy, UNAM wanted to take a step further and create a quasi-autonomous municipality comprising 733 hectares, with the university authorized to impose property taxes on the owners of any land that was sold. The revenue from leased land, from the sale of developed land, and from the property taxes collected would go to build the school's campus and to run the university as such (Díaz de Ovando 1979). A type of Georgian ideal community financed from land rent was conceived.[22] Thus, financial autonomy from the federal government could be achieved, and the threat of subsidy cuts that had haunted the university for the previous dozen years would fade away. Such was the proposal of the designers of the new campus, but the new rector, Luis Garrido Díaz, had more practical plans.

The university held an architectural competition for the campus, and a grand design won the contest (see Figure 6.4), which was an important watershed for architecture in Mexico.[23] Mexico's new president, Miguel Alemán, adopted CU as an emblematic project and poured enormous subsidies into financing the whole development. The university was included in an overall industrialization strategy, as part of the exports-substitution economic model in Mexico, a policy that was to prevail in most of Latin America during the following decades. It was meant to distance the country from the rural economy and the socialist and agrarian reform of President Lázaro Cárdenas's era. Rector Garrido Díaz took advantage of this, negotiating large federal subsidies for UNAM. The work expanded throughout President Alemán's administration, starting slowly in 1947, accelerating from 1950 to 1952, and culminating with an elaborate dedication ceremony at the Olympic Stadium and the unveiling of a statue of the president himself in a commanding position at the center of the campus (Universidad Nacional Autónoma de México 1952).

The dream of total independence had been put to a test. Economic autonomy had not been achieved, and Rector Garrido Díaz was aware of the risk this implied (Domínguez Martínez 2001, 196). From then on, subsidies steadily increased (see Figure 6.2); after construction was finished, autonomy had to be fought for in other ways. The idea of a quasi municipality for the campus developed into a rivalry between Rector Garrido Díaz and Carlos Lazo, the appointed general manager of the construction, who had slowly accumulated a great deal of power. Lazo proposed to reform the UNAM statutes to create a dual government system for the university, with one administration in charge of academic life and another managing the university city, a rector and a mayor. When the new federal administration was established in 1953, President Adolfo Ruiz Cortínez appointed Lazo to the Ministry of Public Works as a prize for his efficient management of building CU. Feeling even more powerful, Lazo took control of the campus from the ministry. Eventually, the following rector, Nabor Carrillo, was able to regain control of the campus, in March 1954.

Territorial autonomy was tested again when pressure came from the academic and administrative communities for housing plots to be established within the CU campus. University authorities were concerned because a serious legal problem had surfaced that could thwart the whole idea of using vast land reserves for future development and sale in the open market. Creating an independent city depended more on resolving that legal issue than on the battle of two rival personalities, Carrillo's and Lazo's, and the academic pressure for housing.

The law of agrarian reform requires an explicit public utility and a specific destiny as the basis of an expropriation; otherwise, the land returns to its original status, becoming ejido property again, no matter how much time has passed. The 733 hectares of ejido land were expropriated for the university and destined precisely for the CU, to build and lodge the schools, faculties, and institutions that depend on the university and nothing else (*Diario Oficial de la Federación* 1946a). Consequently, the university would never be able to use the remaining land for commercial purposes, not even for housing for the academic and administrative staff. Yet all along, plans were being made to develop the extra land; designs were even drawn up.[24] The administrative and academic communities were led to believe they would have accommodations in the new city, which was particularly important because of the distance from their original residences to the school and the initial transport problems the CU suffered (Díaz de Ovando 1979). Only vague references were made to the "legal issue" regarding the property; it was never discussed in the open. Had it been, the university authorities would have found open opposition from students and staff refusing to move to the city outskirts.

The only properties that the university could manage freely were the old buildings in the city center, which could be sold in the open market; those with historic value could be sold to the federal government, which needed centrally located office space. Those properties were quite valuable, and the idea to sell them had existed since 1930, when the university bought the Tecamachalco property, but it was never carried out.[25]

The university was to become an almost fully subsidized entity. Subsidies escalated dramatically in the 1950s and continued to grow in the 1960s and 1970s; they reached their highest level, 96.8 percent of university income, in 1978 and have essentially remained above 90 percent ever since (see Figure 6.2). During this period, the university lost its upper-class image and gained the reputation of a university for the masses—for middle- to low-income students. Thus, the discourse changed as subsidization became justified on social grounds. Autonomy was fought for on the field of academic independence, together with an antiregime political stand and a strong social commitment. In terms of territory, CU—if not by law, very much in fact—eventually became a sanctuary wherein government dared not enter.

The CU campus is not a walled site; it is even used as a public park by local residents. However, it is highly territorialized in a behavioral sense and has a tumultuous history with law enforcement. In earlier times, Mexico's president traditionally inaugurated each academic year; more recently, when a president entered CU, he risked being stoned.[26] Local police do not go on the university's grounds, and the UNAM community still recalls with rancor when soldiers occupied the CU campus in autumn of 1968. The federal police also entered in January 2000 to break up a student strike that had lasted a year, a strike motivated by a proposal to reintroduce tuition for undergraduates.[27]

Land Speculation by Others

The construction of the CU campus represented a major transformation in the urban structure of Mexico City (Cisneros Sosa 1993; Garza 2000). It was located in the southwest, where the most valuable land uses were expanding. The certainty that the government was going to make a major investment created speculation, not only because the university was an important amenity for the middle- and high-income populations at the time of construction, but also because it meant that water supply and drainage systems, as well as roads and public transport, would be extended in the southeast of the growing metropolis (Espinoza López 2003).

Insurgentes Avenue (see Figure 6.5), which went as far south as San Angel, was extended farther, to become the longest avenue in the city. It eventually connected with the highways to the north and south of the country. This avenue cuts through the middle of the Pedregal zone, which had until then acted as a growth barrier due to its lava rock composition and made opening major roads and sewage and other pipelines very expensive. In addition, Revolución Avenue was extended to reach the Olympic Stadium on the east side, and what was to become Universidad Avenue would link CU with the eastern side of the city. The university itself began a bus service, so students, teachers, and administrative staff could get to the distant campus. Soon a whole array of bus lines redesigned their routes to reach the CU campus, which had built its own bus terminal. All this made possible the development of properties that were linked to the city. Although this is a common situation in many cities of the world, it is interesting to look closely at specific cases that reveal how certain actors take advantage of the situation. In the case of the CU campus, it is a story that has not been properly told despite the enormous relevance the CU campus has in Mexico City's culture and history.[28]

Even before the CU campus was built, it was a source of land speculation (Figure 6.5). Insurgentes Avenue virtually divided the Pedregal zone into two large areas. Furthermore, the property was separated from the urban area by a substantial tract of land that lay between the CU campus and Miguel Angel de Quevedo Avenue to the north. Thus, it was surrounded by open land, and speculation took place almost in every direction. The speculation was of three different types: First, land was subdivided by developers on the western and northern sides to be sold as plots for houses suited to high-income families. Second, pirate developers illegally subdivided land on the eastern and southeastern sides to be sold as plots for self-built housing by low-income families. Third, fractions of land in the border areas owned by UNAM were illegally occupied and sold by speculators and developers.

The best example of the first type of land speculation is Jardines del Pedregal, which eventually became almost as large as the CU campus itself. This development epitomizes many of the land ventures characteristic of the time. Speculation then depended on the ability of land buyers to influence decisions and get information about the location of the CU campus, as well

Figure 6.5 **Pedregal Area Showing CU Campus, Main Roads, and Neighborhoods**

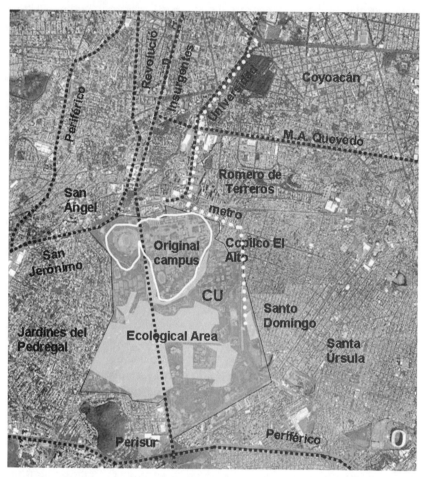

Source: Developed by the authors from the expropriation decree (DOF 1946a) and from an aerial photograph by Aerofoto de México.

as the infrastructure that was going to be built. Evidence of this information circuit seems to lead to the Margain family, one of the large landlords affected by the agrarian reform in the surrounding area of the Pedregal and former owners of the Copilco Hacienda (Oropeza Villavicencio 2001). Some of their remnant property, however, appears to be part of the land assembled for the Jardines del Pedregal; thus, the agricultural land they lost was compensated for many times over with land at an urban value.

Margain family information on the location of the CU and the infrastructure that was to be built could have been gathered through three channels. First, engineering students, who surveyed the land to draw the basic plans for the expropriation in 1943, were lodged at the Margain's hacienda by the prominent Dr. Cesar Margain (Díaz de Ovando 1979). Second, Alejandro Margain was the manager of Luis Barragán's real estate office. Barragán designed Jardines del Pedregal and was one of its major investors, along with the Bustamante brothers, who were well-known land developers.[29] Third, another Margain, Yolanda, was the wife of Carlos Lazo, the appointed general manager for the building of the CU campus (De Cervantes 1952).

Another possible channel of information came from José Villagrán, Mexico's most prominent architectural theorist and an investor in Jardines del Pedregal. He was also a teacher at the School of Architecture and played a crucial role in selecting the project's design.[30] More important, he was an appointed member of the building commission for the CU campus in 1946 before the expropriation decree was signed (Diario Official de la Federación 1946b). During the building commission's meetings with Rector Zubirán, another member, Carlos Obregón Santacilia, insinuated that Villagrán had speculated during another government project years earlier[31] and said that the members of the committee should not use privileged information about the building of CU (Zubirán 1946c). This probably offended Villagrán, but he eventually admitted to the committee that he was an investor in the Jardines del Pedregal project. He argued, however, that the development had started long before and that many plots had already been sold (Zubirán 1946b). This argument sounds dubious; in fact, publicity for the sales of Jardines del Pedregal did not begin until 1949 (Eggener 2001), but property assembly started around the same time UNAM officially petitioned for expropriation of the CU land, in 1943 (Magnano 2001).

Yet another channel of information was Carlos Contreras, an associate of Barragán who helped design the infrastructure of the Jardines del Pedregal development (Ingersoll 2001; Zanco 2001). Contreras was regarded as influential with high government officials and had access to presidents, who had great respect for him.[32] Recognized as the father of urban planning in Mexico (*Enciclopedia de México* 1987a), he had drawn up an early regulating plan for Mexico City, so he knew where major roads and services would be built. He was one of the signers of the technical opinion that recommended where the university should be located specifically (Zubirán 1946c).

The land's increased value was enormous, escalating from $0.03 per square meter to $15.00 and $18.00 per square meter. Barragán eventually acknowledged that he had become rich by 1953 through the Jardines del Pedregal project (Magnano 2001). There was great awareness that land speculation could spring up around the CU campus. Another major land developer look-ing to maximize his earnings, Negib Simón, announced that he was going to build another university city in the area to rival the CU campus.[33] He wanted to challenge UNAM's role in education and bragged about being backed by the president-elect, Miguel Alemán. An aggressive newspaper battle ensued, culminating with José María Luján, a long-time member of the CU campus fundraising team, publicly denouncing Simón's intention to force the govern-ment into inviting him to join as a major patron of the CU campus so that he could later demand to be named developer of UNAM's vast lands in return for the favor. Simón never answered the accusation and retreated from the scene (Díaz de Ovando 1979).

Benefiting from the CU campus, other real estate developments thrived in the 1960s and 1970s, particularly on a strip of land left between the university and Miguel Angel de Quevedo Avenue, in the Copilco and Romero de Terreros areas. This land was developed as a combination of upper- and middle-income housing and high-rise sections for lower-income housing. Even public hous-ing for UNAM workers was constructed in this area through FOVISSSTE (*Fondo de la Vivienda del Instituto de Seguridad y Servicios Sociales de los Trabajadores del Estado*), the housing agency for the bureaucracy. Since the university administrative and academic employees are considered state workers—one of the contradictions of the autonomy of UNAM—this govern-ment agency was called in to build dwellings for university staff. FOVISSSTE probably paid a lot for the land and needed to build at a high density to charge a reasonable amount for each dwelling so university workers could afford them. This is sadly ironic, considering that the university owned sufficient land to develop at a lower density and could afford to give it almost free to the poorly paid staff.

In that same period, and up to the 1980s, the eastern side of the Pedregal area was developed through illegal subdivisions. The area had a mixture of property types: ejido land, communal land similar to ejido, and private property. This part of the city was in the district of the middle-class growth axis but was neglected because of high urbanization costs due to the rocky ground. Thus, the area was to be occupied with no urban services for low-income, self-built housing during the population boom of those decades, when the city became a huge metropolis (see Figure 6.1). Land was subdivided and sold on the black market as in many other parts of the metropolitan area. In fact, in almost every part of the country, land seizures took place in spite of police repression. Due to the strong urbanization process and the market's and the state's inability to offer alternatives to illegal subdivision, subsequent legalization of titles and self-built services with government subsidies became the national way of coping with this problematic pattern of development (Duhau 2003).

Santa Ursula, Santo Domingo, Ajusco, and other communities in the area developed as illegal subdivisions (Mancilla 2000; Azuela, Cancino, and Cruz 1984). However, these communities started to gentrify in the 1980s and 1990s, particularly when the Metro, the underground public transit system introduced in the late 1960s, was extended to the CU campus. The Metro has a major stop in the Copilco area, and the line terminal—together with a large transit bus station that serves most of the southern metropolitan area—is located on the CU grounds. The neighborhood has been urbanized with self-built effort and some aid from the government; and most of the plots have been legalized, so most settlers have property titles. Roads have also been introduced, one even slicing through a piece of the CU grounds to connect the area with the rest of the city's road system.[34]

Gentrification has come about not only from new middle-class residents who improve the existing houses, but also through the construction of a new four- to five-story apartment building sold with a mortgage, for example, which shows that real estate investors and the banking system are coming to the area. It is unlikely that poor settlers have a speculative strategy based on obtaining a land title; it is more likely that the location of this vast settlement within the middle-class sector of the metropolis, right next to the UNAM, enables it to be gentrified. Regarding possible forms of speculation, investors buy land at a low, self-built housing price that takes advantage of the owner having restricted information on the area's potential; thus, they get an above-average surplus by investing intensively through higher density. In addition, the original owners eventually become aware of this potential and translate such surplus into a land rent[35] by selling their lots at higher prices.[36] All of this became possible not only because of the area's location relative to the city as a whole, but also because the university is adjacent to it and became one of the triggers of this type of micro expectation for profit.

Another type of micro speculation that yielded high surpluses must be considered in relation to the CU campus: illegal development in the northwest border zone of UNAM's property for commercial use, known as the Mauna Loa, after the name of a famous restaurant built in the conflicting zone. This type of illegality has a social explanation, possibly to do with fraud. A few meters from the limits of the CU runs San Jerónimo Avenue; a thin strip of private property lies between the limits and the avenue. This was the quarry zone of the Pedregal, which had been used by private as well as ejido owners for a long time. As in many quarries, work on the steep drop developed forward as the excavation advanced. This created the opportunity to argue that an undefined limit existed between the private properties and the CU campus. The situation also had a potential problem to start with: The ejido peasants were allowed to use the quarries as long as the university did not need the land. As the ejido peasants became UNAM workers, this agreement grew less valid—also due to the compensation agreements and the fact that many others were sent far away in the 1950s after they exchanged the remnants of their land for better agricultural ground.[37] It is probable, however, that some ejido peasants or their relatives continued to quarry the area.

All the ambiguity created good conditions for developing an exclusive commercial corridor and even building some high-end mansions.[38] Eventually, in the 1980s, the university claimed its land, and a long legal process followed. The main actors were the developer Camhi, who also represented third parties affected, including the Mauna Loa restaurant, and the Chevarría family, the original sellers of the land.[39] After more than ten years of litigation, the university settled through a complex land reassembling and compensation agreement. The limits of the university property were redrawn (Dirección General de Estudios sobre Legislación Universitaria, "Triángulo").

Land invasions in other border areas of the CU campus (Dirección General de Estudios sobre Legislación Universitaria, "Terrenos de Montserrat") are not as easy to document as the Mauna Loa case. The amount of property involved was little compared with the vast surface area of the CU campus; nevertheless, it had two important characteristics. First, it represented some of the most valuable corners the university owned, which would have become an important source of income if UNAM were given the chance to develop. Second, the reversible characteristic of CU property, explained earlier, and the fact that it does not expire, could eventually be pursued by the agrarian authorities, causing the private owners to lose their now supposedly legitimate property. We do not make a case here on behalf of those property owners, but we raise questions about the university developing its vast properties: Is there a risk of reversion almost sixty years after the expropriation took place? If there is no risk, does the university stand a chance of developing its valuable land and renewing its dream of achieving some financial autonomy through land development?

Land for Private Development or for Science and the Humanities

As we have established, private developers have been interested in buying land from the university. The CU campus is surrounded to the west and the south by very exclusive residential zones such as Jardines del Pedregal, and high-end shopping centers such as Perisur. Developed land commands high prices in the area, around US$1,000 per square meter or even higher; this amount might be doubled on the main avenues. The university's land is divided by Insurgentes Avenue, which commands high prices for high-rise office space.

In fact, the strip that runs along the campus interrupted for many years the expansion of this type of development. However, demand was so high that it eventually jumped the CU and continued in the Perisur area; the pressure to close the gap now comes from both sides.

The university itself has grown quite a lot since the CU campus was developed. The university community had been relatively small, with 33,428 total students in 1954, when most of them moved to the new campus (see Figure 6.1). Fifty years later, the university community had 269,143 students, who accounted for 81.6 percent of the whole community. Student population increased dramatically in the 1960s and 1970s, and then it dropped a little in the early 1980s. Since then it has stabilized at a little above a quarter of a million students. Population for the metropolitan area started to grow even earlier, in the 1950s, increasing rapidly in the 1960s and 1970s, then slowing down a little but still growing at 1.2 percent a year. Specialists have forecast that the metropolis will stabilize at around 25 million inhabitants in the next twenty to thirty years. Until the 1980s, UNAM absorbed a large proportion of the city's as well as the nation's demand for higher education, despite the establishment of a new public university, Autonomous Metropolitan University (UAM), which was set up in the 1970s specifically for the metropolis. Finally, in the 1980s, growth was halted, when UNAM authorities, the government, the economy, and the whole country recognized that the metropolitan area could not be fed endlessly with subsidies and stimuli for growth. A slow decentralization process meant that eventually the urban population would grow in other cities and universities elsewhere would expand.

During the period of rapid growth, UNAM's physical expansion took place elsewhere, not on the CU campus. In the 1960s, the university built nine preparatory schools scattered throughout the city yet still within DF boundaries. In the 1970s, it created six colleges for the sciences and humanities and five large schools of professional education throughout the metropolitan area; each had its own campus, fully equipped with sports facilities and the rest. By that time, the university had become a massive school for the middle- to low-income population, and it needed to bring its facilities closer to the community, in the northern and western parts of the metropolis, where students lived. In the 1990s, UNAM acquired large ranches for the Veterinary Faculty on the periphery of the metropolis that is now within the urban fringe. UNAM did use some of its vast CU vacant land to expand its existing facilities.

There are many stories about decentralization and the way land was acquired, and they are quite different from those of the CU campus. To acquire the land needed, the university had to accept what was donated by the government or buy it at a very low price. It acquired, therefore, poorly located properties, some very far away, some next to garbage dumps, some in areas next to poor settlements, and some so marginal that only squatters wanted them.[40] The design of these campuses is austere. The metropolis was growing fast, and there was little government money to do any elaborate design work like that on the CU campus. In fact, the building of most of these facilities has gone practically unnoticed by historians, and few studies have been made about this decentralization stage of the university (see, for example, Morales Schechinger and García Jiménez 2003).

Construction on CU's campus eventually continued, but less for educational facilities than for the many research institutes; the university TV studios; the national library (which is run by UNAM); the science museum; and a cultural complex with a large concert hall, theaters, cinemas, and chamber music and ballet halls. UNAM always has played an important role in the arts; it even has its own professional philharmonic orchestra, one of the country's top orchestras. UNAM also has commissioned large-scale sculptures that are placed throughout the new sections of the campus. All this development occurred in a scattered pattern across the remaining grounds of the CU campus.

UNAM never built any student quarters. It was understood early on that a high concentration of students on campus would be risky at a university that was increasingly conscious of the country's social, economic, and political structural problems. The university often has played an important role in debating political issues and has even organized large-scale strikes; thus, the decision not to construct student quarters was carefully made in the 1950s (Díaz de Ovando 1979).

In the 1980s, the scientific community within the university, particularly the Faculty of Science, was worried about the way UNAM was expanding on the CU's vacant land. By that time, the campus was surrounded by urban development, which extended far into the mountains. Nothing of the ancient Pedregal remained in its natural state except for what the university had not yet used from its property.[41] The Pedregal is a rare ecological setting with unique flora and fauna that cannot easily be found elsewhere (see Carrillo Trueba 1995).

The scientific community lobbied with UNAM authorities until finally, in 1983, they were able to get Rector Octavio Rivero Serrano to declare protected a natural zone of 123.5 hectares, 16.8 percent of the original CU campus surface area (*Gaceta UNAM* 1983). The zone has been left in its natural state and is in the care of a scientific committee. The area was increased by successive rectors (see *Gaceta UNAM* 1990, 1996a, 1996b), and since 1997 it has covered 177.0 hectares, plus an extra 36.6 hectares that were declared a natural area and act as a buffer zone for the ecological area itself, a total of 29 percent of the original CU campus (see Figure 6.5). Soon after the university declared this land an ecological reserve, the Federal District government also zoned it as an ecological area where no urban land use is permitted. All this put a stop to the university's randomly placing new buildings on its vacant land in what appeared to be an irresponsible pattern of sprawl with little consideration for the environment.

The university now carries out research in the nature reserve; in a way, this scientific use prevents the ecological zone from returning to the ejido type of property. Today, ejido land may become private property due to a controversial constitutional reform that passed in 1992. Although ejido owners must follow a cumbersome procedure, elsewhere in the metropolis they are converting ejido land into private property and obtaining large profits. In addition, they do not always follow zoning regulations in doing so. If the reserve zone were returned to ejido tenure through this complex legal labyrinth and eventually became private property, great pressure would be applied to change zoning regulations, probably for a more profitable use. In fact, landowners might even disobey them as they have done elsewhere, thereby destroying perhaps the only natural green space of significant size in the metropolis, self-controlled by the owner, UNAM.

Land and Territorial Autonomy Today

The university is an institution of such size and complexity that it is capable of creating its own processes of territorial behavior independent of the city's general process of land-use control. The fact that part of its patrimony would be self-declared an ecologically protected area is a clear example of this autonomy. It did not come about readily—for a decade and a half before 1983, the university had been erecting new buildings throughout its grounds on the CU campus, until an interest group that developed inside the university was able to lobby for a restriction on irresponsible land consumption.

Since then, existing occupied areas must be well used before new construction can occur. The building department of the university also must comply with strict norms of conservation of the original buildings and their layout, which are heavily regulated. A commission at UNAM checks that the original section of the CU campus, what could be called the historic center, is preserved so that future generations may enjoy a landmark of Mexico's modern architecture. Therefore, intensification of land use is controlled. UNAM is now engaged in a sort of smart-growth planning process, because interest groups are taking a long-term view that will not allow the developer, in this case the university's building department, to use land in a wasteful manner. All of this has been done without much regard to what the city might say about the issue; however, the DF government eventually validated UNAM's decisions and incorporated them into its zoning plans.

Yet another issue increases the sense of autonomy for the university. All along in its history, UNAM has been able to acquire and retain an important privilege—exemption from paying property taxes to local governments: the Federal District government for the property in its jurisdiction, including the CU campus and the historic buildings in the city center, and the municipalities of the State of Mexico for the property located in their jurisdictions. This privilege came about in 1945, when a university statute reform gave it a general tax exemption (*Diario Oficial de la Federación* 1945). However, with regard to property tax, the legal standing of this exemption now is not very clear. In 1983 a constitutional reform was passed, and Article 115 forbade state legislatures from establishing any exemption for property aside from that in the public domain, be it federal, state, or municipal, including the Federal District's public property (Gutiérrez and Santana 2002). Yet in practice UNAM's land and buildings remained exempt.

Local governments, the property tax authorities as established by the constitution, became aware of this fact and asked the university to pay. To avoid payment UNAM elaborated on a complex argument that puts its autonomy into question once again. The constitution establishes what is and is not considered property of public domain. Property being used by government-decentralized entities, for whatever purpose, may be considered within the public domain if the purpose is so established in its creating statute. Therefore, the university has had to pretend that it is a decentralized entity created to provide higher education, undertake research, and carry out cultural activities. Whether or not it is a decentralized entity, UNAM lawyers were forced to put it in the sphere of a quasi-government entity—if not in spirit, then in practice—so as not to pay the property tax.

The property tax issue does not end there, however. The constitution also established this criterion: Properties used by decentralized entities for purposes not directly involved in activities derived from their statutory mandate have to pay property taxes on them.[42] Local governments have been able to collect property taxes from properties used for office buildings, commercial areas, and parking space, often part of a decentralized entity's facilities, particularly in valuable airport terminals. Considering this criterion, strictly speaking, the university is exempted only for its classrooms, laboratories, libraries, research cubicles, auditoriums, and the like—even the ecological reserve, because scientific research is done there. But other buildings are not strictly educational: the rectory; administrative buildings; cafeterias and small shops scattered on various grounds; a full-size market and department store run by the university's trade union; an academic social club on the CU campus that holds weddings; and even a small building with teachers' quarters, the only housing facility that was built in the 1960s. The value of such property and its land is high, yet those buildings remain tax exempt.

Why they remain exempt is difficult to establish; it could be that the university's lawyers have been clever in disguising the building uses. It could also be that the taxing authorities have been turning a blind eye. If certain land uses were considered to contribute nothing toward the function of the university, the university would have to pay property taxes on them, and then there would be a case for the land reverting to ejido property, as explained earlier. Consequently, accepting those land uses would involve a double risk for the university: It would have to pay taxes on part of its property, and it might lose its ownership altogether.

Other, more political arguments are frequently put forward: The university plays an important role in the community as an educational entity; it provides an important service almost for free; it has imposed on itself an easement, a large ecological reserve, that few private owners are willing to replicate; and it is self-sufficient with regard to such services as security, street cleaning, maintenance of open spaces, water treatment, garbage incineration, and fire service. Thus, tax exemption, self-imposed easement, and self-sufficiency contribute to the perception of autonomy and act as political pressure to prevent any contender, whether it is a taxing or an agrarian authority, from taking action.

Land in the Spirit of the University

The history of UNAM, seen through its land and development, reveals many lessons. The university community had been anxious to become autonomous from the federal government for many years, until it received its independence in 1929. So strong was the ideal tied to a territorial manifestation that the very same year, Rector Ignacio García Téllez launched a national appeal to collect money to buy land and build the Ciudad Universitaria; he was soon able to buy the first piece of land in Tecamachalco. Although that project was frustrated, the acquisition of land in the Pedregal and the building of the CU eventually came about, and the territorial manifestation of autonomy was achieved.

Land has been a symbol of autonomy to many communities throughout the world. For institutions such as the university, land represents much more than economic value, as Massey (1977) explained. The relationship with land is a complex one. According to Harvey (1973), land represents multiple things; has many functional values for those who use it; and though its uses are important, in any given moment they are linked to exchange values, making the dynamic still more complicated.

Land and the university have a complex relationship. In the beginning that relationship symbolized a struggle for autonomy as well as a need to solve practical problems. The historic buildings the university owned in the city center, some since colonial times, not only were inadequate for teaching; much deteriorated; and located in a noisy, congested, and distracting environment, but also represented archaism and a tie to the established order that the university wanted to discard. Later, when the university found itself in a perilous financial situation, it was necessary to sell land but not to lose the dream of territorial autonomy. Nonetheless, as Harvey (1973) explained, owners who bestow use values on their properties sell their land at a price that considers the need to restore the use values through buying a similar property. The university, therefore, sold the Tecamachalco property for pennies.

As Clichevsky (2002) and Smolka (2002) have clearly pointed out, many institutional owners of vacant land, such as the university, are not speculators. UNAM was not an investor that wanted to maximize profit, nor did it retain property to create an economic scarcity that would raise its price. Two facts go against purely economic logic: First, UNAM sold the Tecamachalco property at the same price it had bought it for seven years earlier, in spite of a land-market boom. Second, in the case of the CU campus, it developed the enormous extra land it was acquiring by adopting the least profitable strategy available in those years. It acquired ejido land through expropriation and thus was unable to develop and sell it for a profit without risking restitution to ejido tenure. Had it been a true speculator, the university would have exchanged the land for private property bought inexpensively elsewhere. Land developers commonly used such a strategy at the time, and UNAM could have been advised to do that by its team of excellent lawyers, who could have enthusiastically helped present the best option, and by developers who were part of the committee set up to acquire the land, develop it, and design the best financial strategy. The only benefit UNAM had through expropriation was to acquire land at a very low price, at the agricultural value instead of the speculative price, yet it did not take advantage of that.

The university went through a stage of idealism that reflected the tenets of the mid-nineteenth-century economist Henry George—that is, trying to establish itself as a separate jurisdiction that could live from land rent and land taxes. The ideal was frustrated because the university overlooked the legal issue regarding its property. There is no evidence that those who thought of the ideal were followers of Henry George at that time, even though his ideas were current in many intellectual and political spheres. It would not be surprising if one of the stakeholders had come across a copy of *Progress and Poverty* (1879) or at least had been familiar with its philosophy, considering the academic setting. Not pursuing that ideal shows UNAM as an institution not motivated by the idea of strong economic maximization. Of course, the eventual increase of the federal subsidy did not motivate it, either.

The university, however, represented a major public investment in the southern part of the growing metropolis; it was going to increase property values for its neighbors. UNAM increased land rent in many of its possible manifestations. According to Jaramillo's (1994) classification, it helped to increase the city's overall basic rent—that is, the urban absolute rent—by taking out of the market a substantial portion of land that otherwise would have been developed and would have competed in the market at that time. In addition, the university accelerated a change in the city's layout by making accessible the Pedregal area, as the DF government extended Universidad, Revolución, and Insurgentes avenues and drilled new wells for water supply in the area. In this way, differential rents increased, reducing infrastructure costs to other developers and transport costs to future families, as well as favoring a high turnover for future commercial development. Furthermore, the university unintentionally helped to create residential areas for the elite, thus increasing monopoly exclusionary rent; the CU became part of the propaganda that would help boost prices for the prestigious high-income Jardines del Pedregal. As has been recounted, access to privileged information on locations and public works by specific landowners and investors played a role in the increases in land rents.

None of these land rent increases could be cashed in by the university itself. It did receive a substantial subsidy to build the Ciudad Universitaria, but the money did not come from land value captured by the government, and the subsidy ultimately increased profits for the neighboring developers. The subsidizer was the federal government, whose revenues came from income and sales taxes and petroleum excises. The increased value appropriated by the university's neighbors did not contribute to the development of the CU campus in any way. None of the many value capture instruments described by Smolka and Amborski (2001) have ever been applied for the benefit of the university. The only way value capture has been possible has been via the property tax, but that is a local tax collected through the DF government, and it contributed little to building the CU campus.

The university has abandoned any intention of becoming a developer—that is, living off yields as a landlord or cultivating a culture of real estate speculation. On the contrary, the university has learned that land represents use values in many complex ways: It symbolizes a sanctuary, not only in theory but also in practice, as government authorities do not trespass its borders. In practice, the land is not only an obvious necessity for its buildings but also a source of scientific research as an ecological reserve. It offers opportunities for artistic assets—for example, the large sculptural spaces enclosing fantastic rock formations (see Figure 6.6) and the Olympic Stadium designed

Figure 6.6 **Sculpture Space on the University City Campus**

Source: Fondo Carlos Lazo/Saúl Molina, Archivo Histórico, Centro de Estudios sobre la Universidad, UNAM.

as a crater (see Figure 6.7), both of which took advantage of the Pedregal's volcanic setting.

However, not everything about UNAM's story is glorious or epic. When the university expanded in the 1970s, it learned to accept the same fate that the city as a whole faced: becoming a sprawling metropolis, with populous areas spreading great distances and in tough conditions. The university had to adapt to the times and deal with the same conditions to cope with its own spillover. In learning to play by the rules of a country with many taxing inconsistencies, it has found a way to waive its tax commitments to the city, although compensating the city with much needed open space; low demand for urban services; and free education, artistic activities, and cultural ameni-

Figure 6.7 **UNAM's Olympic Stadium**

Source: Fondo Carlos Lazo/Saúl Molina, Archivo Histórico, Centro de Estudios sobre la Universidad, UNAM.

ties. Yet, before it set self-imposed restrictions on the expansion of the CU buildings, it had sprawled in an irrational fashion and intruded into valuable natural land.

The university's motto, *Por mi raza hablará el espíritu* (On behalf of my race shall the spirit speak), has been followed in a noble way; land has not been used for speculation but has been used to serve science, the arts, and the humanities. The university has managed this voluntarily for the metropolitan community. Perhaps it does not comply with its property obligations, perhaps the community recognizes that what it offers is so valuable that it forgives such obligations, and perhaps the community considers that it deserves such privilege.

Today, the university community reaches far beyond a third of a million students, teachers, research fellows, and administrative staff. Through time, UNAM has produced millions of Mexican professionals and increasingly has educated many of the country's poorer children, leaving behind its elitist origins and becoming a university of the people. Alumni feel a strong connection to UNAM that continues throughout their lives. When the university is in peril, the whole nation suffers for it. Almost no one would accept UNAM losing its property privileges. Youngsters wishing to get into the university want especially to secure a place at the CU campus; it has become the symbol of the university and the symbol of its autonomy. As the motto goes, the nation's spirit is speaking through UNAM's "race" and especially through its Ciudad Universitaria campus.

Notes

1. Data for 2004: students, 269,143; academic staff, 32,498; administrative staff, 28,099 (Secretaría General de la Universidad Nacional Autónoma de México 1989–2004).

2. Surface area, according to the expropriation decree (*Diario Oficial de la Federación* 1946a).

3. Including fifty-seven local government jurisdictions: sixteen delegations of the Federal District, forty municipalities of the State of Mexico, and one municipality of the State of Hidalgo. Estimated by the authors for 2000 based on Negrete Salas (2000) and Garza and Ruiz Chiapetto (2000).

4. The 1997 surface area measured by Grajales (2000).

5. Notice the variations in the subsidy flow throughout the century, as presented in Figure 6.2. A statutory historical fee of US$0.02 per year for undergraduate studies has never been increased because of strong opposition from the students; in fact, it has been the cause of some of the longest and most violent student strikes the university has experienced, causing the resignation of many rectors.

6. The authors wish to recognize the work of Díaz de Ovando (1979), who gathered valuable material about the university's early autonomous history, of which we were able to use various elements for the present study.

7. An appeal by the university was launched earlier, on October 28, 1929 (Díaz de Ovando 1979). However, even before that, the original text of the decree giving the university its autonomy, which had been reviewed by the university community and even approved by the National Congress, included the creation of a university city. It was removed from the final text when President Emilio Portes Gil approved it on June 10, 1929, and published it on August 25, 1929, in the *Diario Oficial de la Federación,* the federal government's official journal. Apparently, the federal government did not want such a commitment.

8. Positions were polarized within the university; at one point two rectors were appointed (in Mexico, the rector is the head of the university). Eventually, the conservative group prevailed, and a new rector was elected, Manuel Gómez Morín (Ramírez López 2001), who eventually founded the *Partido Acción Nacional,* or PAN (*Enciclopedia de México* 1987b), which historically has been the right-wing opposition party, until it won the 2000 election that brought President Vicente Fox into power. The left-wing leader of the university, Vicente Lombardo Toledano, was to found a left-wing party, the *Partido Popular Socialista* (*Enciclopedia de México* 1987d).

9. Currency in Mexican pesos per year, unless otherwise stated.

10. Initially named the *Partido de la Revolución Mexicana* (PRM).

11. There is another variation of this type of property, called communal land, which is land claimed by Indian communities and returned to them as part of the agrarian reform. It had the same legal status as the ejido land until 1992.

12. After the 1992 constitutional reform, ejido land was allowed to become private property by agreement of the ejido assembly; it can then be sold in the open market.

13. This was eventually forbidden in 1970 because of the many abuses committed against ejido peasants.

14. Tlalpan: 364 hectares; Copilco: 62 hectares; Padierna: 102 hectares; and San Jerónimo Aculco: 205 hectares (*Diario Oficial de la Federación* 1946a).

15. The expropriation law at the time established that compensation for private property should be established at fiscal values, which were considerably lower than market value.

16. This was in opposition to the northern cities, which also wanted to develop industry and were politically very strong. The president wanted to reduce their strength by favoring Mexico City's stakeholders (Davis 1999).

17. It was eight times cheaper than the Tecamachalco property. The Pedregal was 87.6 percent rocky land paid at $0.01 per square meter and 12.4 percent arable land at $0.15 per square meter (derived from *Diario Oficial de la Federación* 1946a). These low prices illustrate how former hacienda landlords kept the best land and distributed among the peasants what in this case was mostly nonarable land.

18. Tlalpan ejido was endowed in 1929 (and an extension made in 1938), Copilco in 1938, Padierna in 1938, and San Jerónimo Aculco in 1923 and 1938 (*Diario Oficial de la Federación* 1946a).

19. In the end, the stadium was built for a smaller number of people and later enlarged for the Olympic Games in 1968. At present it has a capacity for 68,954 people (Universidad Nacional Autónoma de México 2004).

20. These prices were reported in 1946 by José Villagrán, co-owner of the nearby Jardines del Pedregal development; Luis Barragán, another co-owner, reported sales in 1950 of between $18 and $22 per square meter. Prices could have been as high as $20 to $25 per square meter, as predicted by José María Luján, who counterattacked the developer Negib Simón in the newspaper in 1946 when Luján denounced Simón's speculative intentions (see details on section about land speculation by others). The university commission, established for the development of the CU campus, was thinking of an even higher selling price, of $30 to $40 per square meter.

21. Total average, including the price paid for the land plus the cost of providing housing and other amenities to the ejido peasants.

22. There is no evidence that Henry George's ideas of a single-tax community, or of such a tax representing 100 percent of the land rent as a basis for financing government (George 1879), influenced this concept. Yet, since George's ideas were still in vogue in many parts of the world in the first half of the century, some of the stakeholders involved in the building of CU perhaps were familiar with his philosophy.

23. The design for a long time was wrongly attributed to Mario Pani, importer to Mexico of Le Corbusier's ideas, and Enrique del Moral, director of the School of Architecture, both fathers of Mexico's modern architecture who increased their prestige from this mistaken attribution (Pani and Del Moral 1979). Three decades later, Enrique del Moral admitted that CU was inspired by the design from a student competition won by Teodoro González de León, Enrique Molina, and Armando Franco (González de León 2003), the first of whom became one of the most renowned architects in Mexico at the end of the century.

24. The Centre for University Studies (CESU) keeps microfilm of some of the designs.

25. Eventually, in the late 1960s, the university changed its policy and started to renew the historic buildings and use them as museums or research centers and for continuous education programs and cultural activities. They constitute some of the most important landmarks of what is now known as Mexico City's Historical Center. Some university properties in this area with little historical value are leased for private use, yet they represent insignificant income to the university.

26. Two anecdotes illustrate this point. First, President Alemán's statue was bombed twice soon after its dedication on the university campus; the remnant was eventually removed. Second, President Luis Echeverría (1970–76), who led a populist government and sought a pro-UNAM policy reconciling UNAM and the government after the 1968 massive killing during student riots in Tlatelolco, visited the university and was injured when a stone was thrown at him from inside an auditorium full of roaring students and a few teachers. This happened in the 1970s, when the university had perhaps its strongest left-wing tendency.

27. Legally, there always has been a tuition fee for undergraduates, but it has been frozen for decades and severely deteriorated by inflation. In 2004, full five-year tuition amounts to only $1.00 (less than US$.09).

28. The work of Díaz de Ovando (1979) brought to light information and documents that are not readily available, yet she does not review them from the land speculation standpoint, which we discuss here. We hope to connect her information with other sources, which, when analyzed together, will allow another interesting story to be told. As many authors have written, the CU campus is a major landmark and a breakthrough in the history of architecture in Mexico. However, those authors do not discuss the speculation that surrounded it, except Vargas Salguero (1994) indirectly; we believe one reason for this is that some of the most prestigious architects of the time were involved in the design and construction, and the authors have avoided staining the image of such architects. Each of these architects has become an icon: José Villagrán, the great theorist; Carlos Contreras, the successful planner; Carlos Lazo, the excellent manager of large-scale works; and Luis Barragán, the most internationally known Mexican architectural designer in history. They all established a highly regarded style of modern Mexican architecture. Tampering with historical icons is not easy.

29. It must be noted that Barragán stated that he decided in 1943 that if he wanted to have creative freedom, he needed to become very rich (Ingersoll 2001; Zanco 2001). His family had been landlords of the Hacienda Los Corrales in the State of Jalisco, which they lost after the agrarian revolution (De Michelis 2001), thus Barragán must have been aware of the economic advantages of landownership.

30. Villagrán is now recognized as the teacher who brought some students' projects to the attention of the architects Pani and Del Moral, who later took credit for the design (Gonzalez de León 2003). See note 23.

31. They were referring to the Huipulco Hospital in Tlalpan, designed by Villagrán, a very important building that is frequently seen to be an example of how his theories of architecture were put into practice. This eclipses any discussion about possible conflicts of interest that could have occurred while it was being built.

32. President Alemán is known to have gone into land ventures, yet it is difficult to link him with the Jardines del Pedregal. We can only say that he appears to have been fully aware of the project. Alemán and Barragán knew each other at the time; the president was photographed in 1948 at Barragán's house at a gathering related to Jardines del Pedregal (Zanco 2001).

33. He recently had sold a large bullring in the middle of one of his developments

farther north on Insurgentes Avenue. That sale gave him enough money to finance half of what was needed to build the CU campus (Díaz de Ovando 1979).

34. This road, Las Dalias Avenue, has not become public property as such; it remains part of the university patrimony and has been on loan to the DF.

35. We are referring to a specific type of land rent—that is, differential rent, type II in Marxist terms, adapted to the urban context (Jaramillo 1994)—that is due to higher capital input that can be invested in the land.

36. Little research has been done in the area under this perspective, though Angeles Zárate is writing a PhD thesis on the topic at Facultad de Arquitectura, Universidad Nacional Autónoma de México.

37. Another characteristic of land speculation of the period was the exchange of ejido land for private property. By that time the law was flexible, and though ejidos remained inalienable, they could be exchanged for better agricultural land even if it was located elsewhere. In that way, land from two of the same ejidos that had been expropriated for the UNAM campus, Tlalpan and San Jerónimo Aculco, was exchanged for land in the distant states of Veracruz, Hidalgo, and Guanajuato, which belonged to or had been bought for the purpose by Barragán and the Bustamante brothers (see, for example, *Diario Oficial de la Federación* 1950, 1951). These developers exchanged poorly located but agriculturally good property for well-located but agriculturally poor property. Consequently, many of the ejido peasants moved away and continued their modest lifestyle elsewhere, while Barragán and the Bustamante brothers sought a large profit.

38. President Adolfo López Mateos (1958–64) lived on the other side of the avenue, and his daughter resided on the side adjacent to the CU campus, apparently barely avoiding an overlap with the UNAM property. Such residents exemplify the high-status location that invited speculation.

39. It is unclear that the Chevarría family were ejido peasants, though they could at least have been related to them. They were exercising some sort of quarry usufruct rights that enabled them to claim or pretend to have some sort of ownership.

40. In fact, part of the Zaragoza School of Professional Studies was lost this way; the university had already built classrooms that were squatted by residents who have occupied them ever since (Morales Schechinger and García Jiménez 2003).

41. Together with a small archaeological area farther south, with the ancient round pyramid of Cuicuilco surrounded by some volcanic lava.

42. After a constitutional reform introduced in 1999 (Gutiérrez and Santana 2002).

References

Azuela, Antonio, Miguel Angel Cancino, and Ma. Soledad Cruz. 1984. "Ilegalidad y Procesos Sociales en Cuatro Colonias Populares de la Ciudad de México." *Revista A* 5, no. 11: 113–48. Azcapotzalco: Universidad Autónoma Metropolitana.

Carrillo Trueba, César. 1995. *El Pedregal de San Angel*. Mexico City: Coordinación de Investigación Científica, Universidad Nacional Autónoma de México.

Cisneros Sosa, Armando. 1993. *La Ciudad Que Construimos: Registro de la Expansión de la Ciudad de México, 1920–1976*. Mexico City: Universidad Autónoma Metropolitana–Iztapalapa.

Clichevsky, Nora, ed. 2002. *Tierra Vacante en Ciudades Latinoamericanas*. Cambridge, MA: Lincoln Institute of Land Policy.

Davis, Diane. 1999. *El Leviatán Urbano: La Ciudad de México en el Siglo XX* (Urban Leviathan: México City in the Twentieth Century; trans. Eduardo Suárez). Mexico City: Fondo de Cultura Económica.

De Cervantes, Luís. 1952. *Crónica Arquitectónica, Prehispánica, Colonial, Contemporánea.* Mexico City: Cimsa.

De Michelis, Marco. 2001. "Los Orígenes del Modernismo: Luís Barragán los Años de Formación." In *Luís Barragán la Revolución Callada,* ed. Federica Zanco, 42–64. Milan: Skira, Barragán Foundation, and Vitra Design Museum.

Diario Oficial de la Federación. 1945. Ley Orgánica de la Universidad Nacional Autónoma de México. January 6.

———. 1946a. Decreto Que Expropia Terrenos Ejidales de los Poblados de Tlalpan y Copilco, de la Delegación de Tlalpan, y Padierna y San Jerónimo Aculco, de la Delegación de la Magdalena Contreras, Distrito Federal. September 25.

———. 1946b. Ley sobre Fundación y Construcción de la Ciudad Universitaria. April 6.

———. 1950. Resolución sobre Permuta de Terrenos Ejidales del Poblado San Jerónimo Aculco en la Magdalena Contreras, DF. January 18.

———. 1951. Resolución sobre Permuta de Terrenos Ejidales del Poblado San Jerónimo Aculco en la Magdalena Contreras, DF. May 14.

Díaz de Ovando, Clementina. 1979. *La Ciudad Universitaria de México: Reseña Histórica 1929–1955,* vol. 10–1. Mexico City: Universidad Nacional Autónoma de México.

Dirección General de Estudios sobre Legislación Universitaria. Various years. "Terrenos de Montserrat." Mexico City: Author, Universidad Nacional Autónoma de México.

———. Various years. "Triángulo de San Jerónimo." Mexico City: Author, Universidad Nacional Autónoma de México.

Dirección General de Patrimonio Universitario. 2004. www.patrimonio.unam.mx/instalacionuniv.html. Accessed October 6, 2006.

Domínguez Martínez, Raúl. 2001. "Historia de la UNAM (1945–1970)." In *La Universidad de México: Un Recorrido Histórico de la Época Colonial al Presente,* ed. Renate Marsiske, 187–260. Mexico City: Centro de Estudios sobre la Universidad, Universidad Nacional Autónoma de México and Plaza y Valdés.

Duhau, Emilio. 2003. "Programas de Regularización y Mercado de Suelo para Vivienda Popular en la Ciudad de México." In *A Cidade da Informalidade: O Desafio das Cidades Latino-Americanas,* org. Pedro Abramo, 43–77. Rio de Janeiro: Libreria Sette Letras, Observatório Imobiliário e de Políticas do Solo, Instituto de Pesquisa e Planejamento Urbano e Regional, Universidade Federal do Rio de Janeiro, Fundação Carlos Chagas Filho de Amparo á Pesquisa do Estado do Rio de Janeiro, and Lincoln Institute of Land Policy.

Eggener, Keith L. 2001. "La Arquitectura Fotográfica de Barragán: Imagen, Publicidad y Memoria." In *Luís Barragán la Revolución Callada,* ed. Federica Zanco,178–95. Milan: Skira, Barragán Foundation, and Vitra Design Museum.

Enciclopedia de México. 1987a. "Contreras, Carlos." Mexico City: Compañía Editora de Enciclopedias de México and Secretaría de Educación Pública.

———. 1987b. "Gómez Morín, Manuel." Mexico City: Compañía Editora de Enciclopedias de México and Secretaría de Educación Pública.

———. 1987c. "Instituto Politécnico Nacional." Mexico City: Compañía Editora de Enciclopedias de México and Secretaría de Educación Pública.

————. 1987d. "Lombardo Toledano, Vicente." Mexico City: Compañía Editora de Enciclopedias de México and Secretaría de Educación Pública.

Espinoza López, Enrique. 2003. *Ciudad de México: Compendio Cronológico de su Desarrollo Urbano 1521–2000.* Mexico City: Secretaría de Educación Pública and Instituto Politécnico Nacional.

Gaceta UNAM. 1983. "Más de 123 Hectáreas del Pedregal de San Angel, Propiedad de la U.N.A.M. Fueron Declaradas Patrimonio Ecológico Inafectable." October 3.

————. 1990. "Acuerdo por el Que Se Redefine la Zona de Reserva Ecológica de Ciudad Universitaria." October 20.

————. 1996a. "Acuerdo por el Que Se Reordena e Incrementa la Zona de Reserva Ecológica de Ciudad Universitaria. March 14.

————. 1996b. "Acuerdo por el Que Se Reordena e Incrementa la Zona de Reserva Ecológica y Se Declaran las Áreas Verdes de Manejo Especial de Ciudad Universitaria." January 13.

Garza, Gustavo. 2000. "Ambitos de Expansión Territorial." In *La Ciudad de México en el Fin del Segundo Milenio,* ed. Gustavo Garza, 237–46. Mexico City: Gobierno del Distrito Federal and El Colegio de México.

Garza, Gustavo, and Crecencio Ruiz Chiapetto. 2000. "La Ciudad de México en el Sistema Urbano Nacional." In *La Ciudad de México en el Fin del Segundo Milenio,* ed. Gustavo Garza, 229–36. Mexico City: Gobierno del Distrito Federal and El Colegio de México.

George, Henry. 1879. *Progress and Poverty.* Repr., New York: Robert Schalkenbach Foundation, 1992.

González de León, Teodoro. 2003. "La Vida del Barrio Universitario." In *Un Destino Compartido: 450 Años de Presencia de la Universidad en la Ciudad de México,* ed. Juan Ramón de la Fuente et al., 113–54. Mexico City: Coordinación de Humanidades and Programa Universitario de Estudios sobre la Ciudad, Universidad Nacional Autónoma de México.

Grajales, Gabriela. 2000. "Uso del Suelo y Conformación Territorial." In *La Ciudad de México en el Fin del Segundo Milenio,* ed. Gustavo Garza, 511–20. Mexico City: Gobierno del Distrito Federal and El Colegio de México.

Gutiérrez, Juan Marcos, and Salvador Santana. 2002. *Artículo 115 Constitucional: Historia y Reformas de 1999.* Guadalajara: Instituto Para el Desarrollo Técnico de las Haciendas Públicas.

Harvey, David. 1973. *Social Justice and the City.* London: Edward Arnold.

Ingersoll, Richard. 2001. "A la Sombra de Barragán." In *Luís Barragán la Revolución Callada,* ed. Federica Zanco, 206–27. Milan: Skira, Barragán Foundation, and Vitra Design Museum.

Jaramillo, Samuel. 1994. *Hacia Una Teoría de la Renta del Suelo Urbano.* Bogotá: Ediciones Uniandes and Instituto Agustín Codazzi.

Magnano, Vittorio. 2001. "Luís Barragán: Diseño Urbano y Especulación." In *Luís Barragán la Revolución Callada,* ed. Federica Zanco, 146–67. Milan: Skira, Barragán Foundation, and Vitra Design Museum.

Mancilla, J. Ignacio. 2000. *Del Pedregal a Santo Domingo: Historia del Proceso de Regularización.* Mexico City: Gobierno del Distrito Federal.

Massey, Doreen. 1977. "Análisis de la Propiedad Capitalista del Suelo: Una Investigación sobre el Caso de Gran Bretaña." In *Estudios sobre Renta del Suelo,* ed. Maite Martínez Pardo, 135–70. Madrid: Comunidad de Madrid, Consejería de Ordenación del Territorio, Medio Ambiente y Vivienda.

Morales Schechinger, Carlos, and Sara García Jiménez. 2003. "La Desconcentración de la Universidad, 1970–2000, y Su Presencia en la Metrópoli de la Ciudad de México." In *Un Destino Compartido: 450 Años de Presencia de la Universidad en la Ciudad de México,* ed. Juan Ramón de la Fuente et al., 211–37. Mexico City: Coordinación de Humanidades and Programa Universitario de Estudios sobre la Ciudad, Universidad Nacional Autónoma de México.

Negrete Salas, María Eugenia. 2000. "Dinámica demográfica." In *La Ciudad de México en el Fin del Segundo Milenio,* ed. Gustavo Garza, 247–54. Mexico City: Gobierno del Distrito Federal and El Colegio de México.

Obregón Santacilia, Carlos. 1952. *Cincuenta Años de Arquitectura Mexicana (1900–1959).* Mexico City: Editorial Patria.

Oropeza Villavicencio, Eduardo. 2001. "Del Obraje de Contreras a la Fábrica de Hilados y Tejidos la Magdalena: 400 Años de Testimonio Textil." Graduate thesis, Instituto Nacional de Antropología e Historia, Mexico City.

Pani, Mario, and Enrique del Moral. 1979. *La Construcción de la Ciudad Universitaria del Pedregal,* vol. 12. Mexico City: Universidad Nacional Autónoma de México.

Perló Cohen, Manuel. 1981. *Estado, Vivienda y Estructura Urbana en el Cardenismo.* Mexico City: Instituto de Investigaciones Sociales, Universidad Nacional Autónoma de México.

Ramírez López, Celia. 2001. La Universidad Autónoma de México (1933–1944). In *La Universidad de México: Un Recorrido Histórico de la Época Colonial al Presente,* ed. Renate Marsiske, 163–85. Mexico City: Centro de Estudios sobre la Universidad, Universidad Nacional Autónoma de México and Plaza y Valdés.

Secretaría General de la Universidad Nacional Autónoma de México. 1960–81. *Anuario Estadístico.* Mexico City: Universidad Nacional Autónoma de México.

———. 1982–88. *Presupuesto.* Mexico City: Universidad Nacional Autónoma de México.

———. 1989–2004. *Agenda Estadística.* Mexico City: Universidad Nacional Autónoma de México.

Smolka, Martim. 2002. "Prólogo." In *Tierra Vacante en Ciudades Latinoamericanas,* ed. Nora Clichevsky, vii–x. Cambridge, MA: Lincoln Institute of Land Policy.

Smolka, Martim, and David Amborski. 2001. "Captura de Mais-Valias para o Desenvolvimento Urbano: Una Comparação Interamericana." In *Cidade em Transformação: Entre o Plano e o Mercado: Experiências Internacionais de Gestão do Solo Urbano,* ed. Abramo Pedro, 37–74. Rio de Janeiro: Observatório Imobiliário e de Políticas do Solo, Instituto de Pesquisa e Planejamento Urbano e Regional, Universidade Federal do Rio de Janeiro and Secretaria Municipal de Urbanismo, Prefeitura do Rio de Janeiro.

Universidad Nacional Autónoma de México. 1952. *Pensamiento y Destino de la Ciudad Universitaria de México.* Mexico City: Author.

———. 2004. Estadio Olímpico, Conjunción de Valores y del Espíritu Universitario. www.dgsg.unam.mx/estadio.htm. Accessed January 10, 2007.

Vargas Salguero, Ramón. 1994. "Los Autores de la Ciudad Universitaria, Urbanismo, Arquitectura y Práctica." In *La Arquitectura de Ciudad Universitaria,* ed. Rogelio Alvarez Noguera, 68–95. Mexico City: Universidad Nacional Autónoma de México.

Zanco, Federica. 2001. "Luís Barragán: La Revolución Callada." In *Luís Barragán la*

Revolución Callada, ed. Federica Zanco, 78–105. Milan: Skira, Barragán Foundation, and Vitra Design Museum.

Zubirán, Salvador. 1946a. Diario de Labores April 9, excerpts from a diary compiled in Clementina Díaz de Ovando, 1979, *La Ciudad Universitaria de México: Reseña Histórica 1929–1955,* vol. 10–1, 413–36. Mexico City: Universidad Nacional Autónoma de México.

————. 1946b. Diario de Labores August 15, excerpts from a diary compiled in Clementina Díaz de Ovando, 1979, *La Ciudad Universitaria de México: Reseña Histórica 1929–1955,* vol. 10–1, 413–36. Mexico City: Universidad Nacional Autónoma de México.

————. 1946c. Diario de Labores May 27, excerpts from a diary compiled in Clementina Díaz de Ovando, 1979, *La Ciudad Universitaria de México: Reseña Histórica 1929–1955,* vol. 10–1, 413–36. Mexico City: Universidad Nacional Autónoma de México.

7

Partnering with Private Corporations to Build on Campus

Yonsei University, Seoul, Korea

GwangYa Han and Wann Yu

Yonsei University (Yonsei) is the nation's largest and oldest private educational institution; it serves approximately 47,000 university people on a 250-acre campus in Seoul, Korea.[1] While the daily "commuter-shed" of the university has expanded as far as thirty kilometers, well beyond the Seoul Metropolitan Area (SMA) edge, since its founding in 1885, Yonsei's internal campus, consisting of 119 buildings, has continued to redefine its functional boundaries with its neighborhood.

The recent southern expansion of Yonsei campus has been driven by a series of research and development (R&D) facility construction projects that began in the mid-1990s: the Yonsei Medical Research Center (YMRC, 1996), the Engineering Research Center (YERC, 1999), and the Science Research Center (YSRC, 2000). These research complexes together make up 15 percent of the total area of university building space (758,000 square meters), and they nearly doubled the density of the south end of the campus.

In contrast to earlier R&D facility development, which has been directly and indirectly funded by national governments in Korea and overseas in previous decades, the dynamics of this development process—its pace, building groupings, and, most important, the development framework—are a product of the university's increased awareness of the practical benefits of developing partnerships with private corporations such as Daewoo, Hyundai, LG, and Samsung. Consequently, this development changes the way the public views the university's function, as well as the way the public sector controls the campus development.

There is considerable debate among policy makers of universities and public agencies over the form and density of such R&D construction and over stakeholders' motives, as well as their role in the development planning and implementation. Among other requirements, research should address how to understand such privately operated corporate R&D activities on academic campuses, particularly from functional and regulatory perspectives, including who are the development participants and what roles should be performed, given the economic benefits for local and metropolitan settings.

This chapter explores the issue of a corporate-sponsored R&D facility development in an academic environment using an in-depth case study of the recent YERC development at Yonsei University. It explores how shifting views and attitudes toward the university's function have influenced this recent development in the academic environment and how its dynamics are guided by the different roles and interests of university, corporation, and public sector. To do this, we explore three broad themes that aim to answer the following questions:

- First, how was the R&D facility development initiated, and what roles are performed by whom? In fact, the YERC project was initiated not by the university administration but by a task force group of the Engineering College, which was motivated not only by a lack of physical space but, more important, by an eagerness to build institutionalized channels for technology transfer and commercialization of corporate-sponsored research products. As for its implementation, YERC was realized through a university-corporation partnership in which the university provided its land and the corporate participants donated financial resources for development costs in exchange for thirty years' building tenancy.
- Second, given recent trends of campus development in general, how can a university accommodate such corporate R&D facilities on campus, and how can it make their uses compatible with those of the adjacent neighborhood as well as the university? These questions concern a campus-wide location screening procedure and space programming of use, circulation, and public access of corporate facilities. For the university's decision makers, however, the fast-growing and continuous, clustered expansion poses a challenge for maintaining integrated campus-wide programs as a decentralizing space strategy, while the typical growth trend of the university's functional boundary has spread evenly from the core toward the periphery.
- Third, how can the public sector understand the changing function of a metropolitan university and attempt to regulate the growing corporate R&D activities on campus in physical and nonphysical ways? In fact,

both the local governing body's and the Seoul Metropolitan Government's perceptions of campus development have shifted from that of educational installation to encompass the university's citywide influence—not only the positive impact of job creation but also of property development as an extremely profitable activity. Thus, there is debate regarding whether corporate R&D facilities on campus can be subject to property and other taxes. The ambiguity of R&D's role, purpose, and benefits to a campus and community and the public sector's lack of regulatory control make it difficult for the public sector to directly influence the physical bulk of R&D development and its economic impacts upon immediate job creation and taxable income.

University Initiative and Corporate Interest

Among such recent R&D facility developments on the Yonsei campus is the Yonsei Engineering Research Center. YERC is a result of the increased demand for academic institutions to collaborate with private enterprises that began in the 1990s. This demand came from Yonsei's pragmatic initiative to attract capital from corporations that were interested in partnering with the university to build research laboratories and office space on its campus. YERC is a US$88 million mixed-use development project with 66,800 square meters of floor area on 4.1 acres of university property (see Figure 7.1). The project involved a two-year planning phase (1993–1995), and construction was completed in 1999.

In early 1993, the faculty of the Bioengineering Department envisioned a private, corporate, R&D platform on the campus because it wanted a channel for collaborating with industry. Soon, this idea struck a chord among several faculty members of the Engineering School. They shared a new view of technology driven by society's increasing demand for technological advances—and the enormous profit potential from the commercialization of intellectual technology, a realization that other universities also had in the 1990s.

The faculties quickly formed a committee, the YERC Task Force (YERC TF), to turn the idea of collaborating with industry into a built structure. Their prompt action revealed two important needs at the engineering college: first, the need for a consolidated complex of learning and research activities, which at the time were scattered across campus; second, the need for an institutionalized setting through which corporate-sponsored research could be channeled for accelerated real-world practical applications.

The project as envisioned required more space than just research facilities and business offices for the private enterprise. It necessitated offices for support services for early-stage ventures and student start-ups, such as an incubat-

Figure 7.1   **Overview of Yonsei Engineering Research Center (YERC), the Yonsei University Campus, and the Conservation Area**

ing center (later named the Yonsei Technology Business Center, or YTBC), and technical support units (later named the Small Enterprise Technology Supporting Group, or SETSG) for technological infrastructure and business management advising services, as well as investment entities for financial resources for the early years of incubating.

In fact, Yonsei was among several Korean universities that were planning on-campus research complexes.[2] But Yonsei had three major advantages over the other universities. The first was the metropolitan location of its campus, which was becoming a regional hub in the northwest of Seoul. The city had been significantly expanding in that direction, driven by the national government's new town developments, such as Ilsan, built in the early 1990s.

The second was the recent opening of a new international airport in Inchon, as well as the renovated domestic airport at Gimpo, which, combined, provided the campus with a powerful national and global reach. Finally, Yonsei had the nation's top medical school, as well as the associated University Hospital of Severance, one of the country's best in quality and physical attributes. Thus, the proposed YERC had much potential to accelerate the transfer of technological innovation into the commercial marketplace, particularly in medical engineering.

At that time, Yonsei's new university president, Ja Song, who had been a professor at Yonsei's College of Management of Business Administration, was focused on accomplishing one major agenda item: to make Yonsei into one of the world's top one hundred universities. The business-minded president aimed to produce and aggressively pursue key strategies to realize that goal. Soon, the new university administration launched the first major initiative—the Yonsei Research Complex Project, which aimed to create an on-campus R&D infrastructure in engineering and science. The plan won strong support from the deans of the colleges of engineering, science, and human ecology, all of which desired their own research facilities.

New campus development has become an important measure of the success of university administrations, and expansion has followed a periodic development cycle at Yonsei. Overall, expansion patterns appear to correlate with the cycle of university presidents. The building construction statistics from the university's Facility Department indicate that new construction follows within one to two years after a new university president takes over. For example, surges of new construction throughout the 1990s, specifically in 1990, 1995, and 1998 (see Figure 7.2), came immediately after the inauguration of a new president: YoungShik Park (1988–1992), Ja Song (1992–1996), and ByungSoo Kim (1996–2000).

The time lag is attributed to the planning process, which includes setting up committees to draw construction plans. A university president's planned construction is typically wrapped up one or two years before the end of the presidential term. This cyclic interval at Yonsei was shorter through the mid-1970s and the late 1980s. Change appears to follow the university presidency at Yonsei in the 1980s; since then, presidents have been limited to no more than two consecutive four-year terms. Transitional years of outgoing and incoming presidents indicate the lowest degree of new construction based upon Yonsei's statistics.

One of the most important aspects of YERC is its project finance strategy. At that time in 1994, YERC TF, in partnership with the university's administration, launched a nationwide drive to solicit donations from major business corporations for the new engineering complex. Yonsei was interested in

Figure 7.2   **Growth Trend of New Building Space, Yonsei University, 1885–2002**

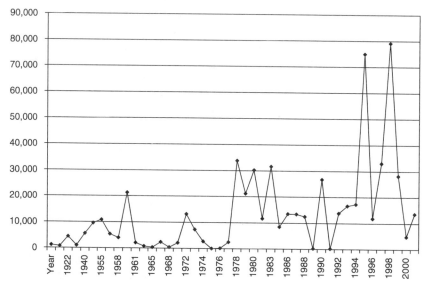

Source: Annual Statistics of Yonsei University, 2003, Seoul, Korea: Yonsei University.
Note: Unit: square meters.

attracting capital from corporations that were interested in partnering with the university to build research labs and office space for their occupancy on its campus. As the project moved into the implementation stage, the new university administration also tried boldly to attract corporate sponsors to the campus.

During the past decade, several major domestic corporations in technology-related fields, such as Daewoo, Hyundai, LG, and Samsung, showed strong interest in opening branch R&D centers on university campuses. For those corporations, being in close proximity to, as well as having a cooperative relationship with, university research centers is quite an incentive, not only for R&D but also from a business viewpoint in the following three respects.

First, the university's cluster of engineering, science, and medicine research facilities is an excellent resource for maximizing R&D operations, not only for the cooperative benefits but also from a competition perspective. Along with its proximity to domestic and international airports, the campus is located close to Sungsan Avenue, a major northwestern artery into a fast-growing region of Seoul. Such regional and global accessibility-plus the attractions of the surrounding town's cultural resources, night life, and intellectual stimulation—are key to attracting young professionals who seek a quality work environment with more geographic freedom than other business entities may offer.

Second, corporations are having difficulty leasing or acquiring research facility space in the Central Business District (CBD) of Seoul due to high building leasing prices. Furthermore, multiple owners often make the land acquisition and site assembly process complex, lengthy, and costly. Thus, despite the advantage of being close to trendy markets as a critical element of successful business, it is difficult for corporations to purchase land or buildings for R&D facilities in the CBD area in a timely way. From a business perspective, if a university provides land and buildings, corporations as tenants can avoid various real estate taxes and bypass the land acquisition hurdles. In addition, being located on a prestigious university's campus heightens a corporation's image in the academic community and beyond, particularly for potential leaders and employees of the next generation.

Third, due to the absence of clear boundaries of on-campus corporate R&D activity, debate has emerged in the public domain about how to define R&D activity: Should it be classified as conventional manufacturing or corporate factory operations in the private domain, or as academic activities of a non-profit organization, the university? Blurred boundaries and the integration of corporate R&D with academic research hold significant implications for regulatory control of these on-campus business operations, which are typically designated as nontaxable zones. From the public sector's view, such ambiguous status helps corporations encroach on the academy for their tax-free private business activities.

Screening Procedure for Site Location

Two basic issues must be addressed regarding corporate R&D facilities on academic campuses: first, where to locate them and how to narrow the potential development sites; second, what factors influence the screening of the site locations, and who is in charge of the location decision.

Three university stakeholder groups directed the development process of the YERC complex: First, the YERC Task Force was the project initiator and promoter; second, the university's administration representative and the university trustees acted as final decision makers; third, the seven private corporations were the funding providers and future tenants.

Immediately after its formation, YERC TF launched a campus-wide search to identify possible sites. It is interesting that it excluded off-campus locations in the early planning stage. Such a locational orientation for developing facilities inside university boundaries reflects a unique mechanism of campus buildings in Korea, given the following issues.

Off-campus extension projects in neighboring residential areas often require years of site assemblage work, particularly when various entities own the land, making for a cumbersome process. Universities often prefer to expand on their own property to expedite the development process.

For on-campus development at Yonsei in general, individual colleges should take responsibility for implementing new building construction from the first idea and throughout the construction. Thus, a college that plans to construct and expand its facilities to meet demand is expected to finance a significant portion of the development itself. The university has historically provided needs-based matching funds without expecting to control or influence the project. It is noteworthy that a construction plan for off-campus locations (not owned by the university) often triples the land-purchasing costs. Accordingly, a college that cannot afford to purchase land rules out off-campus development sites in the very early planning process.

Such a campus development mechanism reflects the importance of a campus-wide long-range development plan that is supposed to be prepared by the university at large. At Yonsei, despite a series of university efforts to create a unified campus environment via a "big development picture" or campus master plan, the overall pattern of campus development has been historically driven by individual building-based projects.[3] Thus, the pattern of development at Yonsei has been piecemeal, as individual buildings have been added in a form of localized development project implementation.

In fact, it was only under the presidency of Ja Song (1992–1996) that the university conducted its first campus-wide development suitability survey for possible sites that could be developed in the near future. Until then, the direction of campus development had been driven by individual colleges' need-based projects and ad hoc constructions rather than a phased planning strategy of deliberate practices with long-term investment strategies.

In the beginning of the planning stage for the YERC, YERC TF made a preliminary site location decision: next to the two engineering college buildings. The site, totaling 4.1 acres and located at the southern edge of the university, was used as tennis courts, underneath which was the university's wastewater treatment facility. From YERC TF's perspective, the site was an ideal location for three reasons: First, it was owned by the university, negating any land purchasing costs for immediate project implementation; second, it was in close proximity to the existing Engineering College buildings (Buildings 1 and 2, as well as Building 3, then under construction), which would ostensibly foster an excellent collaborative R&D environment (see Figure 7.3); third, the site was expandable into the adjacent baseball and soccer fields for future development.

These units, as well as start-up ventures, are mostly managed or comanaged

Figure 7.3   Engineering College Buildings on the Southern Edge of Yonsei University

by the faculties of eleven departments of the Engineering College nearby and create full-time and part-time research involvements for undergraduate and graduate students. Among some of the early start-ups is Yonsei Digital Hollywood (renamed Yonsei Digital), an educational training venture in the field of multimedia digital contents production and Internet applications. It was cofinanced by Yonsei, Hyundai Digital Entertainment, Hynix Semiconductor, and others in 2000.

In May 1993, YERC TF contacted the new administration's University Planning Department to solicit university-wide financial and political support. Concurrently, the group retained a faculty of the Architectural Engineering Department to develop a preliminary site plan for YERC, which proposed a 33,000-square-meter (380,000-square-foot) building. Through a series of follow-up meetings with the group, the university administration accepted the proposed location for YERC with no significant reservation.

Until recently, this type of location screening procedure, particularly with a passive attitude by the university administration, was common practice. In the absence of a long-range master plan, new construction often took place as recommended by the building construction steering committees from individual colleges. When objections were raised from neighboring colleges—mostly over close physical proximity that would block views and sunlight and increase noise—the university administration or ad hoc committee traditionally acted as a mediator to resolve the conflict. New campus construction has become more problematic in recent years as the quality of space and well-being has become a hot-button issue.

After the first campus-wide development suitability survey, conducted in the mid-1990s, the university's decision-making process for campus development began to crystallize. In general, a college steering committee would contact the University Planning Department to propose and promote a new building project. The Planning Department would review the plan and then give a preliminary "go" or "no go," based primarily on the project's compatibility with the administration's vision, along with the proposed site and financing strategy. If the project was considered positively, a board of individual colleges, on behalf of the construction steering committee, would launch an official discussion with the University Planning Department on the proposal.

Subsequently, the proposed project would be reviewed, particularly with regard to its proposed site location and development density, by the Construction and Environmental Advisory Board of the university, which would then make recommendations to the Planning Department. If the Planning Department endorsed the project to the university president, the university trustees would make a final decision (see Table 7.1).

It is interesting to think about the attitude of the university administration

Table 7.1

Decision-Making Procedure for Campus Development

Level	Decision maker	Decision-making process
College	Construction Task Force	• Space demand identified • Construction plan initiated • Preliminary screening of site location • Preliminary construction cost estimate • Funding strategy devised • Design and development proposal
	College Board	• Recommend proposal to university
University	University Planning Department	• Preliminary discussion with college • Official review and recommendation
	Building Construction Advisory Board	• Review of proposal
	Environmental Advisory Board	• Review of proposal
	President	• Preliminary decision
	University trustees	• Final decision

in the YERC's site screening process, since the administration had not considered the campus's southern edge as an ideal location for development. This is because the south end abuts directly to an elevated railroad track beyond which are clusters of heavy retail and commercial use areas including entertainment district businesses. These businesses not only serve the university population but increasingly target the fast-growing northwestern region of Seoul as a major regional activity hub.

Among university officials, it is an accepted norm that the academic environment should be at a distance from neighboring retail and commercial activity. Given that view, university officials regarded the elevated railroad track as a useful neighborhood separator to block the further expansion of the retail and commercial district from the academic environment. Because the district's real estate property ownership is significantly subdivided by individual landlords and building owners, most of whom have inherited the ownership from their parents, it is virtually impossible for Yonsei to expand toward the district.

The campus had expanded its functional boundary toward the east and northeast ends through a series of construction projects during the past two decades. Such campus growth has been accelerated by various nonregular academic training programs such as foreign language, executive training, and children's education, as well as other community service uses that have driven the continuous expansion of campus development toward the adjacent neighborhood.

Several factors led university officials to begin to view the south end positively for YERC. When the new administration came to office in 1992, the physical condition in and around the campus was deteriorating. It was due not to the sudden increase of the college population and new construction, but to a dramatic increase of vehicle ownership because of the economic growth in Korea and the resulting demand for parking spaces and changing commuting patterns, particularly by the students. Furthermore, the activities of professional graduate programs and campus visits by a nonuniversity population exacerbated the situation, particularly during evenings both on weekdays and weekends.

The new administration took the problem seriously and looked for a solution. Eventually, the university decided to make many inner campus roads free of vehicles by minimizing through-campus traffic. To do that, the university considered creating two large parking hubs next to the campus entrances: the first one (the YERC parking facility) next to the university gate in the south end, and the other in the north end (the Sanggyung Hall parking facility). Thus, they not only absorbed significant surface parking spaces, but also removed unnecessary through-campus vehicle traffic generated by students, staff, and visitors.

As the YERC's construction scheme developed through a series of Construction Committee meetings between the YERC TF and the university administration in 1994 and 1995, the maximization of underground parking capacity became a major concern. Subsequently, the committee decided to increase the parking capacity from the minimum of 420 to 550 and finally to 668 spaces. At present, the YERC parking garage accommodates 735 cars, and the Sanggyung Hall parking (completed in 1996) accommodates 364 cars. Two additional parking garages accommodate about 1,100 cars, more than half of the total of 2,000 on-campus parking spaces.

Furthermore, by creating such large parking facilities, the university aimed to generate significant operating cash revenue. In later months, the university adopted a campus-wide pay parking system and hired a private company to manage the parking facilities. Today, on average, 8,800 cars enter and exit the campus daily. In addition, an access road from the northwest gate to the northeast gate has become a popular paid bypass for adjacent community residents, particularly during commuting hours.[4] The demand for daily campus parking and through-campus vehicle traffic generates more than US$26,000 revenue per day.[5] Neighborhood dwellers go through the campus as a shortcut to their destinations, and the university charges a toll to cross the campus.

The corporate participants did not play a major role in YERC's site-identification process. But when the location was finalized, they became involved in the south end project, primarily due to the site's direct access to

Sungsan Avenue, a major road connecting Seoul's fast-growing northwest region, and its proximity to the domestic airport and the newly opened international airport (within an hour's drive).

Development Form and Use Programming

Accommodating the needs of the corporate sponsors of the R&D facilities into an academic campus raised two important questions, particularly for university planners and officials: First, what was the development trend on campus, and in what direction was recent campus expansion heading in terms of development form and density? Second, how could various functions of a corporate facility be integrated with neighboring academic uses?

When YERC was in the early planning stage, three important trends were observed in Yonsei's campus development: First, the scale of individual buildings noticeably increased, with significant commitment to intensive underground space development; second, individual buildings were being grouped due to their users' demand for physical interaction and shared infrastructure installation; third, campus activities were spreading out toward the adjacent neighborhoods, necessitating the decentralization of campus functions.[6]

More than half of the university property is designated as a Scenic Quality Preservation District (SQPD) by the Seoul Metropolitan Government (SMG) due to its highly valued natural topography of varied gentle slopes of vegetated hilly terrain (see Figure 7.4). This is a type of "overlay zone" within a residential zone, and the local governing body of SeoDaeMoon District Government (SDMG), on behalf of SMG, directly controls above-ground development density and bulkage with a floor-area ratio (FAR), as well as building height limits.

These local restrictions on the above-ground development drove planners to significantly increase underground development, particularly for required vehicle parking and for general supporting uses—auditorium, restaurant, and office space—which has been done since the mid-1990s.[7] In fact, 81 percent of all campus buildings today have basements, and most of Yonsei's buildings constructed since 1996 have more than three underground floors.

Such development practices pose two important problems for YERC: First, in order to allow natural light into deep underground levels, typically four basements, the perimeter of the buildings on the ground level must be heavily cut out to create the necessary intermediate access space. Construction not only necessitates heavy access steps and ramps to the building entrance, but also loses a building facade while being isolated from the neighboring buildings and context. These individual, project-based, large-scale developments have made it difficult to create a unified campus image and to achieve

Figure 7.4 **Overview of the Scenic Quality Preservation District, Yonsei University**

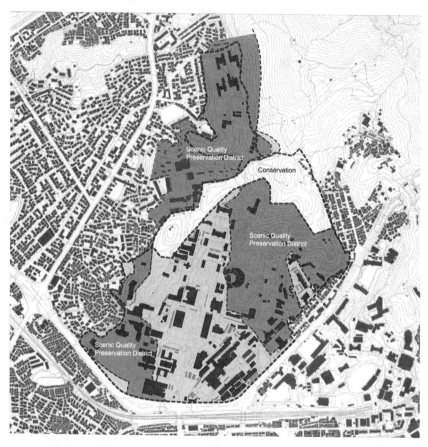

a long-term, campus-wide integrated master plan. Second, as the campus is already nearly built out, it has become increasingly difficult to find available large on-campus sites, and it is necessary to look for properties from local private and public landowners.

The heavy underground development is particularly outstanding in YERC's case, which utilizes a sloped site. In fact, the site of YERC was designated an SQPD; thus, the height of a proposed YERC building could not exceed seven stories above ground. The height control resulted in YERC being four stories above ground and five floors of basement, with a possibility of an expansion of up to three additional stories in the future.

Meanwhile, the corporate donors influenced the building-use programming

Table 7.2

Facilities of the YERC

Floor	Area (m²)	Use	Tenant
4th	4,803	Lab, research units, office	Hyundai, KTF
3rd	5,116	Lab, research units, office	LG/SaePoong/Yonsei
2nd	5,210	Lab, research units, office	Samsung/Yonsei
1st	6,141	Lab, research units, office	Daewoo/Yonsei
Base 1	9,644	Lab, dining, retail, auditorium	PoolMooWon/Yonsei
Base 2	10,603	Lab, parking (207 cars)	—
Base 3	10,673	Parking (225 cars)	—
Base 4	5,268	Parking (118 cars)	—
Base 5	9,373	Parking (118 cars), mechanical, water treatment	—
Total	66,831	Parking (668 cars) + ground level (49 cars)	—

throughout the design development process. The university hired a building design consultant to conduct a series of preoccupancy surveys to identify potential tenants' specific needs for R&D facilities and various supporting equipment, including telecommunication infrastructure and security systems, particularly for intelligent building design, building automation, integrated cardkey systems, CCTV, and office automation.

As a result, YERC became a mixed-use R&D building with a total floor space of 67,000 square meters (721,182 square feet). The building includes retail space and restaurants (7,500 square meters), an auditorium (248 seats), and a four-story underground parking garage for 668 cars, as well as office and R&D space (23,400 square meters) that accommodates forty research units of the Engineering Colleg—-including corporate branch research labs for firms such as LG CNS, Samsung SDI, KTF, and Qualcomm—and features fourteen research centers for the Engineering School plus venture incubating facilities such as YTBC and SETSG (see Table 7.2.).

This dynamic implies that, increasingly, campus planners had to consider the following important campus-wide use programming: first, how to best group R&D facilities so they could expand rapidly and continuously, proximity between buildings also being important for physical interaction in a collaborative scholastic and corporate environment; second, how to best program the corporate R&D and supporting uses to enable easy access to building functions to promote interaction between corporate players and academics yet allow them a certain degree of isolation from institutional uses.

Given such space programming needs, various building support elements that act as circulation mediators became important functional tools for campus planners. They included an overhanging bridge between two buildings, a ground-level arcade, a colonnade, a facade pergola for ground-level buildings, and an underground concourse as a comprehensive connector to academic classrooms, labs, offices, facilities, auditorium, parking, and so forth.

This locally grouped form in a section of the campus is evident in the complex of Engineering Buildings 1, 2, and 3; YERC; and the new technology center complex currently under construction. In particular, due to its functional nature, YERC requires easy public access from outside, yet it contains a corporate climate that is more closed than a university's with regard to access, security, safety, and building management.

In fact, YERC's south end location offers direct access from the street, which serves to minimize access to the campus core yet maximize public street access. Furthermore, since interconnection between buildings was a key for YERC, bridges and basement corridors were added to the design. A walk-through overhanging bridge (funded by POSCO Corporation) was built in September 1999 (immediately after YERC's opening) to connect YERC with other engineering buildings.

Since R&D facilities are becoming popular at Yonsei and on many major campuses in Korea, they have prompted campus planners to develop sound yet flexible planning practices of use programming. For example, various supporting and logistics facilities—such as hotels, convention centers, conference halls, visitor parking, and retail and commercial space—are becoming necessary next to the campus. Thus, instead of a single master plan for an entire campus, more strategic and precinct-based plans for building groups are becoming indispensable. Yonsei is also presently planning to build an underground complex of a guest house and faculty club, as well as a concert and exhibition space next to YERC, under the existing baseball and soccer fields.

Space Ownership and Long-Term Tenancy

The YERC project should address the development concerns of stakeholders to accommodate corporate R&D activities on the academic campus. Such a development illustrates the changing role of a university with a pragmatic attitude as an institutional developer. Meanwhile, private corporations aim to capitalize on their donations beyond their occupancy for operational business activities as long-term investment strategies.

What has made campus development in Korea unique is that the developer does not have the clear-cut role of an investor that is typically observed in the development framework overseas. In fact, a university that holds the ownership of a given project property often finances the development from its various financial resources. This is mainly due to the conservative development culture

Table 7.3

Corporate Donors of the YERC Project

Donor	$ million	₩ billion
Daewoo	7.8	7.0
Hyundai	7.8	7.0
KTF	7.8	7.0
LG	7.8	7.0
PoolMooWon	4.4 + 2.8*	4.0 + 2.5*
SaePoong	1.6	1.4
Samsung	7.8	7.0
Ministry of Commerce and Trade	0.6	0.5
University Matching Fund	22.2	20.0
Total	70.4	63.4

*Noncash donation.

and the public view, in which a university as a nonprofit organization is not supposed to be in the profit-making business. Thus, the university does not want to get a profit-oriented private professional developer involved with its campus development.[8]

In the case of YERC, as the site was being finalized by the university administration, the YERC TF launched a nationwide fundraising drive to secure an estimated project cost of $50 million. Eventually, the total project cost jumped to $87.5 million ($75 million in construction costs, $10 million in earthwork costs, and $2.5 million in design consultation fees). Led by faculty members and acting independently of the university administration, the YERC TF contacted several major corporations via their personal contacts to solicit $7.8 million in donations for securing the building construction.

Two issues in the development scenario deserve further examination from the perspectives of the university administration and the corporate donors: first, whether donations are conditional, that is, whether the donor attaches any strings to it; second, whether a donation is a calculated action to obtain tax incentives from the local district government of SDMG and SMG.

When YERC was in the planning stage, seven corporations expressed interest in giving donations: Daewoo Motors, Hyundai Electronics, KTF, LG Group, PoolMooWon, SaePoong, and Samsung. They did actually donate to YERC (see Table 7.3), and it appears that they did not set any direct requirements for their donations during the planning stage. It also appears that their donations were motivated by faculty members' personal relationships with high-ranking administrators of the donors.

It has been argued that YERC TF members' long personal relationships with decision makers of donor corporations were the single most important factor in corporations' decision to donate. In fact, a few of the seven corporate donors were major beneficiaries of technical innovation and research work previously completed by the task force faculty. Thus, they were willing to help the committee members' fund drive.

In acknowledging the donations, the university decided to award long-term occupancy rights in the new buildings to the corporate donors or their branch affiliates. During this process, the university first established a detailed "guiding principle of donation of building space and return procedure for corporate donors." Under that contract, each donor obtained occupancy rights to 2,000 square meters of R&D space at YERC for thirty years.

It appears that the corporate donations were motivated not by any expectation of direct tax abatement or tax incentive, but rather by advertising promotions and corporate image-making. Corporate business activities in Korea are subject to two types of taxes by national and municipal governments. The first is a "resident citizen tax"—10 percent of a corporation's taxable income—imposed on corporations by the local government. A university construction donation, however, is not subject to any direct tax incentive from the SDMG or the SMG. The second is a national "corporate (income) tax," which is 15 to 27 percent of corporations' taxable income.[9]

In 1995, YERC TF also secured funds from the national government to realize the YERC project. It first received an indirect subsidy of $0.6 million from the Ministry of Trade and Industry for the construction of YERC as a nationwide initiative for technology and industrial infrastructure investment. In addition, the university obtained the indirect subsidy of an income tax abatement from the SDMG for leasing building space immediately after the construction. This agreement required that the prospective tenants should be small start-ups or medium-sized ventures that would collaborate with the university on R&D activities.

Yet, even today, debates rage not only over R&D activities at YERC, but over the relationship between universities and local governments nationwide, specifically about how to define R&D activities performed jointly by nonprofit academic organizations and for-profit corporations. The debate revolves around whether R&D is a taxable profit-making activity. Of significance is, as previously mentioned, R&D's ultimate goal to commercialize the products and processes from science and engineering research.[10]

The debate over taxing academic R&D activities involves two types of taxes imposed on both the university and the corporations. First, although the university is not considered a property tax payer because it is a nonprofit organization, the accommodation of R&D activities on campus should be interpreted as a real estate leasing business activity, which is subject to building property tax and land property tax. Second, corporate R&D activity that aims to pursue corporate profit making should be subject to income tax. Thus, the definition and interpretation of R&D activities on campus have been an important legal issue with regard to conditions and qualifications.

The Public Sector as Development Controller

Campus development at Yonsei is controlled by two levels of regulatory framework enforced by SeoDaeMoon District Government, a local governing body, and its larger metropolitan entity, the Seoul Metropolitan Government. They regulate the physical form and density of development projects, as well as the use and type of activities to take place in the buildings.

The development control of YERC should be observed from the public sector's changing view of university buildings in past years and its influence on the campus development as a direct and indirect development regulator. Important questions include what rationale underlay the public sector's shifting view, and how such dynamics actually have affected development control through which regulatory mechanism.

In recent years, the SMG has recognized that the university provides many benefits to the city and its residents that go beyond the campus boundaries, such as cultural resources, open space, and a regional economic engine. This view requires that campus development be in step with the city's long-range master plan, and thus it should be directly guided by the metropolitan government, rather than by a local governing body, as previously.

Until recently, university construction was regarded as a typical private development for residential, retail, and commercial uses within a community neighborhood. Thus, campus development was directly within local regulatory jurisdiction throughout the development process. Under such jurisdiction, while a final construction permit for campus development was officially issued by the SMG, most of the regulatory controls, such as building permits and architectural codes and design reviews, were administered by a local government. Accordingly, the local zoning ordinance of the SDMG has approved the bulk of physical development on the campus during the past few decades. In fact, a local zoning ordinance classifies 238 acres (963,000 square meters) of the university property into two zones—"Residential" and "Conservation."[11]

The SQPD also directly controls the bulk of campus construction and, in particular, limits building height to three stories, or twelve meters, with a maximum allowance of seven stories, or twenty-eight meters. Today, most of the Residential zone inside and outside of the SQPD appears fully developed. The SQPD has been the most influential regulation to direct the path of on-campus development since its adoption in the late 1970s.

YERC's site, as mentioned earlier, is zoned Residential within an overlay zone of SQPD that allows a development floor area ratio (FAR) of 3 with a maximum seven-story structure. The SDMG's Zoning Approval Board reviewed the YERC proposal for a construction permit to ensure that basic regulatory requirements such as building use, FAR, and height limits were satisfied. Subsequently, the SDMG's Architectural Department also reviewed a series of construction regulation requirements such as the Building Energy Conservation Code and the Fire Code, as well as the guidelines of building color, soil and earthwork, and architectural design. This process was followed by a Traffic Impact Assessment from the SMG, so that the university could obtain final approval for a building permit from the SMG.

However, this campus construction permitting practice underwent a significant shift in recent years. As of August 2002, the Ministry of Construction and Transportation adopted an ordinance that designates higher educational facilities and buildings as "Urban Planning Facilities," along with ports, airports, and parks. In this regard, as the Urban Planning Act states, "The development and installment of an Urban Planning Facility should coincide with the City Management Plan and the Citywide Long-Range Plan."

Such a change highlights that campus building construction is no longer simple individual building construction. All new university structures and buildings must be reviewed within the context of the larger metropolitan region. Thus, they should be directly controlled via an "institutional master plan" by the SMG's Urban Planning Review Committee, instead of by SDMG's board. This change directly involves the density, mass, and height of all campus development by the SMG.[12]

Under the direct control of SMG, the university must pursue two types of permitting procedures from SMG and SDMG, respectively. First, it must submit a campus-wide midrange development plan for SMG approval, prior to any construction. A university that anticipates continuous construction should obtain campus-wide development approval on a regular basis, preferably every two to three years. The approval procedure often takes six months to a year and is intended to focus on campus-wide development density of FAR, building coverage, and height requirements, rather than on individual buildings—similar to a "planned unit development" concept overseas.[13]

Second, the university should also file a request for a construction permit from the local governing body for each building. The request should provide a profile of the proposed building and the Architectural Regulation Code requirement, including building use, setback, height limit, mechanicals, parking, and fire codes. This process often takes one to two months. If the floor area of a proposed project is greater than 100,000 square meters, a Traffic Impact Assessment also is required by the Ministry of Construction and Transportation.

What matters for a university administration under such a thick layer of regulation are the following three obstacles. The first is the overall length of the construction review procedure, which can take from six months to a year or more. In the words of an associate of Yonsei's Facility Management Department, the development of university buildings "is getting more and more difficult than ever before" due to the long permitting process. The direct involvement by SMG makes campus construction scheduling difficult due to the academic calendar, particularly in the case of a semester-sensitive project, such as student dormitories.

The second obstacle is opposition from the neighborhood residents and business owners, particularly if a project involves zoning revision. Under normal circumstances, campus construction proceeds quickly as long as there is no opposition from the neighborhood. In most cases, since the development takes place within the university property, serious public opposition does not occur in the early planning stages. In recent years, the university appealed to the local zoning board to revise the regulation to make it more favorable to campus development in the adjacent neighborhood. The effort ran into opposition from community residents who worried about the possible degradation of the single-family neighborhood by multifamily residential development by private developers.

Third, as R&D facilities are growing bigger and taking on a clustered form in general, public and private properties scattered throughout the campus have been a serious obstacle for continuous and fast-paced expansion of R&D development. In fact, a significant amount of space within the campus boundaries is owned by the SDMG, the SMG, and the national government as a form of right-of-way, easement, or other public use. Further development of or around such land is possible only if the university purchases the land or somehow incorporates it.

R&D facility development is also indirectly controlled in nonphysical ways by the regulation of development-related activities in both property acquisition and property operation stages: The first concerns whether to view R&D facility construction activity on campus as a real estate property acquisition activity; the second concerns whether to view R&D activities as taxable business activities in a property operation stage.

If YERC were viewed as a corporate R&D facility regardless of its physical location in an academic setting, two types of taxes and "exaction" would be imposed in the construction stage. The first is a "real estate acquisition tax" imposed by registering the ownership of the new real estate property of YERC (2 percent plus 0.2 percent of citizen tax of total project development costs). The second is a "real estate acquisition registration fee" (3 percent of total project development costs). In addition, YERC would be assessed a

Traffic Impact Fee (a sum of total floor area of building use multiplied by a trip generation multiplier coefficient) by SMG.

The two real estate taxes and the exaction account for a significant portion of the cost of development, particularly in the construction stage. YERC was exempt from these three direct and indirect taxes because it was viewed as an institutional use of the campus. Otherwise, the operation of YERC would also be subject to corporate income taxes as a real estate business activity. Until recently, such indirect fiscal incentives helped facilitate fast-paced campus development that was mostly limited to within a university's property boundaries.

Conclusion

The modern campus of Yonsei University includes two types of development patterns: first, a campus-wide spread from its core toward adjacent neighborhoods; second, an intensive, localized, dense cluster complex. The dynamic transformation of the campus has recently been accelerated by privately funded R&D facility development, especially at the campus property edge. Such a locational shift is due to, along with land availability, the functional independence of the R&D facility from the existing academic establishments to allow independent public access. Once established, the R&D facility expanded incrementally to the adjacent site to form an independent mega cluster next to the existing engineering and science buildings, illustrating the importance of physical proximity for intellectual and collaborative interaction between scholarship and corporate application.

The R&D facility development represents the university's pragmatic response to the market demand for science and engineering applications with a proactive initiative to channel technology transfer through corporate R&D activities. Yet the accommodation of the R&D facility necessitates various auxiliary and supporting entities, such as convention centers, hotels, retail stores, restaurants, and others.

For university decision makers, such dynamic development poses a challenge to create a model for a new campus plan to manage its ever growing expansion yet to unify the decentralized clusters as a whole. Traditionally, as the university's functional boundaries have spread evenly from the core toward its periphery, dormitories have been an essential element for decentralization of the campus, particularly for residential universities; but Yonsei, as a metropolitan university, is not a residential university and does not plan to be one. It is evident that for Yonsei the time has come to pursue a strategic plan for the inevitable shift from a consolidated, campus-wide master plan to a precinct-based, localization plan of decentralization. Such a change will require an enormous effort to reshape goals, strategies, and decision-making procedures for the university administration.

University campus planners also face the challenging tasks of how to accommodate private corporate R&D facilities and support mixed uses in an institutional setting and how to make them integrated into not only the university but also the physical, social, and cultural environments of the adjacent community. Conventionally, the focus of campus master plans has been the "form-giving" or "image-making" of physical features within an academic setting. The YERC development implies that campus planning should address the issue of use programming that satisfies various users on and off campus. Such a requirement necessitates a wide range of participation from academic, community, and corporate players who can work collaboratively to enhance the quality of use, circulation, and public access for academic and corporate facilities.

This decentralizing development trend has produced a blurred functional boundary between campus and community in a physical context. Recently, several universities in SMA have implemented the construction of various cultural resources such as an auditorium, concert hall, gallery, and museum. Furthermore, they have increasingly made university libraries, student centers, and even major outdoor campus areas accessible to the public in an effort to reach out to the community and embrace it as an integral part of the academic culture.

In that regard, the definition of *campus* today, particularly in a metropolitan area, goes beyond the traditional meaning of the academic campus—a property of grounds and buildings owned and controlled by a university. Thus this chapter proposes a functional definition of the university campus, in which the academic, the corporate, and the community share not only the physical aspect of the campus, but also a variety of educational, social, and entrepreneurial activities in both on- and off-campus settings.

As exemplified by the YERC case, the university is assumed to play two proactive roles: first, of a project initiator to build an institutionalized channel for commercial undertakings; second, of a land provider in partnership development with private corporations that make a contribution to the project cost. This transformation of the roles has changed the way the public views the university's contribution to society, as well as the way the public sector controls campus development. As a result, inevitable conflict has occurred between the academic nature of the university and the business aspect of the corporation in regard to their civic service to society.

Given the positive impacts from R&D activity in general, the important questions are who will benefit from it and how to manage its subsequent impact on the larger-scale community in a metropolitan area. In past decades, what the university tried to obtain from early R&D partnerships with the national government were the benefits from scientific breakthroughs in atomic energy, radar, air flight, and computers. But now the main goals of the university's partnership with the private sector have shifted to the timely transfer and application of science and technology; the creation of collaborative research opportunities for students, graduates, and faculty; and, ultimately, a good economic return from the development investment.

As observed in the case of YERC, the local municipality and the national government have the capacity to control the private R&D development on campus, along with the physical and nonphysical regulatory frameworks such as taxes and zoning regulations. The SMG's recent revision of the regulatory framework for university facility development reflects a considerable interest in its citywide impact on job creation, public well-being, and long-term economic benefits, going beyond the conventional policy on the physical characteristics of the academic environment. Yet the public sector still faces the challenge of assisting the university's interaction with the private sector for their mutual benefit, of making relevant policies more comprehensive and embracing than regulatory and controlling.

Notes

1. Yonsei University consists of 19 colleges, 18 graduate schools, 105 research institutes and hospitals and serves 46,677 people, including 18,839 undergraduates, 9,106 graduates, 1,325 faculty, 472 university staff, and 4,159 hospital staff. Its annual budget is $1.1 billion, which accounts for 10 percent of the combined budget of about 230 private universities in Korea and is 11.3 percent of the annual budget of the Seoul Metropolitan Government. Yonsei was founded in 1885 by Dr. Horace G. Underwood as a center for learning based on Christian principles (*Annual Statistics of Yonsei University*, 2002, Seoul, Korea: Yonsei University).

2. Many public and private institutions nationwide were competing to collaborate with industry to build research parks, including Inha (1994), Dongah (1995), Korea (1996), Joennam (1998), Choongbook (1999), and Hanyang (2000). Their efforts aimed to obtain cooperation from municipal governments as well as corporate business sectors to form a sustained regional research and commercial complex.

3. Such localized campus development plans include the First Master Plan (1915), Yonsei Forward 10-Year Plan (1958), Plan for Yonsei's 100th Year (1972), Blueprint for Yonsei's 100 Years (1974), Preparing Yonsei's 100th Year (1976), and Long-Range Plan (1978).

4. During commuting hours, the busiest entrance gate is the northwest gate, whose incoming traffic accounts for 39 percent of all incoming vehicles (34 percent via northeast gate and 27 percent via the main south gate). The busiest exit gate during the same hours is the northeast gate, whose outgoing traffic accounts for 42 percent (36 percent for the main south gate and 22 percent for the northwest gate).

5. The university has about 3,000 regular daily parking commuters and 5,300 visitor parkers, who park for around an hour for a $5 fee.

6. Most buildings at Yonsei have significantly increased in both floor area and mass. Such large-scale building complexes increased with the construction of Yonsei's Central Library and its Cancer Hospital in the early 1980s. In fact, the average building floor area increased to well beyond 20,000 square meters—for example, the Yonsei Engineering Research Center (67,000 square meters), the College of Business and Economics (29,000 square meters), and the College of Science (22,000 square meters).

7. To cope with development restrictions, several Korean universities such as Korea, Ewha, Sugang, and Gookmin included in their master plan strategies to develop underground spaces, mostly under their athletic fields for bookstores, theaters, galleries, student centers, libraries, parking, and administrative offices. Korea University has successfully completed such a project, and Ewha recently announced a proposal for underground space development in an international design competition.

8. Universities in Korea, as tax-exempt organizations, have historically avoided the roles of investor and developer. They do not commit to aggressive profit-oriented, long-term investment projects that may create a negative public image. Until recently, universities have often taken a passive attitude toward proactive campus development. Thus, the building developments at Yonsei have often been initiated and financed by an individual college rather than the university administration. In most large-scale real estate development projects in Korea, professional developers have no formal role and no control of the project; their typical role is simply to invest financial resources in the projects. A project initiator and coordinator, often called *SiHang-Sa* get a construction company involved in the project. With the construction company's credit, the SiHang-Sa is able to finance the project indirectly by borrowing cash from a bank. In this scenario, the construction company is not only the physical builder but also a financial player in the Korean real estate market.

9. In general, corporations consider donations a type of operational cost, which should be deducted from their profit line; thus, there is a direct incentive for donating. Within this context, corporate donations are generally seen as a type of advertising fee; announcements often appear in newspapers and alumni magazines and other media. In some cases, whether or not they donate as an indirect advertising strategy for image making and corporate identity promotion, corporate donors often cross their fingers in the hope that their donation will have more broad and enduring effects among students. Maximum amounts of donations to nonprofits are based on the objective of the donation: 5 percent of taxable income for direct scholarship and 50 percent for building construction. Once the university receives the corporate donation, it puts the donated money tentatively in an "educational activity fund" for future use.

10. Currently, the District of SungBook and two universities (Korea University and the Korea Institute of Science and Technology) in the SMA are engaged in a legal dispute with regard to the construction of R&D complexes and semiconductor manufacturing facilities and the taxation of R&D activities. The conflict arose when the two universities sought public approval and construction permits from the District of SungBook.

11. The first citywide zoning ordinance was introduced in 1934 by the Japanese colonial government and was revised in 1952 immediately after the Land Reform Act in 1950. The Conservation class was introduced with the first Urban Planning Act, in 1962, by the Ministry of Construction and Transportation of Korea, and was later revised. Most of the university's land is zoned Residential, which accounts for 212 acres (857,900 square meters), or 89 percent, of the campus. The campus development in the Residential zone is more tightly controlled by the Scenic Quality Preservation

District, a type of overlay zone designated by the SMG. This overlay zone regulation aims to prevent excessive high-density development in a Residential area. The SQPD accounts for 116 acres (469,400 square meters), or 54.7 percent, of the Residential zone area within the campus. The rest of the property is zoned Conservation, which covers 26 acres (105,200 square meters), or 11 percent, of the campus. This Conservation zone strictly blocks development encroachment from the campus's environmentally sensitive areas (40 percent or greater slope, eighty-plus meters in elevation, productive soil, and heavy vegetation).

This Conservation zone, along with the SQPD, has been the most critical tool for the public sector to control campus development. After it was adopted by the Ministry of Construction and Transportation in the early 1960s, new campus building projects began to look for locations in the campus's perimeter beyond the Conservation zone, particularly in the east and northeast areas, and primarily the Residential zone, for more buildable space.

12. Such drastic action appears to have resulted from a long dispute between the university and neighborhood residents and businesses that started with the construction of a Seoul National University (SNU) museum in early 2000. At that time, SNU wanted to build its museum next to the university gate, which required the significant cutback of an adjacent hill. This proposal ran into serious objection from a group of environmentalists and from the community and subsequently became a rallying social issue.

13. This system, referred to above as an institutional master plan, is practiced by universities in Boston, whose development process is controlled by the Boston Redevelopment Authority.

References

Bender, Thomas. 1988. *The University and the City from Medieval Origins to the Present.* New York: Oxford University Press.

Duderstadt, James J. 2003. *A University for the 21st Century.* Ann Arbor: University of Michigan Press.

Harvard Magazine. 2001. "The Politics of Campus Planning." March–April.

Martin, Pearce. 2001. *University Builders.* New York: Willey-Academy.

Simha, Robert. 2001. *MIT Campus Planning, 1960–2000.* Cambridge, MA: MIT Press.

Turner, Paul Venable. 1984. *Campus: An American Planning Tradition.* Cambridge, MA: MIT Press.

Yonsei University. 2002. *Annual Statistics of Yonsei University.* Seoul, Korea: Author.

———. 2003. *Annual Statistics of Yonsei University.* Seoul, Korea: Author.

8

Urban and Real Estate Development of the Central University of Venezuela's Rental Zone

Abner J. Colmenares

Since its foundation in 1721, the Central University of Venezuela (UCV) has been a public institution that has contributed not only to the scientific, technological, and cultural development of Venezuela, but also to the urban growth of the city of Caracas. The development of the Caracas University City (CUC), university campus of the UCV, has been a key factor in the city's urban structural and morphological shaping. In fact, the construction of the CUC carried out in the 1940s had a positive impact on the development of the city's Plaza Venezuela–Sabana Grande sector, subsequently fostering the real estate appreciation of that part of the city during the 1950s and 1960s.

The CUC master plan, designed by architect Carlos Raúl Villanueva in 1947, allowed for the creation of a campus with an area of over two hundred hectares and included the creation of the Plaza Venezuela Rental Zone (ZRPV), an extra ten-hectare area for real estate development that would generate resources to financially support the scientific activities carried out by the UCV. To this end, in 1974 the Venezuelan government created the Andrés Bello Fund Foundation for the Scientific Development of the Central University of Venezuela (FFABUCV), which is aimed at developing the ZRPV into a great city-scale business, commercial, and recreational center. This chapter outlines the work of the FFABUCV as it has set out to realize the development goals of the city and the university in the ZRPV. In so doing, the chapter will set the stage for the ZRPV with a description of the development of Caracas University City, followed by a historical overview of the ZRPV and the nature of urban development there, especially planned large-scale development beginning in 1984. The chapter will focus on how well such activity can foster new planning and design processes with which to transform the city conditions and meet the needs of the UCV. The chapter concludes with a consideration of how well the ZRPV can achieve a balance between the need to create public spaces for a capital city and the particular interests of investors, in order to ensure a place with a high quality of life. In the strategic attempt to meet such a balance, can the ZRPV's development be a successful real estate venture, so that the FFABUCV can meet its objectives and accomplish its mission by generating resources for UCV's research funding?

The Plaza Venezuela Rental Zone

The Plaza Venezuela Rental Zone is a large-scale urban project located at the heart of the metropolitan area of the city of Caracas, Venezuela, in the vicinity of the Caracas University City headquarters and campus of the Central University of Venezuela.[1] As to the plot, it is an exceptional portion of land, located at the geographical center of the city and bordering on the main entrance to the CUC. It joins the downtown area with the east and south of the city valley. It enjoys outstanding vehicle and pedestrian accessibility through the city's vehicular and subway systems, including direct connections with one main expressway and three nearby subway stations. This project will foster cutting-edge technology in business, commercial, lodging, and recreational facilities, as well as fully equipped services. It will be built on the land of the rental zone, property of the FFABUCV.

The FFABUCV has been planning the urban and real estate development of the ZRPV since 1984. For this purpose, its board of directors has drafted a set of strategies and actions in line with the Master Plan for the Urban Development and Design of the Rental Zone of the UCV,[2] elaborated by Insurbeca, a consulting firm at the Institute of City Planning of the UCV.[3] The design of the buildings and other elements of the ZRPV has been made in accordance with the zoning regulation of the rental zone sector[4] and the *Urban Design Bylaw*, also drafted by Insurbeca. This zoning regulation sets land uses and construction figures for the entire area, whose specific spatial distribution is based on guidelines of construction design included in the Master Plan. The Urban Design Bylaw "defines the guidelines for architectural or engineering projects for the development of the ZRPV, in order to achieve harmony and integration of the different elements, spaces and buildings of this urban complex."[5] The ZRPV will have a gross floor area of 6,886,400 square feet, a central location, accessibility, great potential for diverse activities, flexibility to adapt to market demands, design and quality controls, and a large variety of land uses. It is bound to become the most important large-scale urban project in Caracas, revitalizing one of the most symbolic spaces of the city: the business and commercial strip of Plaza Venezuela–Sabana Grande (Figure 8.1).

This chapter describes a unique case of long-term planning of a large-scale urban project carried out within the framework of political and economic turmoil and promoted by a public university. It is unique because (1) the ZRPV consists

Figure 8.1   **Proposed Rental Zone**

of land granted by the state to the UCV for the development of a real estate venture; (2) the real estate development of the ZRPV is controlled by a public body; (3) the FFABUCV is a nonprofit corporation whose real estate strategy is based on its association with private investors; and (4) all profits produced by real estate development of the ZRPV (once operation costs have been deducted) are to be transferred to the UCV for its scientific development.

The Andrés Bello Fund Foundation for the Scientific Development of the Central University of Venezuela

The foundation—known in Spanish as *Fundación Fondo Andrés Bello para el Desarrollo Científico de la Universidad Central de Venezuela*—is a nonprofit corporation set up by the Venezuelan state in 1974 to promote scientific development of the Central University of Venezuela.[6] It was endowed by the Venezuelan state with the real estate patrimony of the rental zone of Plaza Venezuela in the city of Caracas.[7] These lands were granted by the state to the FFABUCV, so that it could profit from its real estate development and transfer the revenues to the UCV.[8] For this purpose, and based on its corporate bylaws, the foundation has given priority to the appreciation of its economic value through real estate development of the lands.[9]

The FFABUCV enjoys autonomous management status and submits annual reports only to its tutelary entity.[10] Since 2001, the FFABUCV has been completely under the tutelary attachment to the UCV.[11] It does not receive any type of funding from the UCV. It has raised its capital by renting land or available space in provisional buildings that have been on the plot since the moment of the granting. Additionally, it has raised considerable capital through the granting of the usufruct rights of a land lot to private investors for the development of a shopping mall.

The strategies for the development of the rental zone have been designed by the foundation with the support of the board of directors, a collegiate group that, according to its corporate bylaws, is in charge of approving the operations of the foundation and its development plans and overseeing the accomplishment of the institutional objectives.[12] Since 2003, the FFABUCV has kept a permanent and fluent relation with the UCV through its rector and other authorities, who have been involved in workshops held recently for the definition of strategies and actions for the development of the rental zone.[13]

Development of the Rental Zone and UCV's Institutional Development Interests

The decisions on real estate or financial matters concerning the development of the ZRPV are neither related to nor shall be they affected by the UCV's institutional development interests, due to the foundation's autonomous management status. Moreover, as the foundation's mission and the use of the lands have been statutorily defined, there is no room for a possible influence of the university on such decisions. The UCV authorities have been very aware—and have acknowledged—that the FFABUCV's activities are strongly related to the expectations and demands of the real estate market and to national economic and financial vicissitudes. Nevertheless, since the foundation is aware of the problems faced by the UCV due to its deficiencies regarding the campus infrastructure, it has granted an area of 110,828 square feet in another rental zone, known as Plaza de las Tres Gracias, for the development of educational buildings, so as to provide some of the space needed to carry out postgraduate teaching and research activities.

Development of Caracas University City

Caracas University City, known in Spanish as *Ciudad Universitaria de Caracas*, is a large architectural complex with an area of 498.94 acres.[14] CUC is the headquarters and main campus of the Central University of Venezuela, which is the oldest, largest, most important university in the country, with a population of over 50,000 students, 5,000 professors, and 6,000 employees.

Figure 8.2   **Overview of Caracas University City Campus**

CUC is the masterpiece of the Venezuelan architect Carlos Raúl Villanueva. It comprises 65 buildings, including an assistance and clinical hospital, all surrounded by vast gardens (Figure 8.2). One of the entrances is flanked by the UCV Botanical Garden, which is not only a national park, but also the headquarters of the Institute of Botanical Research and the National Herbarium, with an area of 148.20 acres, additional to the area of the campus. Furthermore, CUC boasts 107 artworks of large dimensions that blend seamlessly into the architecture and public spaces. Sculptures, murals, and stained-glass windows form an outdoor museum of modern art—all part of the project of "Synthesis of the Arts," as Villanueva conceived it.

Conditions in the UCV That Led to the Creation of the CUC

For more than two hundred years, the main buildings of the UCV were located in the colonial Convent of San Francisco, near the National Congress and Bolívar Square, in the old quarter of the city of Caracas.[15] By 1943, the student population had increased fourfold in a ten-year period, reaching 2,380 students that year,[16] but despite efforts to modernize the old facilities, they were simply inappropriate for activities of higher education in accordance with modern teaching and research standards.[17]

The idea of a new university campus for the UCV came to life during the administration of President General Isaías Medina Angarita.[18] It began with the creation of the City University Institute (ICU), which was attached to the Ministry of Public Works (MOP) and aimed at planning and building a modern campus for the university. The ICU was endowed with autonomous legal status, its own patrimony and autonomous management, and it was independent of the decision-making bodies of the UCV. The first task undertaken by the ICU was the design of the university hospital. In addition, a commission was appointed for the selection of the land and the development of the urban complex plan for the university campus.[19] This commission was led by Villanueva as project manager.

Conditions in Caracas That Led to the Creation of the CUC

Caracas's urban form in the 1940s was one of a low-density, rural country just beginning to show signs of the transition from an agricultural economy to one dependent on oil revenues.[20] Between 1906 and 1936, the city faced important changes in growth patterns and urban development. The central, colonial quarter of the city was no longer the focal point of urban growth, around which the town had grown in concentric circles from its foundation in 1567 until 1906.

As a consequence of the automobile boom, there was a chaotic, scattered growth of urban activities, especially to the east of the valley. A number of private initiatives fostered the construction of residential quarters for the middle and upper classes in what had been large extensions of farmlands, bringing about a migration of people from the center to the east of the city. The old quarter still kept political, administrative, commercial, financial, and productive activities[21] and that part of the city was connected to the new subcenters of the east through only one roadway.[22]

In this changing and dynamic urban context, the commission led by Villanueva—after evaluating other locations—proposed for the construction of the CUC the land belonging to the Ibarra Hacienda, an area located right in the geographical center of the valley in an urban sector formerly considered the boundary between downtown and the peripheral area. This land plot adjoined the growing area of Sabana Grande, where new stores began to appear and office buildings were constructed to meet the demands of the emerging middle class. It was also conveniently located near Los Caobos Park (a 103.74-acre area), where the recently built museums of fine arts and natural science—both designed by Villanueva—were located.

Carlos Raúl Villanueva and the Caracas University City Project

The planning of the CUC began in 1943.[23] The different Venezuelan governments that supported its creation granted financial resources for its construction and conducted strict monitoring of the plan and the works.[24] The decisions that gave final shape to the CUC were in fact made by government advisors and technicians, and not by university authorities.[25] The planning and design were originally made through the MOP and then through the ICU. In 1958, after the overthrow of President General Marcos Pérez Jiménez, the Division of Planning of the UCV was created. From that moment on, the university ruled autonomously over planning and enlargement of its headquarters.

In his first proposal of 1944, Carlos Raúl Villanueva designed a university campus with an urban complex plan defined by a neoclassical scheme, in which axial symmetry prevailed for the layout of buildings and green areas. Volumes and outdoor spaces were articulated on a monumental axis beginning with the medical complex and ending with the sports area. The construction works of the first stage began in 1944, the University Hospital and the Faculty of Medicine being the most representative buildings.

The second stage of the CUC started in 1958. Villanueva's new urban proposal for the complex broke with the symmetry of the original plan, changing it radically to a freer and more organic scheme. The project discarded the strict symmetrical definition of the urban complex plan through a new building layout in favor of a clear setting of the boundaries of the functional areas. The CUC was articulated on a flexible distributive scheme, bounded by a system that separated vehicle and pedestrian flow. Covered pedestrian ways allowed people to access any area of the campus protected from the elements. The pedestrian network was a fluent system in which the first floor of every building blended into its exterior. During this stage, the Cultural and Directive Center was also built, comprising the Central Library, the Aula Magna (main assembly hall, providing a seating capacity of three hundred people),[26] the Covered Square,[27] and other important buildings, such as the concert hall and the main administrative building. The Cultural and Directive Center constitutes the heart of the university and is located at the core of the campus, east of the medical area. The importance and transcendence of Villanueva's masterpiece were acknowledged by UNESCO, when in 2000 it included the CUC in the World Heritage List.[28]

Villanueva divided the campus into specific zones: health, science and technology, humanities and arts, and sports. In 1947 he also planned a rental zone that could generate additional income for the university's maintenance.

Historical Background of the Plaza Venezuela Rental Zone

The Concept of Rental Zone

A *rental zone* is historically defined as land granted by the state to national universities to finance their scientific activities, so as to promote financial autonomy through the use of real estate to generate profit.

The notion of rental zone dates back to the transition of the UCV from an institution ruled by royal and pontific statutes to a republican university in 1827. The liberator Simón Bolívar, at that time president of the republic, issued the decree of enactment of the new Republican Statutes, in which he endowed "the UCV with funds from national income and production of some farms granted to the university to assure an appropriate faculty and for the general upkeep of the academy, which is in the path toward progress" (Leal 1981, 29). In addition, Bolívar anticipated the emergence of rental zones when he granted real estate properties to the UCV.

In the 1940s, during the planning of the CUC, one of the most highlighted topics was the financial autonomy of the university. Several options were suggested for income generation, such as the demarcation and exploitation of real estate property.[29] The CUC urban complex plan designed by Villanueva in 1947 established the ZRPV as an extra 24.7-acre area for real estate development. This area would be a source of income for the financial support of the scientific activities carried out by the UCV. To this end, the urban complex plan included, apart from university buildings and the Botanical Garden, "an area between the Carretera del Este (east road) and the Guaire River for rental buildings, as a source of income to the Caracas University City."[30]

Earliest Initiatives for the Plaza Venezuela Rental Zone

Villanueva designed several proposals for the building complex of the rental zone, as seen in the CUC urban complex plan of the year 1947,[31] as well as in the project for the rental zone complex, drafted in 1955 (Figure 8.3).

In 1957 the construction began on the main building of Villanueva's rental zone complex: a fifty-one-floor skyscraper with five additional, basement

Figure 8.3   **Villanueva's 1955 Master Plan for the Plaza Venezuela Rental Zone**

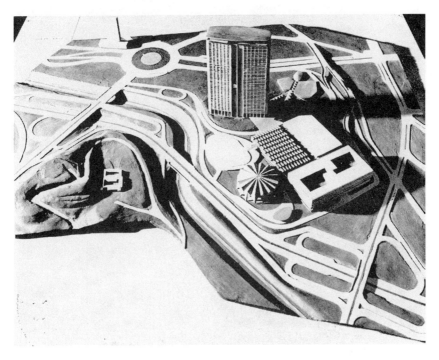

levels and a spacious gross area per floor of 32,280 square feet, with different possible uses such as a hotel, small apartments, offices, restaurants, entertainment facilities, and view terraces. The complex plans also included "large low-rise buildings making up a multipurpose center endowed with theater, halls for national and international conferences and congresses, hotel, stores with covered squares and pedestrian ways separated from vehicular ones, several basement levels, gardens and entertainment facilities" (Zawisza 1977, 65; Figure 8.4). After the overthrow of President Jiménez in 1958, the construction of the main building was stopped. By then, only four basement levels and one service level had been built.

In 1974, the Venezuelan government set up the FFABUCV in order to continue the construction of Villanueva's rental zone complex. At that moment, the ZRPV was a huge abandoned plot in the center of the city. The FFABUCV was completely controlled by the government.[32] The strategy for the development of the ZRPV was based on the sponsorship and funding of governmental agencies.

Ten years later, the FFABUCV renewed Villanueva's project according to

Figure 8.4   **View of the First Tower**

its real estate potential and to the new market conditions. Consequently, and as already mentioned, a Master Plan for the Urban Development and Design of the Rental Zone was created that did not include Villanueva's project. In 1997, after thirteen years of unsuccessful governmental financial backing, a new strategy was set up based on the association with private investors for the financial support of the project.[33]

Urban Development of the Plaza Venezuela Rental Zone

Location and Urban Environment

The ZRPV is located at the geographical center of the city of Caracas, in the sector known as Plaza Venezuela, adjoining the Sabana Grande sector.[34] By the time Villanueva designed the CUC, the area of Plaza Venezuela, Sabana Grande, had become a privileged quarter of tremendous real estate value. Villanueva's proposal for the rental zone visibly depicted the urban adaptability and potential of the area as a zone of high real estate value. The land is separated from the rest of the CUC by the Guaire River and has the ideal conditions for a large-scale business, commercial, and recreational development. In fact, a large number of buildings began to be constructed in the Plaza Venezuela sector in the 1950s, especially for residential and business purposes. Additionally, the Sabana Grande sector, between 1950 and 1970, became the new retail, restaurant, and entertainment center of Caracas.

The Plaza Venezuela and Sabana Grande sectors combined have the potential to be the new business, commercial, and recreational center of metropolitan Caracas. The mixture of land uses—mainly residential and commercial—will generate constant vehicular and pedestrian traffic aimed at the satisfaction of commercial, financial, and working needs. At the moment, there is an approximate daily traffic of 650,000 people going from one place to another either by foot or in private or public vehicles. A wide range of retail and service provision activities are carried out at different hours of the day. This includes restaurants, nightclubs, hotels, and stores selling personal or household goods or providing automobile-related services, as well as private and public offices of metropolitan and regional scale.

In general terms, this sector is experiencing great dynamism at the moment, and there are signs that the deteriorated existing urban conditions will change, mainly due to the intervention of the CA Metro de Caracas, which is constructing a new subway line and the new subway station "rental zone," which will be connected to two existing lines and their respective subway stations within the area. This construction work was due to be completed by the first quarter of 2006. The Plaza Venezuela–Sabana Grande sector can be considered to be the articulating point for one of Caracas's districts with a high real estate venture potential.

Urban and Real Estate Development Potential of the Plaza Venezuela Rental Zone

Due to its central location and easy accessibility from any city point, the ZRPV can be considered a privileged area right in the heart of Caracas. As a consequence, it is feasible to develop a large business, commercial, and recreational complex with a floor area of over 6,886,400 square feet for offices, different types of stores, five-star hotels, centers for conventions and events, recreational and cultural centers, and public squares. It could become a new civic, cultural, and business center of Caracas. The ZRPV, as a large-scale urban project, will have a positive impact on the urban development of the city, not only because of the foreseen total investments and the urban dynamics that will arise as a result of the mixture of uses, but also because of the quality of the buildings and urban spaces that will be built.[35]

From a morphological point of view, its development will comprise three main

Table 8.1

Development Units in the Plaza Venezuela Rental Zone

Unit	Gross area (approx.)
Northern (norte)	225,960 ft²
Southern (sur)	307,520.8 ft²
Eastern (este)	333,560 ft²
Central (central)	247,480 ft²
Total	1,114,520.8 ft²

elements: the border buildings, with a continuous uniform image; the towers, as referential elements; and the Grand Central Square, as a space where people get in contact with the city. All this will be built in a land plot that has been divided into four development units (Table 8.1, Figure 8.5),[36] which can be totally or partially given in usufruct, independently developed, and subdivided again in accordance with the conditions established by the FFABUCV and the market analysis.

Strategy for the Development of the Plaza Venezuela Rental Zone

The ZRPV project is a case of real estate development controlled by a public body, the FFABUCV. The foundation is subject to corporate legislation, so it is able to carry out any type of business, except for land selling. Besides, due to its autonomous management status, the FFABUCV is able to distance itself from the normal problems of the university and to act independently when faced with real estate market issues. Therefore, demands for physical facilities or for space to carry out the activities of the UCV do not influence the foundation's decision making. It is worth reiterating that the FFABUCV is also a nonprofit corporation, and thus all the profit gained—once the administrative and development expenses have been taken off—must be transferred to the UCV and used for scientific development funding. This condition does not affect or make a difference for the administrative and development practices of the rental zone, as the foundation operates in the real estate market and thus interacts with private investors, who will try to get the best possible conditions for their business operations, which results in the application of competitive and efficient practices aimed at playing a positive role within this productive sector.

Real Estate Strategy

In order to meet its statutory objectives, the FFABUCV has designed a strategy for the real estate development of the ZRPV, based on collaboration

Figure 8.5   **Development Units in the Plaza Venezuela Rental Zone**

with private investors. The foundation remains the owner of the land, and the investors are given usufruct rights. These rights allow them to commercially develop and exploit a land plot at their own expense, paying a fixed rent during the usufruct period (between thirty and sixty years). When the contract expires, the improvements made to the rented lands revert to the foundation. Each unit will be put out to public tender for its development and usufruct

Figure 8.6   **First Developmental Stage of the ZRPV Shopping Mall**

once the real estate and financial analyses of feasibility and viability have been carried out.

The usufruct contracts are guaranteed by the following legal instruments:

- Law for the Development of the Rental Zone of the Andrés Bello Fund Foundation,[37] a legislative instrument that regulates the real estate operations of the UCV's rental zone and is the only legislative instrument of its kind in the Venezuelan legal system, not only establishing that usufruct periods will be a maximum of sixty years,[38] but also authorizing the foundation to carry out any type of commercial exploitation of the rental zone except selling;
- Ordinance on Zoning Regulation of the Rental Zone Sector,[39] a legal instrument that regulates urban development at the local level and was created to provide the Master Plan for the Urban Development and Design of the ZRPV with a legal framework; and
- The long-term contracts signed by the parties, which not only reflect the foundation's win-win policy, but also include commercial arbitration clauses for the settlement of conflicts that could emerge.

Development Stages

In the first development stage, once the market and financial feasibility studies had been carried out, the Southern Unit of the complex—an area of 225,960 square feet—was offered for the construction of a shopping mall to be endowed with a hypermarket, a shopping arcade, an entertainment center, and a three-level parking place (Figure 8.6). This area was given by means of a public tender process in the early 2000 to the multinational company *Cadena de Tiendas Venezolanas Cativen SA*, which the French group *Casino*,

Figure 8.7 **Master Plan for the ZRPV, 2000**

the Colombian merger *Cadenalco-Éxito*, and the Venezuelan conglomerate *Alimentos Polar* jointly operate. The investments for the construction works of a floor area of 1,936,800 square feet will amount to US$80 million, and, according to the plans, the inauguration would take place in 2006.

As for the following stages, a number of actions have been planned, aimed at developing the large-scale public infrastructure required to further stimulate development and attract people to the sector from throughout the metropolitan area, thus creating an added value for the other land plots and generating an added value for the offices and stores in the complex. These infrastructure projects that will serve as "poles of attraction" are the Grand Central Station; the Conventions, Spectacles, and Events Center; the Interactive Art, Science, and Technology Center; and the Grand Central Square (Figure 8.7):

- Grand Central Station: This project has been conceived as a center for modal transportation transfer, to be endowed with a number of shopping and support services for short- and long-distance passengers, with services and parking places to be built in the rental zone's underground. It will be integrated into the city's metro system and roadway networks. It will be located on a land plot of 376,600 square feet and have a gross floor area of 1,635,520 square feet, with 236,720 square feet for stores and 4,200 parking spaces. An investment of US$56 million has been estimated. Studies for the development of the Grand Central Station are already being carried out on the basis of an Agreement of Technical Support between the CA Metro de Caracas and the FFABUCV.[40]

- Conventions, Spectacles, and Events Center: This project is aimed at providing the capital city with a central multitasking area that can be easily reached by the citizens and is fitted out for specialized and thematic meetings—something the city has lacked. It has been conceived as a multipurpose center, with a capacity of 15,000 people, where different types of activities can be carried out. The land plot will have an area of 122,664 square feet, a gross floor area of 483,339.2 square feet, and a main hall of 71,016 square feet, which can be enlarged to up to 98,561.6 square feet by integrating an additional open area of 27,545.6 square feet at the square level. It will offer 1,000 parking spaces, and the estimated investments amount to US$30 million. Another land plot of 22,639.04 square feet will be available for construction of a hotel, which could be placed either next to or within the convention center.

- Interactive Art, Science, and Technology Center: This project has been conceived as a public recreational and entertainment center based on the appreciation of art, science, and technology. Its main attraction will be a high-tech theater for IMAX-type films. The land plot for the center has an area of 376,600 square feet. It will occupy a gross floor area of 129,120 square feet, and there will be 250 parking spaces. The estimated investments amount to US$9 million.

- Grand Central Square: This project has been conceived as a large, 5.68-acre public area, where people get in contact with the city; it will become the new center of the metropolitan area, being Caracas's largest square. A public international ideas competition will be announced in order to generate landscaping and urban design proposals to pave the way for its design and development. The competition will be carried out under the auspices of the Venezuelan Association of Architects, the Pan-American Federation of Architects' Associations, and the UCV.

Once this infrastructure has been consolidated, the Northern, Eastern, and Central Units or land parcels will be offered for the construction of buildings that will contain offices, retail stores, hotels, apartments, and related services, so that a new center of tertiary activities of the city will be consolidated. See Table 8.2 for plot and floor areas.

Action Program for the Development of the Real Estate Strategy

The foundation's board of directors recently approved an Action Program to reinforce the above-described strategy.[41] This program sets forth a number of

Table 8.2

Development Areas in the Rental Zone

Unit	Plot area	Floor area
Northern	192,066 ft^2	1,736,126 ft^2
Eastern	288,906 ft^2	1,834,548 ft^2
Central	97,862.2 ft^2	621,390 ft^2
Total	578,834.2 ft^2	4,192,064 ft^2

actions to be taken in order to meet urban quality and real estate needs, including the following: (1) constant assessment of actions and identification of indicators to oversee the urban quality of development; (2) projection of a public image that favors development; (3) development of strategic alliances with third parties; (4) redefinition and promotion of real estate products; (5) redefinition and oversight of financial strategies; and (6) assessment of the foundation's operating structure.

Actions related to urban quality include studies on the impact of development on nearby parts of the city,[42] as well as programs to ensure all-around security in the ZRPV and the adjacent urban area, an all-embracing plan of mass media and strategic alliances, with representatives of the government, business and commercial sectors, and civil society partaking in the development process.

Actions related to real estate include diversification of the strategies for trading real estate products, analysis of the possibilities of creating financial instruments to get resources that would foster the development of real estate projects, preservation of a flexible organizational structure that can be adapted to market ups and downs, and carrying out periodic workshops for updating strategies.

The real estate and financial decisions related to the development of the ZRPV have been made after conducting economic and financial feasibility studies and real estate market studies and assessing the value of the lands considering the market demands. To that end, close ties are maintained with the Real Estate Chamber of Venezuela, the Construction Chamber, and the National Banking Association, on the one hand, so that the state of the real estate sector and the demands of the various market segments can be monitored. On the other hand, one of the most important external advisors of the foundation is *Consorcio Priven SA*, which has given support to the foundation on every aspect related to real estate and financial strategies.

Final Remarks

The large-scale urban project of the ZRPV, aimed at transforming the city of Caracas, is unique among other Venezuelan urban design processes and shall thus be considered an urban planning model. In addition, it is meant to be a successful real estate venture, so that the FFABUCV can meet its objectives and accomplish its mission by generating resources for UCV's scientific research funding.

The FFABUCV has created a novel design and management strategy in order to carry out this large-scale urban venture. The actions included in the operational stage of executing this project can be summarized as follows:

- Establishment of a real estate company as a private-law, nonprofit corporation, independent from the university administration;
- Formulation of the comprehensive Master Plan for Urban Development and Design;
- Definition of the *Urban Design Bylaw* as the guideline for the design of buildings and infrastructure;
- Formulation of the real estate strategy;
- Creation of adequate fiscal and regulatory instruments; and
- Formulation of an Action Program for monitoring the real estate operation.

The ZRPV will contribute to building a complex of high-quality public spaces and private buildings for the city of Caracas that allows for a synergy between the UCV and the city's inhabitants in terms of its shared perception and use.

Notes

This chapter was originally written in Spanish and then translated into English by Ainoa Larrauri. All acronyms used in the chapter are in Spanish.

1. For this chapter we have reviewed a great number of documents of the FFA-BUCV written by its chairpersons, management personnel, and advisors. These documents include technical reports, annual management reports, and minutes of the board of directors.

2. *The Master Plan for the Design and Urban Development of the Rental Zone* is a regulating instrument of the ZRPV, aimed at overseeing the construction and guaranteeing a final product in accord with the urban reality.

3. Insurbeca has been the main advisor of the FFABUCV on issues related to urban and architectural design since 1984, with outstanding work by architects Frank Marcano and Fernando Gonzalo and a group of intern students at the Institute of City Planning.

4. The City Council of the Federal District of Caracas passed the Ordinance on Zoning Regulation of the Rental Zone in 1987. It was published in *Municipal Gazette* no. extra 720-C, November 6, 1987.

5. Insurbeca. 2000. *Master Plan for the Design and Urban Development of the Rental Zone of the UCV*. Amendment to the *Urban Design Bylaw*. Caracas: Institute of City Planning.

6. The corporate bylaws of the foundation were set forth in Presidential Decree no. 581, November 26, 1974, published in Caracas, in *Official Gazette* no. 30.616, February 5, 1975.

7. The Senate of the Republic authorized the grant of the rental zones of the Central University of Venezuela to the FFABUCV; Caracas, *Official Gazette* no. 31.500, August 29, 1978.

8. According to the estimates of the FFABUCV, the development of the ZRPV will have a considerable positive impact on the UCV, becoming the main source of funding for its research programs. In 2002, the FFABUCV asked a real estate and financial advisor to conduct a study on the incomes to be obtained through the development of the ZRPV. This study says that when all the ZRPV's works are concluded—which requires an investment of US\$688 million—the foundation could receive an estimated gross annual income of US\$16,814,453 from payments of the usufruct rights, which would imply that US\$14,514,453 could be transferred to the UCV. This means that if the development of the ZRPV had been fully concluded by 2003, the equivalent of 90 percent of the UCV's research budget or 20 percent of its total regular budget could have been transferred to the university. In addition, those figures would rise after the expiration date of the usufruct terms, between thirty and sixty years. So when the improvements made to the rented lands revert to the FFABUCV, even 55 percent of the UCV's annual budget could be financed by the foundation (report published by *Consorcio Priven, SA*, in September 2002).

9. Article 4 of the FFABUCV's corporate bylaws establishes the appreciation and economic use of the land as the foundation's most important asset. This guarantees the capacity of the FFABUCV to act as a real estate developer.

10. This was set forth in the Rules of Functioning of foundations attached to bodies of the decentralized public administration and in its reformed version, both published in Caracas, in *Official Gazette* no. 33.134, December 28, 1984, and in special *Official Gazette* no. 3.574, June 21, 1985.

11. Right after its creation, the foundation was attached to the Ministry of Education; later, in 2001, it was attached to the UCV, thanks to actions taken by its directors. This change of tutelary entity is defined in a resolution of the Ministry of Education, approved with previous authorization and by decision of the president of the republic. It was published in Caracas, in *Municipal Gazette* no. 37.103, December 20, 2000.

12. The board of directors of the FFABUCV consists of seven members. Representing the UCV: the rector or his deputy, a member appointed by the University Council, and a member appointed by the Council for Development of Sciences and Humanities (CDCH). Representing non-UCV entities: a member appointed by the National Fund of Science and Technology (FONACIT), a member appointed by the Venezuelan Institute of Scientific Research (IVIC), and a member appointed by the National Academies. The president of the foundation is elected by the University Council from three candidates proposed by the rector.

13. In September 2003, the first workshop for the definition of development strategies for the ZRPV took place, with the participation of UCV authorities, president, directors, managers, and advisors of the FFABUCV, and guests of the Construction Chamber of Venezuela, the Real Estate Chamber of Venezuela, and the National Banking Association.

14. "The CUC is one of the largest building complexes to be ever constructed in the country. It took ten years for the project to become a reality and twenty additional years for the complex to be finished" (Zawisza 1977, 5).

15. The UCV was founded as a Royal University in 1721 by Royal Decree of Philip V, King of Spain. Later on, Pope Innocent XIII endowed it with pontifical character. In 1827, Liberator Simón Bolívar and Rector José María Vargas promulgated new statutes for the UCV that made it into a republican and liberal university.

16. The student population of the UCV in 1906 was 162; in 1933, there were 654 students (Leal 1981, 310).

17. By the 1940s, both the physical and psychological environments of the UCV buildings were unsuitable for teaching and research activities. The university expanded into different buildings, transcending the spaces of the convent, but none of those facilities was originally built for educational purposes. There were no laboratories or proper workshops for practical classes. There were no dormitories or libraries.

18. The project of the CUC was a collective work by the government, through the Ministry of Public Works (MOP) and the Ministry of Education (ME), and university authorities. We should highlight the work of Dr. Antonio José Castillo, UCV's rector for the term 1937–43, and engineer Armando Vegas from the MOP, in its creation. Dr. Castillo was not only a zealous promoter of the CUC project from the beginning, but also the first president of the City University Institute, giving the last years of his life to the planning and construction of the CUC (Leal 1981, 311–14).

19. Presidential decree no. 196, which establishes the creation of the ICU, set its functions as follows: purchasing the land, planning and building the campus, administering the funds for the construction, and promoting all activities required to select the best project (Leal 1981, 315).

20. Caracas, the capital city of Venezuela, is located in a narrow valley, which stretches westbound, with a total length of 9.32 miles, a maximum width of 2.17 miles, and a flat area of around 39,520 acres. The average height is 3,280 feet above sea level. The urban settlements grew onto the hills and mountains surrounding the valley, with the exception of El Ávila National Park, a mountain chain that separates the city from the sea, its highest peak (over 8,856 feet above sea level) serving as a majestic north facade to the city. The valley is characterized by a tropical climate, with warm temperatures that barely fluctuate throughout the year, minimum and maximum ranging between 66°F and 90°F and producing an annual average of 77°F. The continuous, clean westbound winds that flow through the valley refresh the environment and carry polluting particles away from the city. A short rainy season and a long dry season, with direct sun, afford great possibilities for outdoor activities.

21. In the book *Estudio de Caracas* (Valmitjana et al. 1990, 91–101) there is a detailed analysis of the historical evolution of Caracas's urban pattern.

22. Between 1926 and 1936, there was a dramatic increase in population and a transformation of the city at a pace never seen in the country's previous 350 years of history. The population doubled, and the urban areas increased threefold. In the book *El plan rotival* (Valmitjana et al. 1991, 21–108) there is a detailed, critical, historical summary of urban growth in Caracas in the first decades of the twentieth century.

23. The role of the UCV in the planning stage for the development of the university campus was limited to the promotion of the works and the definition of programmatic and functional requirements of the buildings aimed at hosting academic and research activities of the university. As mentioned above, the ICU was attached to the MOP and enjoyed autonomous management status.

24. Despite political instability, changes in the administration, democratic or dictatorial governments, the general plan and the construction kept on track during the stages of planning and construction of the CUC, thanks to Villanueva's discreet

but decisive action. In 1941–46 President General Isaías Medina Angarita started the Plan for National Public Works, which guaranteed the financial resources for the construction of the University Hospital, the Medical School, and the Industrial Technical School. Subsequent presidents Carlos Delgado Chalbaud, Rómulo Gallegos, Marcos Pérez Jiménez, Wolfang Larrazábal, and Rómulo Betancourt made the necessary provisions to guarantee the continuity of the project.

25. There is no doubt that the planning of the CUC was carried out by the members of the commission; however, the role played by architect Carlos Raúl Villanueva and engineer Armando Vegas (also on the commission) was fundamental. Villanueva assumed the entire direction and design of the urban and architectural plan of the CUC.

26. The Aula Magna, being one of the world's acoustically most impeccable auditoria, remains the ideal hall for graduations, academic and cultural events, and assemblies of the university community. Villanueva achieved here an innovative "Synthesis of the Arts," in which the floating clouds by sculptor Alexander Calder; the acoustic design by American firm Bolt, Beranek & Newman; and the structural design by Norwegian firm Christiane & Nielsen combine into an icon of modern architecture.

27. The Covered Square is an outdoor museum that boasts a splendid collection of modern art pieces of large dimensions and exceptional quality conceived by some of the most renowned plastic masters of the early twentieth century: Fernand Léger, Jean Arp, Antoine Pevsner, Víctor Vasarely, Wilfredo Lam, André Bloc, Mateo Manaure, Oswaldo Vigas, Pascual Navarro, and Carlos González Bogen. The area becomes thus a perfect rendezvous place for the UCV community, apart from serving as foyer for the Aula Magna, the Concert Hall, and the Ceremonial Hall.

28. The declaration was based on its invaluable architectural, urban, and artistic principles, which clearly represent the modern movement of architecture of the early twentieth century. Its incorporation in this list confirms the exceptional value of the CUC. For reference to the declaration, visit the UNESCO World Heritage Center (http://whc.unesco.org/pg.cfm?cid=31) and select Venezuela on the World Heritage List of countries.

29. The commission led by Villanueva states in one planning report, "The autonomy of the university is the fundamental basis for a proper functioning of the university campus, and in this connection, it is necessary to create appropriate sources of income" (Vegas 1947, 100).

30. As quoted in the CUC project descriptive report, published in the journal *Revista Punto* (AAVV 1970).

31. "In 1947, Villanueva drafted the first proposals for the development of the rental land; back then, it was perhaps considered of great importance for the survival of the university, as it would become a source of income" (Lasala 1999, 66). In the overall designs of 1943 and 1944, the land for the rental zones was thought to be used for the complex of the Industrial Technical School.

32. The FFABUCV's president and most of the members of the board of directors were directly appointed by the government.

33. Villanueva's original project was ruled out by both Insurbeca and the FFABUCV for the following reasons: (1) the reinforced concrete structure does not comply with the current seismic standards; (2) the gross area of each floor of the tower is 32,280 square feet, which, according to market research, makes it difficult to sell due to its large size; (3) the current costs for the construction of a structure made of reinforced concrete are too high for such a high-rise and big building compared to the costs of

construction of a structure made of steel; and (4) adapting Villanueva's original project to the new seismic standards, using steel to allow for a more feasible construction, and modifying the area of each floor to make it suit the market conditions, would mean that, in the end, the structure would be completely different from the one designed by Villanueva.

34. The area is endowed with the city's largest ornamental fountain, which is surrounded by emblematic office buildings such as Edificio Polar, Torre Phelps, and Centro Capriles, as well as other buildings that have become referential elements of the city, such as Torre La Previsora and its famous digital clock, Torre Domus, Torre Lincoln, and Centro Teleport, among others. In additional, the Plaza Venezuela–Sabana Grande sector is surrounded by the Botanical Garden and the Caracas University City to the southern limit of the rental zone next to the Francisco Fajardo Highway. From the ZRPV it is possible to see a number of buildings standing out within the university campus, such as the soccer stadium, the baseball stadium, the gymnasium, and the central library. The site is also near the Science Museum, the Museum of Fine Arts, the Contemporary Art Museum of Caracas, the National Art Gallery, and the Athenaeum of Caracas, which are located in the area of Los Caobos Park.

35. To this end, the *Urban Design Bylaw* has been created as part of the *Master Plan for the Urban Development and Design of the ZRPV*, establishing the standards to guarantee the security of the buildings and public areas to be designed. Moreover, the policy of the FFABUCV provides for the organization of architecture competitions to select the architects and the project designs.

36. These development units, which have been named depending on their location within the ZRPV, are the following: Northern Unit (located near Casanova, Gran Avenida, and Olimpo avenues and the Plaza Venezuela); Southern Unit (located along the borderline of the Plaza Venezuela feeder to the Francisco Fajardo Highway); Eastern Unit (located along the borderline of Olimpo Avenue, between Gran Avenida Avenue and the Plaza Venezuela feeder to the highway); and Central Unit (located in the southern end of Casanova Avenue among the Northern, Southern, and Eastern Units). The old main Rental Building's basement structure of a floor area of over 161,400 square feet comprising five floors is located within this land unit below the square surface height.

37. *Ley para el Desarrollo de las Zonas Rentales de la Fundación Fondo Andrés Bello,* published in Caracas, in *Official Gazette* no. 37.022, August 25, 2000. This law was passed by the National Legislative Commission created by the Constituent National Assembly, in reply to the foundation's request and with the support of the UCV and the Ministry of Higher Education.

38. The *Código Civil de Venezuela* (Venezuelan Civil Law) establishes that the maximum usufruct period is thirty years.

39. *Ordenanza sobre Zonificación del Sector de Espacios Rentales de la UCV,* published in *Municipal Gazette* no. extra 720-C, November 6, 1987. It was passed by the Local Council of the Federal District of Caracas in reply to the foundation's request and conceptually based on the *Master Plan for the Urban Development and Design of the ZRPV*, elaborated by Insurbeca (an enterprise of the Institute of City Planning of the UCV).

40. This agreement was signed on May 24, 2004. It establishes mutual support between FFABUCV and CA Metro de Caracas for drawing up the Terms of Reference for the Grand Central Station project.

41. This Action Program is the result of a workshop carried out in September, in which university authorities; the members of the board of directors; the managers and advisors of the foundation; and special guests from the Venezuelan real estate, financial, and construction sectors took part. The conclusions were assessed by the foundation's Strategy Committee, and then the Action Program was approved in a special meeting of the board of directors held on December 1, 2003, as a planning instrument that should guide the activities of the foundation during 2004.

42. To achieve this goal, the FFABUCV has been working with the Council for Development of Sciences and Humanities of the UCV, fostering the creation of a funding program to finance research on the impact of the ZRPV's development on nearby areas. In this sense, they have already drafted the guidelines to be able to announce a competition for researchers from the UCV that could develop the required projects. The CDCH will finance this research with resources from the Special Projects Funding Program approved by the University Council.

References

AAVV. 1970. La obra de Carlos Raúl Villanueva. *Revista Punto* 40–41. Caracas: Facultad de Arquitectura y Urbanismo, Universidad Central de Venezuela.

Insurbeca. 1984. *Zona Rental Plaza Venezuela. Plan maestro de desarrollo y diseño urbano*. Caracas: Insurbeca, Instituto de Urbanismo, UCV.

———. 2000. *Zona Rental Plaza Venezuela. Plan maestro de desarrollo y diseño urbano. Reformulación del reglamento*. Caracas: Insurbeca, Instituto de Urbanismo, UCV.

Lasala, Silvia H. 1999. *En busca de lo sublime. Villanueva y la arquitectura de la Ciudad Universitaria de Caracas*. Caracas: Facultad de Arquitectura y Urbanismo, Universidad Central de Venezuela.

Leal, Ildefonso. 1981. *Historia de la Universidad Central de Venezuela*. Caracas: Ediciones del Rectorado de la Universidad Central de Venezuela.

Moholy-Nagy, Sibyl. 1964. *Carlos Raúl Villanueva y la arquitectura de Venezuela*. Caracas: Editorial Lectura.

Novoa, María T., et al. 2002. *Ciudad Universitaria de Caracas. Patrimonio mundial. Catálogo de la exposición*. Caracas: UNESCO, Universidad Central de Venezuela.

Valmitjana, Marta, et al. 1990. *Estudio de Caracas. Evolución del patrón urbano desde la fundación hasta el período petrolero 1567–1936*. Caracas: Universidad Central de Venezuela, Instituto de Urbanismo.

Valmitjana, Marta, et al. 1991. *El plan rotival. La Caracas que no fue. 1939–1989 un plan urbano para Caracas*. Caracas: Universidad Central de Venezuela, Instituto de Urbanismo.

Vegas, Armando. 1947. *La Ciudad Universitaria de Caracas. Documentos relativos a su estudio y creación*. Caracas: Editorial Grafolit.

Villanueva, Paulina and Macía Pinto. 2000. *Carlos Raúl Villanueva*. Madrid: Tanais Ediciones.

Zawisza, Leszek. 1977. La Ciudad Universitaria de Caracas. *Revista Punto*, 59, 1–69.1.

9

Development of the Jatinangor University Area, Indonesia

Growth Problems and Local Responses

Wilmar Salim

This chapter traces the development of a new university town, analyzing the ways in which government uses the siting and development of new university campuses to impact urban development in general and higher education secondarily. It is a case of university land development as provincial/regional urban economic development. The argument here is that university land development in developing countries is not always first and foremost about higher education; and where university and government policies are undertaken in such a matter, there are often as many negative as positive consequences, especially for the existing local community. I will discuss the new university town plan, the development of the universities and the town, and the impacts such development has had on the area. This discussion will be followed by an assessment of university-community relations and initiatives taken by universities. The central premise of this assessment is that as a center of "enlightenment," the university bears the burden of initiating and sustaining dialogue between university representatives and local community stakeholders.

Urban Development of Bandung, West Java, and the Relocation of Universities

Jatinangor University Area is located on the eastern fringe of Bandung, the capital city of West Java Province of Indonesia. The western part of Java is the most populated part of the island, due to two reasons. Geographically, the land is fertile, which makes this region a major rice producer for the country. Economically, it has been the location of major urban centers, where metropolitan Jakarta, the nation's capital city and the center of the national economy, is sited. Bandung, located approximately 180 kilometers southeast of Jakarta, is the second-largest urban concentration in the western part of Java and the third-largest city in Java, after Jakarta and Surabaya. It is a colonial city well known for its arts and educational life and was called the Paris of Java with its lined boulevards, art deco buildings, and beautiful scenes inside and outside the city. As a provincial capital city, Bandung has several core functions; it is the center of government,[1] the center of local and regional trades, the center of industrial activities,[2] the center of science and education, and the center of tourism and culture. With all of these functions, the urban development of Bandung accelerated over time, as shown by its population increase. The population of Bandung was just over 1.2 million in the early 1970s, and it had become 2.06 million twenty years later. Rapid population growth and increased economic activity have created many urban problems for Bandung, such as traffic congestion, deficiency of urban infrastructures, water and air pollution, and slum areas.

As the center of science and education, Bandung is home to three national educational institutions (Institut Teknologi Bandung, or ITB, the oldest and most prestigious engineering school; Universitas Pendidikan Indonesia, or UPI, the main teachers school; and Universitas Padjadjaran, one of the biggest social science schools) and other tertiary educational institutions and has thus attracted a number of students coming from other provinces to gain higher education over the years. Between 1977 and 1982 the number of students in tertiary education in Bandung doubled from around 36,000 to 80,518 in about forty public and private colleges and universities (Theresia 1998). The increasing number of colleges and universities in Bandung caused an increasing demand for land to develop new campuses, student housing, and supporting facilities. However, the city boundaries forced the government of West Java Province to reconsider the function of Bandung as a center of higher education and think of finding vacant lands outside Bandung to accommodate those demands.

A proposal to move some universities from Bandung was made by Badan Perencanaan Pembangunan Daerah (Regional Development Planning Agency) of West Java in the early 1980s, in order to deconcentrate the urban development of Bandung to its surrounding regions under the concept of a "counter magnet." Under the theme of "balanced urban development" the counter magnet strategy was adopted by the government (Firman 1996). An unproductive rubber plantation about twenty-three kilometers from the city center, in the Cikeruh area of the District of Sumedang adjacent to the District of Bandung, was chosen as a site for universities.

The decision to choose this area was based not on an analysis of the best location, but merely on the vacancy of the land. For the government of West Java, relocation was necessary to meet the demand for lands for higher education. High land value in Bandung makes it unattractive for universities. Part of the provincial government plan was to relocate four universities from Bandung to this new area, called Jatinangor (see Figure 9.1), and designate it as a university town.[3] Based on decree no. 583 of the governor of West Java in 1989, 534 hectares out of 934 hectares of the former rubber plantation land in the Jatinangor area was formally dedicated for four universities: Universitas Padjadjaran, Universitas Winaya Mukti, Institut Manajemen Koperasi Indonesia, and Sekolah Tinggi Pemerintahan Dalam Negeri. Even though the location was not the best, the decision to relocate would benefit the Bandung city government by easing the burden of having colleges and universities inside the city.

Following decree no. 583/1989, the master plan of Kawasan Pendidikan Tinggi Jatinangor (KPTJ), or Jatinangor Higher Education Area, was designed by the Office of the Governor in 1989 with land divisions of the former rubber plantation as follows (Badan Perencanaan Pembangunan Daerah Jawa Barat, 1999):

- Zone A, for development of Universitas Padjadjaran in an area of 175 hectares
- Zone B, for development of Universitas Winaya Mukti in an area of 51 hectares, including 8 hectares of experimental forest
- Zone C, for development of Institut Manajemen Koperasi Indonesia in an area of 28 hectares
- Zone D, for development of Sekolah Tinggi Pemerintahan Dalam Negeri (STPDN) in an area of 280 hectares
- Zone E, an area of 140 hectares for open space
- Zone F, an area of 66 hectares for recreational forest and campsites
- Zone G, an area of 194 hectares reserved for conservation

This master plan (see Figure 9.2) attempted to integrate the development of four campuses in a total area of about 2,640 hectares, including the 934 hectares of land divisions above. The new university town was designed to house forty thousand students and ten thousand academics plus local residents (Ahmadi 1988). The distribution of land use as planned for year 2005 is outlined in Table 9.1, in which development of built-up areas is shown to be balanced with non-built-up areas.

Impacts of Relocation on Bandung and Jatinangor

As a proposal that was meant to resolve one issue, a limited area for the expansion of universities, the development of Jatinangor town to house the relocation of the universities from Bandung had positive impacts on the source of the problem (Bandung) but more negative impacts on the other end. Initially, this relocation benefited Bandung by lessening the population pressure created by an increasing number of university students, mostly from other regions.[4] For a

Figure 9.1　Orientation Map—Jatinangor Area in the Vicinity of Bandung, West Java

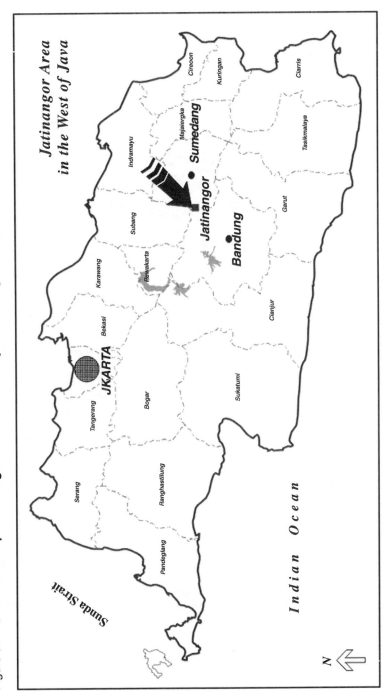

Figure 9.2 **Master Plan of the Jatinangor Higher Education Area**

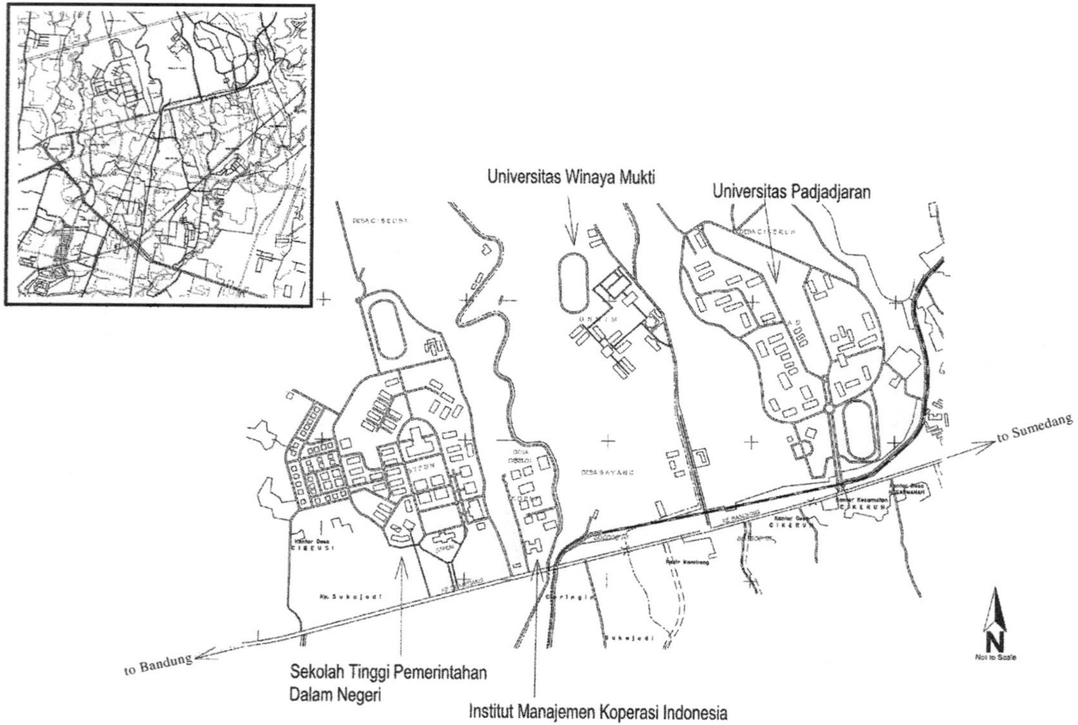

Table 9.1

Land Use Plan of Jatinangor Town in 2005, as Planned in 1989

Built-up areas	50.33%
Residential	18.05%
Commercial	0.65%
Industrial	5.63%
Educational	22.97%
Public facilities	3.03%
Non-built-up areas	49.67%
Agricultural	1.12%
Recreational forest and camp sites	2.50%
Conservation area and green space[a]	46.05%
Total area (approx.)	2,639.9 ha

Source: Modified from Badan Perencanaan Pembangunan Daerah Jawa Barat, 1999.
[a]Includes 140 hectares of golf course.

service city like Bandung, the economic result was more land available for commercial than educational activities. The relocation of universities also helped to reduce the rapid growth of Bandung's population. During the period from 1980 to 1990 the growth rate was 3.47 percent per year (from 1.46 to 2.06 million), while during the period from 1990 to 2000 the rate slowed to 0.41 percent per year (from 2.06 to 2.14 million) (World Bank 2002), which made it easier for the Bandung city government to face issues such as municipal services, poverty and unemployment, slums, and traffic congestion.

On the other hand, the huge land parcel available from the government offered university administrators the opportunity to expand their academic services, in terms of increasing the number of students enrolled in their universities. This relocation would benefit the city as well as the universities. However, as will be discussed, the relocation of universities to the new area subsequently created several interconnected issues that resulted in an overall negative impact on Jatinangor (see Figure 9.3). Based on information compiled for a project with which I was involved a few years ago,[5] we can trace the situation in Jatinangor since the decision to relocate universities, which took place twenty years ago.

Physical and Socioeconomic Changes in Jatinangor

In the late 1970s and early 1980s, land uses in Jatinangor grew mainly as the result of area expansion by business and industrial activities. Jatinangor is located on the major regional road that links Bandung to the eastern part of the province. From the time when the governor's decree no. 583/1989 was

210

Figure 9.3 **Causal Relationship of Issues in Jatinangor University Area**

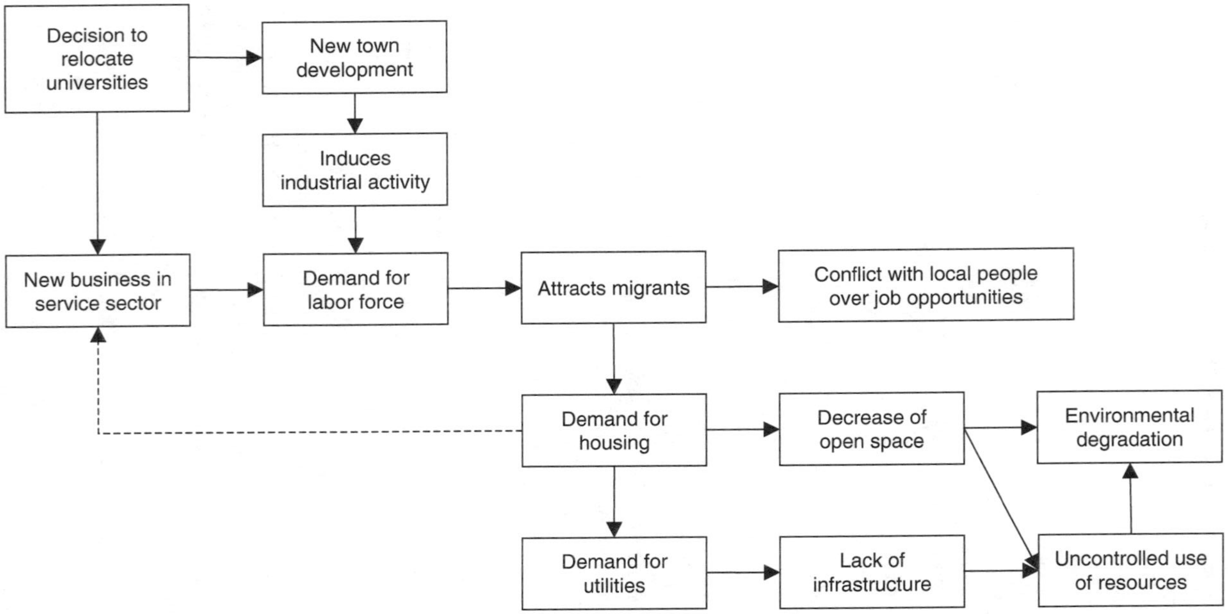

Table 9.2

Land Use of the Jatinangor Area in 1981, 1991, and 2000

	1981	1991	2000[b]
Built-up areas	10.47%	38.69%	59.81%
Residential	9.83%	14.90%	
Commercial	0.18%	0.70%	
Industrial	—	1.30%	
Educational	—	21.01%	
Public facilities	0.46%	0.78%	
Non-built-up areas	89.53%	61.31%	40.19%
Agricultural	29.67%	26.93%	
Forest/plantation[a]	18.82%	5.02%	
Unused (ex-plantation)	41.04%	29.36%	

Source: Modified from Theresia, 1998.
[a]Includes recreational forest for camping ground.
[b]From Pamungkas, 2001; breakdowns are not available.

issued, major urban physical development has taken place in this area, including a land-use change from rural to urban, subdistrict boundary changes, and increasing urban activities. In the past twenty years, this new town has undergone a rapid residential and commercial development as the consequence of the relocation of four universities in the area. Table 9.2 depicts the land-use change between 1981, when the area was first selected to be developed as a university town, and 1991, when all four universities were operating, and includes the estimate of built-up areas for the year 2000.

Table 9.2 indicates a very rapid increase in the development of residential areas, which have expanded beyond the area allocated by the original master plan of the town. Much of this development, particularly in the past decade, has been uncontrolled, which was perhaps unthinkable when the government planned this area. Between 1981 and 1991, the growth of new residential areas was only about 13 hectares per year (Theresia 1998). By 1992, all four universities were operating,[6] which resulted in an increasing number of students and associated facilities to serve students' needs, such as private dormitories, small shops, copy centers, and so forth. The growth of the town was also influenced by industrial activities, which made it more than just a university town, as a result of a national government policy to deregulate development of industrial parks in 1988. The rapid physical change in the area resulted in the consumption of 1,604 hectares for built-up areas by 2000, half of that estimated to be for residential use (Pamungkas 2001).

From the original 1989 division of the lands discussed previously, the current allocation is as follows:

- Zones A, B, C, and D (land for universities): University buildings have been constructed on parts of this land, but major parts of the land remain undeveloped and are used by the Faculty of Agriculture or Forestry for experimental plots. Some land is also distributed to the community for cultivation.
- Zone E: In this open-space zone, an eighteen-hole golf course and a resort have been built.
- Zone F: This area has been developed as a Boy Scout campground.
- Zone G: Some parts of this conservation zone have been used for unplanned settlements, as well as for gardens by local people. Due to these squatter settlements, it is losing its function as a "reserved area."

Development in the area is reflected both in the physical changes and in the socioeconomic transformation. The high level of physical development since 1991 has been followed by large population increases, of students as well as a significant number of people who came to the area to find jobs or start their own businesses. In 1991 the population of the Jatinangor subdistrict was 54,018. By 2000 it was 82,982, an increase of approximately 3,000 residents each year. Almost 90 percent of the population increase is the result of people migrating to the area. Most of the people who migrated to the area were between fifteen and twenty-nine years old and were students in one of the four universities. This is supported by findings that 42 percent of immigrants have graduated from high school, while those who had finished only middle or primary school were only 18 percent and 19 percent of immigrants, respectively (Theresia 1998).

The economic development of the area has also shown periodic increases. The economic growth of the Jatinangor area is the major contributor to the economic growth of the District of Sumedang, in which the town is located. However, this economic growth is mainly a result of manufacturing activities, which contribute almost 50 percent of the gross regional domestic product. Unfortunately, manufacturing does not have much impact on the town's economy, since that industry does not provide many jobs. It is primarily service activities that support the needs of students and provide jobs to people. Private dormitories, restaurants, computer rentals, and other services have been the primary sources of jobs (Mardianta 2001). Thus, the universities have had little direct impact on the local economy despite the apparent indirect impact by way of increasing demands for service jobs.

Emerging Issues in the Area

Even though the relocation of the four universities to Jatinangor area was accompanied by a master plan to develop the area as a new town, the plan

Figure 9.4   **Land Uses around Jatinangor University**

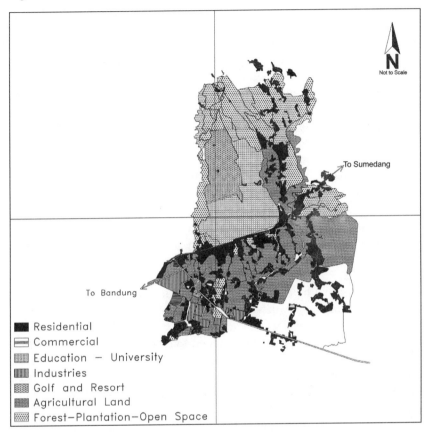

To Sumedang

To Bandung

■ Residential
▭ Commercial
▦ Education — University
▥ Industries
▩ Golf and Resort
▨ Agricultural Land
▦ Forest—Plantation—Open Space

failed to anticipate the rapid change brought on by developers (see Figure 9.4). Moreover, it should be admitted that there was no overall plan that could integrate the campus development with the dynamics of the communities. Rapid residential and social development, as mentioned earlier, caused significant problems to the infrastructure capacity, a decline of environmental resources, and the collapse of community institutions (Departemen Teknik Planologi ITB 2002). The absence of a comprehensive infrastructure plan caused a deficiency in public service provisions, particularly water supply, transportation, waste disposal, and drainage. The occupation of critical land by squatter developments contributed to deforestation and increased sedimentation. The large influx of new settlers threatened employment opportunities for local people, creating tension between them.

Water provision, which relies on surface water, is available to only

30.44 percent of the town's residents. The remaining residents, along with the industries, are forced to use the shallow and shallow-to-deep underground wells (Kolikiana 2003). This led to a lowering of the water table by as much as twenty meters in the six years between 1995 and 2001 (Pamungkas 2001). Thus, access to clean water has become a major problem in the area.

Waste disposal management is another problem faced by residents in this area. Without a waste management agency, the community handles its waste by dumping it into a pit or small stream, burning it, or leaving it in the open, which creates unsightliness and public health concerns. Sewage and drainage create similar problems.

Because this once rural area was converted to urban use without adequately considering the potential ramifications (the increase in residential areas was not anticipated by the existing plan), there is no infrastructure to serve most of the town. Moreover, the lack of solid and liquid waste services has created an environmental disaster, especially during rainy season, when flooding has occurred due to limited drainage and stormwater channels blocked by solid waste deposits.

The provision of housing is another concern in the Jatinangor area. The increased population growth has increased the demand for housing, which is provided by private developers. Development of housing has taken place in several areas, some of which are unsuited for residential development, and some of the housing itself has been inconsistent with good design principles. Furthermore, the encroachment of dwellings in environmentally sensitive areas such as the forested hills in the northern part of the town could disturb the hydrological function of those areas. This massive residential development is inconsistent with surrounding uses and has caused Jatinangor to become an inconvenient and unattractive place to live.

The opening of universities in the area was expected to facilitate local economic development. However, according to a study conducted to discover the impact of the universities' activities on the local economy of the Jatinangor area, most people involved in new businesses related to the provision of students' needs are new settlers rather than residents of the original communities (Mardianta 2001). Thus, the universities provide more economic benefits to the immigrants than to locals. Several factors behind the limited economic opportunities for "locals" are common in developing countries, including a lack of economic capital to open new businesses and difficulty transferring employment skills from the farming to the service sector. In addition, the competitive advantage of locals is weakened by the fact that new settlers bring large capital to be invested in the area, and these new settlers often employ labor from outside of the area instead of providing jobs for locals.

Furthermore, although the development of Jatinangor as a new town involved the provision of land for industrial activities and that sector generates income for the region, that income does not accrue to the locals. Employment provided by the industrial sector involves specialized skills that many locals who were previously engaged in the agriculture sector do not possess. Therefore, the demand for labor in industry is largely supplied by immigrants. That situation has become a significant source of tension between local residents and new settlers. Local residents have blamed the provincial government for not giving adequate attention to such problems, and at the same time they have regarded the inaction on the part of the university as a sign of insensitivity to local conditions.

Theoretical Discussion: Urban Universities and Community Relations

Urban universities are generally regarded as having three main effects on the fabric of city life: (1) they bring economic opportunity, (2) their real estate policies affect neighboring communities, and (3) their research has impacts on urban policy. In the case of Jatinangor, however, these impacts on the local community simply do not exist. First, as discussed, the universities did not bring direct economic opportunity to the local people. Second, it was not their real estate policies that affected the neighboring communities; the decision to relocate the universities was made by authorities at the provincial level. Furthermore, the campuses were built on vacant lands owned by the state; the university administrators did not have their own policies.[7] Third, research conducted by the universities has had less impact on the urban policy of Jatinangor for two reasons: (1) In the limited research conducted by the universities, the focus has been more on larger geographic areas, since these are more attractive and often bring more funding opportunities. A study of highway development that serves several districts is more valuable than a traffic management study for a small town, for example. (2) Jatinangor does not have the autonomy to run its own government since it does not have municipality status. It is considered a subdistrict under the jurisdiction of the District of Sumedang, where all decisions about urban affairs are decided. No research about this area will affect policy unless its results are presented to the local government in Sumedang.

It is also appropriate to discuss the situation in the Jatinangor university town in regard to the four opposite and conflicting values that Barlow (1998) describes: gates versus doors, campus life versus home life, teaching versus research, and local versus global. These opposing values provide a background for the problems in university and community relations.

Gates versus Doors

Universities in Jatinangor, as with most universities in other places, are viewed as "ivory towers." This image is reinforced by urban forms such as walls and gates, which provide a sheltered experience for an elite population rather than "open doors" for the community. As one of the biggest state universities in West Java, Universitas Padjadjaran attracts students from all over the province, as well as from other provinces. Entry into the university is highly competitive, and the annual enrollment of five thousand students is usually filled by high school graduates from urban centers in West Java, especially Bandung, as opposed to its surrounding neighborhood. The Sekolah Tinggi Pemerintahan Dalam Negeri, or the College of Government, is also an example of a college that does not serve local populations, drawing largely from elite groups. This college was opened by the Department of Home Affairs to educate high school graduates who will work for local governments all over Indonesia. Therefore, students are usually those sent by their local governments and selected from many applicants in each district. This reinforces the idea that the universities are exclusive entities.

Campus versus Home Life

The issue of campus versus home life can be illustrated by the fact that Jatinangor as a town fails to provide decent infrastructures, thus making it an inconvenient place to live, as discussed earlier. Since Bandung is not far from Jatinangor, many students and academics choose to commute from Bandung because it has better urban services. Therefore, campus life for students is often not so lively outside their courses; the private boarding houses in Jatinangor are used by those from other regions. The mass of commuters then creates transportation problems that have yet to be resolved by the provincial government, which has authority over regional road networks.

Teaching versus Research

The issue of teaching versus research not only is faced by universities in Jatinangor, but also is a systemic concern of higher education in Indonesia. As Indonesia is a developing country with young people becoming the majority of the population, the primary function of higher education is to produce as many qualified graduates as quickly as possible to enter the labor market. The public demands that universities perform this function well. Therefore, the main focus of universities, including those in Jatinangor, leans toward teaching, with less of an emphasis on research. The number of students enrolled in and graduating from university is more important than the amount of research conducted by academics.

Local versus Global (or National)

The issue of research versus teaching is also related to the last of Barlow's conflicting values, which in this case is seen as local versus national. Research that is of greater value at the regional and national levels than the local level is often more attractive to universities. As state universities, the universities in Jatinangor also feel more important if they are involved in activities at the regional and national levels. The seemingly mundane problems that Jatinangor faces are not appealing in the eyes of university administrators when compared with, for example, a contract to conduct policy research that will be used by the West Java Province or the District or City of Bandung.

A similar situation is faced by other universities in developing and industrialized countries. American urban universities in the 1960s were charged with not addressing their social responsibilities and often exacerbating existing conditions by creating economic barriers for low-income students, uprooting the poor for university expansion, and defending the status quo of urban policies. Confrontations between the urban university and the community were inevitable where a university's land expansion policy and research activities triggered the resentment of its neighbors.[8] It was not until the 1970s that university administrators by and large began to actively address such problems. Reforms had three goals: (1) to educate the urban poor, (2) to establish good community relations, and (3) to develop urban research and related studies. A decade later, some community partnerships based on addressing urban problems, community outreach programs, and improvements in public facilities indicated positive changes, as reported by Grobman (1988) and based on the examples of several urban state universities. A similar path can be observed in Jatinangor.

Collective Action Initiative through Forum Jatinangor

The case of Jatinangor reflects not only the ongoing conflicts in university and community relations but also the absence of community involvement in the decision-making process for area development. Table 9.3 illustrates the level of involvement by government, universities, and community in each phase of the development of the area, whether full, moderate, or none. This table serves to demonstrate the place and influence of three levels of social institutions in the various components of the case. As described earlier, the policy to relocate the universities was made unilaterally by the provincial government, and although

Table 9.3

Roles of Actors in the Decision-Making Process

Phase	Actors		
	Government	Universities	Community
Policy of relocation	■	–	–
Planning	■	□	–
Land acquirement	■	■	–
Construction	□	■	–
University operation	□	■	–
Addressing issues in the area	–	□	■
Collective action initiative	□	■	■

■ = full participation
□ = moderate participation
– = no participation

area development and its implementation were planned collaboratively by the government and the universities to varying degrees, the local community was not involved. Later, as the town grew, problems emerged that have led the community to question the existence of the four universities, criticizing them as ivory towers that have not contributed to solving the problems they helped create. For many years, the community has tried to devise solutions using its own resources; not until recently did the problems attract attention from a wider public. At that point, a collective action initiative was undertaken in the area, involving all three parties (see Table 9.3).

It was not until 1999 that the ongoing problems became apparent to those in the Department of Regional and City Planning at the Institut Teknologi Bandung (DRCP-ITB). Some faculties in that planning school were concerned that the development trajectory of the Jatinangor area was not going as planned. At the same time, the political situation in Indonesia had changed, and grassroot movements for reform were emerging in the context of the decline in government power. The collapse of community institutions in the area was seen as an entry point for DRCP-ITB to be involved in the Jatinangor area. Adopting a model of university and community relations developed by the School of Architecture at the University of Illinois at Urbana-Champaign (UIUC) for the community of East St. Louis through the East St. Louis Action Research Project (ESLARP), DRCP-ITB started its participatory action research in the Jatinangor area in the year 2000.[9] The initiative for collective action was promoted, and several workshops involving the four universities and representatives of the community and local government were facilitated by DRCP-ITB. Within these workshops a collective agreement was reached to examine the problems discussed previously as shared concerns of all the stakeholders.

The Working Group: University, Government, and Community

During the workshop, a stakeholders' forum (Forum Jatinangor) was proposed, and a working group made up of representatives from the universities, the local government, the community, and DRCP-ITB was created. This working group was then assigned to find ways to resolve the shared problems. This partnership model resulted in research, policy advocacy, and an institutional network from the year 2000 on. Several achievements of this collective initiative in each aspect are discussed in the following sections.

Research

Three areas of research—water supply, labor force, and civil society—were identified in the forum as major problems and are the focus of the working group. Research findings were used by the group in proposing a resolution to the provincial or district authority on behalf of the stakeholder parties.

Water Supply

The study on water supply was conducted by a team of hydrologists and geologists led by a faculty member from Universitas Winaya Mukti. Areas of analysis under this study were groundwater capacity, demand for water, and the possibility of intervention programs. This study showed that the demand for water has overwhelmed groundwater capacity, resulting in lowering the water table by approximately three meters per year. Recommendations made were followed by a tree-planting program and the construction of recharging wells, in order to increase the groundwater table and ease the flood threat. The local government, with the support of both the universities and the community, implemented these programs. The government provided the materials, the universities provided the expertise, and the community provided the land and labor.

Workforce Development

With regard to the labor research, the working group together with village councils and heads of villages conducted a workforce survey in the twelve villages in the area. The findings identified most of the local labor force as unskilled or unemployed. Another study was conducted specifically to look at the problems faced by small-scale businesses and entrepreneurs. Common factors faced by that group are limited access to capital and financial institutions, limited access to potential markets, and lack of management capacity. To resolve the problems, the working group mobilized the potential workforce to attend trainings provided either by universities or by other institutions. Some funding has been appropriated from the local government to support the small-scale business start-ups.

Civil Society

Regarding community institutions, the working group concluded that those institutions in the area were not well developed, and that there was a general lack of awareness regarding public affairs. Some elements of the society, such as professionals, laborers, and craftsmen, lacked an institution that could represent their interests. Some of the informal institutions that exist, such as the Village Council or the Mosque Council, run their businesses individually without awareness of the need to combine their efforts to address public issues. This finding was not surprising, given that community institutions have historically been excluded from otherwise public decision-making processes. Ways to empower civil society are described under "Community Institutional Development" below.

Policy Advocacy

Policy advocacy characterizes the strategic program carried out by the working group of Forum Jatinangor. The local governments in the District of Sumedang, the District of Bandung, and the West Java Province have overlapping authorities regarding public affairs in Jatinangor. As those are the decision-making entities, there is a need for policy advocacy as to what would be appropriate and effective to implement in this area. One of the policies currently being advocated is for the local and provincial government to create an "urban management body" to take care of public affairs in the Jatinangor area, especially with regard to public service provision. This body would resemble a development corporation board that consists not only of local government representatives but also of representatives from the private sector, the community, the universities, and nongovernmental organizations and that manages urban affairs. This body is proposed to have a certain degree of administrative authority delegated by the District of Sumedang in order to manage day-to-day affairs. Such a body would ultimately maintain the partnership initiated by the Forum Jatinangor.

Community Institutional Development

The institutional networking conducted by the working group was accomplished by facilitating meetings involving various local institutions. Several community institutions are being fostered and strengthened by Forum Jatinangor, including the Forum for Youth Council, the Association of Village Heads, the Forum for Village Council, and the Forum for Mosque Council. One important achievement was the creation of a University Collaboration Forum, which consists of the four universities and has a goal of building a platform to guide the policy of each university toward the development of Jatinangor. A similar forum was founded in the early 1990s soon after the relocation, but it failed to proceed, resulting in each university having its own policy on this matter, as well as its own relationship with the local community. The situation then was degraded to the condition discussed earlier. The new network development initiative strives for coordination among the decision makers in all four universities by adding a task force to the institutional structure to support the rectors. In the joint decree signed by each rector, there is a provision that each university will contribute to the operation of a joint secretariat and agree upon a joint agenda for research.

This joint decree will strengthen the role of the four universities in actively improving their relationship with the community as more joint events are carried out in accord with their respective capacity. The most recent activities carried out by Institut Manajemen Koperasi Indonesia and Universitas Winaya Mukti were (1) academic forums, "Management of Cooperative and Small-Medium Business" and "Management of Community," which were attended by students, academics, officials of the Jatinangor subdistrict, and business practitioners; (2) research on traffic management to ease existing transportation problems; and (3) an outreach program of computer database training.

These initiatives provided universities with avenues through which to play an active role in improving the condition of the Jatinangor area, including ending environmental degradation and empowering the local community. These efforts were undertaken with the intention of making the area a better place to live, as the universities could share the benefits from improvements in these areas.

Concluding Remarks and Lessons Learned

The case presented here is an example of siting and development decisions conceived and carried out by universities and governments without input from local actors and resulting in negative consequences. But this case could also be unique in terms of the idea, the scale, the problems that emerged, and the sociopolitical changes that led to the problem-solving processes. The idea started with the need to provide lands for site development, which is market driven, then led to the development of large-scale areas, making Jatinangor the only university town that houses four tertiary educational institutions. Some lessons can be derived from this case in terms of the decision-making process, the declining role of the state, the emerging dialogue, the partnership and collaboration among different elements of society, and the impact on university siting decisions in general.

The decision to relocate the universities at the beginning shows how powerful the state was. Faced with the urbanization problem in its main city, the government looked at what functions it could exclude from the city to reduce the problem and chose higher education. Since the state owned and controlled the land and the universities, the government's decision met no obstacles. Plans were generated, buildings were constructed, and universities were opened. The emerging problems were observed only when the town grew substantially, which was not expected, according to the plan. In the absence of a formal institution to deal with the problems, the community tried to address them itself.

In the meantime, the dynamic changes of social and political life in the past couple of decades, not only in Indonesia, have had an effect on the declining role of the state in general. The power of the state in the 1990s was not as strong as a decade earlier. To provide and manage urban infrastructures or an urban economy, the government was relying more upon private entities. The case of Jatinangor is just one example of how the government could not do much in solving the problems. Thus, the civil society emerges in reaction to the declining power of the state. In Indonesia this movement reached its peak in 1998, when President Suharto, a symbol of the powerful state, was forced to step down following the economic crisis.

This political event opened up the initial process to solve the problems that Jatinangor had. Some individuals in the universities and the community played roles as agents of the problem-solving process. The international community also shifted its attention to civil society empowerment and good governance and supported the effort. The increasing needs for dialogue, partnership, and collaboration between elements of the society were felt and followed up. The general lesson from this project was that a university could not be an exclusive entity inside a city. The dialogue between the community and the universities must be sustained as part of the community-university relations. In addition, the partnership and collaborative approach can be a successful model for addressing negative consequences of urban development.

To close this chapter, two general observations need to be made regarding the effect of the university siting decision. First, although the idea of relocating universities from the center of the main city to the fringe areas was followed by other cities in Indonesia (Jakarta with Universitas Indonesia, Semarang with Universitas Diponegoro, and Denpasar with Universitas Udayana), evidence from Bandung shows that the effect of reducing the number of higher education institutions in order to ease the urbanization problem was limited, even though the urban population growth rate slowed. There are currently eighty-four tertiary educational institutions operating in Bandung, which is double the number of institutions twenty years ago. The number of students also increased, to more than 130,000, which is the same as the number of government employees working in the city. This indicates that the policy of relocation as part of a counter magnet strategy failed.

Second, although the participatory planning approach in urban affairs is new in Indonesia, it is spreading to many communities both rural and urban, but especially to urban areas. We cannot tell for sure how successful this approach will be in solving the problems in all areas, or whether it is applicable to all areas, but from the lessons we have derived from other countries and from the initial successes in Jatinangor, we can say that collaboration between universities, communities, and the state could help address acute urban problems. In this era of a declining state and emerging civil societies, universities, as respected elements of the society, must and will always be expected to play an active role in solving the problems of the society.

Notes

I would like to thank several people who helped with the writing of this chapter: Ridwan Sutriadi in the Department of Regional and City Planning of ITB and all colleagues in the Forum Jatinangor for providing the materials (reports, numbers, and drawings) for the chapter; Kem Lowry and Lawrence Rutter at the University of Hawaii at Manoa for editing and proofreading the manuscript; Neel Chapagain and Nurmala for editing the drawings; and all who participated in the discussion during the Author's Workshop at the Lincoln Institute of Land Policy, Spring 2004. Should there be any mistakes or shortcomings in the chapter, I am solely responsible for those.

1. Besides serving as the capital city for West Java Province, Bandung houses several national state-owned enterprises such as the Post and Telecommunication Company and the Railway Company.

2. Industries located in Bandung that contribute a lot to the national economy are the textile, garment, footwear, electronics, and aircraft (Industri Penerbangan dan Teknologi Nusantara, or IPTN) industries.

3. In 1982, the ambitious plan had been to move nine public and private universities from Bandung, but in 1989 the governor of West Java issued a decree to relocate only four of them (Hindersah 1985; Badan Perencanaan Pembangunan Daerah Jawa Barat 1999).

4. The question has been raised of whether the decision to relocate universities to the urban fringe area was a political decision, to remove students far from the center

of government to avoid student demonstrations, as happened in other countries, but that was not the case with Bandung.

5. "Participative Planning in Public Affairs: Strengthening Local Institutions as a Participative Institutionalisation Process. Case Study: Jatinangor University Area," Dept. of Regional and City Planning Institut Teknologi Bandung–University of Illinois at Urbana-Champaign, Ford Foundation, 2001–3.

6. Institut Manajemen Koperasi Indonesia opened in the early 1980s, STPDN opened in the mid-1980s, and the other two universities opened in 1991–92.

7. Three out of the four universities are state universities (funded by the national government); the other is a private university but is under the influence of the provincial government.

8. Berube (1978) presents the case of Columbia University in New York, with its development of a gym in a public park, and the case of Harvard and MIT in Boston, with their ownership of housing in the midst of a low-income housing shortage.

9. ESLARP has a mission to establish and nurture mutually enhancing partnerships between community-based organizations in East St. Louis, Illinois, and students, staff, and faculty members from UIUC. Through these innovative partnerships, ESLARP promotes the revitalization of distressed areas as well as the university's research, teaching, and service missions. Although DRCP-ITB is not located in the Jatinangor area, its role in the initial process of rebuilding this university-community relationship has been essential and is similar to what UIUC does in the community of East St. Louis.

References

Ahmadi, D. 1988. *Pengarahan Lokasi Asrama Mahasiswa di Kota Jatinangor* [Location Allocation for Student Dormitory in Jatinangor]. Tugas Akhir. Bandung: Dep. Teknik Planologi ITB.

Badan Perencanaan Pembangunan Daerah Jawa Barat. 1999. *Buku Fakta dan Analisis, Rencana Umum Tata Ruang Kota Kawasan Perguruan Tinggi Jatinangor* [Fact and Analysis Book: Master Plan of Jatinangor University Area]. Bandung: Pemerintah Provinsi Jawa Barat.

Barlow, M. 1998. "Developing and Sustaining an Urban Mission: Concordia University in Montreal." In *The Urban University and Its Identity, Roots, Locations, Roles*, ed. M. van der Wusten. Dordrecht: Kluwer Academic.

Berube, M.R. 1978. *The Urban University in America*. Westport, CT: Greenwood Press.

Departemen Teknik Planologi ITB. 2002. *Perencanaan Partisipatif dalam Urusan Publik, Studi Kasus Kawasan Perguruan Tinggi Jatinangor* [Participatory Planning in Public Affairs: Case Study of Jatinangor University Area]. Laporan Penelitian. Bandung: Dep. Teknik Planologi ITB.

Firman, T. 1996. "Urban Development in Bandung Metropolitan Region: A Transformation to Desa-Kota Region." *Third World Planning Review* 1: 1–22.

Grobman, A.B. 1988. *Urban State Universities: An Unfinished National Agenda*. New York: Praeger.

Hindersah, H. 1985. *Konsep Pengembangan Tata Ruang Wilayah Integrasi Kota Tanjungsari dan Kawasan Jatinangor* [Integrated Spatial Development Concept of Tanjungsari Town and Jatinangor Area]. Tugas Akhir. Bandung: Dep. Teknik Planologi ITB.

Kolikiana, Y.E.S. 2003. *Penilaian Manfaat dan Biaya Penggunaan Sistem Penyediaan Air Bersih Secara Komunal (Studi Kasus: RW 01 Desa Hegarmanah, Kawasan Perguruan Tinggi Jatinangor)* [Cost-Benefit Analysis of Communal Clean Water Provision System: Case Study RW 10 Hegarmanah Village, Jatinangor University Area]. Tugas Akhir. Bandung: Dep. Teknik Planologi ITB.

Mardianta, A.V. 2001. *Identifikasi Awal Dampak Kegiatan Pendidikan Tinggi pada Ekonomi Lokal di Jatinangor* [Identification of Universities' Impact on Local Economy of Jatinangor]. Tugas Akhir. Bandung: Dep. Teknik Planologi ITB.

Pamungkas, A. 2001. *Analisis Dampak Perkembangan Kawasan Perguruan Tinggi Jatinangor Terhadap Biaya Input Penyediaan Air* [Impact Analysis of Jatinangor University Area Development to Water Supply Input Cost]. Tugas Akhir. Bandung: Dep. Teknik Planologi ITB.

Theresia, H. 1998. *Dampak Kegiatan Perguruan Tinggi terhadap Perkembangan Kota Jatinangor* [Impact of Universities' Activities on Jatinangor Town Development]. Tugas Akhir. Bandung: Dep. Teknik Planologi ITB.

World Bank. 2002. *Urban Sector Review for Indonesia: Bandung City Report—Final Report.* Jakarta: World Bank.

10

The University of Oporto and the Process of Urban Change

An Ambiguous Relationship

Isabel Breda-Vázquez, Paulo Conceição, and Sónia Alves

This chapter analyzes the role of the university as a promoter of urban development in the city of Oporto, in Portugal. The argument is developed as follows: (1) the university is an important operator in urban change; (2) however, the relationship between the university's real estate policy, the territory itself, and urban policies is ambiguous and marked by a gulf between the university's strategies and the specific problems of the urban context; and (3) any interpretation of the ambiguity requires an analysis based on institutions or on institutional relationships and capacities. This argument emphasizes the ambiguous and contingent role played by the university in the process of urban development and recognizes that this role is not always explicitly incorporated into the strategy of the main urban agents, such as the local authority or the university itself.

In the case of Oporto, an understanding of these characteristics requires articulating two theoretical concerns that feature in studies of universities and cities. On the one hand, this involves the whole debate relating to the identification and characteristics of the effects of universities on the process of urban development (see, for example, Indovina 1998). That debate seeks to identify the various levels of relationship between the city and the university and to develop and apply methodologies that can reveal and describe these effects. It is important, above all, to note here that these effects are multiple—affecting the spheres of employment, housing, mobility, leisure and consumer activities, and the economic base and its competitiveness—and that this multiplicity may involve different references or territorial scales.

The idea of ambiguity, on the other hand, is anchored in a whole other debate relating to the role of institutions in urban development and to urban development as a relational and institution-building process (see, for example,

Cars et al. 2002; Gualini 2001). In light of this debate, the specific relationship between the university and the city of Oporto cannot be separated from the process of change taking place in the university itself, or from the process of change in urban planning in the city. The relationship between the university, the state, and the city therefore provides the backdrop for explaining the role of the university as a promoter of urban development.

In this chapter, the connection between these two perspectives is addressed in the following way. First, the main characteristics and evolution of the spatial organization of the University of Oporto are presented, and recent changes are located within the general context of the organization of universities in Portugal. Next, two studies of representative situations are presented: the process by which the university moved its facilities out of Oporto's city center, which is showing signs of urban crisis; and the gradual construction of a new, more peripheral university area. In different ways, both studies reveal the difficult relationship between the university's real estate strategies and the territories where the university's facilities are located. The theme of the ambiguous relationship between the university and the city that emerges from these two studies is examined in greater depth in the final section of the chapter.

The University of Oporto and Its Spatial Strategies

The University of Oporto (*Universidade do Porto,* or UP) has a population of over 30,000 people, roughly 27,000 that are undergraduate and postgraduate students and 3,800 are lecturers, researchers, and nonteaching staff. Currently in the process of increasing its student numbers and diversifying the courses on offer, the university is spread over fifteen different schools (see Universidade do Porto 2004). It is situated in the city of Oporto, Portugal's second-largest city, which, in 2001, had approximately 260,000 inhabitants and was the main urban center in a greater metropolitan area of approximately 1.2 million residents.

The UP is the only public university in the city of Oporto, where it has been based since its foundation in 1911.[1] Until the last decades of the twentieth century, the university site retained its original layout, organized around various buildings in the central (and historic) zone of the city. This model was not based on any clearly defined spatial strategy. On the contrary, it developed through the acquisition and occupation of available buildings, meaning that the university expanded gradually into the surrounding urban fabric and helped structure the social, economic, and symbolic character of the central area of the city of Oporto.

A stronger university presence from the 1980s onward, associated with an increase in student numbers and facilities (following the need for a greater diversity of courses and quality of training), involved a new logic of investment in real estate and urban location. The university reorganized itself spatially within three major areas: the original area in the central historic zone of the city (Area I), the Asprela university area on the northern outskirts of the city (Area II), and the Campo Alegre area in a zone to the west of the center (Area III) (see Figure 10.1). Each of the three zones has its own characteristics of location and urban integration, and involves an uneven development dynamic that will be considered in greater detail later.

In order to understand why this particular solution was chosen, it is important to take into account three fundamental sets of circumstances. The first concerns the strategic decision taken in the 1950s to alter the urban setting of the university. It was proposed that the UP institutions be concentrated in a large outlying area especially adapted for the purpose, in accordance with the principles of "university zoning" in western Europe in the 1950s and 1960s.[2] To that end, a vast area destined for university expansion—the Asprela university zone—was reserved in the planning documents of the time (and has been maintained to the present day). The university therefore held a privileged position in the earliest plans for the city, with a claim on land use.

The effects of this decision—to concentrate the university's facilities in its own area—were not particularly evident in the decades that immediately followed. The Central Administration systematically delayed approving and signing contracts for the new UP building projects in the area (Fonseca 1996), which created difficulties for the university in structuring investments. Issues linked to the financing of the new facilities delayed their installation in the Asprela zone. The same factors hampered investments aimed at improving the existing university facilities in the city center, and thus for decades the UP had to contend with a lack of space and the deterioration of its original installations.

The second set of circumstances, which emerged at the end of the 1970s and essentially involved two dimensions, is also associated with decision-making processes. On the one hand, it was proposed that a new expansion zone—the Campo Alegre zone—be created for the university just outside the central area where the UP was historically established. This meant that a second university zone was defined in the city, in addition to the Asprela zone. A decision was also made to maintain some of the university facilities in the original UP site in the city center.[3]

In short, the university's spatial policy, to group the UP institutions within a single area (the Asprela zone) and involving a move out of the city center, was altered. The final decision established a model of three university areas, on which the current strategy for locating the buildings is based. This change in perspective involved a concern for greater links between the university and the city.

Figure 10.1 The Spatial Organization of the University of Oporto

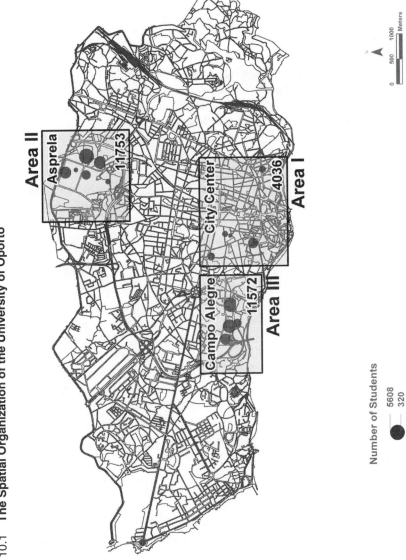

The third set of circumstances is more functional in nature. It concerns implementation of the major real estate development operations in the Asprela and Campo Alegre areas, which began in the 1990s. This was facilitated by greater available funding as a result of Portugal joining the European Union in 1986 and consequently gaining access to the Community Support Frameworks[4] since 1989. On account of greater financial resources, the construction of new university facilities in these areas has occurred gradually over the past few years to meet the needs of increasing student numbers and more diversified course offerings. This process of real estate development has also involved a relocation strategy for some of the university facilities formerly established in the center of Oporto.

As a result of some of the transformations analyzed in this chapter and decisions to use university assets located in the city center for administrative purposes, the central area (Area I) now contains the smallest UP population, approximately four thousand individuals. The schools these students attend occupy the older buildings, which are historically and symbolically associated with the origins of the university. Their historic location within the central urban fabric has helped preserve a strong symbolic and affective character in the area, which is near important monuments and institutions such as the City Hall and the Historic Center of Oporto, a UNESCO World Heritage Site (see Figure 10.2).

The Asprela university area (Area II) represents the most recent and important area of expansion in total surface area occupied (an extension of roughly 120 hectares); it has a population of about 11,753 individuals. Its size and its characteristics of occupation, in addition to its definition as a university land reserve, make this zone distinctly different from the surrounding urban environment.

The semicentral area of Campo Alegre (Area III) represents an intermediary situation in location and capacity, in comparison with the two other areas. There are about 11,572 individuals in its various schools, occupying a group of new buildings that have been integrated in a relatively discontinuous manner into the surrounding urban fabric.

Taken as a whole, the UP spatial organization in three areas expresses the reinforced presence of the university in the city. It is a model that has been constructed over time, bearing witness to the university's relative physical fragmentation in its quest to respond to the needs of development. It is also a model that reflects the relative importance of the three university areas, their structural organization, and the way they are integrated into the urban environment.

The UP's expansion and spatial reorganization have given rise to a wide range of issues concerning the role of the university as an element of urban

Figure 10.2   **The University of Oporto in the City Center**

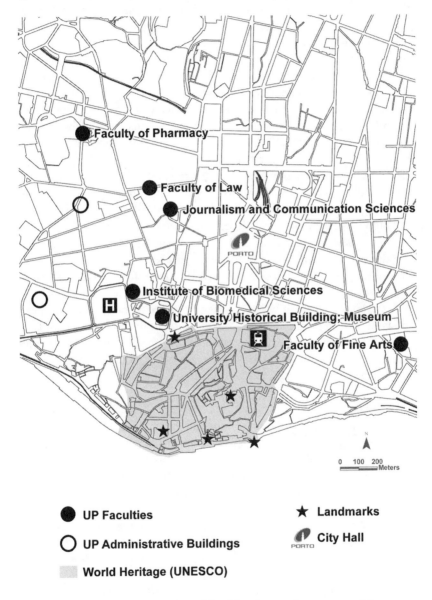

● **UP Faculties**

○ **UP Administrative Buildings**

▓ **World Heritage (UNESCO)**

★ **Landmarks**

🏛 **City Hall**

change. These issues are analyzed in this chapter by means of two representative situations: the transfer of university schools formerly established in the city center to new university areas (Areas II and III), which intensified the physical, social, and economic vulnerability of the city center, as it meant the withdrawal of a significant portion of the university population; and the transformation of the extensive Asprela area into a space that has the characteristics of a university "campus" and is highly distinctive within the surrounding urban fabric.

To provide a framework for these two situations and for any reflections arising from them, it is important to take into consideration some additional factors related to the general positioning of the university within the city of Oporto. The main aspects that should be stressed relate to the importance of the public university (the University of Oporto) as a factor of urban transformation arising from the "weight" of the university population in the city and the role of the UP as a real estate operator.

The university population (staff and students) totals approximately 30,000 people, a figure representing almost 12 percent of the city's residents and roughly 10 percent of the people who work or study in the city.[5] The UP student population (27,000) represents 50 percent of students in higher education in the city (according to Fernandes 2001) and is responsible for around a quarter of the daily travel within the city for study purposes.

These figures allow us to consider the multiple effects of the UP on the urban environment, particularly in socioeconomic dynamics and mobility, which are consistent with what has been observed in other urban contexts. Various studies on the phenomena of interaction of the university population with the urban fabric highlight, in particular, the impacts on local leisure and consumer activities, housing and the use of transport facilities, and infrastructure (Armstrong et al. 1997; Felsenstein 1996; Glasson 2003; Harris 1997; Ricci 1997; Rovigatti 1998).

The urban effects are not, however, consistent. The essential issue seems to be the relative sizes of the university and the city (and the characteristics of the local economic base), as well as the university's more or less dispersed urban location model[6] and, above all, the way reciprocal relationships are established between the university and the city, both on a functional level and in institutional planning and strategy. The two cases analyzed in this chapter illustrate these aspects.

In terms of the importance of the university as a real estate operator, it should be noted that UP investments in the second half of the 1990s represented the most significant share of the Central Administration's investments in buildings in the municipality of Oporto: approximately three-quarters of the investments in buildings over five years. This means that the university's expansion program is far from being a secondary aspect in the "construction" of the urban area, but is, in fact, a fundamental element in its transformation.

This fact assumes even greater importance when it is analyzed in terms of the dynamics of urban transformation. The expansion of the university is taking place at a particularly critical phase in urban development related to a progressive decline in the city's economic base and a sharp demographic reduction. It should be noted that in the past two decades, the city of Oporto, although it has the highest employment density in the greater metropolitan area, has displayed unfavorable conditions in the evolution of total employment in contrast to the situation registered in the rest of the greater metropolitan area. Oporto also has the highest rate of unemployment. In terms of demographics, the city has begun to suffer from the effects of intensive population decentralization (in its center and its surrounding metropolitan area). Certain indicators reflect this process clearly. In the past twenty years, the city has lost a fifth of its inhabitants, whereas the greater metropolitan area has grown by 13 percent, and around 77 percent of this drop in population has been concentrated in the city center. These demographic losses in the city and in its center have intensified over the past decade. During this period, the city and its central area have lost approximately 13 percent and 24 percent of their residents, respectively.

A recent study on the decline in the city's central area[7] shows that this demographic loss has been accompanied by other critical situations: The local population is aged and impoverished, and the housing stock has deteriorated. There is also a significant use of buildings for nonresidential purposes, associated with a decline in the local economy.

It is within this critical context of the city and its central area that the spatial reorganization of the university is being implemented, including its real estate development operations. It is only by taking this context into consideration that we can understand the importance of the university as a fundamental factor of urban transformation.

The Relationship between the University and the State: University Autonomy

The University of Oporto's location strategy cannot be separated from the more general context of change in Portuguese universities and the relationships they have established with the state. This situation can be described in terms of three processes:

- The expansion of higher education in Portugal, with a significant rise in student numbers and diversification of the types of training on offer (universities, departments, courses), which has resulted in objective needs leading to the transformation and expansion of university facilities;
- The process of European integration, which, through the Community Support Frameworks, has resulted in new possibilities for investment in university facilities; and

Figure 10.3   **Number of Students Enrolled in Public and Private Higher Education in Portugal, 1980–2003**

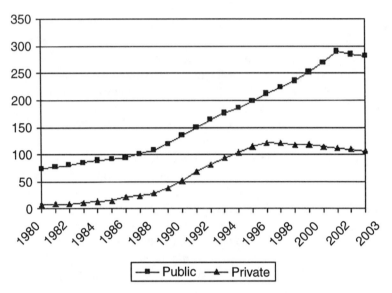

Sources: OCES (2004) and Barreto (2002).

- The increased autonomy of the universities in relation to the Central Administration and the consequent changes in their organization and, possibly, their relations with local communities.

The first significant change relates to the expansion of higher education and public higher education. At the beginning of the 1960s, the number of students enrolled in higher education in Portugal was less than 25,000; by 1980, the number was over 91,000, of which 80,000 were in public schools; and in 2003, the figure was 388,000, of which 280,000 were in public schools (see Figure 10.3). Around 73 percent of these students were attending public universities. Within a European context, this expansion is highly significant. According to data from Eurostat (2003), out of the fifteen countries that made up the European Union at the start of 2004, Portugal registered the greatest rise in student numbers in higher education between 1975 and 2001.[8] During this period, student numbers in Portugal increased by approximately 4.4 times, compared to the average increase for the European Union as a whole, which was by 2.3 times.

The second significant change relates to the consequences of European integration, especially from 1986, the year in which Portugal joined the European Union. As part of the regional policies of the European Union and the provision of aid for the most disadvantaged regions, successive Community Support Frameworks were negotiated, each of which included specific arrangements for support in developing university facilities, with contributions from the European Union amounting to 75 percent.

The third significant change relates to increased university autonomy and the consequent changes in the organization of universities and their relations with the state. The defining elements of this process are the 1986 *Lei de Bases do Sistema Educativo* (Framework Law on the Education System) and the 1988 *Lei da Autonomia Universitária* (Law on University Autonomy, Law no. 108/88). These documents specify the objectives of the universities as centers for education, research, provision of services to the community, and international cooperation and exchange. In addition, they establish the spheres of university autonomy ("statutory, scientific, pedagogical, administrative, financial and disciplinary").

These three changes have important consequences for universities as urban institutions. Within a European frame of reference, Savino (1998) has referred to the relationship between the university and the city in terms of the relative "extra-territoriality" of the universities, which he sees as "introverted and complex" organisms endowed with a high level of autonomy in relation to other urban actors.

One of the explanations for this extra-territoriality is the way universities and university knowledge are traditionally conceived (emphasizing the pursuit of "universal knowledge"), which in Portugal is reinforced by the traditional bonds between the university and the Central Administration. The diverse roles of the university as a center for education, research, and provision of services, as well as the recognition of its relative autonomy in relation to the Central Administration, open up new possibilities for reformulating the relationship between the university and the "community."

For example, the process of constructing university autonomy is accompanied by the development of various "interface" structures between the university and the different social and economic agents linked to the provision of advanced services. Partnership structures have also been established between the university and other local agents, including the local authority, related to the management of particular facilities.

The three changes described above have additional consequences in the way university investment in the area being constructed is programmed. In the case of Oporto, the planning of the various university areas has been developed in very diverse institutional contexts. The Campo Alegre university area is connected with the work of the *Grupo Coordenador das Instalações da Universidade do Porto*[9] (University of Oporto Coordinating Group for

Installations) a Central Administration initiative that includes representatives from the university. The Asprela university area, as we will see, eventually came to be associated with an institutional initiative involving the university and a group of local agents that is particularly focused on access planning. Changes in the location of university facilities have therefore been affected by relations between the various university schools, the university itself, and local institutions.

It may be concluded that (1) the expansion of higher education creates new investment needs, which accumulate over time; (2) changes in the availability of funding explain the exact moment at which the development of new university facilities occur; and (3) in this development, the different roles played by the university and the central and local authorities must be understood in the context of the reorganization of the universities.

The Relocation of University Facilities Away from the City Center

The situation described here refers to the relocation of the University of Oporto's schools away from the city center. The analysis aims to provide a framework for the central focus of this chapter—the relation between the university's real estate policy and its urban context—by focusing on the critical role played by the university in aggravating the existing problems of the central area of the city.

The relocation of the UP facilities took place in 2000 and 2001[10] and involved moving two faculties that had been located in the city center for some considerable time (in Area I) to new installations in the Asprela (Area II) and Campo Alegre (Area III) areas. These faculties provide technological and scientific training and research (engineering and sciences) and in 2000 had a combined total of around 9,800 undergraduate and postgraduate students, corresponding to 36 percent of the total number of UP students and 77 percent of the university students studying in the city center in university institutions (see Figure 10.4).

The relocation of these two institutions created an effective reduction, amounting to about 8,800, of the number of undergraduate and postgraduate students in the center of Oporto.[11] If we add to this figure the number of lecturers, researchers, and other staff who were relocated, it is clear that the city center lost around 10,000 individuals.

For decades, the Engineering and Science Faculties had serious space problems, given the objectives of competitive training and research. The case of the Engineering Faculty is particularly significant: Before it moved out in mid-2000, it housed around 5,500 students (postgraduate and undergraduate)

Figure 10.4   The Spatial Distribution of the University of Oporto Faculties in the City Center, before 2000 and after 2001

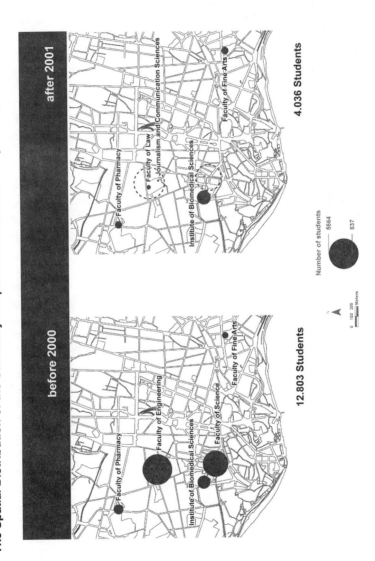

in a group of old buildings[12] amounting to 30,000 square meters[13]—a ratio of almost 6 square meters per student.[14] The new buildings boast an occupied area of almost 85,000 square meters and a ratio of 13 square meters per student.

Overcrowding and the inadequacy of the existing buildings were therefore the main reasons for the relocation strategy. It should be noted that the morphological characteristics of the central zone of the city, particularly the high density of buildings and the strict demarcation of properties and land, make it difficult to build new installations from scratch to serve as teaching and research facilities with high demands for space. The problem of space in the city center, together with the historic character of the properties in the area that belong to the UP, is mirrored in the strategy defined by the UP, which aims to locate in that area only university services and units that require low-intensity space.[15]

The "space crisis" in the two university institutions unfolded in an urban area that has also been marked by crisis. As already mentioned, by the end of the 1990s, the city center was experiencing clear signs of physical deterioration, social vulnerability, and functional instability, which have compromised the local urban dynamics and the city's image, given that its identity is strongly related to the historical heritage of its central area.

The processes of change in the university and change in the city therefore intersect in the traditional and historic center of Oporto. For this reason, we will now seek to analyze the effects of the UP relocation strategy and assess its timeliness and consequences.

The Intensification of Existing Problems in the City Center

Our analysis of the effects of the UP relocation strategy on the functional use and social transformation of the city center focuses on the move of the Engineering Faculty (FEUP) to the Asprela area, which took place in September 2000. To understand how this institution interacted with the surrounding urban area, particularly in terms of the local consumer patterns of the university population, and to understand the main processes of change after the FEUP was relocated, complementary methodologies were used:[16]

- A 2000 survey of 4,891 undergraduate students from the Engineering Faculty, a stratified sample by course, resulted in 336 valid responses on student user habits and perceptions of the city of Oporto.
- Two "focus group" sessions were held with members of the institution (teaching staff, nonteaching staff, and students), and a survey was conducted of commercial companies in the downtown area of Oporto, both in 2003.

The main results will be examined later. In general, it can be said that the relocation of the university institutions, by gradually and steadily removing an important demographic mass from the center of Oporto, has had significant repercussions on the leisure, consumer, and social activities in the area. In fact, the withdrawal of some ten thousand students and staff from the city center was ultimately responsible for a heavy reduction in demand for the urban services it provides, particularly in relation to commerce, leisure activities, and housing.

The reduction in demand has had a significant effect on most of the local commercial businesses. In particular, the businesses that targeted their sales strategies at the younger or student segment of the market, such as the many clothes, fashion accessory, and shoe shops and the cafés that line the avenues, experienced a sharp fall in trade after the university institutions left the area.

In 2000, around 56 percent of FEUP students regularly used the shopping facilities near the UP buildings; those consumer habits were just as marked among the students who lived there only during term time (68 percent said that they shopped in the surrounding area) as among those who were permanent residents of the city (61 percent shopped in the area). Research results confirm that the relocation of university institutions altered student consumer patterns (see Alves and Breda-Vázquez 2003).

The changes in local consumer patterns are significant for three reasons. First, commerce had been the main economic activity in the area from the perspectives of jobs created and land use. Second, city center commerce had little potential to adapt to new consumer patterns, given that it consisted mostly of small and medium-sized family businesses with traditional styles of management. Third, this type of commerce was already experiencing critical instability due to the gradual demographic decline in the city center and the competition from new types of commerce (shopping malls) on the outskirts, which had made it heavily dependent on specific consumer niches such as the university population.[17]

In addition to altering local consumer patterns, the relocation of the university institutions caused a change in interactive behavior and mobility in the city center, since it led to a gradual decrease in sustainable transportation to and from students' places of residence and altered existing urban social patterns.[18] It has, in fact, changed the demand for various spaces in the city center that were sought out for leisure and social purposes. Such activities as "going for a stroll," window shopping or shopping itself, and visiting a café were common leisure and social pursuits among higher education students in the center of Oporto.[19]

The relocation also led to changes in housing patterns for university students, who aim to live near their place of study. This is important for the group of students who stay in the city only during term time. The vast majority of those "uprooted" students live in "rooms" or rented flats.[20] Few live in the

UP residences, as there are not enough places.[21] The gradual withdrawal of this group of students from the city center has led to a change in the use of buildings (favoring services instead of residences and even causing unoccupied buildings), deterioration of existing properties, and increased social vulnerability of the area. The rooms and accommodations in the central zone of the city that used to be rented to university students are now increasingly occupied by a new immigrant population coming mainly from eastern Europe and the Portuguese-speaking African countries, who find the central location and the low rents an attractive option.

This social "reinvasion" of low-income immigrants with precarious employment prospects and limited social relations has exacerbated the unstable balance of the central zone, reinforcing the factors that have made real estate investments and the reversal of this "urban deprivation" difficult. In short, relocation of the existing university facilities has had many local effects, and their significance has been emphasized by the crisis in the city's central zone.

As previously stated, the most serious problems in the city of Oporto—namely, the fragility of the economic base; the physical deterioration of the buildings; the lack of housing and the overcrowding of housing that is available; the aging population; and low incomes, unemployment, and social isolation in family units—are concentrated in the center city. These problems are not recent; they result from processes of demographic and functional decline over the past few decades, together with the more general dynamics of the spatial restructuring of the metropolitan territory as a whole, including the city of Oporto. However, they have made the central zone of the city particularly sensitive to any factors or practices that intensify the condition of urban disadvantage. Decentralization of the university facilities would appear to be one such factor. While the university's location decisions intensified the problems of the city center, they cannot be isolated from other decisions. By the time the university facilities were moved out of the city center, the crisis in the area had already been diagnosed in several studies commissioned by the local authority (see, especially, the studies developed by Breda-Vázquez et al. 1996 2000).

A second dimension emerging from this analysis relates to the difficulties of organizing local responses to the problems that affect the center, in particular, the difficulties of connecting the policies defined by the university to those defined by the local political and administrative authorities.

The Divergence between University and City Spatial Policies

Significant divergences can be found between the university's decentralization policies and local policies aimed at urban renewal. It can even be said that the university's real estate policy and the local authority's urban rehabilitation initiatives have only one point in common: They are both characterized by independent strategies that aim to make the most of the opportunities available.

The urban regeneration initiatives face several difficulties. Local resources are inadequate and are essentially directed at one specific area: the historic zone where the UNESCO Heritage Site stands. In addition, there are almost no national public policies dedicated to urban regeneration in Portugal; national programs aimed at urban areas since the 1990s have been fragmented, restricted in scope, and limited in duration, characteristics that create difficulties and affect the likelihood of public (and private) initiatives (see Breda-Vázquez and Conceição 2002).

The local urban initiatives have, in general, been associated with specific areas of activity and have had significant restrictions in the financial resources mobilized. The programs aimed at housing are an example of this,[22] as reflected in the important work undertaken in the recovery of heritage buildings in the city's historic zone. Public initiatives have aimed to make the best of opportunities provided by European Union initiatives,[23] which involve adopting models and practices that are not always compatible with the nature and dimension of the problems in question. In short, partly due to financial limitations and partly due to the (case-by-case) management context involving possibilities or opportunities for action, initiatives in the city center have been both specific and disjointed.

The only attempt to develop a model of action specifically directed at the central areas of the city of Oporto was part of the Oporto, European Capital of Culture 2001 event. With that event, an attempt was made to combine the cultural agenda with urban renovation and in this way generate the transformation of the city center, particularly its most symbolic features, to promote a new urban image and create functional synergies.[24] This event, which took place in 1999 and 2000, was marked by temporal and institutional constraints that heavily restricted its scope and function. Only some initiatives to rehabilitate public spaces in various areas of the central zone were implemented.

This urban renewal event was developed at the same time the FEUP was implementing its changes. However, even though the University of Oporto was represented in the administration of the Oporto, European Capital of Culture 2001, SA, a public company that promoted the operation,[25] no concerted planning mechanisms aimed at minimizing the effects of the FEUP were established. The university's participation was clearly related to the cultural aspects of the event, given its importance as an urban institution for promoting culture. In this significant relationship between the university and the city's urban policy, concern about the risks inherent in the university's development policy was absent.

As with the local policies for urban intervention, it could be said that the university's development policy was subordinated to opportunistic decisions defined by financial and funding opportunities.

In conclusion, the university's development policy and the urban policies of the local authority have been marked by independent decisions and actions. This clearly indicates a lack of recognition of the role of the university as an agent of urban change and is mirrored in the absence of any interlinked strategy for the institutions in solving the problems of the city center. Furthermore, the fact that the policies of both entities arose from particular (and individualized) funding opportunities, with their own unequal paces of implementation, is not favorable to the organization of collaborative proposals or actions that could address the negative impacts caused by the reorganization of the university.

Urban policy makers' disregard of the effects of the withdrawal of university institutions from the city center and the difficulties associated with creating collaborations between the university and the local authority are important factors in the intensification of the problems in the city center.

The Construction of the Asprela University Area

The second representative study concerns the gradual development of a university area—the so-named Asprela area—on the outskirts of the city of Oporto (see Figure 10.1 above). This section aims to discuss the issues arising from the expansion of the university and the construction of Asprela and to debate the importance of the institutional relations. After analyzing the divergence between the university's development policy and the local authority's urban policies in Oporto, it is important to understand whether the same type of divergence occurs in this context.

The Asprela area occupies approximately 120 hectares and at present contains six University of Oporto schools (Medicine, Economics, Dentistry, Sport Sciences and Physical Education, Nutrition Sciences, and Engineering), with the installation of another (Psychology and Education Sciences) planned. The surrounding area contains two polytechnic schools, two health care units (the S. João District Hospital—one of the two main hospitals in Oporto—and the Portuguese Oncology Institute), and facilities of two private universities (Catholic University's Institute of Biotechnology and the Portucalense University) (see Figure 10.5). The area has been developed over a period of more than four decades. In 1959, the S. João Teaching Hospital was completed, and in 1974, the Economics Faculty was installed. It was in the 1990s, however, particularly the second half of the decade, that the area's physical transformation gathered momentum.

The development that took place in that period became particularly sig-

Figure 10.5   **The Spatial Organization of the Asprela Area**

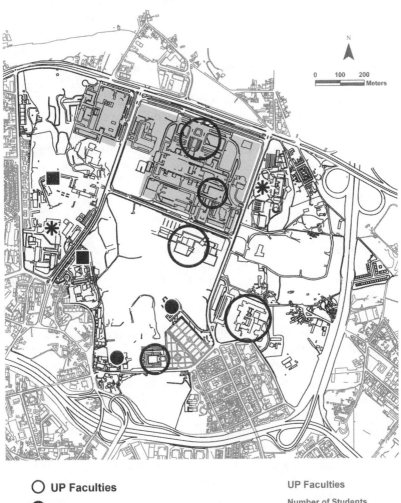

○ **UP Faculties**

● **UP Other Buildings**

■ **Private Universities**

✳ **Polytechnic Institute of Oporto**

▨ **Hospital Institutions**

UP Faculties

Number of Students

nificant, not only for the university but also for the city of Oporto. The total volume of investments (approximately 50 million euros) represents almost four times the average annual local authority's investment in buildings.[26] The total constructed area (roughly 113,000 square meters) corresponds to about 38 percent of the average annual construction projects undertaken by private developers in the city,[27] the building of the Engineering Faculty alone representing over a quarter of the average annual construction work undertaken by private developers. Given its investment capacity and the areas developed, the university therefore constitutes an important agent of change in the city of Oporto.

However, the effects of development in the Asprela area have not merely been a result of the importance of the university as a promoter of urban development. They can be analyzed according to other factors, which take into account the relations established between the university area and the other nearby urban areas, including the following (Indovina 1998; Savino 1998):

- The dynamics of real estate and the supply of accommodations;
- Demands by the universities for various services related to leisure and consumer activities;
- Training and advanced services offered by the university, which may lead to effects on economic activities; and
- The university population's mobility and its effects, the most immediate and visible of which is overloading the existing road system.

The change in location of the university installations has potentially significant effects on student housing, bearing in mind the data relating to the percentage of UP students uprooted from their families. We may therefore ask whether the occupation of the Asprela area by the various UP schools has led to changes in the dynamics of property investments in the area. This question becomes even more important when the effect of the residences provided by the universities themselves is not significant (see Table 10.1).

Table 10.1 does not show a concentration of investments in housing in the areas in question. Even though Paranhos in Oporto and Pedrouços in Maia (a neighboring local authority) have a comparatively high density of new accommodations, a continuous process of growth in housing is not shown—there was even a fall in the rate of new building projects during the period 2000–2002. At that time, the trend was closer to the regression in housing development that has characterized the city of Oporto than to the expansion that characterizes the greater metropolitan area of Oporto.

However, using the same type of data provided by the housing licenses, we have identified more specific indicators within the spheres of housing development. If we compare the investments of the construction firms in the Paranhos parish, where the Asprela area is located, with those of other parishes on the peripheral zone of Oporto, we find clear differences in the types of housing

Table 10.1

New Building Licenses and Density of Accommodations, 1994–2002

	Number of new building licenses			Density of accommodations 1994–2002
Area	1994–1996	1997–1999	2000–2002	(dwellings by sq km)
Metropolitan area of Oporto	35,599	44,215	50,927	171
Municipality of Oporto	3,710	3,940	3,856	305
Paranhos	1,127	1,200	1,018	517
Pedrouços	360	536	518	547

Source: Instituto Nacional de Estatística, Oporto.

available. In Paranhos, accommodations with a smaller number of bedrooms (0 or 1) represent about 36 percent of the total figure. It is interesting to note that the phenomenon of comparative differentiation—even more intense in terms of the amounts being considered—also separates Massarelos (where the Campo Alegre university area is located) from the other nearby parishes. We may therefore hypothesize that these differences are associated with a reorientation in real estate investment toward the type of accommodation sought by the student population.

These differences, which have yet to be studied, confirm likely changes in the relationship between students and accommodations, with the emergence of a market based on buying accommodations (or investing in smaller types of accommodations to rent out), rather than the previous tradition of renting rooms.

A second aspect of the effects of development on the Asprela area has to do with leisure and consumer activities. The study in the preceding section, of the effects of the withdrawal of university facilities from the city center of Oporto, recognized the importance of the university location to the organization of social practices. The absence of strong relations between these elements involves at least three aspects: first, the trend, in each school, toward internalizing certain services that are unavailable in the nearby area, particularly those most directly related to academic activities; second, the relative lack of links between the schools, from the viewpoint of access to shared services and their production; and third, a lack of firm, explicit references in the plans of the university installations to the creation of common areas and elements associated with leisure activities, both for the student population and for those living near the university.

Another effect of the development of the Asprela area results from a concentration of organizations that produce advanced services (e.g., laboratories, research units), whose relationships are predominantly based not on interaction between the different university schools or between those schools and the immediate surrounding area (Cardoso 1990, 1991), but on much broader spatial contexts.

Finally, there are the issues related to accessibility. The gradual occupation of the Asprela area, particularly after relocation of the Engineering Faculty, has led to considerable overcrowding on the existing roads, with a significant increase in the number of trips made. Of all the aspects of the relationship between the university and its surrounding territory analyzed so far, the problem of access arouses the most immediate and visible concern. As we shall see, this problem has led to efforts to coordinate the agents intervening in the area.

The assessment of the situation here highlights two significant difficulties: on the one hand, the difficulty of the university establishing relations with the surrounding territory; on the other hand, the difficulty of creating functional and morphological links between the various spaces that have been constructed (fulfilling the university's role as a "promoter" of the city).

To explain these difficulties it is necessary to describe the institutional characteristics of the development process in the Asprela area (see Domingues and Mealha 2002). The question that needs to be asked is this: Why have none of the many dimensions on which a relationship between the university and its territories could be established worked out?

As mentioned in the beginning of this chapter, the university occupies a territory in the Asprela area that has been reserved since the beginning of the 1950s by the municipal planning system as part of an arrangement for the functional division of space, first for health care and then, also, for university and cultural facilities. Envisaged in the *Plano Regulador da Cidade do Porto* (Urban Plan for the City of Oporto, approved in 1954), structured in the *Plano Director da Cidade do Porto* (City of Oporto Land-Use Plan, approved in 1964), and confirmed in subsequent planning documents, the planning system can be said to have left three fundamental marks over time: the availability of land, due to state demarcation and control, reserved for university and health care institutions; the main road system that structures the area and makes it accessible; and the concept of exclusive zoning, which disallows private real estate development within the Asprela area.[28]

Even though the Asprela site has been reserved since the 1950s,[29] its development has been an example of an incidental process of change, conducted over time, based on the expansion needs of each school and accomplished according to the financing made available by the state.

The relations the university establishes with the city and with the territories nearest to it are restricted by the characteristics of this development process. On the one hand, the principle of the functional division of space and the university's relative physical isolation may be seen as factors that make it difficult to construct links between the university and the territory nearest to it. On the other hand, the casuistic nature of the process of installing the various schools seems to have inhibited the quest for more systematic planning solutions for the area as a whole, whether on the part of the University of Oporto or on the part of the local authority. While these difficulties have arisen partly out of the initial choices of location and the characteristics of the surrounding territory, they nevertheless raise certain issues about the planning system and its organizations.

We have already considered the effects of land-use plans in creating a "reserve" of land for the development of the university area. It is important to note that, particularly within the context of the 1990s, when the changes in the Asprela area intensified, the several agents involved gradually acknowledged the inadequacies of the existing planning tools for the area.

This acknowledgment, which resulted from an initiative to prepare the so-called *Carta de Objectivos Comuns* (Charter of Joint Objectives) between 1996 and 1997, was formulated through a series of diagnoses that referred to the "lack of relevance" of the *Plano Director Municipal* (Municipal Land-Use Plan), the "distressing panorama of urban need and deprivation," and the "marginal role" of the local authority (see Fundação Ciência e Desenvolvimento 1997).

Efforts are now being made to construct—a posteriori?—a collaborative framework for the various agents involved in development of the area,[30] based on the compatibility among initiatives to produce structural elements such as the road system, the building of the rail transit network, and the organization of parking lots and public areas.

The University of Oporto eventually produced a plan to introduce some elements of integration and territorial cohesion, after a major part of the decisions and projects were already in their final phase. However, there remains the question of how to coordinate the municipal responsibilities and spheres of intervention with those of the university. The planning process for the Asprela area is not yet over. Several important interventions relating to access routes are still simultaneously in progress, although it is possible to draw some conclusions.

One factor that stands out, as we have seen, is the difficulty in establishing interaction between the university and the areas around it. This difficulty may be understood in terms of two main aspects:

- On the one hand, based on the characteristics of the municipal planning system, this difficulty involves the existing model of land-use planning (in particular, the concept of zoning that was adopted); it also involves, less directly, the fact that the planning system was incapable of responding adequately to the process of "reserving" the space and later developing and building on it.

- On the other hand, there is the issue of institutional relationships: This difficulty begins with the university's model of organization (and, in particular, the relationships between the various schools, which helps us to understand the case-by-case nature of the installation of these schools in the Asprela area) but also involves a lack of systematic mechanisms for establishing links between the university, the local authority, and other agents that recognize the university's role as an urban institution.

The University of Oporto and Urban Change: An Ambiguous Relationship

This chapter has analyzed the role of the University of Oporto as an agent of change in the city of Oporto. The increase in the number of students and the diversity of courses on offer resulted in the need for transformation and development of the university's facilities. Consequently, the university has gradually reorganized itself within three different areas of the city.

The first point that needs to be stressed in this analysis is that the university is an institution endowed with a high investment and development potential. This fact cannot be isolated from the institution's capacities for funding and its position within the different levels and institutions of the Portuguese administration. After Portugal joined the European Union, the university's capacity for real estate investment and development unfolded within a framework that was highly favorable in terms of availability of financial resources. In addition, the university's relatively autonomous status within the Portuguese public administration has enabled its real estate investment program (and its implementation) to progress independently of the political powers and the local administration.

The second point that emerges from this analysis is the importance of the university as a real estate operator with considerable influence on the dynamics of change in urban areas at a time when several signs of stagnation and even decline were evident in the city of Oporto.

Third, an analysis of the university's role in the spatial transformation of the city of Oporto reveals critical aspects of the interaction between the university's development policy and the urban area and its policies. It can be said that this interaction reflects the central issue explored in this chapter: the ambiguous nature of the university as an agent of urban change.

The university's development policy has unleashed spatial problems, whether by contributing to the critical situation that already existed in the central zone of the city or by promoting the relative segmentation of the Asprela university area in its internal organization and in relation to the surrounding urban areas. The impact of relocating university institutions away from the central area of the city has been shown to intensify that area's problems of physical decay, social vulnerability, and functional instability. The physical transformation of the Asprela area, which involved a significant investment in property and space in the city of Oporto, resulted in a lack of urban cohesion and functional relationships in the area.

The tension created by the university's disinvestment in the central area of the city has not been regulated by any local urban development policies, as previously noted. In the Asprela university zone, the development process was limited to following the functional zoning that was established in advance by the official planning system, which guaranteed that the land would be reserved as a university area. Successive interventions operated within the margins of this formal planning structure, whose underlying casuistic logic actually appears to have hindered the search for more systematic planning solutions for the area in question.

It is within the sphere of the relations between the university and the local authority, and in the way the urban planning system and policies operate, that we may find an explanation for the ambiguous role played by the university in the city's transformation. Difficulties in interaction between these two urban institutions have already been mentioned. The "exceptional" character associated with university initiatives as a result of the university's relatively autonomous status in relation to public administration and the opportunistic nature of those initiatives allowed local planning structures and strategies to be undermined. Moreover, the fragmented nature of local urban policies and the financial and temporal constraints placed on them did not encourage common agendas and mutual cooperation. Both these factors reveal the difficulties inherent in creating joint organizational capacities for the two urban institutions.

However, the frailty of this process of institutional empowerment should not be overstated. It has been clear in the case of Asprela that the university's development initiatives led to experimentation in new forms of interaction between the agents intervening in the area, which resulted in the *Carta de Objectivos Comuns*. In addition, both the university and the local authority are now seeking to overcome the various obstacles and introduce coordinated mutual efforts. Current concerns of the university (Universidade do Porto 1999) include improving the ways university areas are linked to the urban fabric of the places where they are established and actively participating in requalification schemes for the center of Oporto. In turn, the local authority, which is launching an ambitious regeneration strategy for the area, recently began developing contacts with the university in order to define joint commitments.

The learning process involved in the creation of institutional capacities may be seen as an important element of change, as discussion on this issue shows (see, e.g., Amin and Thrift 2002; Gualini 2001; Healey et al. 2002). Since it is an interactive process in which the different types of consolidation and decoding of knowledge play a key role, its development requires time and effort. The analysis contained in this chapter, within its limitations, is intended to contribute to this learning process.

Notes

We are very grateful to Frederico Sá for support in the cartographic productions in this chapter. The authors extend also a special thanks to the FEUP students from the course on planning projects (2003–4) for assistance with the data analysis.

1. The founding of the University of Oporto by decree-law on March 22, 1911, was associated with two higher education institutions that had existed in the city since the nineteenth century: *Academia Politécnica* (Polytechnic Academy) and *Escola Médico-Cirúrgica* (School of Medical Surgery). It is also possible to identify its more remote antecedents in the *Escola de Náutica* (Naval Academy), established in 1762, and the *Escola de Desenho* (School of Design), founded in 1779 (see Universidade do Porto No Date).

2. A concept of zoning that in urban universities refers to the concentration of university facilities in areas on the outskirts of cities. The underlying vision is a rationalist view of university work, in which "the researcher is an isolated being in his laboratory who has no direct contact with society" (Cardoso 1991, 31). In some advanced democratic countries, the physical separation of the university from the city also symbolized the defense of academic freedom and university autonomy (Abercrombie et al. 1974, 20).

3. The new context for decision making is associated with the activities of the *Grupo Coordenador das Instalações da Universidade do Porto* (University of Oporto Coordinating Group for Installations), created in the 1970s by the Ministry of Education to analyze the situation regarding the UP's assets and installations and to propose suitable programs for its modernization and development in future decades.

4. Funds that support development within national territory, negotiated within the terms of the European Union regional policies.

5. This is assessed by the number of daily journeys made for work and study purposes.

6. The "dispersed campus" solution has characterized urban university expansion in other European countries, particularly Italy, where some authors have debated the strategic role of the dispersed urban university in terms of how it has strengthened interaction with the local community, as in the special issue of the journal *Archivio di Studi Urbani e Regionali* (no. 60–61), 1998, dedicated to the theme of "the city and the university."

7. An analysis undertaken as part of a strategic study on urban rehabilitation in these areas. See Breda-Vázquez et al. (2004).

8. This is partly explained by the low level of higher education in Portugal during most of this period.

9. See note 3.

10. The Engineering Faculty moved in mid-2000, and the Science Faculty moved gradually (course by course) up to 2001.

11. Also taking into account the new students arriving in the area due to the recent opening of other UP schools, which will be discussed later.

12. The main building dates from 1937; expansion of the local facilities took place incrementally, by converting properties in the surrounding area as they were gradually acquired from private entities.

13. The figure refers to the total constructed area. The occupied area represents only 13,400 square meters.

14. These days this type of teaching institution (associated with technology) ordinarily has spatial parameters on the order of fifteen to twenty square meters per student (Mariotto 1998).

15. For example, the administrative and symbolic types of services (the Rectory and the University Museum) and the units that do not require much space (the schools associated with law and journalism courses). Several studies on the spatial restructuring of universities in Europe indicate exactly the same options (see Merlin 1995; Pasqui 1998; van der Wusten 1998).

16. For a more detailed consideration of the application of these research tools to the evaluation in question, see Breda-Vázquez and Alves (2003).

17. These factors have led to the recent launch of a program to revive traditional commerce: the *Programa Urbcom,* which began in 2000 and is jointly financed by the central government, the European Union, and the local authority.

18. The relevance of traveling on foot in Oporto's city center should be stressed, particularly for those students who reside there only during term time, roughly half of whom travel between their place of residence and place of study on foot. Those who come from the city and live there permanently most frequently use collective forms of transportation, and a large part of the central urban area is dedicated to the public transportation system (namely, buses and trains).

19. For example, a survey by Fernandes (2001, 240) involving a sample of 875 "higher education students in the city of Oporto" concluded that "going for walks in the city" is something almost all the students did (78 percent frequently), together with "going to the café" (mentioned by 52.8 percent of the total). Moreover, according to Fernandes, "The demand by students for particular places such as the café, the bar, the pub or the discotheque must be understood in terms of their social and relational aspects and not just as a consumer activity. . . . These are leisure areas, since they enable friends to meet up, and they also act as an intermediary between the academic area and the family area" (2001, 241).

20. "Uprooted" from their family home and area of residence. This situation applies particularly to students from beyond the Oporto Metropolitan Area, as students inside this area usually continue to live with their families. As Fernandes (2001) points out, students in higher education in Oporto leave their families later in life compared with those in many other European countries.

21. Approximately 1,347 beds are available for the University of Oporto student population; thus, they serve only 6 percent of the total number of undergraduates (see Breda-Vázquez and Alves 2003).

22. The PER program, created in 1993, and the programs linked to older rented properties developed from 1988 onward.

23. As in the case of the PPUBS, an urban pilot project implemented in a neighborhood in the historic zone at the end of the 1990s.

24. Around 38 percent of the overall budget associated with this event (that is, 86 million euros) was dedicated to urban renewal programs.

25. The university was represented on the company's Advisory Committee, which incorporated a group of renowned individuals from various sectors of society. The committee met as required to give opinions on the programs and projects.

26. Average figures between 1998 and 2002 (Oporto City Council).

27. Average figures between 1998 and 2002 (Instituto Nacional de Estatística, Oporto).

28. The most recent change here is a 2004 development, which involves a hotel, shopping mall, and car park, on land belonging to the S. João Hospital by a private company through a license granted by the hospital authorities.

29. In a context characterized by a functionalist view of planning and the promotion of strategies aimed at rehabilitating the city center, boosting urban expansion, and decentralizing population (resulting, for example, in a series of housing developments in the peripheral area).

30. The Oporto City Council, the *Federação Académica do Porto,* the S. João Hospital, the Oporto *Instituto Politécnico,* the *Instituto Português de Oncologia,* the Oporto Metro, the Portucalense Infante D. Henrique University, and the University of Oporto, which signed the *Carta de Objectivos Comuns.*

References

Abercrombie, N., I. Cullen, V. Godson, S. Major, and L. Timson. 1974. *The University in an Urban Environment: A Study of Activity Patterns from a Planning Viewpoint.* London: Heinemann Educational Books.

Alves, S., and I. Breda-Vázquez. 2003. "Universities and Their Role in Urban Community Development: A Case Study." Universities and Their Role in Urban Community Development, EURA Workshop, Enschede, Netherlands.

Amin, A., and N. Thrift. 2002. *Cities: Reimagining the Urban.* London: Blackwell.

Armstrong, H., J. Darrall, and R. Grove-White. 1997. "Maximising the Local Economic, Environmental and Social Benefits of a University: Lancaster University." *GeoJournal* 41, no. 4: 339–50.

Barreto, A., ed. 2002. *A Situação Social em Portugal, 1960–1999.* Lisbon: Imprensa de Ciências Sociais.

Breda-Vázquez, I., and S. Alves. 2003. *Universidade e Transformação Urbana.* Oporto: Centro de Investigação do Território, Transportes e Ambiente, Faculdade de Engenharia da Universidade do Porto.

Breda-Vázquez, I., and P. Conceição. 2002. "EU Initiatives and Programmes in Practice: In What Sense a New Approach to Urban and Regeneration Policies?" Urban and Spatial European Policies: Levels of Territorial Governance, EURA Conference, Turin.

Breda-Vázquez, I., P. Conceição, L.M. Batista, and L. Branco-Teixeira. 2000. *Contributos para a Definição de Intervenções de Regeneração Urbana.* Oporto: Faculdade de Engenharia da Universidade do Porto.

Breda-Vázquez, I., P. Conceição, T. Marques, P. Moia, and F. Sá. 2004. *Estudo Estratégico para o Enquadramento de Intervenções de Reabilitação Urbana na Baixa do Porto.* Oporto: Faculdade de Engenharia da Universidade do Porto.

Breda-Vázquez, I., P. Pinho, P. Conceição, and J. Ferreira. 1996. *Estratégia de Intervenção para o Centro do Porto*. Oporto: IC/SPTA/CMP.

Cardoso, A. 1990. "A Universidade do Porto e a Cidade: Notas sobre a Expansão da Cidade." *Boletim da Universidade do Porto* 2–3 (November–December): 10–15.

———. 1991. "A Questão da Diversidade." *Boletim da Universidade do Porto* 7–8 (April–May): 31–32.

Cars, G., P. Healey, A. Madanipour, and C. De Magalhães. 2002. *Urban Governance, Institutional Capacity and Social Milieux*. Aldershot, UK: Ashgate.

Domingues, A., and R. Mealha. 2002. "O Confronto entre Duas Escalas Urbanas: Projecto da Área Central do Pólo II da Universidade do Porto." *Sociedade e Território* 33: 130–41.

Eurostat. 2003. *Education across Europe 2003*. Luxembourg: Office for Official Publications of the European Communities.

Felsenstein, D. 1996. "The University in the Metropolitan Arena: Impacts and Public Policy Implications." *Urban Studies* 33, no. 9: 1565–80.

Fernandes, A., ed. 2001. *Estudantes do Ensino Superior no Porto: Representações e Práticas Culturais*. Oporto: Edições Afrontamento e Porto.

Fonseca, M. 1996. *A Construção do Pólo 3 da U.P.: Planos, Projectos e Edifícios*. Oporto: Tese Doutoramento, Faculdade de Arquitectura da Universidade do Porto.

Fundação Ciência e Desenvolvimento. 1997. *Pólo Universitário da Asprela: Objectivos Comuns de Intervenção*. Oporto: Fundação Ciência e Desenvolvimento.

Glasson, J. 2003. "The Widening Local and Regional Development Impacts of the Modern Universities: A Tale of Two Cities (and North-South Perspectives)." *Local Economy* 18, no. 1: 21–37.

Gualini, E. 2001. *Planning and the Intelligence of Institutions: Interactive Approaches to Territorial Policy-Making between Institutional Design and Institution-Building*. Aldershot, UK: Ashgate.

Harris, R. 1997. "The Impact of the University of Portsmouth on the Local Economy." *Urban Studies* 34, no. 4: 605–26.

Healey, P., G. Cars, A. Madanipour, and C. de Magalhães. 2002. "Transforming Governance, Institutionalist Analysis and Institutional Capacity." In *Urban Governance, Institutional Capacity and Social Milieux*, ed. G. Cars, P. Healey, A. Madanipour, and C. de Magalhães, 6–27. Aldershot, UK: Ashgate.

Indovina, F. 1998. "Sinergi Tra Communità e Università." *Archivio di Studi Urbani e Regionali* 60–61: 85–114.

Mariotto, A. 1998. "L'Universitá a Venezia: Scelte Localizzative e Funcion Formative Nelle Politiche Territorialli." *Archivio di Studi Urbani e Regionali* 60–61: 145–62.

Merlin, P. 1995. *Urbanisme Universitaire à l'Etranger et en France*. Paris: Presses de 1´école nationale des Ponts et Chaussées.

OCES (Observatório da Ciência e do Ensino Superior). 2004. *O Sistema do Ensino Superior em Portugal: 1993–2003*. Lisbon: MCES.

Pasqui, G. 1998. "Le Università Milanesi come Attori Urbani: Politiche, Strategie e Processi di Interazione." *Archivio di Studi Urbani e Regionali* 60–61: 115–43.

Ricci, M. 1997. "The Urban Role of a New University: A Case Study of Chieti-Pescara, Abruzzo, Italy." *GeoJournal* 41, no. 4: 319–24.

Rovigatti, P. 1998. "Università e Processi di Transformazione Urbana: Il Caso di Pescara." *Archivio di Studi Urbani e Regionali* 60–61:219–50.

Savino, Michelangelo. 1998. "Università, Città, Studenti: Aspetti Complessi di Interdipendenze non Sempre Note." *Archivio di Studi Urbani e Regionali* 60–61.

Universidade do Porto. 1999. *Guia de Desenvolvimento Estratégico 2000–2004.* Oporto: Author.

———. 2004. *A Universidade do Porto em 2002: Relatório. Factos e Números.* Oporto: Author.

———. No Date. *Breve História da Universidade do Porto.* http://sigarra.up.pt/up/web_base.gera_pagina?P_pagina=2415 (accessed March 20, 2007).

van der Wusten, H. 1998. *The Urban University and Its Identity.* Amsterdam: Kluwer Academic.

Part IV

The University and the Contested City

11

Academic Fortress

The Case of Hebrew University on Mount Scopus, Jerusalem

Haim Yacobi

> *Monumental buildings mask the will to power and the arbitrariness*
> *of power beneath signs and surfaces which claim to express*
> *collective will and collective thought.*
>
> —Henri Lefebvre, 1991

Universities in cities are considered significant urban catalysts, stimulating the development of city centers and neighborhoods economically, culturally, and socially. However, little attention has been given to the political role of universities in constructing a national territorial identity in general or in the Israeli case in particular. In this chapter I will discuss the role of universities in shaping national urban space. More specifically, I will critically analyze the case of Hebrew University on Mount Scopus in Jerusalem through the following perspectives: (1) the *territorial-national* task, (2) the *architectural symbolic* dimension, and (3) the *urban functional* role.

The main argument to be articulated in this chapter is that after the 1967 war the location of the Hebrew University campus had a fundamental role in the Israelization of Jerusalem. Geographically, the campus marked the edge of the "unification" of the city post 1967 and produced a seemingly natural, historically based frontier that enabled the extensive development of Jewish neighborhoods on Palestinian expropriated land that linked Hebrew University to West Jerusalem's city center. Thus, a new cognitive map of a "unified Jerusalem"—the Jewish capital—was produced.

Furthermore, reconstructing the Hebrew University campus on Mount Scopus had a symbolic importance, expressed in its mega scale and architectural forms that aim to dominate the East Jerusalem skyline; it symbolically hegemonized Jerusalem's urban space. This new urban-scale landmark competed with the Mount of Olives skyline, whose towers mark non-Jewish monuments. As a result of the overemphasis on and attention to its political and territorial role, the university left aside its social and cultural (potential) contribution to the community and city daily life.

From a Third Temple into a Military Enclave

This section discusses the historical roots and ideologies—from the 1920s to the 1948 war, which was followed by the establishment of the Israeli state—that caused the erection of the Hebrew University campus on Mount Scopus. This historical period is important in understanding the development of the campus that became an Israeli enclave within the Jordanian territory.

Early Zionist thinkers and activists encouraged the establishment of a Hebrew university in the land of Israel. It is argued (Dolev 1997, 2004) that the Zionist movement identified this issue as being significant on its agenda, and thus the founding of the Jewish/Hebrew University (both names were initially used) was promoted among Jewish communities around the world. It is important to note that in the early stages there was uncertainty as to whether the university should be located in Europe or in Palestine. As the vision shifted from a school to serve the needs of Jewish students in Eastern Europe into a central promotion tool in the Zionist settlement agenda, it became clear that the university should be erected in Palestine.

The cornerstone for the university was laid in 1918 on Mount Scopus. On April 1, 1925, the opening of the Hebrew University of Jerusalem was followed by a ceremony attended by Zionist leaders such as the university's founding father, Dr. Chaim Weizmann; distinguished Jewish academics; and community leaders; as well as respectable British politicos such as Lord Balfour, Viscount Allenby, and Sir Herbert Samuel (Kedar 1997; www.huji. ac.il/huji/eng/aboutHU_history_e.htm). This event, according to a university publication (Susman 1969, 1), had "deep significance for the Jewish people," as also declared by Chaim Weizmann:

> It seems paradoxical that in a land with so spare a population, in a land where everything still remains to be done . . . we should begin by creating a center of spiritual and intellectual development. But it is not a paradox to those who know the soul of the Jew. . . . We Jews know, however, that when our mind is given full play, when we have a center for the development of Jewish consciousness, then coincidentally we attain the fulfillment of our material needs. (Hebrew University brochure 1969)

The importance of the university to the Zionist project is analyzed by Dolev (1997; 2004), who argues that the question of whether the inhabitants of Jerusalem were in need of a university was not brought up at all. In fact, she claims that "the location issue was one of prestige rather than a true need" (2004, 183). She illustrates her argument by mentioning Heinrich Loewe, a delegate at the Zionist Congress, who said:

> Universities are the birthplace of culture and *Bildung:* the European states have understood their value. Now Central Europe is celebrating the hundredth anniversary of the War of Liberation, in which the universities played such an important role. From where was the liberation of Prussia led? From the founding of the University of Berlin! (Loewe 1913 in Dolev 2004, 183)

From an architectural point of view, the construction of Hebrew University on Mount Scopus expressed the national aspirations of the Zionist movement. This is indicated in the attempt to refer to it as the "Third Temple," an approach that appeared in early Zionist texts (Paz 1997; Dolev 2004).

In the scope of this chapter, I will not be able to examine in detail the discourses and images that shaped the architectural form of the Mount Scopus Hebrew University campus.[1] I will emphasize the central value of Hebrew University to the Zionist national project and the university's link to the traditional notion of the Dome of the Rock as the Holy Temple. This link is worth noting, since the issue is significant to the discussion of the Jewish people's return to Israel within the Zionist narrative—the return to the origins of authentic being, both ideational and earthly.[2] This attitude is also expressed in the words of Patrick Geddes,[3] the first planner of the campus (Dolev 1997; Shapiro 1997):

> But the best example, the classic instance of city renewal (beyond even those of Ancient Rome and Ancient Athens), is that of the rebuilding of Jerusalem; and my particular civic interests owe more to my boyish familiarity with the building of Solomon's temple, and with the books of Ezra and Nehemiah, than to anything else in literature. . . . The improvising and renewal of cities might, and should once more, find an initiative, an example, even a world-impulse, at Jerusalem. (Dolev 2004, 185)

This indicates an important link between Geddes's oriental-colonial-biblical aspirations and the Zionist national agenda, which has been discussed by some researchers (Greenstein 1995; Atran 1989). Furthermore, it illustrates Edward Said's (1993) claim that no single person, nor any society, is beyond or outside the struggle over geography, which is fought, he maintains, using not merely weapons but also ideas, images, and imagination. This struggle escalates when the issue is discussed within a context of national space and place. However, due to the complexity of reality, the landscape—whether natural or built—is shared by different groups, and each entity claims exclusive symbolic possession of the landscape. The result of this is the establishment of spatial dominion, which in turn is symbolically exploited to draw the boundaries between "self" and "other" (Yacobi 2003).

But beyond the territorial-symbolic dimension, Hebrew University functioned as an academic institution, and by 1947 it had expanded and established research and teaching programs, including the humanities, science, medicine, and education; the Jewish National and University Library; a university press; and an adult education center. Student enrollment exceeded one thousand, and there were over 200 faculty members (www.huji.ac.il/huji/eng/aboutHU_history_e.htm).

However, the 1948 war left Mount Scopus cut off from Israeli West Jerusalem (Figure 11.1). The university campus became an Israeli enclave within the Jordanian territory, and alternative facilities were found throughout the western part of the city. Indeed, after 1948 the only possibility of development in Israeli Jerusalem was on the west side. During the 1950s and 1960s, there was intensive construction of new, modern neighborhoods such as Kiryat Yovel and Katamonim. They were planned to be in the National Compound,[4] in the vicinity of Givat-Ram, the new site of Hebrew University in Jerusalem. In opposition to the orientalist architecture that characterized the Mount Scopus campus, Givat-Ram, which opened in 1958, was designed as a clear manifestation of a modernistic and functional vision. A few years later, work began on a health science campus in Ein Kerem in southwest Jerusalem, in partnership with the Hadassah Medical Organization. By the beginning of 1967, the number of faculties and schools had been greatly expanded, and enrollment exceeded 12,500 students (www.huji.ac.il/huji/eng/aboutHU_history_e.htm).

"The Exile from Mount Scopus Was Over"

From the top of the mountain a fascinating view is discovered. To the east—the Judean desert, the Dead Sea, and the Moav Mountains. To the west—a bird's-eye view of Jerusalem, the city that became over generations the city of eternity, a center of the cultural world.

—From The Hebrew University on Mount Scopus, 1976

A formal publication of Hebrew University narrates the "return" of the university to Mount Scopus after the 1967 war:

Figure 11.1 **Neighborhoods of Jerusalem, 1949–1967**

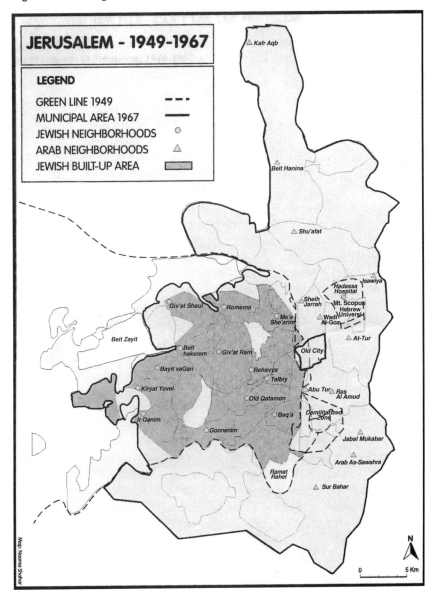

On Tuesday, June 6, 1967, the second day of the Six-Day War, the Israel Defense Forces fought their way through to Mount Scopus and liberated the summit, which for nineteen years had been a Jewish enclave in Arab territory. Three days later, on June 9, the university hoisted its flag atop one of the highest buildings on the hill. The exile from Mount Scopus was over; a new chapter had been opened in the history of the university. (Susman 1969, 13)

Indeed, the most significant turning point, on which this chapter focuses, starts after June 1967, when Israel occupied East Jerusalem, among other territories. Following this, the Israeli government initiated some legislation in order to apply Israeli law in East Jerusalem, despite international objections. Israel then annexed Palestinian land and declared the city of Jerusalem its "unified capital." Yet beyond the rhetoric representing Jerusalem as a unified city, Jerusalem's planning policies were those of the exemplar of an ethnocratic city.[5] Both state and city pursued policies that persistently promoted Judaization—that is, the expansion of Jewish political, territorial, demographic, and economic control.

As has been documented widely,[6] Israel has used its military might and economic power to relocate borders and boundaries, grant and deny rights and resources, shift populations, and reshape Jerusalem's geography for the purpose of ensuring Jewish dominance. Two central Israeli strategies have been implemented: (1) the massive construction of an outer ring of Jewish neighborhoods, which now host over half the Jewish population of Jerusalem, and (2) a complementary containment of all Palestinian development, implemented through housing demolition and the prevention of immigration to the city.

Land-use policy in Jerusalem encourages Jewish growth while inhibiting Palestinian growth in the city. Prior to 1948, Jews owned less than 30 percent of the property within the municipality of Jerusalem. Today, Jewish ownership or control of property accounts for over 90 percent of Jerusalem. This pattern created a physical obstacle on top of the already existing spatial barrier between East and West Jerusalem. What is more, Israelis have maintained control of all infrastructures, including water works and access roads, so that Palestinians have become isolated in their own neighborhoods, cut off from each other (www.afsc.org/middleeast/peace/jerusalem/jeruhistory.htm).

The unilateral unification of Jerusalem challenged Israeli architects and planners, who immediately after the 1967 war were asked "to cover the recently occupied land with 'built facts on the ground' in order to foster the desired unity of the city under Israeli rule" (Nitzan-Shiftan 2004, 231). The architectural form and its symbolic manifestation vis-à-vis the national aspirations of the post-1967 period made powerful symbolic use of the physical environment.[7]

In this context it is important to note that it was a government decision that the university be built on Mount Scopus, emphasizing the symbolic significance of the "return." This attitude infiltrated to the planning discourse at the time and was clearly expressed in the text that accompanied the *Mount Scopus Campus Master Plan:*

> Scopus—site of the dream come true, proud home of the national university of the Jewish people. Scopus—the campus in exile, the vision cherished throughout nineteen long years as we turned our eyes to its distant prospect. Scopus—the measure of our growth and development and now—the challenge of our future.

But beyond its symbolic importance, the planners had to consider the future contribution of the remote university site to the city, a point raised in the master plan documentation for establishing the Hebrew University campus on Mount Scopus (in *Tvai: Quarterly for Architecture and Town Planning* 16, 1976). The decision of returning to the Mount Scopus campus involved answering questions such as these: Which academic units would move to Mount Scopus? What would be the number of students? Which additional activities, besides teaching, would be located there? How could a vivid life be created on the mountain? How could a tight link be kept with the Givat-Ram campus? What would be the optimal solution to issues of housing, economy, and culture?

In 1981 the new campus, designed by some of the leading architects in Israel,[8] was opened, expanding on the hill in the shape of an introverted megastructure with a tower that marks its location from a distance (Figure 11.2). On the way to the isolated site, which was surrounded by Palestinian villages, new Jewish neighborhoods were constructed as part of the wider planning scheme that attempted to Judaize the space between the Israeli western city center and the Palestinian eastern zone.

The struggle over geography mentioned in the previous section is intensified in light of present reality, in which the national state has come to represent the dominant geopolitical order. Despite controversies between different schools of thought that analyze the origins and development of nationalism, all seem to agree that the nation has the potential of provoking deeper loyalty on the part of its members than any other community. This sense of belonging develops over time, as a result of changes and by encouragement of the state and leads to relationships of "us versus them," reflecting not merely differences but also superiority.

In the course of socialization, individuals' interrelations with territory may alter, leading not only to their identification with territorial space, but also to that space becoming a hub of their awareness, defined as a homeland, the "land of our forefathers" or the "motherland" (Fox 1990; Agnew and Corbridge 1995). But the very fact that a nation is not a homogeneous entity dictates

Figure 11.2   **View of Hebrew University's Tower and New Jewish
Neighborhoods**

that national symbols, which embody the freedom of political, cultural, and symbolic choice, be in the hands of those in power. Here the discussion of architecture and town planning as socially constructed symbolic manifestations is central. Just like other cultural representations, buildings are symbols of the political power of the state, which struggles to establish a particular collective identity and no other (Swartz 1997; Vale 1992).

I propose to refer to the immediate consideration of rehabilitating the Mount Scopus campus through this perspective. The university senate appointed a Rehabilitation Planning Committee a day after the end of the war. Its first meeting focused on a suggestion to erect a second campus on Mount Scopus, and the committee members prepared a new plan.[9] A few days after that, in a report of a special committee, the following was announced:

> The Board of Governors records its profound joy at the restoration of Mount Scopus to the city of Jerusalem. . . . It expresses its warmest congratulations to the Israel Defence Forces, whose heroism and self-sacrifice made this possible, and its heartfelt gratitude to the Government of Israel for its understanding of the need and desire for the university to be reunified with its original home.[10]

Archival documents show that different committees within the university dealt with the different aspects of reopening the university on the site.[11] One of the central issues was the search for land for the extension of the campus: "When [the planners] commenced to survey the existing site appropriated by the university, they discovered that the development opportunities are limited because of the shortage of land, and thus every future planning will demand the expropriation of land."[12]

These words are an example of the colonial legacy of perceiving the territory as *terra nullius,* which has been incorporated into the Zionist discourse (Yacobi 2004). Moreover, the potential "available" land that was expropriated belonged to the Palestinian village Isawiyah, which surrounded the area; thus, the situation demanded "state intervention."[13] State intervention was also discussed in relation to the financial aspects of the project. In one of the protocols the following is reported:

> There was a meeting with the prime minister. . . . Three decisions were taken:
>
> a. The government gave a "green light" to implement the first stage of the project and committed itself to finance 50 percent of the expenses.
> b. The minister of finance will locate the other 50 percent . . .
> c. We can immediately go to the next stage of planning.[14]

In a later meeting of the committee, this issue was more clearly raised, and national interests were used as justification for the need to fill the spatial "vacuum"—that is, to rehabilitate the Mount Scopus campus, which was considered an important task "from a national perspective as well as from the university point of view." It was further argued that the "empty space in Mount Scopus and its surroundings must be filled. If we will not fill it, someone else will do [it]."[15]

It seems that the spatial and visual relations between Mount Scopus and the city fabric were central to the design of the campus: "The future development is toward the east. The planning team sees this approach as a symbolic integration of past and future and as a continuation of the dialogue between the university of Mount Scopus and the city of Jerusalem" (*Tvai: Quarterly for Architecture and Town Planning* 16, 1976, 56). This was architecturally expressed by the planners, who thought that controlling the spread of the campus would "preserve the grandeur of Mount Scopus' natural landscape and the magnificent skyline it presents when seen from the city of Jerusalem" (*Mount Scopus Campus Master Plan*).

The architects' terminology relied on hegemonic interpretation, which projected the national Jewish identity and sentiments toward the cityscape and the role of the university in it. Hence, the discussion of the architectural discourse that accompanied the design of the campus cannot be separated from the wider social arena.

This issue was theoretically addressed by Lefebvre (1991), who states that one should observe the complexity of space and recognize not only its physical elements but also its symbolic elements, as well as the ideology that stands behind its production. Lefebvre asks, "What is an ideology without a space to which it refers, a space which it describes, whose vocabulary and kinks it makes use of, and whose code it embodies?" (1991, 44). In order to decipher the symbolic meanings associated with the new campus, one should trace the "vocabulary" used by the architects and planners. In numerous texts and architectural tributes that accompanied the planning stages, and later the construction of the building, their words reflected the concrete architectural practice. I propose that their words manifested the fortified hegemonic interest demanded of every project in the construction of a subjective identity (Khinsky 1993).

From a functional point of view, the planners' vision reflected the desire that the academic life of the future university community would "provide a rare opportunity for both the student body and the faculty to participate in a process of interaction that fosters the growth of the human personality" (*Mount Scopus Campus Master Plan*). Furthermore, the new master plan aimed to create "a campus combining both grace and functionality."

I suggest that the desire of the planners to create a functional campus on the one hand and a symbolic site on the other is problematic. This is manifested in the fortress-like architecture of the campus, which is set against its neighboring environment in order to create an urban-scale landmark vis-à-vis the city fabric (Figures 11.3 and 11.4). It is better manifested in the decision to locate a tower within the campus that primarily aimed to memorialize the site's original significance as the "mountain that looks over."[16] However, the tower is seen from a distance and manifests Israeli sovereignty on Jerusalem's skyline. It is interesting, however, that entrance to this panoptic tower is infeasible because of its military use.

The fortress-like architecture also has a significant effect on the organization of space within the campus. The intensity of the corridors that link the spread-out buildings produces a disorientating space (Figure 11.5). Moreover, the gigantically scaled, introverted complex caused the design of impervious facades. The facade of the university's synagogue, however, is exceptional; it opens toward the old city, framing the Temple Mount.

To sum up this section, it is important to mention that the area of the Hebrew

Figure 11.3   **The University Is Set Apart from Its Neighboring Environment**

Figure 11.4   **The Fortress-like Architecture of the Campus Is Evident**

Table 11.1

Land Area and Built Area of Hebrew University Campuses in Jerusalem

Campus	Land area (square meters)	Built area (square meters)
Mount Scopus	850,000	295,000
Givat-Ram	730,000	174,000
Ein Kerem	56,000	57,000

Source: Hebrew University Properties Department.

Figure 11.5 **Corridors Link Spread-out Campus Buildings**

University campus on Mount Scopus includes 850,000 square meters; it is the largest campus of Hebrew University in Jerusalem. Moreover, as Table 11.1 shows, the intensity of construction on the campus is significant, especially compared to the other campuses in the city.

The University's Urban (dys)Function

Beyond the territorial-national task and the architectural symbolic dimension discussed in the previous sections, it is important to ask what the results are of the spatial processes discussed above and what the urban contribution of Hebrew University—as an urban institution—is to Jerusalem's urban life. Following discussion of these questions, I will focus on the urban functional role of the university and examine the extent to which the decision to return to Mount Scopus contributed to the social, economic, and cultural life of the city.

According to the Student Management Office at Hebrew University, the total number of students in academic year 2004–5 was 24,500. That included 12,000 undergraduates, 8,000 master's degree students, 2,500 doctoral candidates, and 1,500 at the School for Overseas Students and in certification and other programs. From this data and the density of construction and sprawl of the campus mentioned above, one would expect the campus to be a central urban hub in Jerusalem. However, few commercial or cultural urban-scale functions are located in the area. Rather, the mountain is surrounded by an extensive system of roads and infrastructure—isolating it tangibly and symbolically from the urban fabric. Here I would argue that the campus's distance from the city center—its suburban-like location—caused the creation of an isolated urban entity, which cannot produce a significant connection to the daily urban life.

This argument is also raised by a comparison with the Givat-Ram campus, where most community activities take place. In an interview in December 2004, Dr. Shabtay Dover, head of the Center of Community Development at Hebrew University, stated that since the year 2000 there has been a serious attempt to develop a dialogue between the university and the community. This includes various projects, such as a series of lectures that is open to the public, the opening of the sport center to the public, science summer camps, and the opening of advanced laboratories (the Belmonte Science Laboratories Center) for the use of Jerusalem's high schools. The last example, he emphasized, creates an opportunity for Palestinian pupils from East Jerusalem to interact with Israelis from West Jerusalem. The university, according to him, has declared its commitment to the community; nevertheless, the majority of the activities are on the Givat-Ram campus, which is better connected to the Jewish neighborhoods in the south of Jerusalem.

Relevant to the problematic location of the Mount Scopus campus in relation to Jerusalem's city center is a current debate concerning the construction of more student dormitories—named the "Students' Village." The university aims to increase the number of students' rooms by 50 percent. On the one hand, there is an attempt to build these dormitories in the city center so as to contribute to its social, economic, and cultural life, which has suffered in the past two decades from deterioration, both because of planning policy (the erection of shopping malls out of the center) and because of the political situation (the last intifada). On the other hand, there is a faction that wants to build the dormitories by the campus in order to contribute economically and socially to that area. Indeed, it can be argued that one of the significant results of the decision to return to Mount Scopus is the dysfunction of the campus vis-à-vis the urban life of the city.

As I have elaborated in the previous sections, the location of the university had a fundamental role in the Israelization of Jerusalem. This is clearly expressed in the texts that accompanied the design and construction of the campus, as well as in policy documents supporting the claim that national identity—as a political and cultural construct—is related to the formulation of new time and space created by communal imagination processes that intertwine past, present, and future. This course is a manifestation of hegemonic culture, which frames the place while generating spatial transformation, using architecture as an instrument for its realization. Thus is formed the rhetorical landscape, the spatial fabric that "teaches" us about our past and our identity, and within which buildings assume their structured symbolic significance, being justified as representatives of the collective wish and thought. Moreover, as pointed out in this chapter, the preference of the symbolic location of the campus in the name of national territorial identity ignored the broader urban consideration and created an academic fortress—not just from an architectural point of view but also from its (dys)function as a central urban institution.

Notes

1. For a detailed study, see Dolev (1997, 2004).

2. For more details on the notion of "return" within the Zionist context and its relevance to architecture, see Yacobi (2004).

3. Patrick Geddes was a Scottish town planner who was involved intensively in urban planning in Mandatory Palestine. For more details, see Erlich (1984).

4. The National Compound (*Kiryat Ha Leom* in Hebrew) is the area that was designated before the 1967 war to include national official functions such as the Knesset (the Israeli parliament), the Israel Museum, and other governmental institutions.

5. *Ethnocracy* is defined as a distinct regime type established to enhance the expansion and control of a dominant ethno-nation in multiethnic territories. In such regimes, ethnicity, and not citizenship, forms the main criteria for distributing power and resources. As a result, these regimes typically display high levels of uneven ethnic segregation and a process of polarizing ethnic politics (Yiftachel 1999; Yiftachel and Kedar 2000). Urban ethnocracy critically analyzes a situation in which a dominant group appropriates the city apparatus to buttress its domination and expansion. In such settings, conspicuous tensions accompany the interaction between the city's economic and ethno-territorial logics, producing sites of conflict and instability and essential-

izing group identities and ethnic geographies. For further analysis, see Yiftachel and Yacobi (2003, 2004).

6. For details of Israeli Judaizing policies, see, among many others, Yiftachel and Yacobi (2002).

7. This argument is theoretically based on a comprehensive discussion of the role of architecture and urban design in the production of capital cities in Vale (1992).

8. According to Dolev (2004), three people were central in shaping the new design: architects David Reznick and Ram Karmi, and Yoseph Harpaz, the newly nominated general director, who was formerly an army officer. Harpaz became the dominant figure in the university and also took over the Mount Scopus development planning. It is claimed that it was he who pushed toward building a large-scale campus on Mount Scopus that would eventually replace the Givat-Ram campus. For further details on the historiography of Israeli architecture post 1967, see Nitzan-Shiftan (2004).

9. "Meeting of the Mount Scopus Rehabilitation Committee on 12.6.1967," Hebrew University Archive.

10. "Report of the Special Committee on Mount Scopus Protocols, 27–29.6.1967," Hebrew University Archive.

11. "The Vaada Matmedet Protocols, 29.12.1967," Hebrew University Archive; "Summary of the Special Meeting of the Board of Governors of Hebrew University, 8.7.1969," Hebrew University Archive.

12. "The Vaada Matmedet Protocols, 17.11.1967," Hebrew University Archive.

13. Ibid.

14. "The Vaada Matmedet Protocols, 17.5.1968," Hebrew University Archive.

15. "The Vaada Matmedet Protocols, 19.2.1967," Hebrew University Archive.

16. *Har HaTzofim* in Hebrew.

References

Agnew, J., and S. Corbridge. 1995. *Mastering Space: Hegemony, Territory and International Political Economy.* London: Routledge.

Atran, S. 1989. "The Surrogate Colonization of Palestine: 1917–1939." *American Ethnologist* 16, no. 4: 719–44.

Dolev, D. 1997. "The Hebrew University Master Plans 1918–1948." In Katz and Heyd 1997, 257–80.

———. 2004. "Academia and Spatial Control: The Case of the Hebrew University Campus on Mount Scopus, Jerusalem." In *Constructing a Sense of Place: Architecture and the Zionist Discourse,* ed. H. Yacobi, 182–97. London: Ashgate.

Erlich, A. 1984. "The British Architects in Mandatory Retz-Israel." *Tvai: Quarterly for Architecture and Town Planning* 22. (In Hebrew.)

Fox, R. 1990. "Introduction." In *Nationalist Ideologies and the Production of National Cultures,* ed. R. Fox. American Ethnological Society Monograph Series.

Greenstein, R. 1995. *Genealogies of Conflict.* Hanover, NH: University Press of New England.

"The Hebrew University on Mount Scopus, Jerusalem." 1976. *Tvai: Quarterly for Architecture and Town Planning* 16: 56–64. (In Hebrew.)

Katz, S., and M. Heyd, eds. 1997. *The History of the Hebrew University of Jerusalem: Origins and Beginnings.* Jerusalem: Magnes Press. (In Hebrew.)

Kedar, B.Z. 1997. "Laying the Foundation Stones of the Hebrew University of Jerusalem, 24th July, 1918." In Katz and Heyd 1997, 90–119.

Khinsky, S. 1993. "Silence of the Fish: The Local versus the Universal in the Israeli Discourse of Art." *Theory and Criticism* 4: 105–22. (In Hebrew.)

Lefebvre, H. 1991. *The Production of Space.* Oxford: Blackwell.

Nitzan-Shiftan, A. 2004. "Seizing Locality in Jerusalem." In *The End of Tradition?* ed. N. AlSayyad, 231–55. London: Routledge.

Paz, Y. 1997. "The Hebrew University on Mount Scopus as a Secular Temple." In Katz and Heyd 1997, 281–308.

Said, E. 1993. *Culture and Imperialism.* New York: Vintage.

Shapiro, M. 1997. "The University and the City: Patrick Geddes and the First Master Plan of Hebrew University, 1919." In Katz and Heyd 1997, 202–35.

Susman, D.A. 1969. *The Hebrew University of Jerusalem.* Jerusalem: Department of Information and Public Affairs. (In Hebrew.)

Swartz, D. 1997. *Culture and Power: The Sociology of Pierre Bourdieu.* Chicago: University of Chicago Press.

Vale, L.J. 1992. *Architecture, Power, and National Identity.* New Haven, CT: Yale University Press.

Yacobi, H. 2003. "The Architecture of Ethnic Logic: Exploring the Meaning of the Built Environment in the 'Mixed' City of Lod, Israel." *Geografiska Annaler* 84(B): 171–87.

———. 2004. "Form Follows Metaphors: The Case of the New Israeli High Court Building in Jerusalem." *Journal of Architecture* 9: 233–53.

Yiftachel, O. 1999. "'Ethnocracy': The Politics of Judaizing Israel/Palestine." *Constellations* 6, no. 3: 364–91.

Yiftachel, O., and S. Kedar. 2000. "Landed Power: The Making of the Israeli Land Regime." *Theory and Criticism* 16. (In Hebrew.)

Yiftachel, O., and H. Yacobi. 2002. "Planning a Bi-National Capital: Should Jerusalem Remain United?" *Geoforum* 33: 137–45.

———. 2003. "Control, Resistance and Informality: Urban Ethnocracy in Beer Sheva, Israel." In *Urban informality,* ed. A. Roy and N. Alsayyad, 209–39. New York: Lexington Books.

———. 2004. "Urban Ethnocracy: Ethnicization and the Production of Space in an Israeli Mixed City." *Environment and Planning D: Society and Space* 21, no. 6: 673–93.

12

Interface between Academy and Community in Contested Space

The Difficult Dialogue

Frank Gaffikin

This chapter addresses an attempt by one of the two Northern Ireland universities to develop a major new campus in Belfast deliberately designed to ameliorate urban ethno-nationalist conflict and to engage its adjacent neighborhoods in a new form of partnership between academy and community. Such an ambitious project was informed by two processes: the *universal* trends affecting all UK universities; and the *particular* circumstances of Belfast, a "contested" city scarred by over three decades of political violence.

In the case of the former, it is clear that UK universities are at a cusp of significant new opportunity and challenge. First, they face a future of rising student demand. Second, they enjoy an elevated role in the new economy as prominent creators and repositories of knowledge. Finally, as a consequence of this greater visibility, they have secured high priority in the government's policy agenda. Yet they face acute pressures, none more pressing than a long-standing and substantial fiscal gap. Put simply, public funding—the traditional main support for UK higher education—has not kept pace with expenditure. Accordingly, most institutions struggle to maintain, repair, and extend their plant while simultaneously coping with widened student access rates and financing globally competitive research. In turn, such exigencies have informed the definition and delivery of universities' wider social obligation as they extend both their physical and intellectual presence (House of Commons Education and Skills Committee 2003).

This chapter focuses on the implications of these combined features for the relationships between the urban university and its neighborhoods. But it does so in the setting of a city where deeply contested space confounds the politics of land and community. Thus, it begins with a brief contextual section that explores current patterns and policy imperatives. It proceeds to outline the response of a university in Northern Ireland to this agenda in the context of an urban arena marked by deep ethno-nationalist tensions. Through a case study analysis of the University of Ulster's Springvale project, the chapter examines the narrative of a major university real estate venture and the lessons it poses for effective collaboration between tertiary education and communities beset by intense sectarian territoriality. The author's research is based on extensive interviews with all the key stakeholders, multiple seminar sessions and focus group discussions, and collaborative work with colleagues at the University of Illinois that permitted comparative analysis. But it derives also from his deeply embedded participant observation in the process, stretching back nearly a decade.

The Policy Context

In the UK, student intake in higher education has been rising dramatically. Fifty years ago higher education was the preserve of a tiny elite of some 50,000. Now it is moving to a mass system, and the pace of increase is remarkable, from 567,000 in 1989 to approximately double that figure within fifteen years (HESA 2005). Yet resources per student have dropped by 20 percent from the late 1970s to the late 1980s, and by a further 36 percent by the late 1990s (Universities UK 2001; DFES Paper 2003). Notwithstanding the planned real public spending increase for the sector at approximately 6 percent for the next three years, the estimated investment backlog in teaching and research facilities stands at £8 billion (DFES 2003). By the late 1990s, the UK ranked behind its main competitors, such as the United States, Germany, France, and Japan, in share of GDP devoted to higher education (OECD 2002). Thus, as UK universities seek to compete for staff and research funding in a more global environment, their financial base compares unfavorably with that of their counterparts elsewhere.

This trajectory of expansion alongside deteriorating finances can induce universities to generate income from property development and to "cozy up" to corporate donors while demoting less remunerative relationships—for example, with the community sector. Thus, it is not simply that universities in the UK are expanding their role in general economic development (Robson, Drake, and Deas 1998) or in regional development (Charles 2003). These interfaces *between* business and universities are increasing in the UK, supported by arguments about the important new relationship between knowledge-intensive wealth creation and the research capacity of higher education (Goddard 1999; Glazer and Grimes 2004). However, in recent times, the elevated role of business *within* academia has also become evident, particularly in the massive corporate beneficence magnetized to prestigious institutions (Monbiot 2000). Much of this largesse has involved relatively minor physical expansion, such as new research buildings. But, as one example of substantial property development, Cambridge has announced recently the creation of three new colleges, the first expansion of their real estate for a quarter of a century (*Independent,* May 5, 2004). The proposal involves the development of a university-owned 120-hectare site on the city outskirts that will more than double the space occupied by the eight-hundred-year-old institution. Even though it involves land designated as "greenbelt" in an area of "best landscape," the City Council has agreed to incorporate the proposal into its draft local plan, which if endorsed will grant the development process full legal support. Interestingly, the location is close to the West Cambridge Development, a science and technology park that connects to the cluster of high-technology companies now forming a prestigious development corridor in that region. While possibly selling off some of the land to private developers for housing, the university intends a mixed-use project, comprising academic and community facilities including a primary school, shops, parks, and nature conservation area. A spokesman was quoted as promising, "The university is determined to work closely with the local community and Council to achieve environmentally sensitive, sustainable, beneficial development over the next 20 years" (*Independent,* May 5, 2004, 4). Thus, despite its incongruity with government regeneration policy that privileges brownfield over greenfield land and central city over out-of-town location, the proposal has won preliminary approval. Basically, Cambridge's academic and economic weight has prevailed over standard government criteria for sensible development. But Cambridge, with its Ivy League reputation and buoyant property market, is a long way from Belfast, whose reputation is for intractable intercommunal animosity, and whose property market has been deformed by deeply rooted patterns of ethnic turf.

Development in Contested Space

Contested cities like Belfast are marked by sharply defined opposing cultures (Amin 2002) that even when interactive, tend to be polarizing (Cash 1996). In the absence of explicit social markers like skin color, territory assumes the role of ethnic marker (Anderson and Shuttleworth 2003), and such spatial clustering creates a series of contiguous neighborhoods that are at once comfort zones to one tribe and threatening territory to the other. Thereby, these spaces become local manifestations of the macro political divisions (Boal 2001) and acquire meanings and symbolism associated with that broader political canvas. We can see this in the way partitioned Ireland is replicated in partitioned Belfast.

It is useful here to distinguish *two* types of contested city. In one, there are arguments about systematic discrimination in the distribution of power and economic opportunity among groups that are culturally distinct and spatially segregated (Featherstone and Lash 1999; Fenton 2003). But all contending parties acknowledge some common allegiance to the state, and the discourse is about *reformist* strategies to redress racial and social imbalances. We can characterize this as a *pluralist* model. In the other type, like Belfast and Jerusalem, the dispute is more fundamentally about nationalist origins and loyalties, where often the subjugated group challenges the state's very legitimacy and seeks solution in a more *revolutionary* framework that involves the reconstitution of the state's boundaries (Benvenisti 2001). We can characterize this as a *sovereignty* model.

An urban arena torn by pronounced ethno-nationalist rivalry has been designated as a "frontier" city—"a territory of two dreams" (Kotek 1999, 228). Territorial and cultural spaces, embracing the significance of ethnic turf, distinctive identities, loyalties, and symbols, are particularly potent in this kind of contested city. In this respect, Morrissey and Gaffikin (2001) have identified four kinds of territorial/cultural space:

1. *Ethnic:* Ghettoizing by marking tribal territory through the use of murals, flags, and sectarian emblems in a manner intended to deter "trespass" by the other side.
2. *Neutral:* Establishing buffer zones for protected common, though not shared, use. This allows for contact and cohabitation of space with security but does not deliberately foster engagement across the divide.
3. *Shared:* Creating opportunities for dialogue and exchange as a premeditated means of acknowledging, and ideally resolving, the basis of the conflict.
4. *Transcendent:* Promoting common bond through uses and activities that rise above, and thereby diffuse the intensity of, the local tribalism and conflict, usually through designing cosmopolitan space that privileges the global over the parochial.

In any given contested city, all four can be operating. Thus, while Belfast can be seen *mainly* in terms of two competing and mutually exclusive cultural identities (Neill and Schwedler 2001), it hosts alongside these primary identities (Ignatieff 1999) other diversities and fidelities that unite people around transcending cultural idioms, thereby producing multiple identities (Hutchinson and Smith 1996). Nevertheless, ethnic bonding and the related appeal of boundary remain preeminent. Thus, the attraction of segregated settlements in such cities is compelling, appearing to offer *security, solidarity,* and the *scale* to support separate service provision such as education. Any alternative vision, based on integration and common belonging, has to provide convincing added value to both tribes, inclined to view intently all locational and distributional aspects of public policy for their sectarian impact. This inherent "ethnic auditing" makes all interventions into this sensitive arena difficult (Gaffikin and Morrissey 2006).

But in such contexts, planning and development are particularly problematic (Bollens 1999), if only because land lies at the heart of such disputes (Dumper 1997), and planning is concerned with the social construction of space. Most contentious among combatants is the issue of who "owns" the land and whether any change in use of particular real estate represents encroachment by the opposing camp. Accordingly, it would be reasonable to expect that universities, given the many pressing problems of their own, would run shy of getting immersed in such controversy and seek to avoid any new property development in such places. The fact that a university decided to adopt the challenge of locating in the very center of Belfast's violent "Troubles" makes for a remarkable and instructive case study of the capacity of higher education to intervene productively in contested cities.

The Springvale Campus: Straddling the Belfast Peaceline

In the mid-1990s, the University of Ulster in Northern Ireland set about establishing a new campus, known as the Springvale Educational Village, in the heart of North and West Belfast, an area renowned not only for long-standing economic decline and poverty, but also for intractable political violence (Gaffikin and Morrissey 1996). Often urban universities find themselves in locations that have become economically distressed, socially deprived, and conflict ridden and accordingly are induced to support the stabilization of their hinterland if only through self-interest. By contrast, Springvale was deliberately sited in acutely contested territory on an interface between disadvantaged rival ethno-nationalist communities. Moreover, this was not the usual case of a university seeking to bulge out into space contiguous to an existing campus. Rather, this was a completely new location separate from the rest of the institution.

The main campus lies on the outskirts of Belfast, safely removed from the intensity of the conflict. In the city itself, for over thirty years there has been increasing segregation of the two communities into exclusive domains (Boal 2002), with over thirty "peace walls" to keep warring factions apart. Such separatism derives from, and at the same time reinforces, a bitter sectarianism that is rooted in the "precarious belonging" (Dunlop 1995) of the "settler"

Protestants to their Irish setting and the "resentful belonging" (Elliott 2000) of the "native" Catholics to the British connection. Deepening spatial segregation is most acute in the poorest parts of the city, where by the late 1970s, nine in ten households lived in streets that were completely or almost completely of one religious or political persuasion. Such ghettoization occurred in the context of an overall changing demography in Northern Ireland (Anderson and Shuttleworth 2003), which once use to be two-thirds Protestant, one-third Catholic, but which by 2001 had shifted to 53 percent Protestant, 44 percent Catholic, and 3 percent other. Part of this declining Protestant presence is explained by the tendency over recent decades for many young Protestants to undertake their university education in Britain and for many of them not to return. Thus, the undergraduate student population in the two universities in Northern Ireland is now 60 percent Catholic.

The surrounding area to the proposed new campus, North and West Belfast, suffered intensive exposure to political violence during the three decades of conflict, while simultaneously suffering deprivation and underdevelopment. Over 40 percent of deaths resulting from political violence happened in Belfast, even though the city contains about a fifth of the regional population. Certain kinds of violence were even more concentrated—almost half of all sectarian deaths took place in Belfast. The degree of spatial segmentation represented by peacelines and residential segregation is much greater in the city than for other areas of Northern Ireland. Not only have these adversely affected the urban quality of life, they also make institutions less efficient in serving the population and induce "diseconomies of division"—the less than optimal functioning of labor, capital, and property and housing markets. Yet different parts of the city had very different experiences of political violence. The patterning of deaths over time can be seen in Table 12.1.

The concentration of fatalities in the initial period is notable, the first seven years of the Troubles accounting for over half the fatalities. In both the city as a whole and in each sector, there was a significant reduction after the paramilitary cease-fires of 1994. Clearly, violence was also spatially concentrated, with just over 60 percent of deaths of local residents located in the north and west of the city (Morrissey and Smyth 2002). In this area, which accounts for approximately half of the population of 300,000 in Belfast central city, lies a complex mosaic of different religious territories. Heartlands of Republicanism and Loyalism like the Falls and the Shankill are literally side by side.

Spatial deprivation levels more than match the pattern of political violence (see Figure 12.1). In terms of overall deprivation, of the fifty most deprived wards in Northern Ireland (as measured by the degree of deprivation), six are in North Belfast (43 percent of all North Belfast wards), and eight are in

Table 12.1

Political Deaths in Belfast over Time

| Years | Deaths of local residents | | | | | |
	West	North	East	South	Non-Belfast	Total
1969–75	255	233	68	94	179	829
1976–80	104	118	21	17	65	325
1981–85	39	32	9	21	31	132
1986–90	43	42	11	15	31	142
1991–95	49	45	16	25	24	159
1996–99	10	11	0	1	4	26
Total	500	481	125	173	334	1,613

| Years | Fatal incidents | | | | | |
	West	North	East	South	Non-Belfast	Total
1969–75	286	297	61	114	71	829
1976–80	105	127	40	38	16	326
1981–85	51	31	11	23	16	132
1986–90	44	53	20	15	10	142
1991–95	46	46	19	40	8	159
1996–99	7	8	2	5	4	26
Total	539	562	153	235	125	1,614

Source: Morrissey and Gaffikin (2006).

Figure 12.1 **Belfast Area Deaths and Other Characteristics**

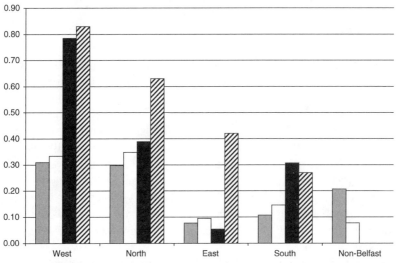

◨ Share Local Res. Deaths □ Share of Fatal Incidents ■ % of Pop. Catholic ▨ % of Wards Deprived

Source: Morrissey and Gaffikin, (2006); Robson (1994).

West Belfast (62 percent of all West Belfast wards). This compares to one in South Belfast (10 percent) and three in East Belfast (27 percent) (Robson et al. 1994). Within these areas, the inner cities are particularly vulnerable, and the persistence of deprivation in the same wards over time is marked (Northern Ireland Statistics and Research Agency 2006). Moreover, it is possible to characterize "two" inner cities—a Catholic one with a younger and expanding population but with high levels of male unemployment and nonpensioner economic inactivity; and a Protestant one, more elderly, subject to population decline and with particular problems of older housing.

The Concept and Financing of the New Campus

In an area that cut through some of the most contentious sectarian geographies in North and West Belfast, brownfield land became available with the relocation of one of the few local sizable private industrial companies. All told, the site involved 689 acres of derelict and underused land that became known as Springvale. Initially, in 1992, a concept plan was drawn up for its development, involving the attraction of a cluster of new industries. When no major new investment was forthcoming, and as the prospect of an end to the paramilitary violence dawned, in 1993 the University of Ulster nominated itself as an ideal anchor tenant, whose presence could deliver:

- Enhanced educational opportunity in an area of educational under-achievement;
- Recreational and other social amenities in cooperation with local groups; and
- The stimulation for inward investment and industrial and commercial development, given its research expertise and general capacity to improve the quality of life in the area.

Moreover, given the politics of the time, based around great optimism that peace was on the horizon, the university stressed particularly the "reconciliation" dimension. It argued that its proposal for a new campus had "the potential to be the most significant single vehicle for bringing the two communities together following the cessation of violence. As a force in the social and economic regeneration of the region, the campus would have a unique role in consolidating the peace in North and West Belfast" (University of Ulster 1994, 2).

But outside of these inventive goals, there was a more orthodox consideration. The university's main campus, on the edge of Belfast, known as Jordanstown, was congested. Student demand outpaced its capacity to supply.

Thus, the university argued that a new campus would capture the excess and avoid much of the enforced student exodus to universities in Britain. The University of Ulster had an existing small campus in Belfast devoted to art and design, but it was not suitable for expansion or conversion for four reasons: It had been purpose built, its refurbishment would be prohibitively expensive, spatial constraints limited further development, and its single faculty form did not permit the desired interdisciplinary format. By contrast, Springvale gave the opportunity to start afresh. For instance, it was billed as the first custom-built "virtual" campus in the British Isles, electronically networked internally and externally and thereby capable of exploiting the economics and reach of leading-edge information technology.

An initial feasibility study specified a land requirement of 82.6 acres to accommodate a full-scale multidisciplinary campus to house 3,750 students (full-time equivalent), offering a comprehensive range of teaching, learning, and research facilities alongside student residences, social and sporting amenities, and parking. With a planned completion date for 2001–2002, phased in two stages, the final development was due to be a high-quality, low-density "university parkland" that would include the landscaping of the river valley that ran through the site. The university was hopeful of a partnership with private developers to secure the necessary student residential accommodation. But, largely, the capital costs were anticipated from the public purse. It was projected that there would be an operating deficit in the first few years, after which the economies of scale derived from the rising student intake and the operational efficiency gains would bring the campus into balance.

Designed not only to be an international model of innovative lifelong learning, but also to contribute to the regeneration and reconciliation processes in the area, the campus was a formidable undertaking. Accordingly, it evolved from the financially untenable original conception in 1994 as a university-only campus with an indicative cost of nearly £100 million (Touche Ross and RJM 1994). Since then, two further unique features informed Springvale's operation. First, a partnership between the university and Belfast's Further Education Institute was created. In the face of convincing argument that an area marked by educational underattainment needed expanded capacity in further education as a pathway to the university level, the government signaled that its support for Springvale was dependent on joint tertiary provision. Second, this cross-institutional partnership in turn partnered with representative agencies of the local Protestant and Catholic neighborhoods, reflecting a commitment to include community interests in campus planning from the formative stage. In short, Springvale was ambitious and distinctive not merely in its multiple objectives, but also in its formal inclusive decision-making process.

Design and Layout

Both the architecture and the layout were intended to convey three key messages: (1) This was a very visible university connected to, rather than apart from, its adjoining communities and natural environs; (2) its facilities were accessible for wider community use; and (3) its very quality testified to its serious and durable contribution to community reimaging and renewal. Belfast had become used to a "fortress" architecture that put a premium on security and deployed materials that could best withstand bombs. But in the case of Springvale, when reservation was expressed about the extent to which its bright and light-penetrating form and extensive use of glass made it vulnerable at least to the pervasive local vandalism, there was a determined resolve to ensure that its design reflected its open and accessible character.

Given all of its other challenges, the last thing the project needed was an additional hurdle in relation to its real estate. Yet that is precisely what it confronted. Simply stated, in its awkward topography and problematic physical access, this site would not have been a conventional choice for university expansion. While there were no decanting costs, since there was no displacement of existing activity, higher infrastructure expense was inevitable due to factors such as soil investigation, decontamination costs, site preparation, and landscaping.

Beyond such physical considerations, Springvale was designed as the first custom-built electronic campus in the British Isles "able from its inception to reap the economies and exploit the opportunities to be derived from up-to-date information technology. In particular, on-line facilities [would] be available to neighboring industry, business and commerce" (University of Ulster 1994, 11).

The Economics of Springvale

An early local economic impact study (Segal Quince Wicksteed Ltd. 1995) listed the potential benefits as follows:

- A total of 444 permanent full-time–equivalent jobs, of which 138 would be taken by local residents;
- A further 90 permanent full-time jobs generated by campus purchases and staff and student spending;
- A total of 200 person years of employment in the campus construction; and
- A focus for new business activity and added value to the activities of existing businesses.

In addition, the report cited greater education access for local residents together with greater access to cultural, sports, and recreational facilities. Such figures were consonant with other analyses of the economic impact of higher education. For example, there was an estimated £1.27 billion output multiplier effect from £1.2 billion of higher education output in the UK (McNicoll 1995).

These estimates were more optimistic than the initial feasibility work, which was felt by the university to be based on flawed modeling. It overestimated costs (by including an unnecessary infrastructural project and by ignoring private-sector contribution to the total resources required) and underestimated benefits by utilizing a low multiplier, which underplayed the advantages of a purpose-designed campus to the residents of the area. Moreover, the costs of each were calculated as *discounted average costs* so that the capital costs of the project were doubly counted for both the higher education and regeneration components. A different calculus would emerge if Springvale was conceptualized as a multidimensional yet integrated project designed to impact on education, deprivation, and intercommunal division. It was this potential dynamism and synergy that conventional appraisal techniques could not capture, since *cross-multipliers* would be achieved, extending beyond the standard linear formula.

The university summarized the economic appeal of its proposal in the following terms:

> This high yield low risk project is the only one which offers cost effective economic and social regeneration with an inbuilt guarantee of stability. For, unlike some private concerns which are capricious and highly speculative, universities, once established, remain: if admitted to Springvale, the university will still be there in a 100 years time. Its plan is unapologetically visionary. . . . (University of Ulster 1994, 17)

Following this appraisal work and further consultations with government, a more detailed plan emerged, comprising the main campus, a Community Outreach Center (COC), and an Applied Research Center (ARC). It became apparent to the two educational institutions that the project's full delivery demanded a still significant investment of £70 million, comprising a complicated portfolio of public, private, and philanthropic funding. Only an initiative aspiring to have an impact on the problems and divisions besetting the most prominent crucible of Northern Ireland's political hostilities could possibly make the requisite funding appeal, especially to government, special European Union and peace funds, and private donors. Government was keen to see something dramatic happen in that part of Belfast to signal the start of a new optimistic era. By the same token, the university was aware that its proposal was the only serious prospect of government being able to deliver a tangible "peace dividend" to that pivotal war zone.

However, to support their characterization of Springvale in these promising terms, the university needed local political and community endorsement. Following a protracted series of formal and informal discussions between the university and local political parties, such support was forthcoming but contingent on continued participatory structures to channel community contributions to decision making. Part of this persuasion process involved bringing over expertise from the Great Cities Institute of the University of Illinois, Chicago, to explain directly to university echelons and to the community the benefits of a genuine partnership between academy and community. This was the start of an ongoing collaboration that brought a valuable U.S. perspective and experience.

This contribution showed how the three main goals of universities—to teach, research, and serve—not only tended to operate in mutual isolation but also involved the residualization of the service component (Stukel 1994). The volatile relationship between town and gown, moving between engagement and detachment (Bender 1988), had seen a rediscovery in recent decades of the relevance and responsibility of academy to society, most particularly perhaps in the United States (DeMulder and Eby 1999). Part of this shift was attributable to U.S. government policy, which had sought to connect the significant power of universities—physical, economic, political, technical, and intellectual—to the assets and capacities of their most needy neighborhoods in a combination that strengthened both partners (COPC 2001; Wiewel and Lieber 1998). The Great Cities model offered the Springvale project a vision of partnership between universities and local communities that went beyond the traditional "outreach" model (Feld 1998; Rubin 1998) to a more ambitious "engaged" model that did the following:

- involved a new scholarship in higher education (Boyer 1996; Schon 1995) that better connected the formal knowledge of academy with the experiential knowledge of community;
- invited universities to change their own purpose and character as a prelude to their more effective response to urban and regional problems (Walshok 1995); and
- created a vision of the democratic cosmopolitan civic university that could function best in partnership with other urban stakeholders (Benson and Harkavy 2000).

These arguments of how academy could rethink its role in the twenty-first century (Ehrlich 2000; Duderstadt 2003), renewing its contract with civil society (Kezar 2004) in a form of mutual engagement (Kellogg Commission 1999; Perry 2005) and equitable partnership (Maurrasse 2001), were communicated directly to the key stakeholders in Springvale by the Great Cities Institute. In so doing, the latter did not seek to underplay the challenges and paradoxes involved in university-community relations (Silka 1999; Baum 2002) or, in particular, the tensions involved in adopting this agenda for those institutions seeking to be research universities in a more marketized and globalized competitive environment (Checkoway 1997; Newman, Couturier, and Scurry 2004). Indeed, in this discourse, the pressures on the contemporary university were examined thoroughly—for instance, the imperative to become more entrepreneurial within a neoliberal framework (Slaughter and Leslie 1998), and to adopt innovative means of expansion in the knowledge age, such as the virtual rather than physical campus (Robins and Webster 2002).

These perspectives raised the level of discourse about Springvale at a crucial time, when the project needed to secure widespread "buy-in." Although internally differentiated, both within and between the two sectarian camps, the community sector in general became convinced of its development potential. Some sections were skeptical about the priority of an "elite" educational resource over the pressing need to improve local schools. But overwhelmingly, the community was persuaded that, far from being a competitor for educational investment in the area, Springvale could be a productive collaborator with the school sector and raise expectations of academic achievement.

Following a series of seminars, workshops, and conferences, a set of guiding principles emerged for the prominent role of community in the new campus, based on partnership and a shared vision (Thompson and Partners 2001). These included:

- Investing in capacity building in the local communities to enhance trust and confidence;
- Providing safe physical access for all sides of a divided city;
- Creating inclusivity by mapping clearly defined progression routes to learning for people of all socioeconomic backgrounds;
- Supporting existing services and resources in the local communities that have a role in local learning and should have a symbiotic relationship with the new campus;
- Balancing academic and community aspirations and connecting local communities to the wider city-region;
- Recognizing and respecting cultural differences among staff, students, and local communities; and
- Operating as a regional flagship project that aspires to become an internationally recognized model for lifelong learning.

Despite the development of such shared principles, some community interests remained critical about the opportunity cost of allocating scarce urban land to an education project rather than to clustered industrial development in an area that had endured significant deindustrialization. But it was persuasively argued that Springvale offered four distinctive contributions to economic regeneration: First, it was considerably more place-bound and thereby connected to the long-term strategic improvement of the area than the typical inward investment from transnational capital. Second, following substantial public subsidy for a series of prestigious developments in Belfast's showcase Downtown and Waterfront quarters, it offered the prospect of the first flagship scheme to be located in the heart of the city's most deprived area. Third, it boosted local employment prospects in an urban labor market that placed an ever greater premium on graduates. And fourth, it offered scope for systemic linkage between research on the one hand and innovation and productivity on the other.

The latter factor had a particular appeal in a regional economy seeking to move into more knowledge intensive production (Gaffikin and Morrissey 2001). Springvale's GDP per capita relative to the UK is 77.5 (UK = 100) (NIERC 2001), and the low-wage, low–value-added character of its private sector impairs its productivity. Knowledge and skill formation are critical to the creation of a regional innovation milieu (Best 2000). Yet, presently in Northern Ireland, knowledge-based sectors comprise only 44 percent of GDP, compared to 56 percent for the UK as a whole. Contributing to this lower investment are factors such as relatively poor performance in ICT (information and communication technology) application, in R&D and innovation, and in business-linked university research (Northern Ireland Economic Council 2001). Thus, the Applied Research Center component of Springvale, directly connected to the economic development needs of North and West Belfast, was to be a valuable instrument for the strategic creation of a new development axis for this historically underinvested part of the city.

Despite the higher capital costs of the Springvale proposal relative to other options identified in an economic appraisal (DTZ Pieda Consulting 1998), there were attractions for government. Apart from direct and indirect multiplier impacts on local employment, it represented a highly visible public intervention to boost educational attainment and urban regeneration in a socially distressed and politically troubled area. Springvale offered the chance to make a major contribution in terms of its enhancement of local physical capital and image and support for local community development. Moreover, in a place noted for symbolism, a learning institution represented the prospect of long-term reconciliation, whereby the force of argument could replace the argument of force. In many respects, this was the main ingredient of its appeal. It became part of the wider peace process. Thus, when President Clinton came to Ireland to leverage further movement by the protagonists toward a settlement, he came to Springvale to herald its symbolism of a new start. At the groundbreaking ceremony for the new campus in September 1998, Clinton proclaimed,

> Indeed, the future has begun. And clearly the best path to a future that involves every citizen of every circumstance in every neighborhood is a strong education. Springvale Educational Village will help you get there. It will be a living, breathing monument to the triumph of peace. It will turn barren ground into fertile fields cultivating the world's most important resources: the minds of your people—providing opportunity not just for the young but for those long denied the chance for higher learning, creating jobs in neighborhoods where too many have gone without work for too long, bringing more technology and skill so that Northern Ireland at last can reap the full benefits of this new economy, creating unity from division, transforming a barbed-wire boundary that kept communities apart into common ground of learning and going forward together.

Sources of Contention

Beyond such high rhetoric, the practical workings of partnership in Springvale proved to be problematic. It became increasingly apparent that neither partner was internally monolithic. Within both there were enthusiastic proponents, while others demonstrated at different stages varying degrees of reservation, ambivalence, indifference, and opposition. For instance, there were two to three senior civil servants, noted for their proximity to the community and their capacity for entrepreneurial public policy, who were indefatigable advocates within government. But faced with, at best, skepticism from senior colleagues, they could not successfully champion the proposal on the basis of a traditional economic appraisal. Rather, as indicated earlier, they relied on one that captured the cross-fertilizing benefits of the combined operation of education, regeneration, and reconciliation objectives. But, to be credible, those benefits, in turn, relied on local community and political support.

Yet this support was difficult to sustain and contributed to protracted negotiation, leading to long periods of indecisiveness, in which Springvale had no guarantee from government about its ultimate destiny. Since there was nothing new to report at these times, communication between the educational institutions and the community became less certain. This perceived lack of clarity led to rumor and strained the trust between partners, which then further complicated relationships.

Beyond the problems the university faced in its partner relations, it encountered local residents' reservations of the kind typically associated with any major property project. For instance, community consultations revealed some ambiguity about the housing provision associated with the campus. Some remarked on how the student intake could prompt speculation and elevate house prices, while others associated an influx of student residents with a supposed student culture of late-hour alcohol parties, likely to depress housing market value. Some anticipated the student presence as gentrification that would change the area's character, while others welcomed the very prospect of a greater social mix. Still others favored a high level of student residence to capture the full economic benefits of their consumption, in contrast to those fearful that the extra housing demand would crowd out local housing need amid the overall shortage of affordable accommodation. In fact, the likely demand for student housing was modest. This was due to a high share of part-time students, a high share continuing to live at home, and another significant share choosing to live in the vibrant and traditional student quarters near the city's other university. Consequently, the accommodation "load" around the campus area was estimated to be 240–250 students. Given the typical ratio of 5 students per house, and the potential for the conversion of local ex-mills for concentrated student apartments, this extra demand was always unlikely to severely stress local housing stock (Mc Greal 2001).

Concerns about transportation, access, and traffic impact featured also. But again, the effect was likely to be moderated by the fact that many students relied on public transport, which was set for improved capacity and more flexible routing in a new strategic transport plan for the city. Moreover, in terms of customized provision of both accommodation and transport such as community taxis, there was scope for local enterprise.

Another consideration is how relationships changed in the different development phases of a long-haul project. For instance, by early 2002—nearly eight years into the concept proposal—when there appeared to be greater certainty about final government approval, some community people expressed concern that the planning process would become internalized into the educational institutions, reducing their influence. In response, the institutions emphasized that there were specific standards and procedures they were obliged to adopt, with respect to academic programs and such like. This debate was associated with a deeper issue about the normalization of such projects. For instance, the community sector had always wanted Springvale to be a "normal" campus, in the sense that it had equal profile, quality, and standards compared to other parts of the university. At the same time, the community wanted it to be different and customized to meet the particular needs of the area. Despite these apparently contradictory desires of unique and normative, Springvale presented itself as able to accommodate its special character without becoming the poor relation of the university.

Nevertheless, this issue became more and more crucial. Many on the community side continued to harbor reservations about how comprehensive and relevant the curriculum would be. From the initial promise that all faculties, all levels of course, and all study modes would feature at the campus, there was greater skepticism about what the buildings could actually accommodate. There was doubt also whether university staff were all signed up for possible transfer into a troubled zone that many had no experience of other than nightly television bulletins about bombs and bullets. Moreover, some continued to suspect that the new campus was largely designed to permit a university "juggling act" among its campuses. The decanting of some Jordanstown staff and students to Springvale would release space and capacity at Jordanstown for concentration on the real high-value activity of science, engineering, and informatics, key areas that government wished to see expanded.

But by early 2002, the partnership had become more locked together in the certainty of the final outcome. By then, following eight years of intensive negotiation and discussions, six main stages had been reached, not all in linear sequence:

- Conceptualization and ongoing refinement of the proposal
- Advocacy and mobilization of support
- Building partnerships between the university and Belfast's Further Education Institute and between both of those and the local communities
- Economic appraisal
- Negotiation with government and other fundraising entities
- Detailed preparation for delivery

It is useful to compare those stages with the typical property development process (based on Ratcliffe and Stubbs 1996), involving the following six stages:

1. Concept, reflection, and initial "critical path" planning
2. Site identification, appraisal, and feasibility study
3. Finance availability
4. Detailed design and assessment
5. Contract and construction
6. Marketing, occupation, and management

The differences are illuminating. In Springvale's case, the site came first. Moreover, the process was complicated by the political and community engagements necessary for its approval. By 2002 the so-called Millennium Community Outreach Building was operational, but no other building had started. Yet the message was still positive. In March 2002, the recently appointed vice chancellor continued to describe the project as a pioneering initiative, based on values of social inclusion. But all was to change drastically.

Springvale: The Retreat

In autumn 2002, the university withdrew from the proposal for a new campus and related applied research center. At first, some assumed that this move was a bluff on the part of the university to leverage more funding support from the government, which was beginning to press certain concerns about long-term viability (DEL 2002). Surely, an institution that had invested such time, cost, and credibility could not walk away so readily. But the announcement was no bluff. Behind vague references to the need for new appraisals lay the reality of retreat.

Following this decision, the university's intention is now to withdraw from the company known as Springvale Educational Village Ltd., jointly owned with the Further Education Institute, thereby leaving the one existing building on the site—the Community Outreach Center—in the institute's sole proprietorship. The primary reason given at the time of this announcement was financial affordability. The university claimed that further appraisal of the revenue costs of the new campus had indicated a significant shortfall that risked skewing its overall budget to the detriment of its other campuses. Specifically, compared to original projections that the university would gain an extra three thousand full-time equivalent (FTE) students, the most plausible current aggregate estimate was for six hundred FTEs, and that reduced total would have to be shared with the Further Education Institute.

In an interview, the new pro-vice chancellor charged with managing the university's withdrawal from the scheme acknowledged to me that the decision had repercussions for the relationships established delicately over the near decade of its development. He felt that the bruised relations with the Further Education Institute would mend over time as they continued their collaboration in other ventures. With respect to the impact with the local community, he emphasized four factors:

1. Protests by activists needed to be distinguished from adverse reaction from the community itself. No spontaneous outburst of community anger was yet evident.
2. Withdrawing from a financially unviable project was not the same as "pulling out" of North and West Belfast, from which the university would continue to attract students.

3. The decision would not blight the area's regeneration, which depended less on university degrees than on improving skills and educational underattainment, interventions that were more germane to further education's mission.
4. The project had tended to be seen as one for Catholic West Belfast, with the Protestant community remaining skeptical about physical access; North Belfast interests had always felt that they had been added to the catchment area to impress funders with a wider geographical reach.

Pressed further, the pro-vice chancellor accepted that their ultimate misgivings about the venture were not reducible to funding issues. First, under the new vice chancellor, the strategy was to deploy the flexibilities of communications technology to create virtual campuses and networks of distance learning rather than necessarily to invest in costly new plant. Second, there was now greater appreciation that if the university agreed to a demand from any specific community to locate a campus in its vicinity, the same logic could bring pressure to build a similar facility in other areas, an untenable proposition.

Third, and particularly significant, the formidable challenge of winning community consent to Springvale had drawn the previous pro-vice chancellor incrementally into unsustainable commitments about new forms of governance involving the community. Shrewd negotiators in an area noted for its sophisticated community capacity had secured unprecedented influence in the university's decision-making system. But forensic examination of these arrangements had caused the institution to realize just how unfeasible it was to have a university in effect run by the community. Indeed, the pro-vice chancellor asserted that this model had never obtained the imprimatur of senior management. Yet, despite the absence of such a mandate, the university had become drawn in so deep that retreat was problematic. If such a radical dispensation had been conceded, similar demands could have been generated with respect to the institution's other campuses.

Fourth, this process of community engagement was undertaken at a time when the university's overall culture was conducive to such quasi-autonomous initiatives. Under new direction, the university saw the imperative for more rigorous management of such enterprises, as part of a general drive for greater discipline, efficiency, and focus. Finally, it was considered now that the Springvale project was conceptually oversimplistic in its assumed impact on reconciliation and regeneration in a troubled community. Rather than developing organically, it had been an external proposal driven by the previous vice chancellor, keen to make a dramatic impression on the macro peace process. Though, in retrospect, that had been naive, the university had learned lessons—particularly, of the need to avoid overselling a concept, thereby getting entrapped in its amplified rhetoric—and was now stronger for the experience.

Community Response

As indicated earlier, the initial community response to the Springvale proposal was cautious. The West Belfast Economic Forum described the prevailing attitude thus: "The community did not initially welcome the proposal with open arms as it was proposed to build on land zoned for industry [that could] create much needed employment in the area. After a very hard sell by the University of Ulster the community gave its conditional support to the campus proposal on condition that it met the social and economic needs of the local community and tackled educational underachievement in the area" (West Belfast Economic Forum, Briefing Paper, November 2002).

When the announcement came from the university about its withdrawal, community representatives claimed to have no prior knowledge of financial or other problems. One responded as follows:

> The community of West Belfast are rightly furious at the announcement yesterday in relation to the proposed campus at Springvale. A number of issues need to be raised.

1. The community representatives on the board were first made aware of these "issues of affordability and sustainability" at the meeting yesterday. . . . At no stage at any board meetings were such difficulties raised.
2. The process by which the community was informed was not only ill mannered but was also dishonest and disingenuous. The community representatives were being informed of the review proposal at the same time as the media was being briefed.
3. If this is an issue of technicalities in relation to the Outline Business Case why then was there a need for the huge media drama that was created? Why is there a need for a fundamental review of the whole proposal?
4. Three economic appraisals have already been carried out on this project. Is more public money going to be spent on further appraisals?
5. The community has actively engaged in consultation on this proposal for the last decade. The Springvale Board knows what this community wants and needs and must deliver it now. (West Belfast Economic Forum, October 2002)

Summary and Conclusion

Springvale came about through a contingency. The relocation of a rare landmark factory in North and West Belfast created an opportunity site. Left derelict indefinitely, such a site could become a symbol of decline and neglect in a politically sensitive locality whose residents' confidence was pivotal to any prospect of conflict resolution in Northern Ireland as a whole. Coincidentally, the University of Ulster was seeking to expand its capacity to optimize its share of a growing student applicant pool at a time of limited government capital funding for new university plant. At the same time, it was keen to make a distinctive contribution to the healing processes of peace building in Northern Ireland, and a North and West Belfast location offered the most impressive opportunity.

What followed from this initial concept was an exhaustive process of brokering and building partnership with the community, lasting nearly a decade. A set of complexities and contradictions, real or imagined, confounded the process. For one thing, relationships between the university, Belfast Institute, and the community were complicated by the internal differentiation within each. For instance, within the community interest, there were notable differences between the following factions:

- *Protestant and Catholic,* with an ongoing perception on the part of some of the Protestant community that the student intake was likely to be overwhelmingly Catholic, thereby advancing Catholic territory in a contested sectarian space
- *North and West Belfast,* with some in the North side believing that the campus location in West Belfast privileged the latter in the project's "ownership"
- *Organized and less organized sectors,* with some interests arguing that they were underrepresented at the table and less included in the ongoing consultation
- *Large and small groups* even within the "organised" section, with some of the latter disgruntled about the relatively greater influence of the area's three main strategic partnerships

In addition, some of the partners could be perceived as potential competitors as well as collaborators. For instance, a campus that risked centralizing further education provision in the interests of rationalization and efficiency might undermine the locally based adult education provided by some community agencies. Such suspicions could be allayed by clarity of intent. Yet the hesitancy felt by some in institutions like the university arguably demanded some ambiguity about the ambition of the whole project to avoid their disaffection from its formidable challenge.

In a similar vein, many other tensions demanded mediation. How could a partnership based on trust be built, while having to negotiate a legalistic relationship in the formation of a new campus? How could parts of the community sector be encouraged to move beyond criticism to constructive co-responsibility, while respecting the disadvantaged power position that fostered their frustration? How could a real sense of local community ownership be afforded in the case of a campus that like all third-level institutions was under increasing pressure to be global in its focus?

How could a campus be created that respected its distinctive identity and mission in North and West Belfast and at the same time offered a sufficiently orthodox and robust academic program to counter any accusation that it was "dumbing down"? How could an elite institution operate in a deprived community, and how could it balance the role of professional expertise with the imperative for local empowerment? How could the tertiary institutions involved contribute to community capacity building, while recognizing that institutional capacity for change and social engagement also needed to be enhanced?

Many of these tensions are typical of the interface between community and institutions like universities. But they are made more difficult in the context of contested space. Thus, the university found itself drawn into intricate processes of alliance and conciliation, which it came to perceive as injurious to its autonomy. The retreat was sounded once the university itself underwent regime change. A new vice chancellor was much less personally committed than his predecessor, who had prominently championed the concept. The agenda of the new incumbent was different, with a focus on creating a few centers of research excellence in the fields of bioengineering and information technology. Springvale risked deflecting scarce university resources from that objective. A new pro-vice chancellor was appointed to the task of withdrawing from the Springvale Educational Village. Indeed, among some of the newly promoted senior officers, there was a sense that the previous pro-vice chancellor charged with implementing Springvale had "gone native," lost sight of the university's primary interest, and conceded too much to community demands in the process. To the advocates and activists in the university who saw in Springvale the epitome of a new relationship with community, the new regime offered a colder climate for such engagements.

Springvale was sited in what is currently ethnic space. To fulfill its mission, it had to reshape that into at least neutral and preferably shared space that could facilitate engagement and reconciliation across the community divide. Over time, it might have been able to create transcendent space by opening up the campus for events like international summer schools that could help extend activities, participants, and perspectives beyond the parochial. But, as it discovered painfully in its long process, major real estate projects like Springvale can be examined by people within both communities not for their formal goals or intrinsic merits, but rather for their inadvertent dislocation of socio-spatial relations between rival sides. Thus, universities, which tend to regard themselves as beyond partisan associations, can be drawn reluctantly into such difficult discourses. This was part of the uncomfortable landscape for the new university regime.

Paradoxically, the community in general had become ever more committed to Springvale. However, the university's withdrawal allowed those community interests that were initially cynical to proclaim vindication of their prognosis. Given the protracted and exacting process, many on the community side lament their wasted investment of time and effort, and the opportunity cost for their other priorities.

It is difficult to overestimate the negative impact of this outcome. The prospect of stirring energies for a flagship cross-community venture of this kind has suffered a huge setback. The university calculated that the differentiated nature of the community, between Protestant and Catholic and between North and West Belfast, would dilute the protest, and, to date, they have been proved right. The ineffectual community reaction testifies to the debilitating impact of rivalries and divisions in contested cities.

Meanwhile, government has been relatively silent. Springvale arrived at a high point in the peace process. It was imbued with significant political meaning as a project that resonated well with the new dispensation. Since then, the peace process itself has faltered. But the conflict now operates at a lower intensity. Sinn Fein, representing republican/Catholic interests in the area, has protested loudly about the Springvale debacle, but it is not going to retreat from its shift to constitutional politics on such an issue. In its early days, Springvale was notably helpful to government in promoting a milieu of more peaceful politics in places like North and West Belfast. But its dissolution is not significant enough to disturb the uneasy peace that has since been generated.

The denouement of the Springvale saga offers no glib lessons for other universities trying to make a positive impression in contested cities. It could be said that Springvale was overambitious in its scale, problematic site, contested location, and complicated innovative new governance. Yet without that ambition it was unlikely to win the necessary combination of community consent, international kudos, and government financing. Certainly, such ambition demands patience for a long haul rather than a quick fix. Yet the long time involved risks, including the turnover of key personnel within its partnership, a serious occurrence when such projects demand most of all a continuity of leadership. Once some of the project's advocates among senior civil servants moved on, and in particular once a new authority arrived at the university, this vital leadership condition was compromised, with fatal effect.

References

Amin, A. 2002. *Ethnicity and the Multicultural City: Living with Diversity.* Report for the Department of Transport, Local Government and the Regions and the ESRC Initiative, University of Durham, Durham, England.

Anderson, J., and I. Shuttleworth. 2003. *Spaces of Fear: Communal Violence and Spatial Behaviour.* Cambridge: University of Cambridge, Center for Research in the Arts, Social Sciences and Humanities.

Baum, H. 2002. "Fantasies and Realities in University-Community Partnerships." *Journal of Planning Education and Research* 20: 234–46.

Bender, T., ed. 1988. *The University and the City: From Medieval Origins to the Present.* New York: Oxford University Press.

Benson, L., and I. Harkavy. 2000. "Integrating the American System of Higher, Secondary and Primary Education to Develop Civic Responsibility." In *Civic Responsibility and Higher Education,* ed. T. Ehrlich. Washington, DC: American Council on Education and Oryx Press.

Benvenisti, M. 2001. *Sacred Landscape.* Berkeley: University of California Press.

Best, M. 2000. *The Capabilities and Innovation Perspective: The Way Ahead in Northern Ireland.* Research Monograph 8. Belfast: Northern Ireland Economic Council.

Boal, F. 2001. "Urban Ethnic Segregation and the Scenarios Spectrum". Paper presented at Conference at the Lincoln Institute of Land Policy, Cambridge, MA.

———. 2002. *Shaping a City: Belfast in the Late Twentieth Century.* Belfast: Queen's University, Institute of Irish Studies.

Bollens, S. 1999. *Urban Peace-Building in Divided Societies: Belfast and Johannesburg.* Boulder, CO: Westview Press.

Boyer, E. 1996. "The Scholarship of Engagement." *Journal of Public Service and Outreach* 1: 11–20.

Cash, J.D. 1996. *Identity, Ideology and Conflict: The Structuration of Politics in Northern Ireland.* Cambridge: Cambridge University Press.

Charles, D. 2003. "Universities and Territorial Development: Reshaping the Regional Role of UK Universities." *Local Economy* 18, no. 1: 7–20.

Checkoway, B. 1997. "Reinventing the Research University for Public Service." *Journal of Planning Literature* 2, no. 3: 307–19.

COPC (Community Outreach Partnerships Centers). 2001. *COPC Annual Report 2000.* Washington, DC: U.S. Department of Housing and Urban Development.

DEL (Department of Employment and Learning). Minister Moves on Springvale Project. www.delni.gov.uk (accessed September 26, 2002).

DeMulder, E., and K. Eby. 1999. "Bridging Troubled Waters: Learning Communities for the 21st Century." *American Behavioral Scientist* 42, no. 5: 892–901.

DFES (Department for Education and Skills). January 2003. *The Future of Higher Education.* White paper. London: Author.

DTZ Pieda Consulting. March 1998. *Further and Higher Education in Northern Ireland and the Regeneration of North & West Belfast: An Economic Appraisal.* Belfast: Department of Education, Northern Ireland.

Duderstadt, J.J. 2003. *A University for the 21st Century.* Ann Arbor: University of Michigan Press.

Dumper, M. 1997. *The Politics of Jerusalem Since 1967.* New York: Columbia University Press.

Dunlop, J. 1995. *A Precarious Belonging: Presbyterians and the Conflict in Ireland.* Belfast: Blackstaff Press.

Ehrlich, T., ed. 2000. *Civic Responsibility and Higher Education.* Washington, DC: American Council on Education and Oryx Press.

Elliott, M. 2000. *The Catholics of Ulster.* London: Penguin Books.

Featherstone, M., and S. Lash, eds. 1999. *Spaces of Culture: City, Nation, World.* London: Sage.

Feld, M. 1998. "Community Outreach Partnership Centers: Forging New Relationships between University and Community." *Journal of Planning Education and Research* 17, no. 4: 285–90.

Fenton, S. 2003. *Ethnicity.* Cambridge, UK: Polity Press.

Gaffikin, F., and M. Morrissey. 1996. *A Tale of One City?* Belfast: University of Ulster, Urban Institute.

———. 2001. "Regional Development: An Integrated Approach." *Local Economy* 16, no. 1 (February): 63–71.

———. 2006. "Planning for Peace in Contested Space: Inclusion through Engagement and Sanction." *International Journal of Urban and Regional Research* 30, no. 4 (December): 873–93.

Glazer, L., and D. Grimes. 2004. *A New Path to Prosperity? Manufacturing and Knowledge-Based Industries as Drivers of Economic Growth.* Ann Arbor: Michigan Future, Inc., and University of Michigan.

Goddard, J. 1999. "How Universities Can Thrive Locally in a Global Economy." In *Universities and the Creation of Wealth,* ed. H. Gray. Buckingham, UK: Open University Press.

HESA (Higher Education Statistics Agency). September 2005. *Higher Education Statistics for the United Kingdom, 2003/04.* Cheltenham, UK: Author, Department for Education and Skills.

House of Commons Education and Skills Committee. 2003, *The Future of Higher Education: Fifth Report of Session 2002–03,* vol. 1, HC 425–1, July 10. London: Stationery Office.

Hutchinson, J., and D.A. Smith, eds. 1996. *Ethnicity.* Oxford: Oxford University Press.

Ignatieff, M. 1999. *The Warrior's Honor: Ethnic War and the Modern Conscience.* London: Vintage.

Kellogg Commission on the Future of State and Land-Grant Universities. 1999. *Returning to Our Roots: The Engaged Institution.* Washington, DC: National Association of State Universities and Land-Grant Colleges.

Kezar, A. 2004. "Obtaining Integrity? Reviewing and Examining the Charter between Higher Education and Society." *Review of Higher Education* 27, no. 4: 429–59.

Kotek, J. 1999. "Divided Cities in the European Cultural Context." *Progress in Planning* 52: 227–37.

Maurrasse, D. 2001. *Beyond the Campus: How Colleges and Universities Form Partnerships with Their Communities.* New York: Routledge.

McGreal, S. 2001. Student Accommodation at Springvale. Unpublished paper, University of Ulster, Belfast.

McNicoll, I.H. 1995. *The Impact of Strathclyde University on the Economy of Scotland.* Glasgow: University of Strathclyde, Department of Economics.

Monbiot, G. 2000. *The Captive State: The Corporate Takeover of Britain.* London: Macmillan.

Morrissey, M., and F. Gaffikin. 2001. "Northern Ireland: Democratising for Development." *Local Economy* 16, no. 1 (February): 2–13.

———. 2006. "A New Synergy for Universities: Redefining Academy as an 'Engaged Institution.'" Unpublished paper, Contested Cities and Urban Universities Project, Queen's University, Belfast.

Morrissey, M., and M. Smyth. 2002. *Northern Ireland after the Good Friday Agreement: Victims, Grievance and Blame.* London: Pluto Press.

Neill, W.J.V., and H.-U. Schwedler, eds. 2001. *Urban Planning and Cultural Inclusion: Lessons from Belfast and Berlin.* Basingstoke, UK: Palgrave Macmillan.

Newman, F., L. Couturier, and J. Scurry. 2004. *The Future of Higher Education: Rhetoric, Reality and the Risks of the Market.* San Francisco: Jossey-Bass.

NIEC (Northern Ireland Economic Council). 2001. *The Knowledge Driven Economy: Indicators for Northern Ireland.* Report 136. Belfast: Author.

NIERC (Northern Ireland Economic Research Center). 2001. *Northern Ireland Economic Outlook: 2001–2010.* Belfast: Author.

Northern Ireland Statistics and Research Agency. 2006. Data for neighborhood deprivation in Belfast. www.nisra.gov.uk.

OECD (Organisation for Economic Co-operation and Development). 2002. *Education at a Glance* (now known as Education Statistics). Paris: Author.

Perry, D. 2005. "The Engaged University." Unpublished paper, Great Cities Institute, University of Illinois, Chicago.

Ratcliffe, J., and M. Stubbs. 1996. *Urban Planning and Real Estate Development.* London: UCL Press.

Robins, K., and F. Webster, eds. 2002. *The Virtual University? Knowledge, Markets, and Management.* Oxford: Oxford University Press.

Robson, B., M. Bradford, and I. Deas. 1994. *Relative Deprivation in Northern Ireland.* Belfast: Policy, Planning and Research Unit.

Robson, B., K. Drake, and I. Deas. 1998. *The National Committee of Inquiry into Higher Education.* Report 9. Manchester: University of Manchester, Center for Urban Policy Studies, Higher Education and Regions.

Rubin, V. 1998. "The Role of Universities in Community-Building Initiatives." *Journal of Planning Education and Research* 17, no. 4: 302–11.

Schon, D. 1995. "The New Scholarship Requires a New Epistemology." *Change* 27: 26–35.

Segal Quince Wicksteed Ltd. January 1995. *Springvale: Feasibility Study.* Belfast: Author.

Silka, L. 1999. "Paradoxes of Partnerships: Reflections on University-Community Collaborations." *Research in Politics and Society* 7: 335–59.

Slaughter, S., and J. Leslie. 1998. *Academic Capitalism: Politics, Policy and the Entrepreneurial University.* Baltimore: Johns Hopkins University Press.

Stukel, J. 1994. "Urban and Metropolitan Universities: Leaders of the 21st Century." *Metropolitan Universities* 5, no. 2: 87–92.

Thompson and Partners. June 2001. *Creating a Better Future Together: Springvale Educational Village, Community Planning Workshop, 15–19 June 2001.* London: Author.

Touche Ross and RJM. 1994. *The University of Ulster Springvale Feasibility Study.* Belfast: Author.

Universities UK. 2001. New Directions for Higher Education Funding. http://www. universitiesuk.ac.uk/funding/report3.asp.

University of Ulster. 1994. *Review of Springvale Proposal.* News update. Belfast: Author.

Walshok, M. 1995. *Knowledge without Boundaries: What America's Universities Can Do for the Economy, the Workplace, and the Community.* San Francisco: Jossey-Bass.

Wiewel, W., and M. Lieber. 1998. "Goal Achievement, Relationship Building, and Incrementalism: The Challenges of University-Community Partnerships." *Journal of Planning Education and Research* 17: 291–301.

Part V

Lessons Learned

13

The University, the City, and the State

Institutional Entrepreneurship or Instrumentality of the State?

Wim Wiewel and David C. Perry

The cases in this book describe the extraordinary vitality and growth of universities throughout the world. Each of these chapters displays the creativity, tenacity, and commitment of leaders in growing their institutions, regardless of national differences. Often they do this in harmony with larger local, regional, or national priorities or global trends. Other times, the pursuit of institutional priorities is quite conflicting.

At the most general level, our argument is that the growth of universities is a result of sheer population growth, as well as a manifestation of the increasing importance of the knowledge economy, including the strengthened role of urban regions (essentially agglomerations of knowledge sectors and workers) as units of global economic competition. Not surprisingly then, urban universities are at the core of these change processes, which is reflected in their physical appearance and functioning.

But ultimately this book is about how this plays out in detail. Which aspects are universal, and which differ by country, for reasons of history, culture, politics, or economic circumstances? In this final chapter, we pull together all of the case studies to return to the questions raised in the introduction. At their simplest level, those questions are as follows:

1. *Why* are universities expanding? Within the context of globalization and devolution, how important are such issues as urban decay, the need for new science and technology facilities, and enrollment pressures in shaping the university's expansion agenda?
2. *Where* is their growth taking place? Do the location decisions of universities reflect primarily their own strategic priorities or local or

national development strategies, or are they simply pragmatic, based on land availability and price?

3. *How* do universities structure the growth and development process? Do they use intermediaries, or partnerships with the private sector? How do they structure their financing? Who within and outside the university community is involved in the process?

4. What is the *impact* of their growth? Do the original rationales for campus expansions in fact get served by the final products? As institutions interwoven in the urban fabric, what are the effects of these developments outside of the institutions themselves?

5. What are critical *success factors?* Which projects succeed, and which fail, and can we identify what seems to work best?

Throughout, we will also deal with the question of how the *relationship between the university and the state* affects all of these issues.

Why Are Universities Expanding?

Thomas Bender emphasized the urban nature of universities in most of the world, in contrast to the idealized Anglo-American pastoral tradition. In light of the rapid urbanization of the world's population, it is not surprising then that universities are deeply implicated in urban growth. However, Bender's point is deeper than a matter of mere location. He emphasizes the long historical legacy of the university as an urban institution in terms of its engagement with the people, institutions, and businesses of the city, as well as with its challenges and celebrations. As we pointed out in the introduction, that engagement is also seen, at least by some, as an advantage to research and pedagogy. Perhaps most important, the urban location and the centrality of universities to the nature and well-being of cities means that cities and countries can be expected to turn to their universities as part of strategies to respond to the new challenges and opportunities that global economic competition poses for urban regions.

Our cases show these factors at work, often in very explicit ways. In Finland, the University of Helsinki developed new campuses in suburban areas to complement its aging and inefficient downtown campus. City government might have opposed this because of a stated policy preference for continued strong central development. But the suburban campuses, while contributing to the creation of a multinucleated metropolitan area, were an explicit part of the city's strategy to profile itself as a globally competitive place for science and research. Similarly, in Scotland the national economic strategy identified its cities, and the universities within it, as the key engines for global economic competition in the area of science. Expansion plans by the universities of Dundee and Aberdeen were developed and implemented within this context. In South Korea, the development of new engineering, science, and medical research buildings at Yonsei University was part of increased public-private collaboration for industrial development and also part of an explicit strategy to position the university among the world's top one hundred universities.

In other places, urbanization per se, as well as population growth and expansion of the proportion of the population attending university, is a more immediate reason for campus expansion. For instance, in Indonesia, the number of students attending higher education in Bandung increased from 36,000 to over 80,000 between 1977 and 1982. In response, the provincial government encouraged the development of a new multi-university campus on an unproductive rubber plantation twenty miles away from the city. In Lüneburg, Germany, the combination of student growth and inadequate facilities in the center of the city led the university to redevelop a former military base outside of town. The University of Oporto, in Portugal, and the University of Helsinki cases also cite growth in the number of students as driving factors for their expansion projects.

Along with growth, obsolescence of existing buildings played a role in requiring campus expansion in the cases of the universities of Oporto and Helsinki. In typical European university style, the universities grew up over time through the aggregation of departments and institutes, all located in downtown areas but without a single, identifiable campus. Indeed, one of the charms of many of these towns and universities is precisely the intermingling of uses and people, perhaps in university districts, such as the area around the University of Oporto, but by no means in exclusive zones. However, the aging of buildings, the demands of modern science and technology, and the sheer growth of the universities make this model difficult to maintain. Hence, in Helsinki, Oporto, and, much earlier, Mexico City, certain colleges and departments moved to new campuses on the outskirts of the city; generally, science, medical, and engineering departments seem most likely to move to the new spaces, while the social sciences and humanities stay behind in the heart of the city. In Oporto, this appears to have had a clear negative effect on the central city.

The University of Ulster and Hebrew University represent an entirely different set of motivations. In both places, a new or expanded campus was explicitly justified on the grounds of national political purposes. In Belfast, the University of Ulster proposed the development of the Springvale campus, right between the Catholic and Protestant communities of West Belfast, as a way to transcend the deep divisions between the two populations. Of course, the need to provide higher education to an area that was woefully lacking and suffered from low tertiary education completion was also cited, but the campus was primarily pitched as a symbolic and real contribution to the peace-making process. In Jerusalem, another conflicted city, Hebrew University had initially been started on Mount Scopus, just outside Jerusalem proper, as early as 1917, as an explicit part of nation building. Lost from Israeli control in the war following Israel's declaration of independence in 1948, it once again became part of the country after the 1967 war. While a new campus had been developed in another part of Jerusalem during the intervening years, plans to expand the Mount Scopus campus began within days of its liberation by the Israeli army. Chapter 11, by Haim Yacobi, argues that the spatial logic in that case was one of territorial control and national symbolism rather than educational functionality.

The National Autonomous University of Mexico provides an interesting counterpoint to those two cases. Its history, at least in most of the twentieth century, has been one of gaining autonomy from government, rather than har-monizing with government's agenda. This was expressed spatially through the creation of a new campus, which was indeed seen as so autonomous that the incursion by the federal military in 1968 to put down a student strike is seen to this day as both a rallying cry and a grievous violation of the university's independence.

On the whole, though, we see clear evidence of the close relationship between urban universities and the economic, cultural, and political agendas of their host communities. In most cases, there is significant convergence. Universities are definitely part of their locales' economic strategy, and in two interesting cases contribute to a political agenda. The preservation of at least a partial downtown location, as in Helsinki and the case of the Scot-tish universities, contributes to the culture and "sense of place" of the cities. The Tokyo case shows that even as national strategies shift, from an effort to decentralize the city to one of recentralization, the university moves with the shifting tide. But there are also examples of divergence. The University of Oporto's move to the suburbs had a distinct negative effect on the old central city, while the National Autonomous University of Mexico's University City is a clear case of attempted independence from, rather than harmony with, the government.

Where Is Growth Taking Place?

Because of the focus of this book, the universities we are dealing with have primarily urban locations. But within that general similarity, they exhibit a vast variety of locational specifics, ranging from one of the most central loca-tions in Caracas to an unproductive rubber plantation on Java, an abandoned military base in Lüneburg, and a highly contested hilltop outside of Jerusalem. We have already discussed the motivations for expanding or building a new campus at all. But what considerations have gone into the selection of the specific sites? Are they sites that maximize available space and accessibility at the lowest cost? Do they bestow prestige or other intangible advantages? Do they primarily meet the universities' own needs and location criteria, or do they fit a local or national agenda? Reviewing the cases, it is clear that site selection primarily reflects the priorities of university leadership, but that the leadership often positions these priorities in the context of local and national needs. However, sheer availability and cost considerations act as important constraints.

The central city, and indeed the downtown area, was the original location of almost all of the universities described in the book. The only exceptions are Yonsei University, which was started in the nineteenth century outside of Seoul but has since been engulfed by suburban development; the University of Ulster, which from its inception has been located in a Belfast suburb but has sought to create an in-city branch campus; and Hebrew University, started just outside Jerusalem but forced to relocate into the city during the 1948–67 period when Israel lost control over the area. The urban location of most of the universities reflects the continental European tradition, with its close interweaving of the academy with the church, the state, and other segments of society, given physical shape in universities consisting of faculties or colleges dispersed throughout a downtown rather than isolated on a campus. This tradition was transplanted to South America and many places in Asia, as well.

But this original locational model started undergoing changes in the 1950s and 1960s. New and expanded facilities could not always be easily accommodated in or near the traditional locations, necessitating a search for new sites. The searches were influenced by the increased accessibility of suburban sites, as well as by the Anglo-Saxon bucolic campus model, the increased emphasis on hard sciences and their specific space needs, and a model of the separation of science and researchers from direct involvement with the rest of society. Thus, as Isabel Breda-Vázquez and her co-authors, and some of the other authors note, throughout Europe there has been a tendency for new science buildings, especially, to be located in new suburban areas. In Oporto, suburban land was set aside in the 1950s, even though a new engineering building wasn't constructed until several decades later. In Helsinki, city government had wanted the university to move out of its prestigious downtown location to the new suburb of Meilatha as early as the middle of the nineteenth century, but not until the 1960s did science departments go there.

In Japan, many universities moved to suburban areas, responding in waves to the destruction caused by the 1923 earthquake and the Second World War, as well as a national policy to decentralize the Tokyo Metropolitan Area. Suburban rail lines provided access to many new areas, and universities responded to the developmental strategies of several towns that billed themselves as new university cities. In one of the clearest examples of the effect of national economic conditions and policies on university location, this pattern has begun to be reversed in the past two decades. With the national economy stagnating, universities have been encouraged to return to central locations in Tokyo and to maximize interaction with the corporate sector to facilitate innovation and technology transfer. Universities have responded to this, not so much by wholesale relocation, as by the creation of centers and branch campuses in strategic central locations.

In Indonesia it was the provincial government that took the lead in decentralizing universities from overcrowded Bandung. An unproductive rubber plantation was designated to house four universities that moved twenty or thirty miles from Bandung. Overcrowding in the city center was also a major motivation for the Autonomous National University of Mexico (UNAM) to seek a new location. As Morales Schechinger and García Jiménez recount, it might have made sense to locate close to the major population concentration of the working-class students that were the university's major target group; however, a site closer to the path of middle- and upper-middle-income residential expansion was chosen, and the campus became a magnet (and tool) for major land speculation.

Another interesting aspect of the Mexican case is the issue of land as a source of income and symbol of autonomy. UNAM was allowed to purchase lands owned collectively by farmers at a very low cost, essentially just providing replacement agricultural land in a remote location. The amount of land acquired was far in excess of actual space needs, and the university was allowed to resell some of it at the much higher value for residential development. It was anticipated that other parts of the land would be used for future profit-making development, as well. In Caracas, Venezuela, the university was similarly granted land beyond its needs, with the explicit provision that it could use the proceeds from development to subsidize its operations. For the university there, full development of twenty acres in a prime downtown spot would indeed generate significant resources, estimated at perhaps 20 percent of the total university budget. In the case of UNAM, income from the real estate turned out to be a negligible fraction of the institutional budget. However, the land became an important symbol in the attempt to maintain the university's independence from the federal government—in spite of the university's dependence on the government for funding. The university governs its campus with many of the same powers a city government would have.

The most explicit cases of political consideration in site selection are, perhaps not surprisingly, in Belfast and Jerusalem. As noted above, Hebrew University was founded as an expression of national aspirations even before the country was established. In 1967, the original location on Mount Scopus was surrounded by Arab villages and was not very accessible. Nevertheless, the campus was renovated and significantly expanded as part of the process of establishing a clear Jewish presence on that side of the city.

In the language of Frank Gaffikin, this establishment of ethnic space is the opposite of what the new campus of the University of Ulster was intended to achieve. The Springvale campus was seen as an avenue for reconciliation. Its location precisely on the boundary between the Protestant and Catholic communities of West Belfast would be open to both communities, at least as shared space, and hopefully even as transcendent space, that would diminish the intensity of hostility by encouraging interaction and common bonds. Clearly, both of these cases represent institutional entrepreneurship by universities seeking to respond to perceived needs and opportunities at the national political level to advance their interests. Indeed, the Springvale initiative unraveled when new university leadership decided that the project did not serve university interests: The concessions made in the process of planning the Springvale campus had become too onerous and costly and deviated too much from normal operating practices.

As several of these cases show, availability of land is a constraint but hardly a definitive one. It took the Israeli army to make Mount Scopus available for development, and no doubt the army continues to be critical to its security. Collective farmers were cheated or, at best, taken advantage of in Mexico City. While those cases are extreme, they suggest the political dimension of site location decisions. Elsewhere, location decisions are intertwined with the common processes of suburbanization and central city renewal, with the university's site decisions not so different from those a private corporation might make: moving to the suburbs in the 1960s and 1970s, and retaining (and perhaps returning) symbolic and highly interactive functions in the central city in the subsequent decades.

How Do Universities Structure Their Development Process?

University real estate development is often described with reference to partnerships and public-private collaboration. In reality, most of the cases in this book represent institutions acting relatively autonomously and independently, albeit within a range of often complex institutional and legal arrangements. Since all but two of the universities are public, they are officially under the control of a larger state entity. In fact, public status alone does not determine the degree of autonomy, as the cases illustrate. They can be arranged along a continuum of relative autonomy, although no one dimension can adequately capture the complexity of inter- and intra-organizational relationships.

Three universities represent substantial autonomy. The foundation that controls the land grant real estate for the benefit of the Central University of Venezuela has managed to obtain great freedom to pursue market-rate development on its twenty-acre site. The foundation was established in 1974, first as an entity of the Ministry of Education and since 2001 as an entity of the university. Its board consists of an equal number of university and nonuniversity representatives, with a president appointed by the university. However, in its development decisions the foundation is expected to act on the basis of market considerations and seek to maximize long-term financial returns, rather than serve any other university or governmental priorities. In the development of its site with 7 million square feet of mixed-use projects, the foundation primarily leases the land for thirty- to sixty-year periods to private developers. Once fully developed, the project is expected to yield perhaps up to 20 percent of the university's budget.

The Yonsei Engineering Research Center at Yonsei University in South Korea also was developed with considerable autonomy from both the university and the government. At Yonsei, individual schools and departments are expected to initiate development projects, including the identification of land on and off campus. A group of engineering faculty members who sought to enhance collaboration with industry were able to obtain gifts of $8 million each from seven corporate sponsors, primarily on the basis of personal relations between faculty and corporate leadership; the university provided an additional $27 million. In exchange, the companies received the use of 20,000 square feet each in the 700,000-square-foot building adjacent to the existing engineering building. For the companies, the main purpose was general brand advertising and goodwill, as well as regular access to engineering faculty and students. Since the building was on the campus, there were fewer regulatory barriers than would otherwise have been the case.

In Portugal, the University of Oporto's ability to pursue its own agenda is codified in law that provides a certain amount of autonomy from the central government and no subjugation to local government at all, a situation described as a form of "extraterritoriality." Because of the university's access to funds from the European Union, this independence is not circumscribed unduly by dependence on central government funds, as is the case with many other public universities. In its development planning, the university is primarily driven by where space for growth is available. Even though the university was involved with the city in various programs aimed at enhancing the attractiveness of the downtown area, that did not influence its strategies regarding decentralization and the move of many units to the suburbs. Only belatedly, the university established a collaborative planning process for its new suburban site, involving the city, the public transit agency, and other major institutions in the immediate area. This was done after most major construction was completed and was primarily intended to remedy some of the problems of the uncoordinated development that had already taken place.

The cases from Indonesia and Israel represent the other end of the scale. In Indonesia, the move of several universities from Bandung to a new town appears to have been initiated, planned, and executed primarily by the provincial government, with little evidence of much influence from either the institutions themselves or other sectors. In Israel, Hebrew University seems to have worked hand in glove with the national government in redeveloping its Mount Scopus site. Clearly, the university had to rely on government, first to militarily retake the site for Israel, and subsequently to expropriate land from the Arab villages surrounding the campus for further expansion.

Not surprisingly, most cases represent a mixed model. For instance, in Lüneburg, Germany, the university is quite dependent on the state, but the entire development process appears to have gone so smoothly and harmoniously that any conflicts or fault lines remain invisible. The Federal Properties Administration was in charge of marketing surplus sites, including military bases made redundant by the end of the Cold War. Preference was given to regional and local governments, and the specific site available perfectly met the needs of the university, which had recently been thwarted in its attempt to expand adjacent to its present campus. The project obtained quick support from politicians up and down the ladder and was eligible for significant federal subsidies, as well. A state-owned but privately run company was retained for construction management, and the entire project, involving renovation of military barracks and construction of several new buildings for a complete new campus of over five thousand students, took only four or five years.

In Scotland, management of a university's real estate has been mandated by the central government to play a central role in university decision making. While universities have a great deal of autonomy (including the right to enter joint ventures with the private sector for real estate development), they must coordinate closely with local government on their planning. They are also expected to produce master plans, landscaping plans, and so forth. Still, the harmony between the University of Dundee's plans and the development strategy of the city is described as "serendipity" rather than the result of deliberate planning.

In Belfast, development of the new Springvale campus was lodged in a separate corporation, Springvale Educational Village Ltd., a joint entity of the University of Ulster and the Belfast Further Education Institute. However, this came about only after years of political maneuvering involving the University of Ulster, key supporters in government, and several community organizations. Indeed, the development process there has characteristics of a campaign or social movement, with constantly shifting coalitions, frequent negotiations and shifts in tactics, and extensive interventions by external parties (including the government, foundations, and universities of the United States). In the end, though, both the initial impetus for the project and the decision to abort it were clearly the university's.

Just as the central government in Scotland is paying more attention to the role of real estate in university growth and development, so is the government in Finland. There, however, government exercises more control by assigning the ownership and control of most university real estate to a state entity, called Senate Properties. Since 1994, universities have had to pay rent, first at about one-third of the market value and since 1999 at full market rates. Presumably, this creates a competitive environment, which would change the incentives for universities to engage in development themselves or to partner with others. Development cases described in chapter 2 largely predate this new regime, however, so the effects are not yet clear.

More subtle is the way the planning process is used in Japan to achieve national development goals. Takeuchi describes how as long ago as around 1900, public universities were deliberately distributed throughout the country to create balanced development. Private universities were not subject to this, and they concentrated in the cities with the highest population density in order to maximize their potential market, since they depend on tuition income. After the Second World War, the rapid growth in higher education was primarily met by private institutions, leading to an overconcentration in the Tokyo Metropolitan Area. This led, in turn, to legislation in 1959 that effectively halted the construction of new university space in central Tokyo; at the same time, suburban municipalities competed with each other to attract universities. When economic and population growth halted thirty years later, the restrictions on central locations were mitigated and ultimately repealed. New programs were put in place to encourage universities to focus more on science and technology for economic development, and favoring urban universities, which presumably would yield the greatest benefits of agglomeration economies. Thus, over a period of a century, planning incentives and regulations were used to steer the development of universities, apparently with noticeable effect.

Thus, there clearly is a wide range of opportunities and constraints facing universities in their development processes. Public or private status alone does not seem to make a decisive difference, nor does the degree of funding obtained from the central government. Traditions of autonomy clearly matter; but those traditions can be changed by legislative decree, as is evident in Scotland and Finland.

These issues are not unfamiliar in the United States. City governments wrestle with the question of how to support universities for their economic benefits while mitigating their effects on surrounding neighborhoods. Cities are handicapped in their power, given that most public universities are entities of state government and are therefore exempt from many city regulations. Private universities are easier to regulate, although the largest and most prestigious ones usually have significant endowments and powerful connections that afford them power vis-à-vis local governments.

What Is the Impact of Growth and Expansion?

Since most of these universities have been part of their cities for centuries, their impact, or the impact of any particular new development, is not easy to disentangle. Clearly, they have been major contributors to the social, cultural, and economic life of their cities, particularly the downtown areas.

The new real estate developments described here have mostly taken place away from the traditional campus locations, with a few exceptions. At Yonsei University, new engineering and R&D space was built on campus and served to enhance the university's capabilities in those areas without much direct physical effect on the rest of Seoul. In contrast, in Caracas, the university has been involved in a commercial development project immediately adjacent to campus. Intended to generate revenues for university use, the project languished for decades, creating a blight on a central urban location. Its current redevelopment should finally take advantage of its economic potential, to the benefit of the city and the university.

The other projects largely involve the development of new buildings or entire campuses away from the original university location. Obviously, this creates possible effects on both the old and the new locations. Given the rapid growth of universities during recent decades, expansion has largely occurred without taking much, if anything, away from the original location. The only exception to this appears to be the University of Oporto, in whose case the move of many departments from the city center had significant negative effects on the commercial viability of the downtown. Everywhere else, however, the new campuses (such as in Bandung, Mexico City, Helsinki, and Lüneburg) were built to accommodate new growth, and other local demand was strong enough that there were no significant negative effects on the old locations.

The effect on the new locations is more complicated and ranges from positive in most cases to quite negative. The main example of the latter is described in chapter 9, on the Jatinangor University Area in Indonesia. Wilmar Salim describes in detail how the decision to relocate universities from Bandung to a new town created many problems for the host area. New businesses and residents were attracted without sufficient infrastructure to service them, housing shortages developed, and deforestation and problems with the water supply occurred.

Indonesia, of course, has the greatest development challenges of any of the countries represented here, so it is not entirely surprising that such problems should occur. Indeed, none of the other cases give evidence of such infrastructure issues. In both Helsinki and Oporto, the location of new branch campuses in suburban areas enhanced the stature of those already attractive places. As Breda-Vázquez and co-authors point out, the new campus of the University of Oporto has little direct effect on surrounding neighborhoods, since most services are provided internally. Similarly, in Helsinki the suburban branches of the university do not share the openness and publicness of the downtown campus; instead, they can be characterized as "privileged space"—not entirely private but accessible only to those who are invited. In Lüneburg, as in Helsinki, the new campus, on a converted military base, was accompanied by new student housing, so there were few effects on the surrounding suburban residential neighborhoods.

Increased housing demand by students was indeed one of the objections raised against the University of Ulster's plans for its new Springvale campus, along with the fear of increased traffic. In almost every other respect, the plans for the new campus were generally received positively, albeit with a certain amount of skepticism and suspicion. It was widely recognized that the West Belfast area to be served did need more education resources, as did Northern Ireland as a whole. However, it was not as clear that a university was best positioned to provide them, since few secondary school students had the required qualifications. In a later modification of the plans, the campus was intended to consist of a partnership between the university and the Belfast Further Education Institute, a lower-level tertiary education entity. Of course, all concerns, as well as hopes for the new campus, became moot when the project was cancelled.

Two other cases give evidence of significant problematic issues. One is the oldest case, that of the new campus of the Autonomous National University of Mexico. We already referred to the expropriation of the land from the collective farmer ownership. This drove the farmers from their land, only recently acquired in the land reform of the early twentieth century; or, depending on one's perspective, gave the farmers access to more productive replacement land far outside of the metropolitan area. Chapter 6 provides more detail on another aspect of the siting of the campus, namely, the land speculation that it engendered. Apparently, this speculation, ranging from using insider knowledge about the likely location of new infrastructure to taking advantage of clouded property titles for lands adjacent to the new campus, continued for many decades.

Expropriation was also part of the expansion of the Mount Scopus campus in Jerusalem after the 1967 war. Land surrounding the original campus was owned by Arab villages, but the Israeli government supported its acquisition in order to provide space for the campus and connect the entire area explicitly with a Jewish Jerusalem.

As has been noted previously in regard to university development, "there is no such thing as vacant land" (Calder, Grant, and Muson 2005). The reutilization of the abandoned military base in Lüneburg is perhaps the most harmonious example of a development welcomed by everyone, positive in its symbolism as well as its actual effects. Other projects exemplify minor and major issues. Nevertheless, with the exception of the Springvale campus, which was never built, all of the projects achieved their goals of expanding educational opportunity, as well as providing greater research capacity.

What Makes for Success?

The cases in this book were not selected to be a representative sample, nor do they provide many examples of failed projects. Nevertheless, it is possible to draw some conclusions about key factors that seem to play a role in making projects work or, conversely, creating obstacles.

The overriding issue for almost all of the universities in this book has been to accommodate rapid growth in the number of students. This is the result both of sheer population growth and of the increased importance of the knowledge economy and hence the proportion of the population attending university. Even in some of the earliest university developments alluded to, such as the initial projects in the 1940s at the Central University of Venezuela, rapid growth constituted a major driver for university expansion. As several of the authors point out, this clear need is a key factor in the success of any project, since universities compete with other public needs for resources.

Perhaps the most successful project represented here is the conversion of the military installation in Lüneburg into a new main campus for the University of Lüneburg. Katrin Anacker and Uwe Altrock identify the key factors that made the process go quickly and with little conflict: There was a clear need due to the university's growth; the recently abandoned military base was available, and there were no clear alternatives; there was consensus between the university, city government, and regional and federal authorities; conversion projects were eligible for significant federal funding; and the project was outsourced to a private-sector management company. Less than ten years passed from the identification of a need to the completion of a new campus for four thousand students in an attractive environment with no noticeable negative effects.

Relative speed also characterized the development of a new campus for several universities moved from Bandung in Indonesia. The plan to move universities out of the crowded city was first raised in the early 1980s, but the specific site was not selected until 1989. Within a few years, four universities were operating in the new location; and the population grew by 60 percent, or thirty thousand people, mostly students, from 1990 to 2000. However, in this case the speed and size of the project caused serious infrastructure problems. While it achieved its goal of relieving pressure on Bandung, it caused great problems in the new locale.

Strikingly absent from almost all of the cases is a discussion about individual leaders, or leadership in general. In our previous work, we had identified this as a key factor: "Given the complexity of real estate development, it is not surprising that strong leadership seems to be a critical success factor in many of the projects described here. The preferences and style of the person in charge (usually the chancellor or president) will affect the type of projects undertaken and how relations with the community, the city, or the private sector are handled. Regardless of preferences or style, commitment to the project is often essential to get it completed at all" (Perry and Wiewel 2005, 303).

There is virtually no evidence of this in the present cases. Indeed, one could almost argue the opposite. In the one clear case of failure—the never-built Springvale campus of the University of Ulster—one of the factors cited as explaining the failure is the project's close association with one university leader; once he left, the project was abandoned. What is striking about the present cases is how embedded they appear to be in the structure and institutional relations of their institutions. Only in the two Latin American cases do we even learn the names of key institutional leaders; elsewhere, institutional priorities and actions appear to reflect broad, ongoing planning processes more than individual agendas.

We did anticipate this possibility in the earlier work: "At a small number of institutions leadership seems to have been sufficiently institutionalized that, even without much evidence of direct intervention from the top, projects proceed. . . . The highest achievement, however, may be to inculcate the vision, objectives, and approach in an organizational structure so it can be implemented consistently and steadily" (Perry and Wiewel 2005, 304).

Perhaps the longer history of these universities, combined with their status as units that are affiliated with the national government, contributes to this sense of greater institutionalized, rather than individual, leadership. Related to this is the nature of their chief executives compared to U.S. higher education leadership. Many universities outside of the United States have titular heads, sometimes appointed for a defined period of time, with limited power. Real power and authority rest with professional managers, operating under the direct or indirect control of a larger public bureaucracy, such as a Ministry of Education, whose political leadership may change from time to time but is unlikely to become engaged in specific development projects at individual institutions.

Several chapters emphasize the complex institutional relationships between the university and the public sector as an integral part of the success of university expansion projects. In Finland, for instance, the university has benefited from a close relationship with the national government, which has at times protected the university from local government plans, while providing it with resources to finance the development of new campuses. Similarly, in Portugal the university was able to access, through the national government, significant funds from the European Union; university investments were almost equal to all investment by the City of Oporto itself. In Israel, Hebrew University was seen as an integral part of the very nature of the state, and hence its expansion received the highest priority, starting within days of the end of the 1967 war.

Final Comments

University real estate development across the world clearly exhibits many similar characteristics. While the details and specifics vary, and some cases stand apart, it is nevertheless possible to make some general observations:

- The main reason universities have been expanding in recent decades is that they need more space to accommodate growing numbers of students. This growth results from the increased number of people in many places, but even more from the increase in the proportion that pursues higher education.
- A second important reason for development of new university buildings is the obsolescence of the current stock, combined with the growth in science and engineering, which have very specific space requirements.
- Political reasons play a very minor role in most cases (with Hebrew University the major exception), but political, economic, cultural, and social reasons may be used strategically and opportunistically by universities to justify expansion.
- The primary location for expansion is available land on the edge of urban areas. In some cases, that land was originally set aside long before expansion became a reality.
- Universities pursued and implemented their expansion projects as independently and autonomously as possible, based on their own needs and their analysis of opportunities and constraints. With three or four

exceptions (Hebrew University, University of Ulster, Jatinangor University Area in Indonesia, and perhaps Tokyo), congruence with local, regional, or national strategies was opportunistic or serendipitous, rather than deliberate and intentional.

- While striving for autonomy, universities nevertheless must negotiate complex governing, planning, and regulatory structures; the complexity both constrains and provides opportunities for entrepreneurship and autonomy.
- It is reasonable to expect that as universities grow in importance as part of the knowledge economy, their power and need for autonomy will grow; but as their physical and economic presence increases, the desire of local governments to exercise some measure of control will also grow. Thus, it seems likely that conflicts between universities and local governments will increase in the future.
- Most university development is funded by the public sector. However, there is an increasing emphasis on the importance of market dynamics and partnerships with the private sector.
- New developments have a significant effect on their immediate area. Generally, this is positive, but in some cases (UNAM in Mexico City, Hebrew University, and Jatinangor University Area) there are significant negative effects on particular groups.
- Universities' new growth and expansion are largely additive and appear to take away little from the original or main locations.
- A key factor in the success of development projects is the strong demand from students and researchers, which provides a clear justification for additional space.
- Most projects appear to be planned and implemented in the course of regular, institutionalized, long-range planning by professional managers, rather than as short-term entrepreneurial initiatives of individual leaders.

Most of these conclusions echo those with which we concluded our previous study on U.S. universities (Perry and Wiewel 2005). The main deviation is the much greater role of individual leadership in the U.S. cases and the greater institutionalization we see elsewhere. Relations with the immediate community also appear to be more important in the United States, or at least the cases presented in this study do not dwell on it as extensively. The American traditions of individual leadership, as well as grassroots democracy and local autonomy, clearly create differences in the way universities operate. In the end, though, the similarities across countries are far greater than the differences and bespeak the globalization of growth of the urban knowledge sector.

References

Calder, Allegra, Gabriel Grant, and Holly Hart Muson. 2005. "No Such Thing as Vacant Land: Northeastern University and Davenport Commons." In *The University as Urban Developer: Case Studies and Analysis,* ed. David C. Perry and Wim Wiewel. Armonk, NY: M.E. Sharpe.

Perry, David C., and Wim Wiewel, eds. 2005. *The University as Urban Developer: Case Studies and Analysis.* Armonk, NY: M.E. Sharpe.

About the Editors and Contributors

Editors

David C. Perry is Director and Professor at the Great Cities Institute, University of Illinois at Chicago. He is the author of more than one hundred reports, articles, nine books, and most recently edited *The University as Urban Developer: Case Studies and Analysis* along with Wim Wiewel. His research interests are in urban policy and the political economy of urban institutions, particularly universities in the comparative and global contexts.

Wim Wiewel is Professor of Public Affairs and Provost and Senior Vice President for Academic Affairs at the University of Baltimore. He was previously Dean of the College of Business Administration and Dean of Urban Planning and Public Affairs at the University of Illinois at Chicago. He is the author / editor of seven books and over fifty articles and chapters on economic development, suburban sprawl, and university real estate. He is a former president of the Association of the Collegiate Schools of Planning.

Contributors

Uwe Altrock is a Professor of Urban Regeneration and Planning in the School of Architecture, Urban and Landscape Planning, University of Kassel, Germany.

Sónia Alves is a Ph.D. Student in Sociology at the Instituto Superior de Ciências do Trabalho e da Empresa (ISCTE), Lisbon, Portugal.

Katrin B. Anacker is a Post Doctoral Fellow at the Metropolitan Institute at Virginia Tech Alexandria, Virginia, United States. She is also the Senior Editor of the Housing Policy Debate.

Isabel Breda-Vázquez is an Associate Professor in the Department of Civil Engineering, Planning of the Territory and Environment, at the University of Oporto, Oporto, Portugal, and Researcher at the CITTA- Research Center for Territory, Transports and Environment, at the same university.

Abner J. Colmenares is a Professor in the School of Architecture at Caracas, Central University of Venezuela, Venezuela. He is also the President of the Andres Bello Fund Foundation for Scientific Development at the Central University of Venezuela.

Paulo Conceição is an Assistant Professor in the Department of Civil Engineering, at the University of Oporto, Oporto, Portugal. He is attached to CITTA, the Research Center for Territory, Transports and Environment.

Frank Gaffikin is a Reader in the School of Planning, Architecture, and Civil Engineering at Queen's University in Belfast, Northern Ireland. He is also the Director of Research at the Institute of Spatial and Environmental Planning, Queen's University. He is currently directing a major international research project, known as Contested Cities and Urban Universities (CU2).

Anne Haila is a Professor of Urban Studies at the Department of Social Policy, University of Helsinki, Finland.

GwangYa Han is an Assistant Professor of Urban Design and Planning in the Department of Architecture at Dongguk University, Seoul, Korea.

Sara García Jiménez is an Assistant Professor in the School of Architecture at the National Autonomous University of Mexico, Mexico City, Mexico.

Carlos Morales Schechinger is a Professor in the School of Architecture, at the National Autonomous University of Mexico, Mexico City, Mexico. He is the author of many articles and reports and is a frequent research contributor as well as faculty member at the Lincoln Institute of Land Policy.

Deborah Peel is a Lecturer at the Department of Civic Design in the University of Liverpool, Liverpool, United Kingdom.

Wilmar Salim is a Ph.D. Candidate in the Department of Urban and Regional Planning at the University of Hawaii at Manoa, in Honolulu, Hawaii, United States.

Yuichi Takeuchi is Vice President at the Institute of Behavioural Sciences in Tokyo, Japan.

Haim Yacobi is a Lecturer in the Department of Politics and Government at the Ben Gurion University of the Negev, Beer Sheva, Israel.

Wann Yu is Professor Emeritus in the Department of Urban Planning and Engineering, Yonsei University, Seoul, Korea.

About the Lincoln Institute of Land Policy

The Lincoln Institute of Land Policy is a private operating foundation whose mission is to improve the quality of public debate and decisions in the areas of land policy and land-related taxation in the United States and around the world. The Institute's goals are to integrate theory and practice to better shape land policy and to provide a nonpartisan forum for discussion of the multidisciplinary forces that influence public policy. This focus on land derives from the Institute's founding objective—to address the links between land policy and social and economic progress—that was identified and analyzed by political economist and author Henry George.

The work of the Institute is organized in four departments: Valuation and Taxation, Planning and Urban Form, Economic and Community Development, and International Studies. We seek to inform decision making through education, research, demonstration projects, and the dissemination of information through publications, our Web site, and other media. Our programs bring together scholars, practitioners, public officials, policy advisers, and involved citizens in a collegial learning environment.

The Institute does not take a particular point of view, but rather serves as a catalyst to facilitate analysis and discussion of land use and taxation issues—to make a difference today and to help policy makers plan for tomorrow. The Lincoln Institute of Land Policy is an equal opportunity institution.

L LINCOLN INSTITUTE
OF LAND POLICY

113 Brattle Street
Cambridge, MA 02138-3400 USA
Phone: 1-617-661-3016 x127 or 1-800-LAND-USE (800-526-3873)
Fax: 1-617-661-7235 or 1-800-LAND-944 (800-526-3944)
E-mail: help@lincolninst.edu
Web: www.lincolninst.edu

Index